The Meaning of Myth
in World Cultures

The Meaning of Myth
in World Cultures

MICHAEL BUONANNO

McFarland & Company, Inc., Publishers
Jefferson, North Carolina

LIBRARY OF CONGRESS CATALOGUING-IN-PUBLICATION DATA

Names: Buonanno, Michael, 1954– author.
Title: The meaning of myth in world cultures / Michael Buonanno.
Description: Jefferson, North Carolina : McFarland & Company, Inc.,
Publishers, 2019. | Includes bibliographical references and index.
Identifiers: LCCN 2018036971 | ISBN 9780786497126
(softcover : acid free paper) ∞
Subjects: LCSH: Myth.
Classification: LCC BL304 .B86 2019 | DDC 201/.3—dc23
LC record available at https://lccn.loc.gov/2018036971

BRITISH LIBRARY CATALOGUING DATA ARE AVAILABLE

ISBN (print) 978-0-7864-9712-6
ISBN (ebook) 978-1-4766-3392-3

Front cover: a wooden Papa Legba statue (from author's
collection, photograph by the author); background photograph
of ancient alphabets carved on a stone plate © 2019 iStock

Printed in the United States of America

McFarland & Company, Inc., Publishers
Box 611, Jefferson, North Carolina 28640
www.mcfarlandpub.com

Table of Contents

Preface

This study examines mythology from a global perspective. Mythology, disseminated in sacred stories (myths) and their reenactments (rituals), is the basis of a society's religion. And religion is an essential key to identity: the articulation of an individual's belief system and the personal store of wisdom that resides there. In fact, the elaboration of identity is a major function of mythic rhetoric: mythology's ability to make, convey, and sanction meaning. And culture provides the essential metaphors which mythic rhetoric employs. These metaphors are at once ecological (associated with the way in which a society exploits its environment), sociological (based in an indigenous network of social relations), and ideological (couched in the terms of a society's worldview). But tellingly, these metaphors are consistently incorporated into the personages of anthropomorphic spirits, fostering a deep sense of identification with those spirits as well as a deep sense of affiliation among those who share in one's spiritual devotions.

While presenting material from a wide array of societies in order to exemplify these observations, I illustrate the primary concerns of this study through in-depth examinations of several cultural traditions. These examinations are paired: San and Euahlayi culture allow us to look at the ecological imperatives that pervade the mythologies of foragers; Iroquois and Lakota culture allow us to consider Native American traditions and two momentous religious movements: The Code of Handsome Lake and Ghost Dance; Jewish and Hindu culture allow us to explore the two religious traditions which, together, are the fountainhead of the vast majority of the world's worshippers; Sicilian and Haitian culture allow us to consider the intermingling of mythic traditions on islands which stand at the center of significant sea routes and tumultuous histories. Such a selection of traditions attempts to offer a representative sample of various cultural regions and ecological strategies without including such a large spread of examples that they become entirely lost to memory. Thus, societies extensively covered in this study—while relatively limited in number—include foraging, agricultural, and mercantile strategies, and come from Africa, Asia, Europe, Oceania, and Native America as well as diasporic societies extending from the Old World to the New.

Though depending upon the work of a large number of cultural analysts—particularly anthropologists, folklorists, journalists, and historians—in describing these traditions, I have whenever possible sought out adherents of the various spiritual traditions explored here and engaged them in conversation. As a result of that strategy, I would like to acknowledge the many individuals who shared their thoughts with me. They include Sicilian, Haitian, Iroquois, Lakota, Tunisian, Indian, Yoruba, and Thai respondents as well as African Americans from coastal Florida, Italian Americans from western New York, and Jewish Americans from up and down the eastern seaboard.[1] So many individuals have been so generous with their time that it would be impossible to name them all but I would like to mention at least a few: Gui shared with me the stories of Papa Legba, Ezili Freda, and the strange mysteries of zombification while Louis told me tales of the Haitian Revolution and the role that the Vodou religion played in it; Bobbi shared with me the happy memories of a vibrant Jewish American community as well as some less than happy moments marked by the starkest of prejudices while Leah expressed to me the excitement that (despite worries over her facility with Hebrew) she experienced as her Bat Mitvah approached; my grandmother, Lucia, shared with me the divination and healing rituals she employed against the evil eye (even if she wouldn't divulge the secret incantation which was the key to her healing practice); Maria told me of the ancient rivalry between the preeminent Carolingian knights, the saintly Roland and the rebellious Renaud, and explained why it was that Charlemagne—the Holy Roman emperor, God's "sergeant" on earth—always took the lesser knight's part; Hitendra conveyed to me the excitement he felt as he accompanied a giant effigy of the elephant-headed god Ganesha to the seashore so that it might be bathed in the holy waters and explained how such an act was yet another of the many varieties of *puja*: ritual veneration of the deities; Gregory tutored me in the mysteries of the Seven African Powers and High John the Conqueror and allowed me to understand why remembering Africa could be so personally empowering; Eleanor told me about the spiritual power of tobacco first brought to Turtle Island when Grandmother Sky Woman fell from the Sky World. But her sister, Ginny, told me about the trauma wrought upon her nation by tobacco's terrible counterpart: alcohol.

What these generous respondents have allowed me to understand is a basic principle of mythic rhetoric and its ramifications on the interpretation of mythology. Historically, when a myth was viewed from a global perspective, there was a natural tendency to base interpretations on contemporary theoretical debates, often leading to some sort of astronomical, psychological, or religiously charged interpretation: the story attempted to explain the movement of celestial bodies; the story remembered the ancient assassination of the primal father; the story reflected inborn archetypes; the story confirmed the historicity of the universal flood. But here, following the anthropological tradition of cultural contextualization, we find that mythology must be understood indigenously before it can be productively emplaced in a global context; that mythology—despite being the inheritance of our one human family—has little significance if we do not account for the local ecological and sociological metaphors which flesh out a given society's philosophical abstractions; that mythology must be explored in its native context if we ever hope to understand its ideological impact, its social function, and perhaps even its spiritual significance globally.

Introduction:
A Story Is Medicine

Mythology

"Listen," the medicine man told me, a tinge of exasperation shading his voice, "the first thing you need to get rid of is this idea of the Indian legend. There's no such thing as an Indian legend." Then, softening his tone so that I might sense the import of what he was getting at, he added, "A story is medicine. You come to me and I see something is wrong. It's my job to find out what's wrong. When I figure that out, I have to find the right story. I tell you the story." He paused slightly and then added, almost brusquely, "Maybe you're kind of *dense* and don't get it the first time, so I tell you another story." Then, looking at me so pointedly that I shifted uncomfortably in my seat, he concluded, "Maybe you're *really* dense." I was feeling a bit put upon at this point, to say the least. "I'll tell you stories all day long if I have to."[1]

I have been told innumerable stories and—being a tad dense, I suppose—it has taken me quite a while to figure out why they, among all the various products of human culture, are so continuously intriguing. What I finally realized is this: I have always wanted to know why a member of a society—my own or any number of others—might approach an issue in a way that seems so markedly different from the way I myself might approach it. Of course, the answer to that question hinges upon the concept of culture. As a member of a particular group (a family perhaps, a community, or even an entire society), each of us is subject to the subtle influence of that group's culture: the system of belief and behavior that the group acknowledges in order to sustain itself. And it is often this influence that governs our own particular take on an issue.

It may be that mythology, more than any other feature of culture, speaks directly to the question of why we come down on one side of an issue or another because myth, like any other story, incorporates that issue in an entire nexus of issues—or, to borrow the language of Clifford Geertz, catches that issue up

6   Introduction

in a web of significance—which enables us to pull it out and examine it singly, then in the context of the various strands that connect it to other issues, and finally in the context of the entire constellation of issues to which it is connected. But further, myth—unlike other stories—sanctifies that issue through situating it in the realm of the sacred. Nowhere else in the arena of cultural signification, I believe, is an issue so thoroughly contextualized, so thoroughly examined, so thoroughly enshrined as a societal value than in myth. And it is probably because of the intensity of the contextualization and sanctification of issues in myth that mythologies have such a profound impact on the cultural identity of real living, breathing human beings: allowing us at times our most profound insights and at times our most incomprehensible squabbles.

But what exactly are myths? They are stories dealing with spirits: gods, demigods, ancestors, ghosts, saints, angels, demons, fairies, monsters, even souls and supernatural forces. As such, they are the central facet of a society's religious traditions, so much so that it would be hard to imagine what religion would even be, what form it could possibly take, without myths. Who could imagine Judaism without the stories of Adam and Eve; Cain and Abel; Noah, Abraham, and Moses; David, Solomon, Elijah and Esther? What would Egyptian religion mean without the story of Isis, Osiris, and Horus? And what would be the significance of the Hindu religion if we did not know the tale, reported by Joseph Campbell, of the eternal creation of the universe? "Vishnu sleeps in the cosmic ocean, and the lotus of the universe grows from his navel. On the lotus sits Brahma, the creator. Brahma opens his eyes, and a world comes into being, governed by an Indra. Brahma closes his eyes, and a world goes out of being. The life of a Brahma is four hundred and thirty-two thousand years. When he dies, the lotus goes back, and another lotus is formed, and another Brahma." And another Indra. "Then think of the galaxies beyond galaxies in infinite space, each a lotus, with a Brahma sitting on it, opening his eyes, closing his eyes."

Campbell continues: "There is a wonderful story in one of the Upanishads about the god Indra. Now, it happened at this time that a great monster had enclosed all the waters of the earth, so there was a terrible drought." But Indra, unleashing a thunderbolt, destroyed the monster and, upon doing so, "the waters flowed, and the world was refreshed." Then, pleased with his victory, Indra, thinking, "What a great boy am I," takes himself to the peak of "the cosmic mountain," the spiritual center of the world, and determines to there erect a palace worthy of his own magnificence. Vishvakarman, carpenter to the gods, sets to work on the project, "but every time Indra comes to inspect it, he has bigger ideas about how splendid and grandiose the palace should be. Finally, the carpenter says, 'My god, we are both immortal, and there is no end to his desires. I am caught for eternity.' So he decides to go to Brahma, the creator god, and complain." On telling Brahma his sad tale, Vishvakarman is told to return to his task while Brahma arranges a resolution to the dilemma. Brahma, climbing down from his lotus, "kneels down to address sleeping Vishnu." Vishnu gestures listlessly, as if he might be brushing away a fly that is troubling his sleep. But the next morning, before the gate of Indra's palace, "there appears a beautiful blue-black boy," Vishnu himself, "with a lot of children around him, just admiring his beauty." The porter, seeing Vishnu from the palace gate, "goes running to Indra," who instructs the porter to bring the boy in:

> The boy is brought in, and Indra, the king god, sitting on his throne, says, "Young man, welcome. And what brings you to my palace?" "Well," says the boy with a voice like thunder rolling on the horizon, "I have been told that you are building such a palace as no Indra before you ever built." And Indra says, "Indras before me! Young man—what are you talking about?" The boy says, "Indras before you. I have seen them come and go, come and go.

And even as Vishnu speaks, "an army of ants parades across the floor. The boy laughs aloud when he sees them, and Indra's hair stands on end." But unable to contain himself, he asks the boy, "Why do you laugh?" And the boy admonishes that he should not ask if he does not wish to learn a hard lesson. Yet, Indra, persistent, says, "I ask. Teach." Thereupon, "the boy points to the ants and says, 'Former Indras all. Through many lifetimes they rise from the lowest conditions to highest illumination. And then they drop their thunderbolt on a monster, and they think, 'What a good boy am I.' And down they go again."[2]

There is an entire philosophy here contained—of life, death, rebirth; illumination, pride, desire; ascents and descents—which could only with difficulty be conveyed outside the context of the story of Indra, Brahma, Vishvakarman, and Vishnu. For instance, reincarnation is explicitly referenced in the image of the army of ants. Though most would claim that our incarnations are innumerable, one woman provocatively told me that ants represent the first step of the reincarnative process, having been taught by her grandmother that "each soul has 100 lives. The first life is that of an ant. The hundredth is that of a human. At the hundred and first, the soul becomes a god or a star." Perhaps no more than a lesson an elder would offer a child, this woman's claim nonetheless depends on the same notion as the story of Indra: that ants represent a lowly rebirth. Vishnu's laugh too is philosophically laden. It alludes to a long folkloric tradition, described by Kirin Narayan, of the laugh of the enlightened *sadhu* (holy man) who lives at the interstices between material and spiritual realms. His cosmic laugh jars the senses of the unenlightened householder, thoughtlessly busying himself with the affairs of the world. It thereby begins to crack the darkness which hides the fissure between *maya* (illusion), that which causes us to cling to desire, and *dharma* (divine order and its duties) in which desire has no meaning. Likewise, *karma*—the doctrine that one's actions have consequences in this life and those that follow—is visualized in the many sad incarnations of Indra. As if to underscore this fact, another visitor comes to Indra in the story: Vishnu's counterpart, Shiva, in the guise of a *sadhu* with the matted hair upon his bare chest looking worn and patchy. He reveals to a frightened Indra that each time a hair falls from his chest, an Indra dies and an ant is born.[3] Such is the natural order of things.

We find the same processes at play in the Mayan creation myth, the *Popol Vuh*, as in the story of Indra and Vishnu. Here, the twin war gods, Blow Gun Hunter and Little Jaguar, are summoned by the lords of Xibalba, the Underworld, for incessantly playing ball on Xibalba's roof, the earth's surface, and disturbing their peace. But once in Xibalba, the twins take advantage of the summons to avenge the death of their father and uncle who were likewise summoned—and killed—by the lords of Xibalba before them. Little did the merciless deities of the Underworld know that the boys' father, whose head had been affixed to a Calabash Tree upon his execution, and there became indistinguishable from the other calabashes, spit into the hand of Xquic—the daughter of one of Xibalba's lords—and thereby impregnated her. He thus aptly provided the very means of avenging his death. Back on the earth's surface, where Xquic had taken refuge from her father's outrage, the twins were nurtured into manhood by their aged Grandmother: she who had unsuccessfully attempted to keep their father's ball gear from them until, through their incessant trickery, they obtained it and—along with it—their inevitable summons to Xibalba. And though the lords of Xibalba killed Blow Gun Hunter and Little Jaguar, as they had their father and uncle before them, the two miraculously

Chichén Itzá ball court (Wikipedia, photograph by Bjørn Christian Tørrissen).

resuscitated themselves and came back in disguise to perform a magical dance before the lords. First, Little Jaguar killed a dog and brought it back to life. The lords of Xibalba were intrigued. Then, he killed a man, cutting open his chest and displaying his beating heart for all to see, before bringing him back to life. The Lords of Xibalba were ecstatic. Finally, Little Jaguar killed his own brother, Blow Gun Hunter, and brought him back to life. The Lords of Xibalba were beside themselves and, in their excitement, they demanded that Little Jaguar next kill them. But they forgot to request that he afterwards restore them![4]

What significance would the great monuments of Mayan civilization hold if not for the existence of the adventures of Blow Gun Hunter and Little Jaguar? The ubiquitous ball courts, pyramids, and ceremonial platforms—these last sometimes adorned with representations of human skulls, a conscious evocation of the skull racks the Maya used to commemorate their sacrificial victims as well as the Calabash Tree from which hung the skull of the Twins' father—all speak to the Twins' primal descent into Xibalba. In the Mayan mind, these architectural features were deeply intertwined in the sacrificial complex that insured the continued veneration of, and support for, the Mayan aristocracy on the basis of one of its primary ritual duties: the reenactment of Blow Gun Hunter and Little Jaguar's defeat of the Lords of Xibalba. Central to this complex is the ball court. Though the ballgame may have been played by many—if not all—segments of Mayan society, when undertaken in conjunction with sacrifices and ritual dances, it was apparently the prerogative of the aristocracy which, selecting members from its own ranks to reenact the feats of Blow Gun Hunter and Little Jaguar in the Underworld, used the extravagant displays to justify its very existence. Notable in this context would be the sacrifices which the aristocracy oversaw: often from a platform placed high upon a pyramid's imperial staircase. From such a perch, members

Ball court goal (Wikipedia, photograph by Kåre Thor Olsen).

of the aristocracy, like Blow Gun Hunter and Little Jaguar before them, might open their victims' chest cavity by cutting them along each side of the torso from the armpits down and lift aloft their still beating heart, allowing them (in the words of the *Popol Vuh*) to receive the embrace of the Sun God, Tohil— he who was daily carried across the sky in the mouth of Gukumatz, the Feathered Serpent. Conversely, the sacrificial victim's body might be thrown in a sacred cenote, a water-filled sinkhole thought to be the portal to Xibalba, as an offering to Chaac, the Rain God. As the archaeologist Takeshi Inomata suggests, many "Classic-period stone monuments (AD 250–900) depict Maya rulers in elaborate costumes dancing, conducting rituals or playing ballgames in public spaces. These theatrical acts were primary duties for Maya kings and an important base of their power. The notion of a ruler dancing in public may sound strange, but political leaders' public performances, in different forms, are an essential part of political mechanisms in modern societies as well. The president, for example, is not just a political decision-maker—through public speeches and official ceremonies, he embodies the ideals of the nation and fosters a sense of social integration."[5]

Chichén Itzá pyramid with feathered serpent shadow that appears at each equinox (Wikipedia, photograph by ATSZ560).

Myths, Legends and Folktales

Though myths may be at the center of religious signification, one often finds elements of a society's religious traditions embedded as well in legends, the stories of a society's culture heroes, and folktales, stories which—like European fairy tales—are considered fictitious but which nevertheless are infused with the religious values of the community. For example, *The Iliad* and *The Odyssey*, though legends dealing with the Greek cultural heroes Achilles and Odysseus, offer much discussion of the nature and deeds of the Olympian gods: Athena, Hera, Zeus, Apollo, Poseidon, and Hermes, among them. Further, Achilles and Odysseus themselves, inasmuch as they are the exemplary Greek culture heroes, are infused with religious significance. Not only are they, as are all the world's culture heroes, viewed as ancestral genii but their spiritual import is continuously underscored by the relationship they both maintain with Athena as their personal daemon, or tutelary deity. It seems almost certain that ancient Greeks learned as much of their spiritual lore from their legends as they did from their myths: stories so secretive that, in fact, we know very little about them today and tend to refer to *The Iliad* and *The Odyssey* when speaking of Greek mythology.

In fact, we are alerted to the religious impact of Greek legend when, in the opening passage of *The Iliad*, Agamemnon—he who has sponsored the Greek war against Troy in order to regain his brother's wife, Helen—robs Achilles of his war prize: the girl Briseis. Achilles, "furious, his heart within his shaggy breast divided over whether to draw his sword and kill Agamemnon on the spot or to restrain himself and check his anger," is stayed by none other than Athena herself. She "came down from heaven and—visible to him alone—seized Achilles by his golden hair."

> Achilles turned in amazement and, by the fire that flashed from her eyes, knew at once that she was Athena. "Why are you here," said he, "Daughter of Aegis-Bearing Zeus? To see the pride of Agamemnon? Let me tell you—and it shall surely be—he shall pay for this insolence with his life." And Athena said, "I come from heaven to bid you stay your anger. Hera, who loves both of you alike, has sent me. Cease then this brawling and do not draw your sword." "Goddess," answered Achilles, "however angry a man may be, he must do as you two command him. This will be best, for the gods ever hear the prayers of him who has obeyed them."

But the religious implications do not end here. They rather continue throughout the story. Achilles is Greece's preeminent hero and his heroic mien is most vividly displayed when his beloved comrade Patroclus is killed by the Trojan hero, Hector. Achilles' single thought thereafter is avenging Patroclus' death—despite the fact that an ancient prophecy foretells that his own death will follow hard on the heels of Hector's. When the hour of Hector's death arrives, a most peculiar aspect of the Olympian gods is betrayed: though Zeus is the most powerful of the gods, he is nonetheless subject to a kind of consensus that could best be termed Fate: an amorphous compendium of the wills of all the gods in unison. As Achilles, the best of the Greeks, and Hector, Troy's champion, came face-to-face to do combat, "Zeus, the Father of All, balanced his golden scales in his mighty hand and placed a doom in each of its equally weighted scalepans, one for Achilles and the other for Hector. As he held the scales by the fulcrum, the doom of Hector fell down, deep into the house of Hades." Thereupon, Apollo, who had been fighting at his side, "left Hector forthwith." And with Hector dead, the Olympians were left free to plot the inevitable fall of Troy.

If Achilles is the very model of Greek heroism, the preeminent Greek trickster is "wily Odysseus." It was Odysseus who, in the guise of a beggar and under Athena's tutelage, entered Troy itself to steal from its sanctuary the sacred statue of Athena which, it was prophesied, would protect Troy from ruin for as long as it remained within the city walls. And with this statue in hand, he

The walls of the Hisarlik, the likely site of Troy (Wikipedia, photograph by CherryX).

constructed the ruse that would lay the city in ruin, sending abroad the rumor that the Greeks had left off their siege when the Goddess herself, infuriated that her image had been stolen from its Trojan sanctuary, cursed the Greeks saying that they would never now be able to take the city. Further, according to Odysseus' ruse, she commanded that if the Greeks ever wished to reach their homes in safety, they should leave an offering in compensation for their sacrilege: a wooden horse but one too large to bring into the city unless the Scaean gate was torn down. The Trojans, of course, fell for the trick—breaking the lintel of the impregnable gate—to bring the horse, filled with the pick of Greece's most valiant warriors, into the city. But they would have never done so had it not been for the fact that the gods on Olympus clouded their reason and rendered them vulnerable to resourceful Odysseus' schemes. Thus, when the Trojan priest Laocoön warned, "Trust not this horse, O Troy; I fear the Greeks, though gift on gift they bear," they ignored him. And when in punishment for his attempt to thwart their design, the gods sent a monstrous two-headed serpent racing in from the sea to ensnare Laocoön and his two young sons, the Trojans interpreted their deaths as evidence of the horse's sanctity, redoubling their efforts to bring the horse within Troy's wide ramparts.

Then, with Troy in ruins and its unhappy survivors scattered abroad, Odysseus played his most famous trick, getting the Cyclops Polyphemus drunk on undiluted wine and piercing the single eye that chillingly sat in the middle of his forehead. But, in doing so, Odysseus earned the undying hatred of the Cyclop's father, Poseidon. It was Athena who finally convinced Zeus that, Odysseus—in his ten years of wandering to get home from Troy—had suffered enough: "Father, Son of Kronos, King of Kings," Athena lamented, "It is for Odysseus that my heart bleeds, when I think of his sufferings, far away, poor man, from all his friends. He is tired of life and thinks of nothing but how he may once more see the smoke of his own hearth. But you take no heed of this. Yet when Odysseus was before Troy, did he not propitiate you with many a burnt sacrifice? Why then should you remain so angry with him?" And Zeus concurred, saying, "My child, what have you said? How can I forget Odysseus? There is no more capable man on earth, nor more liberal in his offerings to the immortal gods that live in heaven." Thus it was that Zeus mustered the courage to override his brother's mandate against Odysseus, finally sending the unhappy wanderer back to his own home and hearth. And it was Athena as well who arranged Odysseus' vengeance against the suitors who were—out of keeping with Zeus' own sacred law of hospitality—eating Odysseus out of house and home, shamefully slaughtering his sheep and draining his casks of wine, even as they wickedly insisted that Odysseus' faithful wife, Penelope, choose one of them as her husband's replacement. When Odysseus finally achieved his homeport on the island of Ithaca, Athena hid his strength and beauty beneath the rags of an old, decrepit beggar and then set him to his work.

Antinous, the worst of the suitors, rather than offer the charity to a beggar that Zeus' mandate required, mocked Odysseus and even went so far as to throw a footstool at him, hitting him in the shoulder. But Odysseus took it all in humility, even joining the wicked suitors as they laughed at his mistreatment. Thus, when Penelope—at Athena's behest—suggested a contest, the suitors' fate was sealed. Penelope proclaimed that whoever could string Odysseus' bow—which he had left behind when he embarked for Troy—and send an arrow flying from it, would gain her hand in marriage. As the ghost of one of Penelope's dead suitors reported: "Not one of us could string the bow—nor nearly do so." But when Odysseus stepped forth and—his strength and beauty revealed—strung the bow with ease, the suitors' death was at hand. One by one, Odysseus slaughtered them, starting first with Antinous, who, all unknowing, "was about to take up a two-handled gold cup," for a draught of wine. "The arrow struck Antinous in the throat and the point went clean through his neck, so that he fell over and the cup dropped from his hand, while a thick stream of blood gushed from his nostrils." Then it was that Hermes "summoned the ghosts of the suitors, and in his hand he held the fair golden wand with which he seals men's eyes in sleep or wakes them just as he pleases. With this he roused the ghosts and led them, while they followed whining and gibbering behind him."[6]

Achilles himself is a demigod—the child of a goddess and a mortal—and, as such, draws attention to the fact that even our culture heroes carry within themselves a spark of divinity. And the same can be said of the preeminent Greek trickster, the "wily Odysseus," even if his mother is, like his father, a mere mortal. Not only are these two heroes' exploits continuously touched by the gods but the heroes themselves function as cultural progenitors for the Greek people and, as such, they—like Athena, Hera, and Zeus—take their rightful place in the world of mythology. Fascinatingly, the idea of Greek (as well as Trojan) heroes as mythic progenitors was retained throughout European history. For instance, the Spanish aristocracy claimed descent from none other than Hercules himself: aggrandizing themselves not only in their own eyes but (not unconsciously, I suspect) in the eyes of their subjects.

Just as Greek religion is partly imparted in legends, so too is Native American religion imparted at times in folktales. Throughout Native America, a number of stories which deal with a young boy's or girl's interaction with a supernatural being, often in the form of a spirit-animal ally, are to be found. The protagonists of these tales are often poor "No Account Boys" or "Ash Girls." They are scapegoats, who like the European Jack (berated for selling his family's single cow for magical beans) or Cinderella (whose name is compounded from the root, *cinder,* ash, and the feminine diminutive suffix *ella*), are disdained by family and community alike. An intriguing tale of this sort is told by the Iroquois: agriculturalists who cultivated the classic Native American corn, beans, squash complex and lived communally in bark longhouses in what is today Western New York. Here, an unnamed "No Account Boy," poor and disdained by the village's war chiefs and somewhat bumbling in his comportment, inadvertently accepted the wampum belt proffered by the village's High Chief. The belt represented the High Chief's assignation to go out in search of a cannibal-monster who was destroying his people: Nyagwaihegowa, the Naked Bear. The War Chiefs, too frightened at the mysterious deaths afflicting their fellow villagers to accept the assignation, laughed out loud when such a lowly member of the community—an impoverished youth living at the outskirts of the village with no family beyond his aged grandmother—took the wampum belt. But the High Chief upbraided them for their arrogance.

Thereupon, the No Account Boy went to his grandmother for advice. She reached up to the loft tucked beneath the rafters of their bark longhouse and "pulled out an old bark-case all covered with dust. This she put on the floor. Out of it she drew an old headdress," a crown with one large eagle feather at the center and "trimmed with many small plumes of downy eagle feathers." When she placed the headdress upon her grandson's head, the "plumes seemed to wave as if a soft wind were blowing upon them." She then took from the loft "a long bow, black with age," and so thick that no ordinary man could bend and string it. "This she gave to him, saying, 'If you can string this bow, then you are good enough to use it.'" When he effortlessly strung the bow, the No Account Boy's grandmother rejoiced to see that her grandson "had become the man that she so often wished him to be." After following a trail of human bones and gore to the Naked Bear's lair, the No Account Boy falls into a deep slumber—whereupon the monster comes to him in a dream and pleads for his life. The Naked Bear, frightened by the spiritual power of the once lowly boy, begs that he be allowed to remove himself to the west where he will no longer menace people with his violent presence. He even leaves one of his teeth as a token of the promise he has made. The one-time No Account Boy, now exalted, becomes the model for a new sort of chief—a Peace Chief who will promote alliance rather than enmity and institute the Hand-in-Hand Dance to celebrate "the ending of war amongst people and the taking of the scalp."

The Iroquois tale is explicit in the import of its message: the lowly become the exalted. When the No Account Boy accepts the wampum belt from the High Chief, the War Chiefs mock him. But he alone is able to accomplish what they are too fearful to attempt. And the villagers who, in these ancient times did not know that they were to be generous to those less fortunate than themselves, learned the essential nature of reciprocity in all their undertakings. The same message is at play in a justly famous tale told by the Zuni: agriculturalists who, like the Iroquois, raised corn, beans, and squash in their gardens but lived in a strong adobe Pueblo in what is today New Mexico. In this tale, a poor Ash Girl, who lives alone at the outskirts of Zuni Pueblo with her aged grandfather and seems reticent to take a husband, is disdained by the Zuni warriors who are always going out on the hunt but do not think to share their meat with the impoverished pair. Thus, the girl—wanting to savor the smell of roasting meat—goes out to hunt rabbits. While doing so, she is set upon by the cannibal-monster Atoshle: Old Lady Granduncle in Dennis Tedlock's chilling translation. Just as the rabbit hunter routed about in the burrow with her outstretched arm in order to extricate its rabbits, so Atoshle routed about in the cave where the frightened girl took refuge. But Old Lady Granduncle was, happily, noticed by one of the twin Zuni war gods, the younger Ahayuuta brother, who not only killed the monster but also took the Ash Girl back to her village where he taught the people the benefits of reciprocity. And it was not simply rabbit that he brought back to the Pueblo. Rather he returned each evening carrying a rack of deer meat on his back. Thereafter the Ash Girl, rather than hunt on her own, knew that it was more proper to marry in order to have meat on her table, and the Zuni always, in accord with the lesson imparted by the Younger Ahayuuta, shared out any meat taken in the hunt with all of their fellow villagers.[7]

Whether dealing with heroes or tricksters, No Account Boys or Ash Girls, or even—as we later will see—Biblical figures or saints, we are dealing with characters which, lacking divinity themselves, carry a touch of the divine within them. This is the reason they find themselves so often in the company of gods. And this too is the reason why myth alone is not large enough to encompass the entirety of a nation's spiritual lore. Beyond gods and goddesses, then, we will be concerning ourselves with ancestors and ghosts; demigods, saints, and angels; heroes who become mythic progenitors and scapegoats who come to the rescue of their nations; witches, sorcerers, demons, and an almost innumerable cast of frightful monsters. These disparate beings may inhabit the celestial realm with the gods or prefer to move quietly and unseen among us here in our earthly realm. Sometimes they are entirely ethereal and sometimes they exist as demigods who may be, just as their name implies, half god: the child of a god and a mortal. Yet again, they may be the all too human vehicles by which celestial dictates are accomplished. Many of the Biblical figures answer to that definition as do Achilles and Odysseus. Though explicitly human, according to the Torah, Noah undertakes the very acts that Utnapishtim, the Mesopotamian god who is his counterpart, does. And Odysseus, without a divine parent at all, plays as important a role in the Trojan Cycle as does Achilles.

Thus, I will—as I go forward—draw a distinction between myth, on the one hand, and mythology, on the other. When I say myth, I will generally be sticking closely to the usual meaning of the term—a religious story—but when I say mythology, I will be going a bit further afield, considering those other stories—legends and folktales—as well as accounts of visionary journeys, recitations of religious codes and, even at times, stories which contain mythic overtones but would unlikely be considered religiously charged such as tall tales, jokes, and personal anecdotes. Perhaps, in the service of clarity, I can add that—whether classified as a myth, legend, folktale, or some other narrative genre—if the story deals with an ostensible first, or ancient, time, before the world came to be as it is, and thus offers an explanation for the creation of the world and an ideal pattern for human behavior modeled on the behavior of the gods themselves, we are dealing with a society's mythology. Further, I should add that just as myth spills some of its substance into stories that are not— strictly speaking—religious, religion likewise spills some of its substance into ostensibly non-religious arenas: magic, witchcraft, and sorcery, for instance. While not necessarily the subject of teachings that might emanate from a church, a temple, or a synagogue, magic, witchcraft, sorcery, and even the arcane accounts of monstrous beings such as vampires and werewolves deal with spirits and spiritual inclinations and we will thus consider them here.

One more clarification: whereas myth often means something that is untrue in everyday parlance, in the study of mythology, it means a sacred story with no assessment as to its literal truth. Nonetheless, because of its more mundane use, the term myth is sometimes fraught with controversy and would be looked at askance by a number of groups—for instance, most Evangelical Christian denominations or Native American nations—which consider their myths to be holy and immutable. The popular usage for the term myth most probably results from, at best, an inherent skepticism or, at worst, an ethnocentric disregard of alternate religious systems. Unfortunately, there really isn't any other term than myth with which to describe our subject matter. Thus, it seems worthwhile to reiterate the fact that despite the use of the term myth to mean that which isn't true in everyday speech, the term here means, simply put, a sacred story, a story whose truth is immutable and not subject to the usual rules of empirical verification. In other words, the validity of myth must be granted as we undertake this study even if sought in realms other than the mere historical. Generally, we will rather find that the validity of the stories that we will consider here would be described by their adherents as a matter of faith.

But what is it that we wish to accomplish through the exploration of mythology? It is the discovery and explication of indigenous philosophies: singular approaches to the world born of specific societies and their particular cultures. Thus, as we go forward, we will draw attention to the fact that every society's culture is a product of its two-fold environment: the physical environment that it exploits in order to gain its livelihood and the social environment by means of which it distributes—equitably or inequitably as the case may be—the resources that its physical environment affords. Further, we will draw attention to the fact that a society's mythology is intimately entwined with this two-fold environment: liberally borrowing from it the various metaphors—ecological and social—with which it embodies the abstract concepts that comprise its ideology: that is, its culturally inscribed worldview. It seems, in fact, that the physical embodiment of the conceptual world that is accomplished in myth is the very essence of religious signification and responsible for establishing the meaning of all the various artifacts of culture—not only verbal but also behavioral and material—which find their way into our religious life. That is to say that each of us, *in mythic language,* whether that "language" is spoken, enacted, or embodied in items of manufacture, figures out—or at least attempts to figure out—the significance of every element of our existence that, in one way or another, perplexes us: life and death; sickness and health; culture and nature; friendship and love or enmity and hate; poverty and happiness or affluence and malaise; obedience and orthodoxy or rebellion and transcendence.

Thus, as we proceed in our analysis, we will continuously pay attention to the various ecological adaptations and social configurations which simultaneously formulate and are formulated by our mythologies, hoping—as we do so—to answer a number of questions that will concern us in our attempt to unravel the mysteries of our spiritual life: What exactly is religion and why is it found in every society? Why does it universally consist of a set of stories (myths) and communal reenactments of these stories (rituals)? Why does it center so intensively on anthropomorphic spirits and why do these spirits— along with the landscapes they inhabit—look so eerily similar to those entities and landscapes that populate our dreams? Why do our rituals universally consist of communal vocalizations and movements—often accompanied by some rhythmic if not percussive sounds? Why are the shamans and priests who perform the religious functions of their societies, cross-culturally and despite different ecological adaptations, predominately men? And why do women, in the face of male dominance of official religiosity, so often carve out for themselves special niches of female spirituality? Why do our myths continuously borrow the metaphors with which they trick out abstract concepts from the arena of ecological adaptations and social structures and why do we need the philosophical

constructs that our mythologies provide through such metaphorical construc-
tions? Finally, what do our mythologies accomplish with regard to our culture
as a whole? In essence, all these questions are contained in one final question:
Why is religion and the form that it takes universal to human existence?

Celebrating Buddha's Birthday

What we will find as we attempt to answer that final question is this: the
reason that the study of mythology is so essential is because the religion that
mythology generates contains within itself the entirety of culture: its biological
underpinnings, its singular history, its ecological and sociological concerns, its
ideological orientation, and—most importantly—its ability to totally inhabit
one's sense of self: an ability we cannot help but notice when falling into conversation with someone whose religion is different from that in which we ourselves were schooled—as I one day did: "Buddhism," she patiently explained
to me that day, "is very easy to understand. The Buddha asks of us one thing
only: that we be kind to one another." But a great deal of thought, gathered in
the deep meditative moments of the Enlightened One himself as he contemplated the meaning of existence beneath the Bodhi Tree, lies hidden behind
that simple dictum of compassion.

As a boy, Siddhartha Gautama's father—tormented by a prophecy which
said his son was destined to be either a resplendent prince or a wandering holy
man—cloistered his son in an opulent palace. Nonetheless, as a young man,
Siddhartha witnessed four momentous sights: an old man, a diseased man, a
corpse, and a wandering hermit. While the first three sights horrified the young
man's sensibilities, the fourth—suffused as the hermit was with a quiet con-
tentment—offered Siddhartha a way out of his distress. Thus, he took up the
life of an ascetic, wandering—along with a small group of mendicant sages—
the back streets of villages and the unbeaten forest pathways in rags, bearing
only a simple bowl with which to beg some small nourishment. But when, near
the point of death from practicing the most extreme austerities, he was given
a small bowl of rice by a young woman, Sujata, he was—not unlike Jesus in a
justly famous incident—criticized and finally abandoned by his fellow hermits.
It was then that he found his way to the famous Bodhi tree beneath which he
would become the Buddha, the Enlightened One. Yet, first, understanding the
danger to his existence such enlightenment presented, the demon Mara—in
another incident which Joseph Campbell reminds us is uncannily similar to one
experienced by Jesus—unsuccessfully tempts Siddhartha. First, he attempts to
frighten Siddhartha with an apocalyptic eruption of the forces of nature. Next,

he attempts to distract Siddhartha with sensual desire. Finally, he attempts to foster in Siddhartha the sin of pride. But banishing the demon from his presence, Siddhartha achieves his goal and—not long thereafter—encountering the hermits who rejected him, accepts them as his first disciples, thereupon instituting the kernel of the Sangha, the brotherhood of Buddhist monks.

Buddhism, avoiding both the extreme asceticism of holy men and the conventional materialism (desire) of householders (members of the laity), opts

The Buddha (author's photograph).

rather for the Middle Way encapsulated in the Four Noble Truths and the Noble Eightfold Path. The Truths consist of the following principles: (1) life is suffering; (2) the source of suffering is desire, anger, and ignorance; (3) suffering can be overcome by taming desire through the practice of detachment, displacing anger through the cultivation of compassion, and dispelling ignorance through the pursuit of truth; and (4) the Noble Eightfold Path permits one to do so. The Eightfold Path consists of attending to the following precepts: (1) Right View, or the acceptance of the Four Noble Truths; (2) Right Thought, or the determination to cultivate compassion, dispel ignorance, and abjure desire; (3) Right Speech, or using one's words to further harmonious relations among one's fellow human beings; (4) Right Action, or behaving in a manner that, likewise, promotes harmonious relations; (5) Right Livelihood, or pursuing an occupation which betters, rather than harms, society; (6) Right Effort, or encouraging healthful urges while taming those that are disruptive to one's spiritual well-being; (7) Right Mindfulness, or maintaining awareness of the present moment as it impacts the delicate balance between body and spirit; and (8) Right Concentration, or perfecting focus—perhaps through meditation—in order to contemplate the ultimate nature of reality. Notice how the Four Noble Truths and the Noble Eightfold Path intersect one another in the fourth Truth and the first precept of the Path and consider the idea that attending to the Truths and the Path allows one to achieve liberation, understood as the comprehension and perhaps even the achievement of Nirvana: escape from the otherwise endless round of life, death, and rebirth.

Though veneration of the Three Gems—the Buddha (the Enlightened One), the Dharma (the knowledge encapsulated in the Four Truths and the Eightfold Path), and the Sangha (the brotherhood of Buddhist monks)—is a universal Buddhist principle, Buddhism (like Christianity) adapts itself readily to local cultural circumstances. Thus, basic Buddhist precepts must always be viewed in the context of their local, indigenous, applications. For instance, in Japan, Shinto's underlying belief in an almost innumerable host of *kami* (deities)—most good, some bad, others moderately troublesome—explained good or ill fortune on a day-to-day basis. The *kami* therefore needed to be propitiated through comportment, ritual, and worship at the Shinto shrines which dot Japan's landscape with their characteristic *torri*, or entrance gate, and *honden*, or altar house. Nonetheless, the teachings that emanated from Buddhist monasteries—which also define the contours of the Japanese landscape with their five-tiered pagodas, perhaps serving as a reliquary for some especially revered *bodhisattva* who had deferred salvation for the sake of humanity—continuously served to remind one of the impermanence of what, even in Shinto ideology, was thought of as a fleeting world situated precariously upon the primordial sea. Into that roiling sea the Shinto *kami*, Izanagi and Izanami, standing upon the floating bridge of heaven, dipped their jewel encrusted spear and spirited into existence the island of Onogoro whereon they gave birth to the Sun Goddess, Amaterasu, she who invested the imperial clan with the Japanese throne.[8] But given such a tenuous origin, it was as if creation in its entirety could, without warning, submerge itself and the world—as we know it—disappear, revealing, once and for all, its essential impermanence.

And a Chinese folktale speaks of the Buddha who, exhausted from his search for and harvesting of the "vegetable of longevity," dropped to the ground and fell into a deep sleep. But as he slumbered, a lion crept upon his treasure and devoured it. Thus, the Buddha had to coax the lion to give up some of his newfound bounty to mankind. Today, upon the New Year, in Shanghai and Hong Kong, in New York and San Francisco, the Lion Dance—during which extravagant white lions, coaxed by a Buddha impersonator, twist their way through the streets to the clamor of drums, cymbals, and gongs—is to be seen. When one finds himself in the midst of clanging cymbals and reverberating drums, the explosive reports and billowing clouds of smoke let off by strings of firecrackers, and the jubilant crowd pressing upon the line of Gung Fu practitioners staving off the onlookers with their martial prowess, it is nearly impossible not to get caught up in the exhilaration of the moment. And, as the Buddha draws the lions—with their rolling eyes, their snapping jaws, and their bobbing heads—from locale to locale, inviting them to devour an offering of lucky greens and leave behind themselves their blessing, the remnant of their ancient repast—it is impossible not to be impressed by the lions' calculated movements: they kowtow, they bend and undulate, they sniff their prey, and—finally—they pounce.[9] In the instance that I stumbled upon, their quarry was a small pyramid of perfectly formed heads of cabbage set out on a table. The two lions swallowed the cabbages whole and then deftly spit the shredded leaves high into the air.

And Thailand's Buddhists, like Buddhists in the religion's homeland of Northern India or the many regions—Sri Lanka, the Himalayas, Japan, China, Korea, Southeast Asia—to which it was transported, have their own pantheon of "saints, ghosts, deities, and spirits."[10] Saints may include among their ranks *bodhisattvas* and particularly revered monks while ghosts may take the manifestation of "ancestral spirits who refuse to be reborn because they want to protect their living family members" or marauding murderers intent on punishing "those that offend them." Parichat Jungwiwattanaporn suggests that, while "Buddhism preaches the awakening from ignorance through mindfulness," indigenous Thai religious practice rather "preaches building congenial relationships" between the living and the dead.[11] And Justin McDaniel aptly illustrates this precept through his analysis of the illusory relationship between the spirit of a deceased Buddhist monk, Somdet To, and a troubled ghost, Mae Nak. Mae Nak, who some 100 years ago died in childbirth, was so devoted to her husband that she convinced him she was still living—always avoiding the sun which might betray her as a decaying corpse. And when fellow villagers attempted to warn her husband of his wife's true nature, Mae Nak would slay them in the night so that she became coated in the blood and gore of her victims. Finally, Somdet To—he whose holiness was so profound that he could publicly check the excesses of King Rama IV (the king depicted in *Anna and the King of Siam*)—found a way to contain the restless spirit and relieve her long-suffering husband. Adept in Pali (the northern Indian language in which the earliest Buddhist texts are written), Somdet To knew just the mantra which would induce Mae Nak to accept burial under a Takian tree at Bangkok's Wat Mahabut where she is, to this day, offered monthly funerals by the resident monks.[12]

The notion that life is suffering and illusory may seem antithetical to the ideals espoused in our optimistic and relatively affluent self-help, achieving your full potential, positive-thinking age. But suffering was a pressing reality in a number of traditional—and perhaps especially preindustrial mercantile—societies. In Sicily, for instance, life was said to consist of misery (*miseria*): an existence without enough food, sufficient work, or decent housing; an existence characterized by an unending scramble to make a hard living. And in Haiti, the same concept (*mizè*) expressed the same anxieties which Sicilians suffered. Under such circumstances, does Buddhism not offer a means of not only explaining but also dealing proactively with suffering? Does bringing desire under control not allow one a sense of control over his or her existence in its entirety? Could it not give us some sense of satisfaction over existence *as it is* rather than asking us to futilely strive after some illusory expectation of how we have been told it should be? And, when coupled with the doctrine of compassion, could it not be that we might at times more easily defer out of sympathy and kindness to someone else's needs over our own?

Though sometimes difficult to fathom, especially for those of us who have been accustomed to thinking our own theology singularly correct and therefore others not worthy of respect, there is a simple pleasure in breaking a Ramadan fast with a small bowl of cold white beans garnished in a light carrot sauce, followed by a bit of bitter chocolate and sweet Turkish liquor, or dining on a plate of rice and cabbage smothered in a sweet yellow curry after dancing before Krishna, or—indeed as I often did with my friend who told me that Buddha's one requirement was that we be kind to one another—celebrating Buddha's birthday with a plate of spring rolls and a bowl of coconut soup. My role in the celebration was simple and straightforward. I was given a shopping list and sent off to the local Asian grocery store to shop for the dinner's ingredients while my friend spent some quiet moments in contemplation before turning to cooking the delicacies and distributing them to coworkers (since there was no monastic school whose monks and nuns could receive the offerings nearby). I remember thinking how singular it was that I was shopping for Buddha's birthday and wondering how many non–Buddhists found themselves so engaged. Who could possibly deprive oneself of such a pleasure as celebrating the Buddha's birthday simply on the grounds that recognizing another deity would be sinful? It seems, in fact, that this is precisely the message which Herman Melville wished us to contemplate in charting—within his mythically charged novel *Moby Dick*—the budding friendship of Ishmael and Queequeg. Ishmael, having spotted Queequeg in the little Nantucket chapel where whalers worshipped before setting out for two or more years upon the perilous seas, was loath to refuse the tattooed harpooner's invitation to worship the little idol which he packed from his South Sea island homeland in a small rucksack. But he finally came to the conclusion that the dictum to "do unto others as you would have them do unto you" was the more compelling to a loving god than that which declared that "thou shalt have no other gods before me." And he shared in his new friend's religious practice.

This brings us to a sensitive point. If it is the nature of religion to inhabit every fiber of one's being, mythology, the central facet of religion, becomes an especially essential—but particularly fraught—study. For while mythologies—and the religions they engender—are among the most imaginative, creative, and even transcendent elements of human culture, they are also at times the most untempered, mean-spirited, and angry cultural products imaginable. I think that it is in the complex of metaphoric signification—what I refer to as mythic rhetoric—that we find the answer to the sometimes bifurcated gift that is mythology, the understanding that though mythology at times seems to divide us and set us against one another, it at others gives us insight into how we all share with one another the human condition: how we all exploit an environment for our resources, organize ourselves into a society to better collect, process, and distribute those resources, and how we all postulate the existence of spirits who aid us in this enterprise of environmental exploitation, material production, and resource distribution. And this understanding can be positively medicinal—for it allows us to make sense of what might otherwise seem an incomprehensible jumble of disparate facts. And it might even help us cultivate a greater compassion for our co-religionists—even if they do follow a different rite than our own. But in order to better appreciate the salutary effects that might accrue to us as a result of such an understanding, let's offer some discussion of the analytic context in which we will situate mythology: culture.

1. Origins: The Dance and the Dream

Culture: Biology and History

Culture is the result of a commingling of universal human biological characteristics with localized historical circumstances. Put more simply, we can say that biology and history collude in order to allow a particular society—a group of people—to elaborate its own particular culture. Thus, anthropology—the academic discipline that takes culture as its central focus—attempts to consider both culture's biological underpinnings and historical development in order to understand its ecological imperatives, sociological functions, and ideological ramifications as well as its major mechanism of transmission: language. Biology, in this context, is a function of evolution.

Charles Darwin's idea that adaptive traits, traits that allow an individual to thrive and reproduce, are more readily passed on to a species' next generation than maladaptive traits is known as natural selection. Indeed, Darwin suggested that, over time, adaptive traits would become more prevalent in a species and could, eventually, lead to the development of new species. This idea was augmented by Gregor Mendel's observations on genetics. Mendel postulated that units of heredity, genes, are passed on from one generation to the next according to predictable rules. One's genes—a random assortment of one's mother's and father's genes, commingled upon conception and acted upon by mutational processes—govern every facet of one's biological existence: not only physical appearance and bodily functions but even a remarkable array of behaviors. Significantly, a number of these behaviors predispose humans to be culture-using animals. Together, natural selection and genetics came to be the central focus of the concept of evolution: the process of biological change which allowed us to recognize the biological lineaments of our own species as well as the interrelatedness of all life forms.

Because of the biological origins of at least a portion of human behavior, a number of late 19th century analysts—E.B. Tylor, for instance, or Émile Durkheim—viewed culture through the lens of evolution, conflating biological change with cultural history. They, thereby, mistakenly viewed human societies in a hierarchical manner beginning with foraging societies (small, egalitarian groups which, rather than producing food, lived as nomadic hunters and gatherers), transitioning through agricultural societies (in which every member was directly involved in food production through farming, herding, or a combination of the two), and culminating in mercantile societies (large groups whose complex division of labor gave rise to full-time specialization, occupational classes, markets, and trade). But such analyses were too focused on mere biology despite the fact that only a fraction of our behaviors are the result of genetics. Much of what we do is rather the result of invention (the spontaneous development of a behavior, perhaps as a result of some environmental need) and diffusion (the historical exchange of behaviors from one society to another). The movement from foraging, through farming, to mercantile societies is among the most essential that humanity has experienced—and one which had a profound impact on our global mythologies—but it is a historical rather than an evolutionary movement.

On the basis of such observations, a school of thought that looked at human behavior as the result of invention and diffusion began to emerge in the early 20th century and is anthropology's inheritance from Franz Boas. Rather than biology, history was seen as the more compelling force in human culture: history perhaps lost to us in the preliterate (and thus prehistoric) phases of cultural development but history nonetheless. Boas and his students, postulating that infants were "blank slates" upon which almost all behavior would be "written" by other members of their society, overcompensated for some of the excesses of the early "cultural evolutionists" but these new "historical particularists" offered a needed corrective to the interpretation of culture.

Still, one of the most useful observations made by anthropology is that we humans are not separated from the rest of the animal kingdom by so remarkable a degree as we sometimes imagine. Probably being attentive to other cultures and their religious views predisposes the discipline to this observation. Consider the words of a Wintu woman when trying to distinguish the view of the Native American from that of the European American as regards the world around her:

> The White people never cared for land or deer or bear. When we Indians kill meat, we eat it all up. When we dig roots we make little holes. When we burn grass for grasshoppers, we don't ruin things. We shake down acorns and pine nuts. We don't chop down the trees. We only use dead wood. But the White people plow up the ground, pull up the trees, kill everything. The tree says, "Don't. I am sore. Don't hurt me." But they chop it down and

cut it up. The spirit of the land hates them. The Indians never hurt anything, but the white people destroy all. They blast rocks and scatter them on the ground. The rock says, "Don't! You are hurting me." But the white people pay no attention. How can the spirit of the earth like the white man? Everywhere he has touched it, it is sore.[1]

Such a communication asks us to think about humans and human culture as they relate to earth's teeming biological diversity. And it asks us to look at ourselves as part of—rather than apart from—the animal kingdom.

The Biological Underpinnings of Mythology

The study of non-human primates and, in particular, that ape that is our closest relative—the chimpanzee, perhaps 99 percent genetically identical to ourselves—allows us to begin to see what is biological, as opposed to what is learned, in our behavior. In fact, the easiest means of determining if there is some degree of biological (i.e., genetic) inscription in our behavior is to ask if the behavior under consideration is not only universal to human societies but also shared with closely related species. In other words, if we humans universally do something that apes and perhaps even monkeys do, it seems reasonable to say that there is some degree of biology at play. Perhaps most remarkable of all primate studies, in this regard, is Jane Goodall's of the chimpanzees of Gombe National Forest in Tanzania, East Africa. The Gombe chimpanzee community, numbering about 100 individuals, inhabits a 30-mile stretch of mountainous forest running along the shore of Lake Tanganyika. During the course of her studies, Goodall continuously found the Gombe chimps doing things that were strictly attributed to humans, not the least of which was hugging, kissing, patting one another on the back or the head, and holding hands, for precisely the same reasons that humans do: to show affection and to reassure one another. Further, Goodall discovered the chimpanzees' penchant for making and using tools—for instance fashioning a probing stick with which to extract termites from their earthen mounds—and even undertaking territorial warfare.

Another observation arising out of Goodall's studies involves chimpanzee hunting and, its constant corollary, sharing. Chimps don't typically share their normative foodstuffs—fruit, leaves, and shoots—but rather special foods, particularly meat. The sharing of meat seems to result from the fact that chimps are not, anatomically speaking, particularly effective predators. They're not very fast and though their canines are markedly larger than ours, they pale in comparison to those of true predators such as lions or wolves. What the chimps lack, however, in speed and killing ability, they make up in terms of cooperation. Chimps, especially dominant male chimps, hunt in a group, tracking, driving, flanking, and eventually killing their prey together. Because chimps hunt cooperatively, it becomes imperative that they share meat. Otherwise, no cooperative hunt would occur in the future. Interestingly, though the dominant males do most of the hunting and thus share the carcass, for the most part, among themselves, subordinate males, females, and even youngsters get a share of the meat through begging. With hand outstretched, sometimes only inches away from the dominant males' mouths, and amidst mounting whimpering, pant-hoots, and—finally—frantic shrieking, the other chimps within the troop get to taste the meat through sheer persistence![2]

Chimpanzees and humans shared a common ancestor, a quadrupedal ape living in East Africa, until perhaps six million years ago. This date is so close to the earliest evidence of bipedal apes, our first known human ancestors, that it seems increasingly likely that the mutations which gave rise to bipedalism were probably not in the foot, legs, or pelvis but rather in the brain and inner ear. In other words, mutations that allowed some apes to more easily maintain their balance while walking upright is likely the first step to bipedalism and this emergent bipedalism is the first step in human evolution.[3] However, the brain of our early bipedal ancestors—who radiated out from their likely homeland in East Africa to inhabit the greater part of Sub-Saharan Africa—is still apelike (some 350 cm^3) in size. The bipedal apes which dominated at least half of the human evolutionary process are likely to have been as efficient hunters as are contemporary chimps but they, unlike chimps, also regularly scavenged carcasses of animals that died of natural causes or had been killed by other, more adept, predators. It is possible that concerted action—and the use of tools, such as clubs—might have allowed them to steal prey when the predators were still present and feeding. Further, those bipedal apes ancestral to ourselves struck out of the forest, which is the normative environment for apes, and into a savanna environment—perhaps to take advantage of greater hunting and scavenging opportunities—rather early in their evolutionary history. In this context, bipedalism may have been an aid in the provisioning of essential resources as the nuclear family structure emerged. Males more adept at bipedal locomotion could more easily transport quality foods—such as scavenged carcasses—to a home base where they could provision females and their young.[4]

By 2.5 million years ago, we see enough cranial capacity (brains measuring some 750 cm^3) to view our ancestors as human, or pertaining to our own genus: Homo. Homo habilis, our first well known human ancestor, was still apelike in stature (with arm to leg ratio similar to that of a chimp). But, importantly, Homo habilis was regularly chipping stone tools which allowed it to butcher its prey more efficiently than its bipedal ape ancestors. Though little more than crude chips broken off a stone cobble, creating cutting flakes and crushing choppers, Oldowan tools allowed Homo habilis to get at the nutritious bone marrow encased by long limb bones and crack open skulls to get at the brain. And by two million years ago, we humans had achieved a sizable brain (1000 cm³), a relatively modern skeletal structure (with a leg to arm length ratio similar to humans rather than chimps) and the complex Acheulian stone tool culture characterized by finely crafted hand-axes which emerged as chips were carefully knapped away from either side of a stone core: what archaeologists call biface production. Homo erectus, representative of this time period, was a big game hunter whose invention of clothes and fire allowed it to expand into Europe and Asia. Moreover, at about 500 thousand years ago, late Homo erectus displays anatomical features that suggest the capacity for speech.

Then, as early as 400 thousand years ago, the robust Neanderthal (Homo neandertalensis), with a brain at least as large as our own (1,350 cm³) and not unusually larger (1,600 cm³), began to inhabit both temperate and glacial environments in southwest Asia and Europe where it continued to thrive until perhaps 40 thousand years ago. Neanderthal's complex Mousterian toolkit, like Homo erectus's Acheulian before it, allowed a continuation of a big game hunting strategy: an absolute necessity to Neanderthal who, as a result of its brawny physique, probably required significantly more protein to survive than do we. But whereas Homo erectus' Acheulian spears were simple wooden shafts, perhaps with a fire-hardened point, Neanderthal's Mousterian spears were likely among the first composite tools, comprised of a stone point somewhat akin to the Acheulian hand axe affixed to a wooden shaft with sinew. Such a spear could accomplish a more deadly strike. Finally, around 200 thousand years ago, anatomically modern humans (Homo sapiens) emerged in Africa and—thanks to their advanced hunting technologies which included the atlatl, the harpoon, and the eventually ubiquitous bow and arrow—left their African homeland between 100 to 60 thousand years ago. Spreading throughout the Old World, they eventually displaced both the last vestiges of Homo erectus in East Asia and Neanderthal in Europe. Yet, their very success at big game hunting (complicated by a rapidly changing environment) spelled the end of that singular subsistence strategy.

The exploration of human evolution, like that of primate behavior, offers us insight into our genetic inheritance. One of the most striking alterations to occur in the process of human evolution—beyond the movement from quadrupedalism to bipedalism and the expansion of cranial capacity—is the minimization of dominance hierarchies and their socially disruptive tendencies. Contemporary human foraging societies are universally characterized by egalitarianism: a relative equality among adult males, often extending to adult females as well. Even the children in foraging societies are generally treated with quite a bit of indulgence. This de-emphasis of dominance hierarchies is probably related to more regular meat use: apes, and probably especially bipedal apes, are not anatomically constructed to be especially efficient hunters. Therefore, they must hunt cooperatively. In order to ensure continued cooperation in the hunt, they must share meat. Egalitarianism in foraging groups is the means by which sharing (or reciprocity) is effectively maintained. It seems likely that as our early bipedal ancestors moved out of forested and into savanna environments, perhaps four million years ago, and as meat was becoming more essential to our diet, egalitarianism must have been simultaneously becoming more essential to our social structure. We might fairly describe this alteration as the "self-domestication" of the human species. Certain biopsychological factors— behavioral manifestations of genetically governed neurological processes— attended this self-domestication: more regularized pair bonding; the appearance of the nuclear family (and its various expansions); dependence on social ritual to facilitate group bonding; and the development of language in order to facilitate intragroup communication. Among these are a number of factors that seem to be preadaptations to our religious life. Preeminent among such factors are those that demarcate us as social animals, dreaming animals, and especially speaking animals.

Social Animals

For instance, when considering ourselves as social animals, we cannot help but wonder if the repetitive dominance and submission gestures that maintain social hierarchy among animals are a potential source for the behaviors that comprise our religious rituals. Perhaps most interesting among such "social rituals" are the threat behaviors observed, again by Jane Goodall, among chimpanzees. Not only do dominant male chimps, with hair bristling and arms thrashing, stand erect and charge their adversaries bipedally, but they further enhance their threatening displays through shaking vegetation, shrieking and pant-hooting, and even moving into a near dancelike performance during which they sway from side-to-side, repeatedly stomp the ground, and occasionally drum on tree trunks. Remarkably, these chimps display the same behaviors when confronting the potent elements—thunder, lightning, wind, and rain— that periodically sweep into their rugged lakeside habitat, as if such phenomena are of the same order as the appearance of threatening male chimps.[5] When Goodall first witnessed this unforeseen "rain dance," undertaken by the dominant male Goliath, she wrote, "With a display of strength and vigor such as this, primitive man himself might have challenged the elements."[6] Yet, a less frantic social ritual overtakes the chimps when, dispersed throughout the day in order to forage effectively, they come together in the evening to construct their nests high in the forest canopy. Then, the chimps settle into their nests amidst a chorus of pant-hoots that start with some of the dominant males, spread throughout the troop, and gradually subside until they are altogether overtaken by the quiet of the nighttime forest.[7]

Yet, chillingly, such chimpanzee sociability comes at the expense of others. Though there is a cohesiveness within the troop, that cohesiveness doesn't necessarily extend beyond the bounds of the troop's territory. When speaking of her discovery of territorial warfare, Goodall said:

> I started off studying one community and in 1972 that community divided into two. And one part of it moved down into the south of the range that the whole community had shared. Two years later, a series of events began which were amongst the most horrifying we have seen at Gombe. The males of the larger Kasakela community, the ones that we are studying today, systematically began to hunt down individuals of the smaller southern community and to attack them when they found them on their own or in small groups.

Within a year, Goodall reports, "every one of the seven males and at least one of the three females who had moved to the south had disappeared." Tellingly, Goodall adds, "And I think it's a bit horrifying to consider that just because we now know how aggressive chimpanzees can be, this makes them even more like us than I had previously believed."[8]

Like our nearest animal relatives, we humans tend to affiliate strongest with those whom we have known for the longest time: our parents, siblings, grandparents and grandchildren, perhaps even our aunts, uncles, and cousins, as well as other members of our immediate community. And, at least initially, the opposite of affiliation—fear and perhaps even loathing—is strongly correlated with a lack of familiarity. It is likely, then, that group cooperation is at least partially dependent on intergroup competition. Edward Wilson views this dynamic as part of our human inheritance of eusociality: a camp-based organization in which a small group of hunters goes out in search of game while another segment of the community, mainly women but potentially including adult men as well, collectively tends to the well-being of the young at the home base. Such an organization depends on a finely honed skill of reading social intentions: a skill which allows "us to evaluate the prospects and consequences of alliances, bonding, sexual contact, rivalries, domination, deception, loyalty and betrayal. We instinctively delight in the telling of countless stories about others as players upon the inner stage."[9] Troublingly though, the competition that defines intergroup relations worms its way into the community—as if an occasional insider is viewed as an intrusive outsider. The inevitable result is scapegoating which, chillingly, is its own sort of bonding ritual.

It's tempting here to suggest that the "dance" which still centers chimpanzee dominance/submission behaviors was coopted by our emergent spiritual selves, subsuming its hierarchical social tendencies in the service of increasing social cooperation. And, indeed, Michael Winkelman and John Baker describe the social rituals associated with the establishment of dominance hierarchies, the facilitation of mating, or the maintenance of group solidarity as preadaptations to religious life: adaptations that do not in and of themselves indicate religion but—when carried over from our earliest bipedal ancestors to our own human selves—became, with time, religiously charged.[10] Such a view seems unassailable. Yet, while the behaviors under consideration bring to mind our own ritual life, they have little to offer us on the elucidation of mythology or the manner in which ritual and myth work collaboratively to help us make sense of the world around us. Thus, we need to look beyond ritualized behavior in animals in order to learn how the biological becomes embedded in the spiritual.

Dreaming Animals

This is where our nature as dreaming animals comes into play. Chimpanzees dream. So do most, if not all, mammals. But what we'll perhaps never know is what chimps and the rest of the animal kingdom make of their dreams. Humans, on the other hand, and particularly humans who grow up in societies which don't dismiss dreams as psychic nonsense, often consider dreams to be spiritually charged. In fact, one of anthropology's progenitors, E.B. Tylor, suggested in the late 1800s that religion arose out of the human perplexity over the physiological fact of dreaming. Tylor, noting that many traditional societies believed that not only humans but also animals, plants, topographical features, celestial bodies, even items of human manufacture contained spirits or souls, believed that this circumstance—which he referred to as animism (from the Latin word, *anima*, or soul)—represented the incipience of religion. Animism arose, Tylor believed, at some point in the evolutionary history of humans because it served to explain a number of natural phenomena: shadows, reflections in water, and most notably dreams and trances. In essence, then, the *anima* (soul or spirit) was the ephemeral manifestation of a living body that was released each night as we slept, that is, during the "little death," and perhaps eternally when we entered that great, unending "big sleep," death itself. This ephemeral manifestation (perhaps we might call it the *alter ego*, the other self) existed in another plane of existence, a spiritual plane, whose landscape was eerily evocative of the dreamscape. Inasmuch as the soul or spirit looked and behaved suspiciously like an entity in a dream, the dream became for Tylor the source of religious belief. This way of viewing religion was likely suggested by reports of Australian Aboriginal religion which sometimes referred to the ancient mythic times when the world was being created as the Dreaming.

The singular relationship between dreaming and notions of spirituality suggested by Tylor is probably best expressed by T.M. Luhrmann when she suggests that "as an anthropologist, I set out to understand the way people experience the spirit." Whereas she found that evangelical Christians in the United States were likely to interpret unusual dream events by means of naturalistic explanations, such as "sleep deprivation," evangelical Christians in Ghana and India were more likely to interpret these events spiritually, believing for instance that God called out to them in their sleep. "It seems likely," Luhrmann suggests, "that the way our culture invites us to pay attention to that delicate space in which one trembles on the edge of sleep changes what we remember of it."[11] Another telling example of the intersection between the physiological reality of dreaming and the spiritual conceptions of human societies is offered by the Iroquois Dream Guessing ceremony.[12] In this, one's family, friends, and fellow villagers would ask questions of the dreamer in order to allow him or her to "straighten out" the dream: that is, to make sense of it and thereby understand the spiritual mandate that it embodied. And this ceremony still remains active, at least in my experience, in the Iroquois tradition of discussing one's dreams first thing in the morning.

Let us think about the nature of the dream for a moment. What are its constant integers? They include representations of the living, the dead, and various phantoms at play upon a stage that includes all the normative elements of our world—landscapes, celestial bodies, plants, manufactured items, and animals—all in a decidedly more ephemeral form than that in which we are used to seeing them during our waking hours. Further, one can suddenly become enveloped in an amorphous sense of well-being or dread while at play in the dreamscape. Among the living, notably, is one's self, always the center of one's own dreams, though, at times, one can sometimes look like someone else even as he or she knows it for himself or herself. Or one can suddenly realize that the self who is being dreamed about is somehow different than the one who is at home, in bed, doing the dreaming. But what do these, the constant integers of our dreams, have to do with spirituality?

Inasmuch as our dreams are defined by the appearance of ourselves, the quick and the dead, phantoms, and sensations of well-being or dread, we might reasonably ask if these same integers are to be found in our mythologies. Certainly, the occasional perception that the dreamer (the living, breathing human being at home, in bed, dreaming) and the dreamed one (the self that one sees in a dream) are somehow separate entities seems to offer an especially cogent explanation for the manner in which we comprehend the soul—if not for its actual origin. And it would be difficult to deny the fact that the circumstance of dreaming one's self as somebody else—while knowing it is nonetheless one's self that one is dreaming—seems to be a potential source of beliefs in reincarnation. But further analogies between the dream state and mythologies may be found if we turn to two singular societies: the foraging San of Namibia and Botswana and the agricultural Dani of New Guinea. The spiritual agencies that are recognized in these societies' mythologies include souls and ghosts, spirit-animal and anthropomorphic deities, monsters and amorphous spiritual forces. San myth is, not surprisingly given the San's foraging ecology, heavily populated with spirit-animal deities, while Dani myth, as seems appropriate to a nation of farmers who have little commerce with wild animals, seems to be especially centered on anthropomorphic deities. For instance, the San have a major cycle of myths which follow the ancient adventures of Beautiful Python Girl, Elephant (her father and the encampment headman), Kori Bustard (her husband), and Jackal (her sister and occasional nemesis). Even the San's major anthropomorphic deities, Gangwanana and Gangwa Matse, retain the term for Praying Mantis (Gangwa) in their names. Conversely, the Dani—while recognizing spirit-animal deities such as Bird and Snake who contend for dominion over mankind's mortality—particularly venerate a Sun Goddess even as they hedge her about with secrecy. Like Dani women during victory celebrations after the death of an enemy warrior, she wears typical Dani war gear: shells, feathers, and yellow clay markings. And she appears to be the same deity who is viewed throughout New Guinea as a culture founder: a goddess who, in the distant past, handed out pigs and sweet potatoes as she traversed New Guinea's interior highlands from east to west.

Still, while venerating both spirit-animal and anthropomorphic deities, San and Dani alike display a continuous preoccupation with souls, ghosts, and the interrelationship between the two. In both cases, ghosts send illnesses among the people which affect the victims' souls. In the case of the San, the ghosts invidiously attempt to lure the souls of the living to the realm of the dead in the Western Sky. In the case of the Dani, the collective agitation of the ghosts over losing a relative in warfare causes the souls of the living to migrate from the solar plexus to the small of the back—bringing on an illness which can only be alleviated by killing a member of an enemy alliance. Further, both San and Dani mythologies—like those of all other societies—are pervaded by monsters: for the San, marauding sorcerers who, in the guise of lions, maul people in the night; for the Dani, witches who might poison a man's sweet potatoes or otherwise send illness against him. Likewise, both San and Dani mythology recognize amorphous spiritual forces that animate the universe: *num,* or medicine, and *twe,* or sickness, for the San; *wusa,* which is sanctifying or dangerous depending upon the context in which one encounters it, for the Dani.[13]

These two instances—as well as numerous others that we will consider—suggest that souls (the mythic analogue to the dream's representative of the living) and ghosts (the mythic analogue to the dream's representative of the dead) along with the addition of monsters (the mythic analogue to the dream's phantoms) and impersonal spiritual forces (the mythic analogue to the pervasive sense of well-being or dread that impinges on the dream state) are the basic integers of human religion. It may be that, over time, the spirits of the dead split into two lineages: benevolent ancestors and malevolent ghosts. Supporting this supposition is the fact that where ghosts alone populate our mythologies they tend to manifest a bifurcated nature, encompassing both benevolent and malevolent tendencies. And ancestors, in their turn, may have split into two lineages: spirit-animal deities (particularly critical to active foragers) and anthropomorphic deities (increasingly critical to those who become removed from foraging ecologies). Supporting this supposition is the fact that both spirit-animal and anthropomorphic deities behave, if not look like, human beings and both are considered ancestral to mankind in a number, if not a majority, of our global mythologies. Finally, as societies moved away from egalitarianism and developed rank or class, anthropomorphic deities became hierarchalized. In fact, there is no way that a hierarchy of spirits—running from spirit-animal deities, through anthropomorphic deities, to the appearance of a preeminent god, a high god, or a king of the gods—could have been an element of religion in its incipience. There can't, after all, be a hierarchy of gods until society is hierarchically organized. There can be no king of the gods, an Indra or a Zeus, let alone monotheism, where the king of the gods has displaced all other gods, until there is a live, flesh-and-blood, king. That said, I want to be clear on one point here. In describing the profound analogies between our dreams and mythologies, I am not suggesting that religion is some trick of human biology, the result of mistaking dream imagery for spiritual phenomena. Rather, I wish to suggest that dreams may offer us a means of comprehending—or, perhaps better, communing upon—the spiritual. As Professor Dumbledore responded to Harry Potter's query as to whether what was happening to him after his cataclysmic battle with Voldemort was real or all in his head, "Of course it is happening inside your head, Harry, but why on earth should that mean that it is not real."[14]

Tellingly, the spare remnants of ancient ritual offer us a slight glimmer of the manner in which our early spiritual ideas were expressed, suggesting the belief in a soul within the living being that is released upon death to some sort of afterlife, to some amorphous realm for the spirits of the deceased. Our first evidence derives from Neanderthal burial sites which allow us to infer something of Neanderthal religiosity. In Shanidar Cave, in Iraq, a man's body, buried some fifteen meters from the cave's mouth about 60 thousand years ago, was discovered. Found lying on his left side, somewhat flexed at the hips and knees into a partial fetal position, his left hand near his face, his right hand near his left elbow, Shanidar IV was perhaps 40 years old at his death and stood about five feet, four inches tall.[15] His burial site was marked by a rough stone boundary, covered over with new soil, and possibly embellished with flowers—including, on the basis of the pollen extracted from the site, a number with medicinal qualities such as daisies, yarrow, cornflowers, grape hyacinth, and hollyhock.[16] It seems incontrovertible that Shanidar IV, like other Neanderthals, was being readied not simply for his exit from the material world but significantly for his entrance into a new spiritual world. The existence of grave goods, particularly finely artificed Mousterian hand axes sometimes found with Neanderthal remains, strengthens the suggestion that Neanderthals maintained a belief in an afterlife and the needs that might be there encountered.

Beyond this evidence of a potential belief in the promise of a spiritual existence following hard upon the heels of a mere material one, we have some indication—through artistic representations on outcroppings of rock or rock faces in the interior of caves dating to as early as 40 thousand years ago—that with the emergence of our modern Homo sapiens selves and our early migration out of Africa into Eurasia, the shamanic complex was already in existence. The best example of this complex, characterized by a shaman's performance of healing medicinal songs and dances presented to him or her by a spirit-animal ally, is to be found in a depiction painted on the ceiling of a cave in southern France. The Sorcerer of Trois-Frères Cave depicts, some fifteen feet above the cave floor, an elk-like entity in a bipedal dancing posture. Prominently visible in the figure is a set of human, rather than animal, genitalia suggesting the blending of animal and human traits that characterizes shamanic healing powers on an almost universal basis. Such depictions characteristically occur deep within caves, in areas not used as shelters, and are often accompanied by images of local game animals and abstract patterns created in red, yellow, and black pigments. The abstractions appear curiously similar to entoptic phenomena: hallucinatory images that can be engendered through the use of hallucinogens, meditation, or any number of techniques—such as exhaustive dancing accompanied by percussive music—employed in order to enter an altered state of consciousness. As William Haviland points out, the images would be familiar to those who suffer migraines. They appear as squiggles and geometric forms in different colored lights at the periphery of one's vision, sometimes moving toward the center, and at times culminating in a figural image, perhaps that of an animal, or a shaman, or a deity, at the center of one's vision. Thus, it is likely that the images which adorn cave interiors, both of animals and abstract patterns, are depictions of the visions that a shaman (and perhaps young initiates) experienced during ritual seclusion within the deepest chambers of the living earth. Further, since similar images of a similarly early date have now been found in Indonesia as well as Europe, it seems likely that the distant origins of the shamanic complex were to be found in Africa, suggesting that it had already developed before humanity left its original homeland.[17]

Winkelman and Baker suggest that the incorporation of animal imagery in religious ritual is natural to a species that depended so extensively on the hunt through much of its evolutionary history. The ability to imitate and deceive prey and even to "disguise hunters as animals" would have been an integral addition to early hunting strategies and would have been easily transferred from a pragmatic to a more esoteric use, particularly if magic were believed to be of help in the taking of prey. Animal imagery incorporated into chanting and dancing, often along with the use of percussive instruments such as drums and rattles, has been a mainstay of shamanic ritual even into the 21st century; likewise, the belief in the efficacy of songs and dances presented to the shaman by an animal-ally for both hunting and healing magic. Thus, the ancient dance which solidified group life among our non-human forebears was incorporated into our human spiritual legacy. But there was something more than augmenting group cohesion in this dance. Beyond taking on alternate— particularly animal—personae, participating in ecstatic dancing, chanting, and drumming, and perhaps augmenting such procedures with the deprivation of food, sleep, and even companionship, the shamanic complex was (and is) almost universally characterized by the shaman's propensity to enter an altered state of consciousness (ASC) during which he or she is said to experience shamanic flight.[18]

The accounts of shamanic flight display marked similarities to one another despite the sometimes significant cultural divides that separate those who recount them. The San shaman Kxao Giraffe once reported, "Just yesterday, friend, the Giraffe came and took me again." He, further, spoke of traveling to the realm of the gods by means of a great river. "My feet were behind, and my head was in front. That's how I lay. Then I entered the stream and began to move forward." And, issuing forth into the sky world, he heard the gods singing. He joined their dance and was presented with a medicine song which he carried back to his own world in the Kalihari desert of southern Africa.[19] And Black Elk, the famed Lakota shaman, speaks of being escorted to the realm of the gods in the sky by two geese who become men and fly like arrows slanting upward. He thereupon enters a tepee through a flaming rainbow and encounters the gods in the form of the Six Grandfathers who give him the gifts which will allow him to cure the illnesses of his people. And as he descended to his encampment, escorted now by his new spirit-animal ally, the Spotted Eagle, he reports that "I saw my own tepee, and inside I saw my mother and my father, bending over a sick boy that was myself. And as I entered the tepee, someone was saying: The boy is coming to; you had better give him some water."[20] While Kxao Giraffe and Black Elk traveled to the Sky World, Inuit shamans dropped to the bottom of the sea where they encountered the goddess of sea creatures.

An ancient Inuit story tells of a maiden whose rejection of her suitors brought upon her and her father the vengeance of Raven. While tossed upon a violent sea in their kayak, the father was forced to throw his own daughter overboard to save himself and when she—in desperation—clung to the kayak's gunnel, he chopped off her fingers with a stone axe: sending her to the bottom of the sea and creating the sea mammals, over whom the maiden would from then on rule, from her broken fingers. When the Inuit are not successful in their hunt, it is because they have slighted the maiden—Takánakapsâluk— who is withholding the sea mammals in her agitation. Thus, the shaman must travel through magical tubes to the seabed in order to placate the troubled god- dess. Within a darkened igloo, the shaman engages all his petitioners' senses using—among the many strategies at his disposal—ventriloquism so that the sounds within the igloo become spatial: "In the darkened house one hears only sighing and groaning from the dead who lived many generations earlier." Their "sighing and puffing" sound to the people in the igloo, "as if the spirits were down under water, in the sea," like "marine animals," for "in between all the noises one hears the blowing and splashing of creatures" as if they are coming up to a breathing hole in the ice in order to take a deep breath before they sink once more beneath the water's agitated surface. Sounds give rise to images in the darkness, and—as if to accentuate the feelings of his petitioners—the sha- man's sleight of hand may send his own clothing and even the clothing of others, all of which had been unfastened and loosened in preparation for the shaman's journey, flying about the room. Sight, sound, and feeling are thus all engaged in a tumult of sensory perception as the shaman—having dropped to the bottom of the sea and negotiated such perils as crushing stones and a snarling dog— approaches Takánakapsâluk in her lodge and lovingly combs her hair, cleansing it of the collected filth that has accumulated there as a result of the breech of taboos. With the soothing of Takánakapsâluk and the shaman's assurance that she has not been purposefully slighted by the people, that the taboos were bro- ken inadvertently, the shaman will reascend to the igloo and Takánakapsâluk will release the sea mammals back to the people who will, thereby, live on for yet another difficult season.[21]

Speaking Animals

The Dream Guessing ceremony, with its emphasis on asking questions to elicit responses from the dreamer, underscores another facet of the role of biology on human spirituality: not only are we dreaming animals but also speaking animals. Chimps are capable of learning language and using it in novel ways. For instance, Roger Fouts, along with a research assistant, Sue, worked with a female chimpanzee named Lucy, teaching her American Sign Language. Lucy's word for "poop" was "dirty-dirty." One morning, when Fouts came to see her, he discovered that Lucy had defecated on the floor, whereupon the following exchange took place:

FOUTS: What's that?
LUCY: Lucy not know.
FOUTS: You do know. What's that?
LUCY: Dirty-dirty.
FOUTS: Whose dirty-dirty?
LUCY: Sue's.
FOUTS: It's not Sue's. Whose is it?
LUCY: Roger's!
FOUTS: No! It's not Roger's. Whose is it?
LUCY: Lucy dirty-dirty. Sorry Lucy.

Lucy learned to combine her words into novel sequences in order to create her own words (for instance, "cry-hurt-fruit" for radish) and perhaps even simple sentences. What's more, Lucy—along with another signing chimpanzee named Washoe—would use their word for "poop" as a swear word: thus taking a word out of a purely denotative context (naming an item) and giving it connotative (figurative) value. Washoe would complain about the monkeys who resided with her at the Institute for Primate Studies in Oklahoma calling them "dirty monkeys." And Lucy, when annoyed by an aggressive cat, referred to it as "dirty cat." Both Lucy and Washoe independently hit upon one of the most common human mechanisms for expressing anger: swearing at someone (or something) and, moreover, using the same sort of excremental swearing strategy that we humans tend to universally use ourselves.[22]

But while chimpanzees can master a number of elements of human language, they do so only with human coaching. We humans may thus be the only true speaking animals: animals who use language rather than calls in order to communicate one to the other. Further, our self-domestication may have played an integral role in our development as speaking animals. As humans became less dependent upon their physical environment and more dependent upon their social environment for their well-being, the function of calls—to express, perhaps, the possibility of danger or the proximity of a food source or to emplace oneself in a dominance hierarchy—became freer. With the ability to "loosen up" on the biological imperatives and, thus, the rules that governed calls, more complex vocalizations could occur.[23] It is likely that a relaxation of the rules governing calls allowed us the great variety of utterances which could eventually carry not only symbolic communication but also nuanced symbolic communication—vocalizations which could carry connotations as well as denotations, vocalizations which could be used figuratively to communicate abstract ideas, vocalizations which were capable of carrying—to borrow linguist Deborah Tannen's term—metamessages: messages deployed as much by contexts (both grammatical and social) as by a mere string of words.[24]

We may never know precisely when the calls that characterize communication among our non-human relatives began to fall into disuse and the grammatically nuanced utterances that characterize human speech began to emerge. But we do know that, once it did, language allowed humans something beyond the ecological adaptations and societal structures that characterize group life among other complex mammals: ideology, a system of thought that can be communicated *in language* from one member of a group to another. Language thus became the integument which held our ecological adaptations and societal structures together, that knit them into the unified whole which is at the base of human culture. In fact, so intimately bound up with the notion of culture is language that it is not altogether clear that culture can exist without language. Or, put another way, it is not altogether clear that culture is something entirely distinct from language. The evolutionary biologist, Ursula Goodenough, suggests, "While language competency is inherited, the languages themselves are transmitted via culture. Also transmitted via culture are understandings, such as technological ways of doing things, that are framed as language-based explanations." Thus, one would "expect a robust co-evolutionary trajectory between language competency and culture." Our early ancestors "capable of the first, and presumably rudimentary, versions of protolanguage would have better access to cultural understandings, and cultural understandings, conveyed in protolanguages that children's brains could readily learn, were more likely to be transmitted."[25] Something of Goodenough's assertion is suggested by the regular sequence in which the world's children undergo language acquisition. As described by Marcel Danesi, first they will begin to create cooing sounds

(12 weeks) followed by the appearance of consonants (20 weeks). At six months they will begin to use monosyllables (da), "over 60%" of which "will develop into nouns," 20 percent into verbs. Then, at twelve months they will start to double them (da-da). At this point, a "pivot class" and an "open class" of words begins to emerge, setting the stage for a rudimentary grammar. The pivot class is a small group of basic words which allows the infant to pivot to a word in the open class, a larger set of terms usually naming things. Danesi gives the example "all-gone" (from the pivot class) and "milk" (from the open class). By 36 months, the child has added function words, such as prepositions and conjunctions, to his or her vocabulary which now contains around 1,000 words.[26] It is difficult to imagine this process simply as language acquisition without the idea that enculturation, or the introjection of a particular culture into one's psyche, is at play as well.

Given the essential relationship between culture and language, it would seem reasonable to suggest that culture is dialogic: arising out of the polyphony of voices that characterize society. And it is precisely culture's dialogism that allows a society's members to both formulate and communicate the deep layers of signification without which there would be no possibility of mythic thought. With the recent discovery of the mysterious and little understood Area 55b, a region of the brain that becomes particularly active when listening to stories, it seems increasingly likely that the act of telling tales itself was somehow essential to the human evolutionary process and remains essential to contemporary human biopsychology. I suspect, in fact, that myth arises organically with our storytelling abilities: just as telling stories about one another in the encampment seems likely to have been an early function of language, so too did the relation of our dreams to fellow encampment members. And the two types of stories, so similar to one another inasmuch as they centered on human characters, maintained one major distinction: the human protagonists of gossip were seen in one's waking hours while the human protagonists of dreams were encountered only when one was asleep. Further, given the essential relationship between the content of dreams on the one hand and our mythologies on the other, it seems likely that it was in the act of relating dreams among our ancient human selves that mythology had its birth.

Émile Durkheim drew our attention to an essential aspect of religion: though human biology may be at the base of our penchant to affiliate with those familiar to us and to mistrust strangers, the deep cognition—or sense—of affiliation which is so essential to the well-being of a social group was most firmly entrenched in the psyche of the community by religious ritual in which the participants literally performed their sense of affiliation in the reenactment of their primal myth of genesis. Yet, inasmuch as the elaboration of this myth so entirely depends upon language, our ability to enact community through reenacting myth—like our ability to turn dreams into myths—depends upon the fact that we are animals that use language. Thus, it is language which knits together the dance and the dream that lie at the base of our spiritual life and makes of them a unified whole: religion.

The Historical Development of Mythology

We humans are genetically predisposed to be culture-using animals. And religion is a seminal element of culture. Thus, it stands to reason that we humans are genetically predisposed to be religious animals: making myths and reenacting them in our religious rituals, sanctifying both the physical and social environments upon which we depend by elevating their essential features in order to construct a constellation of metaphors, and using those metaphors to communicate to one another the abstract ideas that comprise our worldview. If so, then mythology, for animals like us, seems inevitable. But as Franz Boas rightfully insisted, culture is not simply the product of biological but also historical processes. Certainly, our human penchant to use culture to adapt to a particular environment, to create our own particular social ecology, is genetically inscribed but so much of *how* we exploit our environment is the product of invention and diffusion: a function of the fact that historically individuals have come up with unique responses to problems and various societies have come into contact with various other societies and borrowed from them. In a way, we could probably say that culture—much like our own personal idiosyncrasies—could be looked at as arising from the accidents of history.

Yet, because so much history arises in the preliterate past, we must depend upon archaeology to recover it and archaeology doesn't have access to all the arenas of culture. It proceeds rather to arrive at a general understanding of culture at large through its excavation of material culture: that is artifacts, items of human manufacture and processing. And largely on the basis of such artifacts, along with the happy addition of genetic analysis, archaeology has broadened our understanding of how we anatomically modern humans, Homo sapiens, came to dominate the entire globe during the course of the Paleolithic: the period of early Homo sapiens expansion.[27] Conditions were difficult when we first left our African homeland 100 to 60 thousand years ago. A cool, dry climate led to a separation between southern and northern African populations and a drop in human population to as low as 10,000 people. Two possible routes out of Africa have been mapped. One, running up the Nile Corridor, enters Southwest Asia in the region of the Sinai and, from there, pushes further eastward.

A second, running across the Bab al-Mandab Straits between the Horn of Africa and the southern Arabian Peninsula, pushes through the Persian Gulf region into South Asia and beyond. It seems then that our single human family, in its early history, consisted of three branches: Southern African, Northern African, and Eurasian. Australian Aborigines split off from their early Eurasian ancestors, arriving in Australia as early as 50 thousand years ago. Thereafter, they—along with the inhabitants of the interior of New Guinea—were shut off from any influx of new genetic material.[28] Further, Australian Aborigines were cut off from the inhabitants of New Guinea perhaps as early as 35 thousand years ago and, from that time, maintained a remarkably stable ecology until about four thousand years ago. Then, a new technology, an influx of genetic material, and the Dingo, were introduced to Australia by a seafaring people: most probably Indian. In fact, about 10 percent of some Aboriginal groups' DNA results from this relatively recent South Asian migration.[29] Further genetic studies suggest that Europeans and East Asians split off from one another some 45 thousand years ago, whereupon humanity embarked on the final steps of the outward migration here charted: the settlement of the New World, emanating from Siberia—where the last common ancestors of Asians and Native Americans lived some 20 to 16 thousand years ago—by means of the Beringian land bridge; the expansion of Siberian Arctic populations into the New World between 5 and 4 thousand years ago; and the settlement of Polynesia, emanating most probably from Taiwan or the scattering of islands north of New Guinea, some 4 thousand years ago.[30]

Paleolithic: Dolní Věstonice

With particular regard to religion, not only the cave paintings described above but also a proliferation of Venus figurines characterizes Paleolithic Homo sapiens populations. Among these figurines, the most famous are the Venus of Willendorf, from Austria, and the Venus of Dolní Věstonice, from the Czech Republic. Both images date from 30 to 25 thousand years ago and depict human figures with accentuated feminine attributes: dramatically enlarged breasts, hips, and buttocks. Though we will never know with certainty, the proliferation of these figurines—particularly when contrasted with a dramatic lack of any analogous male figurines—strongly suggests a concern with fertility embodied in an image which will, among later populations, be associated with the great mother: the Earth herself.

Another image found at Dolní Věstonice, this consisting of a woman's face, is particularly interesting inasmuch as it may represent (unlike the Venus figurine) an actual member of the community. A woman, who lived somewhat apart from the rest of the community, manifests a facial asymmetry that is reiterated in the small ivory carving. It seems not unlikely that the carving is a representation of this mysterious woman whose burial suggests she may have been the repository of shamanic powers. She was interred beneath two mammoth scapulas which were pitched like a roof over her body. Her bones were tinged in ochre: a mineral pigment widely used in funerary rituals and not infrequently symbolic of blood. A flint spearhead was placed in her grave. And, even in death, she held a fox in her hand, suggesting that—if she were indeed a shaman—the fox might have been her spirit-ally. Nearby the grave, Barbara Tedlock reports, an earthen lodge containing a large oven was discovered. The oven contained clay representations of "human feet, hands, and heads" as well as numerous animal figurines. It seems likely that the woman's unusual burial goods—along with the pre-ceramic industry of the lodge nearby—signified some sort of relationship with spirit-animal allies as well as the ability to heal various human maladies. The existence of a potential female shaman offers an enigmatic clue to Paleolithic religion: not only may it have venerated the earth as a nurturing mother but it may also have placed the assurance of the earth's continued fertility firmly in the hands of women.[31]

Yet another curious burial at Dolni Věstonice consists of three skeletons arranged in a distinctive manner. Three youths are interred together, two males flanking an individual once thought to be of indeterminate sex though today accepted as a male: light-boned and with perhaps some degree of intersexuality. The central figure, lying on his back, faces the figure on his right, lying face down. These two seem to have their arms entwined. The figure on the left lies on his side, facing the central figure, and has his hand resting on the central figure's genital area. All the figures' heads were anointed in red ochre as was the pubic area of the central figure.[32] The careful arrangement of the bodies suggests that the spirits of the deceased were not only sent to their afterlife with necessary grave goods but also certain enigmatic behavioral attributes and even that ineffable gift of companionship. It is not, apparently, unlike our penchant for sending the souls of our deceased to the beyond in an attitude of slumber.

The inhabitants of Dolni Věstonice were, like other Paleolithic populations, big game hunters. In fact, they so depended on mammoth that not only did they adorn their shaman's grave with mammoth scapulas and adorn themselves with mammoth ivory necklaces, but they also built their domed huts with mammoth bones. Still, their total adaptation to a mammoth hunting ecology—an adaptation which we will see reiterated in the Lakota total adaptation to bison hunting—was destined to collapse. By twenty thousand years ago, when anatomically modern humans were well established throughout the Old

World and on the verge of entering the New, environmental change colluded with human technological advancement in a most unexpected manner. As the world became progressively warmer and wetter in the face of successive retreats of the Würm glaciation and global topography became, therefore, characterized by more forest than savanna and tundra, human technological advances had almost universally replaced the jabbing spears used by our Homo Erectus and Neanderthal forbears with such complex tools as the harpoon, the atlatl (spear launcher), and—most remarkably—the bow and arrow, dramatically expanding our hunting toolkits and allowing us to kill game from a safer distance. As hunting became more effective and less dangerous, the severe ecological pressures exerted by glacial retreat began to take their toll on the big game animals that are better adapted to savanna and tundra (which provide them their forage) than forest. Big game became, not surprisingly, less abundant.[33] And human population density was apparently increasing at such a rapid pace that it began to outstrip the carrying capacity of the local environmental conditions. Thus, the emerging environment, along with alterations in human technologies, was having a profound effect on the trajectory of human prehistory leading us away from Paleolithic big game hunting, through a brief, interstitial Mesolithic period characterized by broad-spectrum foraging (that is, augmenting big game with alternate protein sources), to the Neolithic agricultural revolution.

Mesolithic: Natufian Culture

A particularly telling instance of a Mesolithic broad-spectrum foraging society is presented by the Natufians who lived in present-day Israel some 13 to 9 thousand years ago. Inhabiting permanent villages, sometimes consisting of conical stone, wood, and brush structures built within the mouths of caves, Natufians relied on naturally occurring stands of wheat, barley, peas, lentils, and chickpeas, as well as small game, such as tortoise and hare, in order to augment the protein provided through the hunting of gazelle, deer, and boar. Intensively reaping wild grains with their flint-blade sickles, Natufians would be compelled to adopt a sedentary lifestyle because a bountiful harvest, eminently collectible and readily stored, would not be amenable to easy transport. In the context of such an ecological adaptation, nomadism, which had heretofore characterized all human societies, was no longer tenable.

Interestingly, human exploitation of grains (particularly harvesting with flint sickles and grinding with mortars and pestles) gave rise to another impediment to nomadism. Alongside the stands of wild wheat and barley upon which Natufians depended, new stands of domestic wheat and barley began to appear.

These domestic varieties emerged—accidentally—as a result of human processing. Wild wheat and barley are characterized by brittle stalks which allow self-seeding. When the seeds are ripe, a brisk wind or rain will allow the stalks to break along fragile axes, scattering the seeds to the ground. Likewise, thick husks keep the scattered grains protected until the winter rains conducive to germination have returned. But within these stands of wild wheat and barley, as within any plant or animal community, genetic diversity exists. Some plants are characterized by less brittle stalks and thinner husks. And these variants were more regularly, if not consciously, selected for consumption. Domestic wheat and barley could not, like its wild progenitors, easily promulgate itself. Its stalks had become too elastic (the result of successive generations of reaping with sickle blades) for self-seeding and its grain husks had become too thin (the result of successive generations of scorching and grinding the grains) to survive periods of dry weather unsuitable to germination. These new variants, our first domesticated plants, promulgated by human activity and establishing themselves in middens and food processing areas within the village bounds, became with time a more prevalent feature of Natufian settlements and a food source not easily abandoned. In other words, the Natufians—in a grand accident of history—were altering the evolutionary trajectory of the grains they were exploiting and thereby creating an environment for themselves that was simply too rich to leave. In fact, significant stores of grains, both wild and domestic, were maintained in storage pits at a number of Natufian sites. It is likely that a single family could collect as much as a metric ton of cleaned wheat or barley in the relatively short window during which harvesting could take place, rendering storage facilities an integral feature of Natufian life and sedentarism an absolute imperative.

Yet permanent village life gives rise to an ecological problem. Abandoning nomadism for the sake of a more dependable food source leads to a population explosion, often more than doubling the birthrate by some counts, and the expanded population has to find a means of feeding itself.[34] This is where agriculture comes into play. Taking those once wild, now domesticated, grains and purposely planting them in gardens, these early agriculturalists were able to maximize their grain output and feed their burgeoning numbers. The Natufians are one candidate for the earliest agriculturalists who made the transition from wild grains, through domesticated grains, to actual farming (defined as tending to cultivated gardens), perhaps to provide for a growing population or to overcome seasonal food shortages. But an important caveat: we expect this transition did not occur without trouble. In other words, it is likely that expanding populations gave rise to tensions over feeding everyone. And when tension occurs in human communities, particularly tension over the allocation of resources, violence often results. The quickest mechanism for alleviating this violence is to fission: one group splitting off from another and moving.[35] It is likely that people exploiting wild and domestic grains were pushed out of those areas which provided adequate stores of such resources and it may be these people who, transporting not only technologies but also seeds, were the world's first true farmers: attempting to recreate their previous bounty through the construction of gardens.[36] Tellingly, both the Iroquois and Zuni speak of transporting sacred seeds—the first from the Sky World, the second from the Earth's Womb—as if a primal memory of the diffusion of agriculture throughout the world is mythically retained.

As fascinating as the glimpse into the possible origins of agriculture offered by Natufian society is a finding that impacts our discussion of religion in a most direct manner. "To date, more than 450 skeletons have been unearthed" at numerous sites which manifest "several characteristics conceptually similar to modern cemeteries."

> At each, at least several dozen burials were found in a delineated and densely used area. The unprecedented density of graves and the great variety of inhumation practices in these sites represent some elaboration of earlier traditions and a wide variety of innovations. The new forms of burial include the combination of individual and multiple graves, flexed and full-length postures, patterned orientations, head and body decoration with beads, removal of the skull after body decomposition, use of ochre-based pigments, provisioning with grave goods and offerings, and possibly an association with funereal feasts.

Moreover, the first unequivocal instance of the use of flowers in funereal practices occurs among Natufians. On the slopes of Mount Carmel, four bodies were laid out upon a bed of flowers, notably including sage and other plants with "colorful and aromatic" springtime blossoms—some with reputed medicinal qualities.[37] Flowers, symbolic to this day of the rebirth of the Earth herself after the harsh winter and therefore a seemingly perfect symbol for the rebirth of her human children as well, seem likely to have served a similar function for Natufians as they do for us. And it is particularly telling that Natufians seem to have preferred (at least, in those four graves upon Mount Carmel) springtime blooms for their burials.

Intriguingly, a Natufian grave has been discovered that is likely to have housed another early shaman. And this shaman, like her predecessor at Dolní Věstonice, is also a woman. The grave is about twelve thousand years old and its occupant, "a petite, elderly, and disabled woman," is surrounded by an array of grave goods that are unique among the numerous Natufian burial sites excavated to date. The woman's disabilities are substantial and "would have affected her gait," perhaps causing her to either limp or drag her foot. Further, they would likely have "given her an unnatural, asymmetrical appearance." Her grave goods include "50 complete tortoise shells" arranged "under the skull, the pelvis, and at the perimeter of the grave," a fragment of a basalt bowl in conjunction with "a complete, male gazelle horn core," the wing tip of a golden eagle that would have supported "the eagle's large and colorful primary feathers" and "a complete human foot," items which suggest esoteric knowledge including perhaps that of maintaining animal familiars. She was interred in a small cave in lower Galilee, a region in northern Israel, in a burial ground where at least 28 other individuals were buried. But, even among those burials, her treatment was distinctive. Beyond the unusual grave goods, the grave construction itself was unique: the walls of the shallow basin in which she was laid to rest was plastered with "mud collected immediately outside of the cave" and "small limestone slabs were pressed into the mud walls to create a strong foundation. Further, "several large limestone slabs lined the floor." The woman herself was placed in an extraordinary position: though she lay on her side, her legs were spread open flat upon the grave bed and her knees bent inward so that her feet nearly touch one another. Further, a number of heavy stones were placed over her head, her arms, and her pelvis as if to maintain her corpse in this unusual posture.[38]

Neolithic: Çatal Hüyük

It was out of broad-spectrum foraging strategies centering on wild grains that agriculture emerged. And this emergence occurred at various places in various times in both the Old and New Worlds. Southwest Asia and Mesoamerica were early centers: the former cultivating wheat, barley, peas, and lentils as early as 10 thousand years ago; the latter the classic Native American complex of corn, beans, and squash nearly as early. Egypt, India, China, Southeast Asia, and Peru were also early agriculture centers with at least some degree of farming present by nine to seven thousand years ago. Europe, Sub-Saharan Africa, and Native North America were soon to follow, adopting agricultural practices some six to three thousand years ago. But wherever and whenever it happened, the results of agricultural production were remarkably uniform: increased sedentarism, population expansion, and a greater need to manage animal as well as vegetal resources. In fact, just as sedentarism accelerated population growth, it necessitated the domestication of animals—for the preferred game animals would be quickly hunted out in territories close to permanent villages. Early attempts at managing animal populations were, not surprisingly, simple: burning forest to create pasturelands for herding animals such as antelope, deer, cattle, sheep, and goats and, with time, attempting to control their movement.

Such tentative strategies likely served as precursors to actually corralling and selectively breeding livestock. Some animals, conversely, seem to have self-domesticated through foraging on the scraps that were an omnipresent feature of sedentary villages: dogs, taking advantage of the refuse left over from human kills; cats, preying on the rodents which harried our newly established stores of grain; and, perhaps as well, pigs and chickens which would avail themselves of any of our garbage. Domestic sheep, goats, cattle, pigs, dogs, and cats—still the mainstay of Old World domesticates—were all present in Southwest Asia as early as eleven to nine thousand years ago. Chickens and various transport animals—horses, donkeys, and camels—joined the repertoire of Southwest Asian domesticates some six to four thousand years ago.[39] Oddly, while animal deities are the mainstay of foragers' mythologies, with the domestication of animals or, one might say, with the *commodification* of animals that was the inevitable result of domestication, the exalted position of spirit-animal deities suffered a substantial diminution.

The earliest domestic animal is, almost assuredly, our best friend: the dog. The "symbiotic," or co-evolutionary, relationship between humans and dogs began some 15 thousand years ago in Southwest Asia. It is very likely that the origin of dogs is not to be found in just any wolf population but rather in a population of wolves that had already become habituated to human presence by virtue of their habit of scavenging on human refuse. Perhaps wolf pups, from these already distinct populations, that were a bit less fearful of humans were occasionally carried back into the settlement and, over time, these significantly "tamer" wild animals were molded by their human interactions. Analysts have long noted the significant ability of dogs to take verbal and visual cues from humans—something relatively lacking among wolves, foxes, and even chimpanzees; likewise, dogs' eagerness to please their human companions.[40] These traits are likely the result of (first unconsciously, later with purpose) selecting dogs for traits particularly useful to human tasks. Tellingly, the interaction of humans and dogs not only affected the trajectory of canine evolution but also the trajectory of human cultural development: the ability to live safely in permanent villages (dogs being helpful in alerting humans to predators) and the differentiation of status (dogs, kept for hunting, being an early mark of prestige) likely had profound implications with regard to both the safety of sedentary existence and the seeming inevitability of status differentiation. No wonder that the domestic dog spread rapidly from pre-agricultural Southwest Asia where, among the Natufians, we find men buried with their dogs at two sites, to Africa and Eurasia and, eventually, to Native America and Oceania.[41] But what of our other pal: the cat? It was in the agricultural centers of Southwest Asia some 10 thousand years ago that cats were first (more or less) self-domesticated. The earliest evidence of this process is attested to by a 9,500-year-old burial of a cat in a human grave on Cyprus. Inasmuch as Cyprus did not have an indigenous population of wild cats, it is likely that domestic cats were transported to the island "by boat, probably from the Levant."[42] As rodents harried our stored grains, cats were naturally attracted. We tolerated their presence inasmuch as they safeguarded our grain stores but rarely interfered with their behavior. Thus, they never really, like dogs, evolved to take cues from humans. Cats, treated with aloofness by their human hosts, not only treated us in kind but seem to have bettered us in the art of indifference! Still, their presence—along with that of dogs—among the grave goods of Eastern Mediterranean societies so early in their history as domesticates is significant of the human regard that they early on garnered.

Illustrative of a Neolithic (or early agricultural) ecology is the village of Çatal Hüyük in southern Turkey. The term *hüyük*, in the Turkish language, signifies a mound where a village or city—characteristically constructed in sunbaked mud bricks—once stood. The Hebraic equivalent is *tel*, the Arabic *tall*. The mound that comprises Çatal Hüyük is composed of "12 superimposed building levels," all representative of a single society which occupied the site without interruption from 8 to 7 thousand years ago. The village was never apparently subjected to destruction from outside forces, but fires marked the end of one occupation layer and the beginning of another. As James Mellaart, the archaeologist who excavated Çatal Hüyük, explains, with "numerous hearths and ovens and the high winds of the region, a disastrous fire about once a century is no more than could be expected." Though Çatal Hüyük was a Neolithic community, wild animals—including wild cattle, red deer, wild asses, wild sheep, boars and leopards—were still hunted. Sheep and cattle were both domesticated (as evidenced by different skeletal remains for wild and domesticated varieties) and probably goats and dogs as well. Carbonized remains of cereal grains, particularly wheat and barley, were prevalent at the site as were grain bins (found in almost every house). Mortars and pestles were likewise abundant. Beyond grains, peas, lentils, and bitter vetch were cultivated and nuts, fruits, and berries were regularly collected.

Houses at Çatal Hüyük were constructed of sunbaked mud bricks, were rectangular in shape, and often had small storerooms attached to them. There was no evidence of access, such as roads or lanes, between the houses which often shared common walls. Houses were entered by a hole in the roof, always situated "on the south side of the dwelling," probably covered by a canopy to keep out rain and outfitted with a fixed ladder running from the roof to the house's interior. A movable ladder which could be let down to admit a person to the roof and then drawn back up behind him or her was probably how people entered the village as a whole. Outside, the village "presented a solid blank wall," likely offering villagers protection from the raids of nomadic herders, but cattle and other livestock seem to have been kept in corrals at the edge of the village. Within the houses, two raised earthen platforms ran along the eastern wall and were "used for sitting, working, and sleeping." The smaller platform, at the northeast corner of the house, seemed to be reserved for the family's father; the larger platform, toward the center of the eastern wall, for its mother and children. A hearth, and sometimes an oven and kiln as well, was regularly located at the southern portion of the house, apparently to let its smoke out through the roof hole above.

From burials, we know something of how the people of Çatal Hüyük dressed and, importantly, how they viewed the afterlife: "Male dress consisted of a loincloth or a leopard skin, fastened by a belt with a bone hook and eye; the men appear also to have worn cloaks fastened with antler toggles in the winter. The women wore sleeveless bodices and jerkins of leopard skin, with fringed or string skirts—the ends of the strings being encased in copper tubes for weighting. The women used bone pins for fastening garments." Corpses were placed under the earthen platforms that stretched along the eastern wall of the village's houses. The corpses were usually, but not invariably, "those of women and children," suggesting that adult males often died away from the village, perhaps while hunting or participating in territorial raids. "It appears to have been the practice before final burial to strip the body of flesh by a preliminary interment, or by exposure to vultures, insects or microorganisms on an outdoor platform, sheltered by gabled structures built of reeds and mats." Once interred under the platforms, the corpse was placed in a fetal position, often lying on its left side, with its feet pointed toward the east wall and its head toward the west. These corpses were sometimes anointed in red ochre and often buried along with grave goods: finely carved wooden bowls containing "berries, peas, lentils, eggs or a joint of meat." Men were buried with weapons, including polished stone maces, spears and arrows (both with obsidian points), and flint daggers hafted on bone handles. Jewelry, mainly worn by women and children, included beaded "necklaces, armlets, bracelets and anklets" as well as "pendants in a great variety of stone, shell, chalk, clay, mother-of-pearl" and, in later levels, "copper and lead." Even signs of cosmetics, prepared from red ocher, blue azurite, and green malachite as well as "mirrors of highly polished obsidian" were recovered in burial excavations.

Such burial arrangements, like those at Dolni Věstonice and Natufian sites, likely signify the idea that the body was being outfitted for rebirth. But a further clue to beliefs in the afterlife at Çatal Hüyük is offered by the numerous shrine rooms that have been excavated within the confines of the village. These rooms are decorated with clay bull head effigies, generally adorned with a pair of horns, situated on a wall or on a pillar in the midst of the room. Further, on the western walls of these shrine rooms, frescoes depicting the major deity of Çatal Hüyük, the personage denominated by Mellaart as the Great Goddess, are found. Sometimes depicted giving birth to a bull, she is often accompanied by a bearded god, her Consort, who is always shown astride a bull—as if the bull whom she herself bears and her Consort are one and the same deity. She is likewise accompanied by a young girl and boy, likely the daughter and son of the Great Goddess and her Consort. No other deities appear. In some of these frescoes, which are painted predominately in a red ochre pigment that leads Mellaart to term them "life scenes," we find "an enormous red bull surrounded by minute jubilant people" and matrices of red hand imprints. On the shrine rooms' eastern walls appear frescoes of a very different sort. Denominated "death scenes" by Mellaart, these frescoes depict in dark, charcoal pigments, "vultures attacking headless human corpses," women's breasts containing vulture skulls, the "lower jaws of wild boars," and "the heads of foxes and weasels—all scavengers who devour corpses." There is also a "depiction of a great black bull" and hand matrices in black.[43]

It is likely that a complex fertility ritual, expressing the abiding concern of those societies who came to depend upon their own agricultural prowess, dominated the religious life at Çatal Hüyük. The Great Goddess—perhaps the lineal descendant of the Venus figurines that proliferated during the Paleolithic and Mesolithic eras—seems to have been she who generated all, including her consort, the charging bull and/or the bearded deity who rides him, he who—once born—impregnates the Great Goddess, providing her with her offspring: the boy and girl, perhaps the progenitors of the people of Çatal Hüyük itself. Interestingly, generation—the bringing forth of life—seems not to be considered the opposite of death at Çatal Hüyük but rather life and death seem to be viewed as alternate manifestations of a single process. Only then can we make sense of the mirroring of a number of the western "life" symbols upon the morbid eastern "death" walls: the Bull, for instance, or the matrices of hands. The mirroring especially seems to represent an esoteric way of saying that death is in actuality rebirth. If indeed life and death are not opposites but rather two manifestations of a single process, then it is likely that the red bull and the black bull are the same deity—the Great Goddess' Consort—in alternate guises. It is as if to say that inasmuch as life depends upon generation, death does as well; that though we die, we are thereby generated once again into a new world which, perhaps, hovers somewhere in west: toward the setting sun. What could be perplexing about the mythic imagery at Çatal Hüyük is the fact that the west, the direction of the setting sun, seems to be associated with life—

red pigments and celebratory images—while the east, the direction of the rising sun, seems to be associated with death—black pigments and harrowing images. The opposite is inevitably the case in our global mythologies. But what could be perplexing is rendered eminently comprehensible when one considers that, because the sole source of light in the houses at Çatal Hüyük is the hole in the southern end of the houses' roofs, the light of the rising sun is cast on the western, "life," walls of the houses' interiors while the light of the setting sun is cast on the eastern, "death," walls. Thus, the usual association among east, the rising sun, and life and west, the setting sun, and death that prevails in world mythology is reversed in the deeply interior life of the inhabitants of Çatal Hüyük.

Mesopotamia: The Epic of Gilgamesh

From the circumstances created by agriculture—sedentarism, large and more densely populated towns and regions, and the increasing productivity of farming techniques in order to feed burgeoning populations—mercantilism and its symptom, the city-state, exploded upon the world. Mercantile ecologies occur wherever the means of agricultural production have become so intensive that a portion of the population can provide the society's subsistence needs. Thus, the labor of a segment of that society is freed up for non-agricultural activities such as manufacture or the provision of services. Mercantile societies, then, are defined by a complex division of labor and full-time specialization, trade (either directly through barter or indirectly through market exchange) and—inevitable when there are numerous occupations each of which carries its own store of prestige—class. Not surprisingly, since class—including that class at the apex of the social structure, the monarchy—emerged in the context of mercantilism, mercantilism and the city-state exploded upon the world not with a celebratory hymn but rather with a lament:

> Two-thirds of him is god; one-third of him is human.
> The onslaught of his weapons verily has no equal.
> By the drum are aroused his companions.
> The nobles of Uruk are gloomy in their chambers:
> "Gilgamesh leaves not the son to his father;
> Day and night are unbridled his arrogance.
> Is this Gilgamesh the shepherd of ramparted Uruk?
> Is this our shepherd, bold, stately, wise?
> Gilgamesh leaves not the maid to her mother,
> The warrior's daughter, the noble's spouse!"[44]

The *Epic of Gilgamesh*, the oldest secular story to come down to us from the ancient world, opens with the peoples' complaint as to the overbearing behavior of their priest-king, Gilgamesh, who ruled over the city of Uruk some 5,200 years ago. Gilgamesh, whose mother is a goddess but whose father is mortal, is running rampant with the young men of the city. He is impiously sounding the tocsin, an instrument apparently meant to summon the gods when Gilgamesh ascends the holy ziggurat so that they might, at his summons, shower the people of Uruk with their blessings. He is also demanding sexual favors from the city's women before they marry and (apparently most shocking to the epic's ancient audience) he doesn't even seem to consider whether the women are nobles or commoners. Only when the gods, at the behest of the harried masses of Uruk, create for Gilgamesh his complement and near equal— Enkidu who, while Gilgamesh is a mingling of the essence of god and man, is a mingling of the essence of man and animal—is the priest-king's arrogance tamed. Gilgamesh loved Enkidu as he would a wife and when the jealousy of Ishtar, the Goddess of Love, sent Enkidu his death, Gilgamesh would not release his beloved comrade's body until it became bloated and maggots began to drop from its nostrils. Inconsolable, and wishing to thwart death, Gilgamesh sought out Utnapishtim, the Faraway, he who had survived the flood by building an ark, filling it with all the animals of the world, both wild and domestic, as well as the craftsmen of the city, and thus restored humanity to the ruined world, earning immortality as his reward.

As he seeks him out, though, Gilgamesh encounters Siduri: "Beside the sea she lives, the woman of the vine, the maker of wine; Siduri sits in the garden at the edge of the sea, with the golden bowl and the golden vats that the gods gave her. She is covered with a veil; and where she sits she sees Gilgamesh coming towards her, wearing skins, the flesh of the gods in his body, but despair in his heart, and his face like the face of one who has made a long journey." When he tells her that he desires to learn the secret of immortality from Utnapishtim, she benevolently advises him to give up his hopeless quest: "'Gilgamesh, where are you hurrying to? You will never find that life for which you are looking. When the gods created man they allotted to him death, but life they retained in their own keeping. As for you, Gilgamesh, fill your belly with good things; day and night, night and day, dance and be merry, feast and rejoice. Let your clothes be fresh, bathe yourself in water, cherish the little child that holds your hand, and make your wife happy in your embrace; for this too is the lot of man."[45]

Nonetheless, Gilgamesh continues his quest and, finding Utnapishtim, hears from his own lips the ancient tale of the flood:

> For six days and six nights the winds blew, torrent and tempest and flood overwhelmed the world, tempest and flood raged together like warring hosts. When the seventh day dawned the storm from the south subsided, the sea grew calm, the flood was stilled; I looked at the face of the world and there was silence, all mankind was turned to clay. The surface of the

sea stretched as flat as a roof-top; I opened a hatch and the light fell on my face. Then I bowed low, I sat down and I wept, the tears streamed down my face, for on every side was the waste of water. I looked for land in vain, but fourteen leagues distant there appeared a mountain, and there the boat grounded; on the mountain of Nisir the boat held fast, she held fast and did not budge. One day she held, and a second day on the mountain of Nisir she held fast and did not budge. A third day, and a fourth day she held fast on the mountain and did not budge; a fifth day and a sixth day she held fast on the mountain. When the seventh day dawned I loosed a dove and let her go. She flew away, but finding no resting-place she returned. Then I loosed a swallow, and she flew away but finding no resting-place she returned. I loosed a raven, she saw that the waters had retreated, she ate, she flew around, she cawed, and she did not come back. Then I threw everything open to the four winds, I made a sacrifice and poured out a libation on the mountain top. Seven and again seven cauldrons I set up on their stands, I heaped up wood and cane and cedar and myrtle. When the gods smelled the sweet savor, they gathered like flies over the sacrifice.

The gods made Utnapishtim one of their number as a result of his survival of the flood but Gilgamesh, distraught at seeing his own impending death in the destruction of the only man he thought of as his equal, was sent home by Utnapishtim nearly empty-handed. The gods had ordained immortality to only one mortal, Utnapishtim himself. However, Utnapishtim, in his benevolence, did provide Gilgamesh with some solace: a plant which would restore youth. But even this was not destined to remain in Gilgamesh's hands. A serpent, slithering up from the deep, swallowed the plant as Gilgamesh slept, sloughed his skin, and slithered away.[46]

It should probably come as no surprise that the ancient tale of Gilgamesh should speak of a king who is unable to comprehend the nature and limits of his power. It descends from a time when kings first appeared in the world. Previous to the emergence of the political organization which engenders the king—the state—people resided in nomadic foraging bands whose political leader, the headman, is one among equals and has no political capital above prestige. That is to say, the members of his band would tend to defer to him inasmuch as he was an experienced elder but he could not tell them what to do. Likewise, people who lived exclusively by farming relied on chiefs to lead their alliances of agricultural villages. Here, chiefs enjoyed the prestige of foraging headmen, but they enjoyed privilege as well, certain activities incumbent upon their office: usually the collection and redistribution of excess agricultural produce. Only with the emergence of mercantile states do we find kings who enjoy not only prestige and privilege but also power, the ability to coerce others. It was five thousand years ago that these mercantile states first emerged—simultaneously in Mesopotamia and Egypt and, shortly thereafter, in India and China and then, yet again, in Mexico and Peru—with their vibrant cities and apparently despotic kings.[47]

Egypt: Osiris, Isis, Horus

Egyptian civilization, among the earliest mercantile states, emerged five thousand years ago with the unification of Lower Egypt (the Nile delta) and Upper Egypt (the territories abutting the Nile below the delta and above the first cataract at Aswan). Over the three and a half millennia during which it thrived, Egyptian civilization encompassed three periods of stable governance (the Old, Middle, and New Kingdoms) followed by three periods of relative political instability and decentralization (the First, Second, and Third Intermediate Periods), after which it fell successively into the hands of Persia, Greece, and finally Rome. But Egypt, in its imperial glory, was a stunning power: prosperous, influential, and nurtured by the annual spring flooding of the Nile which deposited a rich silt upon the river banks and insured a generous crop year after year. So generous, in fact, was the gift of the Nile's annual flood that a good part of the Egyptian populace was freed from the drudgery of agricultural labor and enabled to embark upon the various arts of manufacture and service that so defined ancient Egypt: architecture, trade, craft production (including the production of luxury goods and art), religious service, record-keeping, construction (including the construction of irrigation and other large-scale public projects), military conquest, and dynastic rule.

With the first stirrings of unification, a single king of one of the many kings who presided over the various towns and cities that dotted the Nile Valley made himself a king of kings—that is, a Pharaoh—and the place of Egypt on the stage of world history was forever thereby ensured. With time, Pharaonic rule was solidified: first, by claiming that one god or another had placed the Pharaoh on the throne; finally, by claiming that the Pharaoh was a god himself. At times, it seems that certain Pharaohs even claimed that there was only one true god and, thus, no other king could legitimately challenge the authority of a Pharaoh on the basis that another, perhaps more powerful, god was his sponsor. It may be thus that monotheism made its first appearance in the world. Among the most important myths that underlie and sanctify the power of the Pharaoh is that of Osiris, Isis, and Horus. For one thing, it exists as a spiritual allegory for the continuous agricultural rebirth of Egypt as a result of the springtime inundation of the Nile. For another, it authorizes the ritual practice of embalming in preparation for the journey to the Afterworld. In other words, the Pharaoh's power seems to be solidified by the belief that the agricultural well-being of Egypt as well as the promise to every Egyptian who lives a charitable life of an afterlife rests firmly in the personage of the Pharaoh as the incarnation of the first mythic king of Egypt: Osiris.

The best-known version of the myth of Osiris is largely based on that reported by Plutarch: Upon the birth of Osiris, "a voice was heard to proclaim that the lord of creation was born," and—within due time—Osiris ascended to the throne of Egypt. He "devoted himself to civilizing his subjects and to teaching them the craft of" husbandry. Further, "he established a code of laws and bade men worship the gods. Having made Egypt peaceful and flourishing, he set out to instruct the other nations of the world. During his absence his wife, Isis," ascended to the throne, incurring the wrath of Osiris's brother, the wicked Set, who began to lay a trap with which to slay Osiris. Having "secretly got the measure of" his brother's body, "and made ready a fair chest," he induced Osiris "to lie down in the chest, which was immediately closed by Set and his fellow conspirators, who conveyed it to the mouth of the Nile," whence it was "carried by the sea to Byblos." There, it was "gently laid by the waves among the branches of a tamarisk tree, which in a very short time had grown to a magnificent size and had enclosed the chest within its trunk. The king of the country, admiring the tree, cut it down and made a pillar for the roof of his house of that part which contained the body of Osiris. When Isis heard of this she went to Byblos, and," telling the queen of that country her sad tale, begged to be given the trunk of the pillar which contained her husband's body. Then, transporting the chest back to Egypt and hiding it in what she thought to be a safe locale, she returned to the throne, pondering within herself what steps to next take. But Set, one night "hunting by the light of the moon, found the chest, and, recognizing the body, tore it into fourteen pieces, which he scattered up and down throughout the land. When Isis heard of this she took a boat made of papyrus—a plant abhorred by crocodiles—and sailing about she gathered the fragments of Osiris's body." Only her dead husband's penis was lost for, when he dismembered his brother, Set tossed it into the Nile where it was swallowed by a fish. Nevertheless, Isis fashioned a golden phallus and, upon embracing her dead husband's body, she conceived his posthumous son, Horus, who, slaying his wicked uncle, ascended to the throne in the visage of his dead father, Osiris.

While Osiris, in this story, represents the eternal return of the floodwaters of the Nile and, along with them, Egyptian fertility, Set—Osiris's evil brother— represents the continuous encroachment of the sterile desert upon Egypt's agricultural well-being. But despite Set's numerous efforts against his brother, Osiris endures: even engendering his son in death. Likewise, the floodwaters of the Nile inevitably recur, insuring Egypt's agricultural bounty. Further, throughout much of Egyptian history, Osiris represents the Pharaoh in death, while his posthumously conceived son, Horus, represents the Pharaoh in life. Thus death, inevitable as the desert sands, is not a permanent state. Just as the floodwaters of the Nile will predictably return so too will Osiris return in the personage of his son: Horus. Death is as transitory, then, as is the brief period which precedes the yearly inundation of the Nile. With the return of the flood waters and the bountiful agricultural cycle, like the incarnation of the old Pharaoh (Osiris) in the personage of the new (Horus), Egypt returns to life. Notably, the lynchpin of this continual return—of the Nile's floodwaters and human life—is the miraculously restorative power manifested in the embrace of Isis: the eternal Mother whose original diadem, the throne of Egypt, is replaced with the diadem of Thoth (the ibis-headed god of wisdom) consisting of a pair of cow horns holding aloft the disk of the sun, Amun-Ra.[48]

2. The Physical Environment and Ecological Metaphors

Ecology

Little wonder that the annual inundation of the Nile River Valley, that single ecological factor that so governed ancient Egypt's agricultural productivity, became such a powerful idiom in Egyptian mythology: investing both pharaonic rule and belief in the afterlife with its own mysterious energy. After all, ecology—the exploitation of a physical environment in order to obtain resources—influences every other aspect of culture: economy, family and community organization, political structure, and—most certainly—religion. That which the environment beneficently offers up for our sustenance takes on greater significance than that of simple foodstuffs. Taro, the staple crop of Hawaiians, becomes not only an element of the people's diet but also of their worldview: simultaneously symbolizing their ancestry and continued welfare. Being the elder, but disabled, brother of the progenitor of the Hawaiian people, Taro was destined to nurture and, in turn, be nurtured by his innumerable generations of nephews. In fact, so sacred is Taro, based on his ancient kinship to the Hawaiian people, that genetic modification of the plant in order to safeguard it from blight seems a sacrilege.[1] Corn, Beans, and Squash are not simply something the Iroquois cultivate and eat but also benevolent feminine deities who so preserve the Iroquois that the three—referred to collectively as the *Diohekon* (*These Sustain Us*)—pervade Iroquois religion. Cattle are so ecologically essential—and so sacred—to India, the country that boasts the highest head of cattle and produces the most milk in the world, that their slaughter is nearly unthinkable and has recently led to politically charged legislation as well as religious violence.[2] Think about this in the context of Christianity, the dominant religion in American society. Though modern food production and distribution systems have diversified American diets to such an extent that Americans no longer have a true staple, the time when wheat—baked into loaves of bread—was the preeminent Mediterranean staple has found its way into American society through the use of bread in Christianity's central ritual: Communion.

Today, there is only one species of humans, Homo sapiens, left in the world. But that one species, despite the fact that it is over 99.9 percent genetically identical, has adapted itself to a wide array of disparate environments. And while some degree of human genetic variation results from each society's adaptation to its own unique environment, the cultural adaptations that each society makes in so adjusting itself will, in their turn, exact some further degree of variation on that society's genetic makeup. In other words, we are so entangled with our local ecologies that not only do we humans transform the environment as we cull from it the various resources upon which we come to depend but also the environment, which we have so transformed, transforms us in its turn: at times exerting upon us profound biological pressures. In those regions of the world, for example, where our environmental exploitation has included the domestication of cattle—northern Europe, for instance, or East Africa—human populations have developed adult lactose tolerance: the ability to digest milk past infancy.[3] Likewise, some populations of farmers who depend upon starchy grains or tubers—but not foragers from tropical forests or the arctic, nor a number of societies that depend upon animal herding for their livelihood—have extra copies of a gene which produces amylase: an enzyme that is found in saliva and aids in the process of breaking down starches.[4] Then again, some West African farming societies, which have cleared forests for yam cultivation, have inadvertently created an environment more conducive to the Anopheles mosquito which transmits malaria. In these groups—when compared to neighboring groups which have not so extensively cleared forest lands—there is a greater incidence of the "sickle-cell" genetic trait which, though it can carry its own devastating health effects, does as well confer a significant line of defense against malarial infections.[5] In essence our interior ecology becomes a function of our exterior ecology.

The main point with regard to the environment, then, is this: human groups live in an environment that in one way or another constrains them—excess aridity or rainfall, rocky terrain or sandy loam, the presence of ungulates or marsupials, the danger of the tsetse fly or the beneficence of deer and black bear, a surfeit or a deficit of fatty fish, extreme cold or heat, high or low altitude. No matter what the environmental conditions, there will be certain factors that the culture which a society develops will have to consider. Foraging, for instance, prevailed into modern times in areas that were simply too arid for agriculture such as the Kalihari Desert in Southern Africa and much of the interior of Australia. Cattle and other draught animals were not heavily used in West Africa where the tsetse fly was too great a risk to their health. Thus, hoe agriculture centering on root crops prevailed. But where relatively rich environments tended to push populations to the upper limits of the land's carrying capacity (that is, the number of people an environment could feed given a society's technology), plow, fertilization, and irrigation could be adopted in order to maximize agricultural production. In all these various cases, both the benefits and constraints of the environment have exerted profound effects on every aspect of our culture and—probably because we have to have a sense that we cannot only comprehend but also control the environment upon which we depend—we humans have universally come to see ourselves as living in a kind of union, both physical and spiritual, with the environment. This perception seems especially notable in foraging societies but can be quite marked as well in agricultural societies: particularly those which, like the Iroquois, historically involved themselves in hunting. But with the advent of agropastoralism, in which both plants and animals are domesticated, and (even more so) mercantilism, in which only a portion of the society is intimately involved in farming, the notion of union, even kinship, with the environment—and the various plants, animals, topographical features, and celestial bodies that inhabit it—begins to erode. And as this erosion progresses, the plants, animals, and other resources we exploit are less often venerated and more regularly commodified.

Yet in either case, whether we venerate or commodify our resources, our global mythologies speak most directly to the environment which we not only depend upon for our survival but which we also have incorporated into the biological fiber of our being. For instance, the nomadic herding of sheep and goats which so defined the ancient Hebraic ecology was sanctified in the Torah. Even though, by the time of the Torah's composition some three to two thousand years ago, a portion of the Hebraic population was living in fortified towns with a distinct mercantile economy, and agriculture proper—the raising of wheat, barley, peas, and lentils—was well established, much of the village populace, in an attempt to gain a living in a sometimes harsh environment, depended heavily on pastoralism. Thus, herding—whether nomadic, sedentary, or transhumant—as an ideal ecology became embedded in Hebraic myth, so much so that the shepherd was the very model of the perfect man. The tiller of the soil, conversely, was not so highly honored, a disparity made explicit in the myth of Cain and Abel:

> And the man knew Eve his wife; and she conceived and bore Cain, and said: "I have gotten a man with the help of HaShem." And again she bore his brother Abel. And Abel was a keeper of sheep, but Cain was a tiller of the ground. And in process of time it came to pass, that Cain brought of the fruit of the ground an offering unto HaShem. And Abel, he also brought of the firstlings of his flock and of the fat thereof. And HaShem had respect unto

Abel and to his offering; but unto Cain and to his offering He had not respect. And Cain was very wroth, and his countenance fell. And HaShem said unto Cain: "Why art thou wroth? And why is thy countenance fallen? If thou doest well, shall it not be lifted up? And if thou doest not well, sin coucheth at the door; and unto thee is its desire, but thou mayest rule over it." And Cain spoke unto Abel his brother. And it came to pass, when they were in the field, that Cain rose up against Abel his brother, and slew him. And HaShem said unto Cain: "Where is Abel thy brother?" And he said: "I know not; am I my brother's keeper?" And He said: "What hast thou done? The voice of thy brother's blood crieth unto Me from the ground. And now cursed art thou from the ground, which hath opened her mouth to receive thy brother's blood from thy hand. When thou tillest the ground, it shall not henceforth yield unto thee her strength; a fugitive and a wanderer shalt thou be in the earth."[6]

It seems hard to imagine this myth arising out of a society that prefers agricultural to pastoral production. Ancient Hebraic society's sense of well-being rather seems, on the basis of such a myth, to have arisen out of the belief that not only would the people's flocks sustain them but also that their deity had so ordained it.

But it was not simply ideals of the appropriate sacrifice that arose out of the Hebraic pastoral ecology. So too did ideals of what (and, just as importantly, what did not) constitute edible food. The extensive dietary prohibitions that characterized Hebraic society, and still inform many notions of ritual purity in Judaism today, arise—according to Mary Douglas—out of a profound and careful reading of ancient Israel's pastoral ecological adaptation. Douglas, in discussing the *Abominations of Leviticus*, the various prohibitions covered in the books of *Leviticus* and *Deuteronomy*, suggests that that which was prohibited—the abomination—was almost invariably something which did not neatly fit into the Hebraic classification of the natural world (i.e., the Hebraic ecology). For example, Hebraic peoples were herders of animals that had parted hooves and which chewed cud (the regurgitated contents of their stomach): sheep and goats, for instance. Pigs, who though they have parted hooves do not chew the cud were an anomaly to the Hebraic ideal of domestic animals and were therefore considered unclean. From Douglas's perspective, the taboo against eating pork had little, if anything, to do with health issues (such as the avoidance of trichinosis) or even the issue that pigs in arid environments might wallow in their own urine and feces to cool down. It rather had to do with the structurally anomalous position inhabited by pigs in the Hebraic worldview. Notably, Douglas claims, the term abomination is not a good translation of the Hebraic concept of the anomaly. She rather translates that which is an abomination as a "confusion" of categories. In essence, Douglas maintains, animals which fit unambiguously into their category—cud-chewing mammals that move with split hooves of dry land; fish with scales, fins, and gills that swim in the waters; and non-predatory birds capable of flight—are clean and thus edible. This excludes animals such as unhooved rabbits and hares, scaleless eels, and flightless carrion-eating birds. From Douglas's perspective, this set of seemingly irrational rules was a continuous, *rational*, reminder to a pastoral people—who had to, in their earliest nomadic history, cull many of their food resources from the arid wilderness around them—of the divine order ordained by the deity for the good of his chosen people. In essence, the rules offered a continual reminder to remember God's creation and to, as one was expected to do on the Shabbat (Sabbath), that day which celebrated creation itself, "keep it holy."[7]

Of Sheep, Goats and Sacred Cows

Christian mythology, so heavily informed by Hebraic myth in its incipience, continues to make use of pastoral imagery. In *The Gospel According to Matthew* we read the following:

> When the Son of man shall come in his glory, and all the holy angels with him, then shall he sit upon the throne of his glory: And before him shall be gathered all nations: and he shall separate them one from another, as a shepherd divideth his sheep from the goats: And he shall set the sheep on his right hand, but the goats on the left. Then shall the King say unto them on his right hand, "Come, ye blessed of my Father, inherit the kingdom prepared for you from the foundation of the world: For I was an hungred, and ye gave me meat: I was thirsty, and ye gave me drink: I was a stranger, and ye took me in: Naked, and ye clothed me: I was sick, and ye visited me: I was in prison, and ye came unto me." Then shall the righteous answer him, saying, "Lord, when saw we thee an hungred, and fed thee? Or thirsty, and gave thee drink? When saw we thee a stranger, and took thee in? Or naked, and clothed thee? Or when saw we thee sick, or in prison, and came unto thee?" And the King shall answer and say unto them, "Verily I say unto you, inasmuch as ye have done it unto one of the least of these my brethren, ye have done it unto me." Then shall he say also unto them on the left hand, "Depart from me, ye cursed, into everlasting fire, prepared for the devil and his angels: For I was an hungred, and ye gave me no meat: I was thirsty, and ye gave me no drink: I was a stranger, and ye took me not in: naked, and ye clothed me not: sick, and in prison, and ye visited me not." Then shall they also answer him, saying, "Lord, when saw we thee an hungred, or athirst, or a stranger, or naked, or sick, or in prison, and did not minister unto thee?" Then shall he answer them, saying, "Verily I say unto you, inasmuch as ye did it not to one of the least of these, ye did it not to me." And these shall go away into everlasting punishment: but the righteous into life eternal.[8]

How are we to make sense of the central metaphor that inhabits this mythic passage? Very simply in fact. In the Mediterranean world, shepherds often pasture their sheep and goats together. One shepherd, two flocks, simply isn't logistically possible. Further, the shepherd, when bringing his flocks to a new pasture can send his goats in the first day. A plant that might simply sicken a goat could kill a lamb. If the goat doesn't sicken after a day of pasturing, it is more likely safe for the shepherd to send his sheep along with his goats into the one pasture the next day. Yet, no matter that the shepherd can pasture his sheep and goats together and, thus, more readily manage his family's livelihood. At night, when he returns his flocks to the fold, he will do best—if he wishes to avoid mayhem—to place his tractable sheep and unwieldy goats in separate pens.

If images of sheep and goats pervade Judaism and Christianity, images of cattle are at the center of Hindu signification. While it is certainly true that the Hindu religion precludes the slaughter of cattle on the basis of its sacred nature, Marvin Harris maintains that there are as well solid ecological reasons to avoid slaughtering cattle. While the milk and milk products provided by cattle are often more valuable than beef, Harris points out that the Zebu cattle, most commonly raised in India, do not provide as much milk as, say, Holstein dairy cattle and, further, that their milk output is especially negligible in times of drought: something to which many parts of India are historically susceptible. Cattle nonetheless do provide India with invaluable milk and milk products:

Shepherds from Sagrada Familia, Barcelona (author's photograph).

for instance, *ghee*—clarified butter—which is not only used in Indian cuisine but also *puja*, the worship of Hindu deities. Moreover, cattle provide two extremely important resources to Indian farmers: manure for fertilizing their fields, fueling their ovens, and heating their homes (one cow providing all the fuel necessary for a family of four), and traction for plowing their fields. Harris further points out that while it might be feasible in the short-run, especially in a time of drought, to slaughter cattle for nutritional reasons, the taboo serves to stave off the potential wholesale slaughter of cattle in a period of extended drought to insure that, when the drought ends (which, after all, it always does), it is possible to resume the highly productive form of plough agriculture which has served India well for centuries. Harris points out an even further surprising factor arising from the complex interdependency of people and cattle in India. Whereas in most of India, oxen—castrated male cattle—are used for plowing, water buffalo are used in parts of Kerala state instead:

> In the Trivandrum district of the state of Kerala in southern India, farmers told me that they obeyed the Hindu prohibition against the slaughter of cattle and that they never knowingly did anything to shorten the lives of their animals. Yet in Kerala, the mortality rate of male calves is almost twice as high as the mortality rate of female calves. In fact, male cattle 0 to 1 year of age are outnumbered by female cattle of the same group in a ratio of 67 to 100. The farmers themselves are aware that male calves are more likely to die than female calves, but they attribute the difference to the relative "weakness" of the males. "The males get sick more often," they said. When I asked them to explain why male calves got sick more often than females some farmers suggested that the males eat less than the females. A few farmers even explained that the male calves eat less because they are not allowed to stay at the mother's teats for more than a few seconds. But no one said that male cattle were not as valuable in Kerala as they are in other regions of India, where they are used in plowing dry fields. In Kerala, where rice, the principle crop, is grown in postage-stamp-size fields, oxen are at a disadvantage. They tend to get stuck in the mud and break their legs. Water buffalo have no such problems and are thus preferred over oxen to prepare the fields for planting.

Thus, Harris points out, "cattle sex ratios are systematically adjusted to the needs of the local ecology and economy through preferential male 'bovicide.' Although the unwanted calves are not slaughtered many are more or less starved to death."[9] In this case, the exception made on cattle slaughter seems to confirm the rule because the sacred nature of cattle—even in a region of India where male cattle are not particularly valuable—is sustained. In fact, the special place of cattle in India, authorized by millennia of holy writings which view cattle as emblematic of a beneficent life-giving force not unlike the Iroquois *Diohekon*, underscores the essential ecological symbiosis between humans and cattle that defines India's agricultural practices. Only with this knowledge in hand can we make sense of the significance of Nandini, "the Cow of Plenty, capable of granting every desire." Possessing "large eyes, full udders, a fine tail, beautiful hoofs, and every other auspicious sign, and yielding much milk," she "roamed about" freely in "sacred and delightful forests," and he who drank of her "sweet milk" remained "a youth for ten thousand years." Further, we might understand how the theft of such an auspicious cow from the *Rishi* (Sage) into whose keeping the granddaughter of Brahma had given her could condemn Bhishma, an immortal son of the River Ganges, to the harsh life of a mortal and death in the cataclysmic battle—which we will later consider— over the throne of Hastinapura.[10]

But every bit as important as the symbiosis between Indian farmers and their cattle is that between Indian farmers and their gardens. Fertilizing their gardens with manure from their farm animals and relying on irrigation systems employing ground wells and streams as water sources; canals, ditches, dams, locks, and waterwheels to divert water; and reservoirs, tanks, and ditches to store excess seasonal rains, India's half a billion plus farmers raise both rice and wheat as well as a multitude of vegetables: potatoes and tomatoes; okra, onions, chick peas, peas, and lentils; soybeans, cottonseed, and sesame. Fruit as well, bananas and mangoes, for instance, is tended in groves at the garden's edge or hard by the farmer's house. Taken as a whole, Indian agro-pastoralism, though marked both by dramatic successes and dismal failures, may be the most extensively practiced agricultural ecology the world has witnessed to date. But the complex is under intense pressure partly as a result of India's burgeoning population but also its further entanglement with a modern market economy. Throughout India, farmers are forced to take out micro-loans to keep their farms afloat. But after several seasons of drought, the loans—the lifeblood of a globalizing economy—become the snare that traps the Indian farmer in a debt from which there is often no easily apparent escape. Still, the fact that farming, as difficult as it can sometimes be, is the lifeblood of Indian agricultural practice is reflected in the fact that Manu, he who (as we will later see) builds an ark to prevent the utter destruction of Brahma's creation, safeguarded in that ark not all the beasts of the forests and fields but rather "all the different seeds which were enumerated by regenerate Brahmins in days of yore." He, thus, safeguarded Indian agricultural practice from inevitable destruction.

It is the unique function of myth to speak directly to the union of a society and the environment it exploits—perhaps because it is myth's unique function to generate the ritual which will offer society a sense that it has some degree of control over the environment upon which its well-being so entirely hinges. Let us look, therefore, at some examples of how thoroughly various societies' mythologies have come into consonance with their ecologies. What we will notice almost immediately is this: myth will borrow the most essential integers of the local ecology—for instance, taro; corn, beans, and squash; sheep, goats, and shepherds; cattle; antelopes and buffalo—and make of them the various metaphors with which it will express the abstract concepts that populate its religion. In the passage from the *New Testament* cited above, for instance, the metaphors are sheep, goats, and shepherds. The abstract concepts are charity and stinginess as well as salvation and damnation. Interestingly, to the Hebraic people who were Jesus's audience, the metaphors are eminently knowable and, thus, apt vehicles for the abstract concepts. To the vast majority of contemporary Christians, on the other hand, the metaphors are nearly incomprehensible. What do we, after all, know of sheep and goats? Thus, the metaphoric heft of the passage is nearly lost on us and we immediately center our attention on the abstract concepts of charity, stinginess, salvation, and damnation. Though, oddly, the notion of unfettered charity (a concept perhaps more honored in the breach than the observance) that is the explicit message of this passage is often overlooked in favor of the less socially conscious concepts of salvation and damnation.

The San of the Kalihari[11]

A particularly intriguing use of ecological metaphors occurs in the mythology of the San: a society of foragers who reside in the northern Kalihari, a semi-arid desert straddling the border of the Southern African nations of Botswana and Namibia. San society, like that of other foragers, is characterized by a number of essential features: a gender-based division of labor in which men hunt and women gather; an emphasis on reciprocity; egalitarian social relations; a nomadic existence anchored by temporary encampments; and—most important to our concerns—a deeply engrained knowledge and even veneration of their environment and all that it contains. Recently, two intriguing lines of evidence have converged, simultaneously giving us a greater understanding of the prehistory of the San people and the emergence of our modern Homo sapiens forebears. One suggests that there is greater genetic diversity to be found among populations which have lived in a locale for a longer period of time, less among more recent populations. The second suggests that there are more phonemes, distinctive sounds, present in the languages spoken in those areas where modern humans have resided the longest, fewer in those areas that we have settled most recently.

Both lines of evidence have pinpointed Southwest Africa, particularly where the present-day countries of Namibia and Botswana meet "in the San homeland," as the birthplace of modern humanity. As Sarah Tishkoff explains,

African populations display "the highest levels of within-population genetic diversity," while "genetic diversity declines with distance from Africa." Further, three foraging groups, including the San, were among the five African groups that displayed the "highest levels of genetic diversity."[12] When we turn to language, we find that the San are speakers of Khoisan, a language family characterized by a number of clicks. Khoisan languages, it turns out, are terrifically complex, being characterized by over 100 phonemes: distinctive sounds out of which words are constructed.[13] These numerous sounds, which include four distinct clicks among the San, contrast with the relative paucity of phonemes among more recent populations. Native South Americans, the Inuit, and Polynesians, who arrived in their homelands near the end of the great migration out of Africa, manifest phoneme counts ranging from the teens to the twenties. Major European languages—such as French, English, Russian, and German—contain phonemes numbering from the '30s through the '40s.[14] Tishkoff, beyond pinpointing the San homeland as the place from which the "modern human migration originated" also suggests that the point of embarkation, from which Homo sapiens first left Africa, is likely "near the midpoint of the Red Sea," equidistant, of course, between the Bab al-Mandab Straits and the Sinai, the two routes out of Africa that archaeological data corroborates.

The ancestors of the San, who most likely spoke a click language, dominated the African continent—and formed the bulk of the global population—in the early periods of Homo sapiens history. But the first anatomically modern humans to leave Africa were likely members of a smaller offshoot of this group. The ancestors of contemporary Bantu speakers, separated from their parental population by a changing climate some 150 to 100 thousand years ago, came to dominate northwest Africa. And it was their descendants, an even smaller lineage of early Homo sapiens, who were the earliest modern humans to enter Asia. Once there, they met—and, to a limited extent, interbred—with the remnants of an even earlier dispersal out of Africa: not only Neanderthal but also a recently discovered contemporary of Neanderthal that lived in East Asia: the Denisovans.[15] While the San themselves, inasmuch as they are our contemporaries, are not the remnant of some ancestral Homo sapiens population, they do seem to be among the most direct descendants of the early Homo sapiens who spread across East and South Africa between 200 and 100 thousand years ago.

Richard Lee describes the climate of the San homeland, the Kalihari, as oscillating between an intense summer heat when temperatures can exceed 100 degrees Fahrenheit and the moderate winter months when temperatures might reach 80 degrees during the day but fall to near freezing at night. Further, it oscillates between a rainy summer and a dry winter. Thus, the San seasonal cycle revolves around periods of high mobility when temperatures are warm, seasonal water supplies are plentiful, and there is an abundance of both animal and vegetal foods, to periods of low mobility when temperatures can become painfully cold, the terrain is arid and lacking in many of the preferred foods, and foraging is further constrained because it must occur within the range of a permanent waterhole. The cycle begins with the first appearance of the spring rains in October and November, "triggering growth in plants and reproduction in animals," and transforming "the parched landscape" into one marked by "lush greenery." The San take advantage of the plentiful seasonal pans— or waterholes—that gather in-between the dunes in the upper elevations of the Kalihari or in the flats below. They, therefore, tend to disperse in small, widely scattered, encampments.

San hunter (Wikipedia, photograph by Ian Beatty).

Then, with the advent of the main summer rains, lasting from December through March, the San exploit "migratory ducks, geese, and other waterfowl" which "flock to the seasonal pans," as well as "elephant and buffalo" which "migrate from the Okavango swamps," some 150 miles to the east. Further, the "major summer plant foods—fruits, berries, melons, and leafy greens—also make their appearance." San encampments, still "widely distributed at seasonal waterpoints in the hinterland," are able to take advantage of the rich, varied, and widely distributed summer food sources. Next comes a brief autumn, running from April to May, during which the rains have ended but the cold weather has not yet returned. The San may "converge on the larger summer pans that still hold water," perhaps near the hardpan, the terrain which dominates the lower elevations within the Kalihari. Summer foods are still plentiful and the April harvest of the Mongongo nut "puts a major new food into the diet." Then comes the "cool dry" winter, running from the "end of May through August."

The San winter camps, situated "around a permanent waterhole," generally near a low-lying Molapo (dry river course), "are well stocked with firewood to burn though the cold nights," and staples, including "the Mongongo fruit and nut, baobab, and many species of roots and bulbs," are available. Since the San are relatively sedentary at this time of year, being constrained to stay near a permanent water source, friends and "relatives at distant camps" are often visited—and medicine dances more frequent. And though "good tracking conditions encourage more hunting and the setting up of snarelines," plant foods are becoming increasingly scarce as "a wider and wider" collecting radius around the permanent waterhole becomes depleted. Finally, the spring dry season

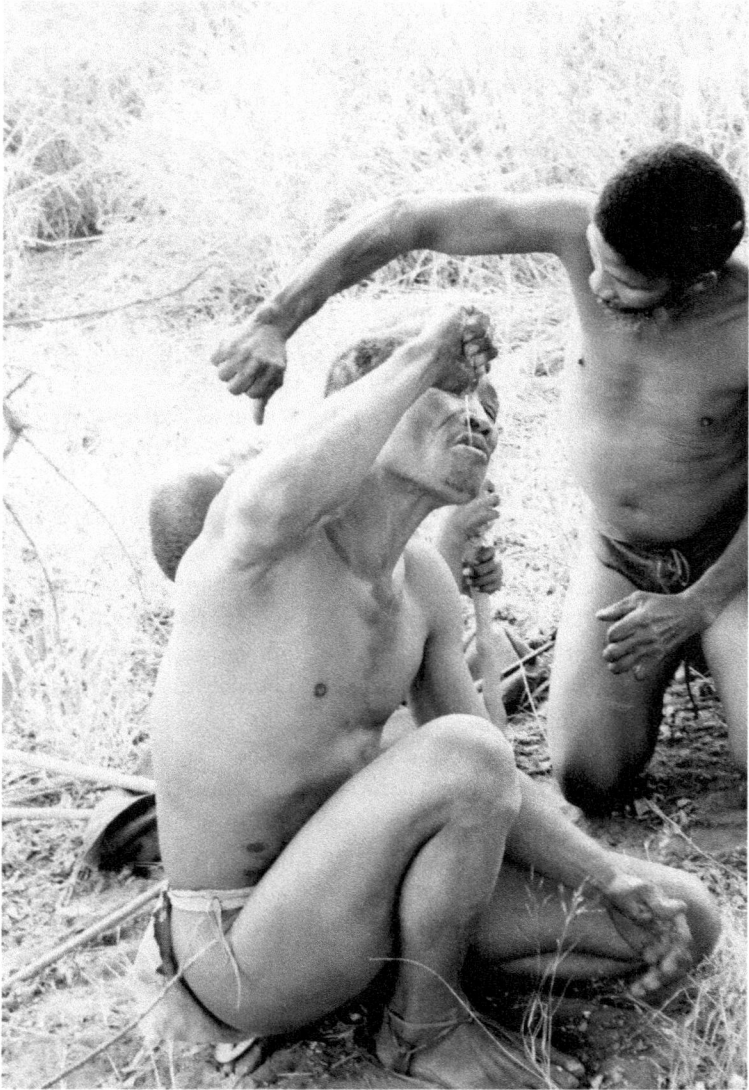

San men extracting water from bulbs (Wikipedia, photograph by DVL2).

arrives in late August and lasts through October or early November. High temperatures make this the least attractive time of the year with highs ranging from "92 to 110 degrees Fahrenheit in the shade." Rendering it an even less hospitable season is the fact that "better foods may be available only at a distance from camp." Thus, the "widest variety of plant food" is exploited, including "fibrous roots, ignored at other times," which are "dug and eaten without enthusiasm." It is a harsh season which the San seem to patiently wait out.

The San are intimately engaged with the animals with which they share their environment and upon whose flesh they depend, attributing to them a spiritual as well as a physical existence. They live with, and name, some 260 species including 50 mammals, 90 birds, and 25 reptiles and amphibians, but their hunting strategies center on ungulates: particularly antelopes such as the steenbok, duiker, kudu, wildebeest, and gemsbok. They also regularly hunt the warthog and a number of smaller animals, particularly the "ant bear, porcupine, springhare, and scrub hare." Other animals commonly exploited by the San include the ostrich, which is not characteristically hunted but whose eggs are collected for both its content and its shells (the later making good canteens), various species of bird, wild honey, and the grub of the chrysomelid beetle which is used for poisoning hunting arrows. This last provides a "slow-acting but highly effective poison" which kills a "wounded animal in 6 to 24 hours."

The San maintain the characteristic foraging division of labor whereby women gather (as well as carry water, cook, and build houses) and men hunt (while engaging in some limited gathering duties). While women's sharing of vegetal foods is primarily within the family, rules strictly stipulate with whom each hunter shares the various cuts of meat from the animal he takes. In other words, sharing of meat is obligatory. In fact, what Lee came to find during the course of his studies with the San was that reciprocity was the strictest of rules among themselves—though it did not necessarily obtain when dealing with members of other groups. One could, without suffering recrimination, profit off an outsider. But, even if one did profit, it was a temporary state of affairs because for the San, getting gifts was always a precedent to giving gifts. Further, as Lee was eventually to learn, one could never gloat over what he gave. Lee once, to thank the San for their hospitality, purchased a fat ox with which to sponsor a feast. For days before the killing and butchering of the ox, the San chastised Lee for being duped into buying such a miserable beast. It would surely turn out to be a sack of bones, hardly worth the effort of butchering and cooking it. Yet, when the ox was butchered and turned out to be filled with luxuriant fat, Lee learned the San practice called "insulting the meat." The San didn't allow anyone to get a swollen head simply because he happened to be a better hunter or perhaps because he had happened to have more luck than another hunter. Whenever a man took a game animal, his fellows would insult the meat. If they didn't, the hunter's pride might eventually cause him, according to the San, to act as a chief and order other people around. It might even cause him to become so "hot" that he might kill someone. So the San always opted to "cool" overbearing natures down through insults such as saying, upon being taken out to the bush to butcher an animal, "You mean you have dragged us all the way out here to make us cart home your pile of bones? Oh, if I had known it was this thin I wouldn't have come. People, to think I gave up a nice day in the shade for this. At home, we may be hungry, but at least we have nice cool water to drink." And adding to his indignity, the butt of the jokes was even obliged to join in: "You're right, this one is not worth the effort; let's just cook the liver for strength and leave the rest for the hyenas. It's not too late to hunt today, and even a duiker or a steenbok would be better than this mess."

"Insulting the meat is one of the central practices," among the San, "that serves to maintain egalitarianism," according to Lee. And egalitarianism, likely a necessity to a society whose very existence hinges on reciprocity, is characteristic of San social organization. Yet, within the framework of egalitarian social relations, the San acknowledge relations characterized by traditional deference or, conversely, the lack thereof. Every San person maintains a number of deferential, or respect, relations with a number of members of the encampment as well as a number of peer, or joking, relations. In fact, each person stands in either a respect or joking relationship with every other member of the encampment. As Lee explains it: "A woman jokes with her sisters but respects her brothers. She jokes with her grandparents and grandchildren and respects her parents and children. A man jokes with his brothers but respects his sisters. He jokes with his grandparents and grandchildren but respects his parents and children."[16] Further, within one's own generation, a woman will maintain joking relations with all save her brothers and brothers-in-law and a man will maintain joking relations with all save his sisters and sisters-in-law. Notably, the respect a woman owes persons of her parent's generation are particularly marked with her mother-in-law and especially her father-in-law. Likewise, a man's respect relationships are particularly marked with his father-in-law and especially his mother-in-law. So marked, in fact, are these avoidance relations that not only do they disallow joking but also sitting together, entering one another's dwellings, and even using one another's names. This last rule necessitates the use of a system of respect terms—titles or metaphoric alternatives—to which a speaker makes recourse if he or she is not permitted to use a person's name.[17]

Respect relations are characterized by reserved speech whereas joking relationships are characterized by open and even ribald speech. Lorna Marshall's suggests that while non-sexual jokes can be made by anyone, "sexual jokes and insults" are reserved for use between those who maintain joking relationships: "Men accuse each other of excessive preoccupation with sexual intercourse or of having genital organs of excessive size or abnormal condition," while "men accuse women with whom they joke of being ugly, slovenly, or wanton. The women retaliate, perhaps accusing the men of being worthy only of castration or of unfaithful wives."[18] It seems likely that such a system serves to mitigate some of the natural fault lines that exist in San society, places where an undue degree of social tension could undermine the cooperation and reciprocity that are the hallmarks of San culture. It may as well be that such a system serves to solidify the bonds between individuals among whom cooperation is an absolute necessity: for instance, a group of age mates who might hunt or gather together. Not surprisingly, egalitarianism, reciprocity, and the subtle attention to the language which underpins respect and joking relations find their way most exactly into San mythology. In fact, a central tenet of San myth seems to be that social conflict leads to a breakdown of the cooperation and sharing that are so essential to San social life.

Beautiful Python Girl and the Spring of Creation

The San refer to their myths as "stories of the old people." Megan Biesele explains that they are "set in a long-ago time," when the Creator set the world in motion, the Trickster "walked upon the earth," and the "animals were people."[19] The Creator, after creating himself, gave himself the name Gangwanana, Big Big God, and then brought the Trickster into being, naming him, after himself, Gangwa Matse: Little God. He then set about creating the other gods; the earth, sky, sun, moon, and stars; thunder, lightning, wind, rain, and waterholes; humans, plants, and animals. Creator and Trickster each have a wife and children, and each are attended by a number of lesser gods as well as "the spirits of the dead," the Gangwasi—or Ghosts. "All these beings live in the sky."[20] The Creator lives, along with the spirit-animals over whom he is master, in the eastern sky, in an encampment presided over by a great tree too sacred to name. From this tree, he hangs the "spirit, heart, and blood" of anyone who has died, smoking them with a sacred medicine which transforms the deceased person into a Ghost. The Trickster lives in the western sky, in an encampment presided over by two trees which may be named, and he appears, along with the Gangwasi, in the whirlwind. The Creator "sends both good and bad fortune to the people" through the Trickster and the Gangwasi. But the Creator has, likewise, provided the people with a medicine, *num*, with which to combat bad fortune—and particularly illness. And though the Trickster is said to bring illness, the

San attribute illness mainly to the maliciousness of the Gangwasi. Further, inasmuch as the Trickster is named for and by the Creator, the two—as namesakes—maintain a joking relationship with one another.[21] A singular aspect of the San perception of deity is presented by the fact that the Creator, the Trickster, and the Ghosts all have the same root—Gangwa (literally, Praying Mantis)—in their name. Though all are anthropomorphic, the San sometimes perceive of the Trickster as a Praying Mantis (or, perhaps, a man named for the Mantis).[22]

A seminal episode of San mythology centers on Beautiful Python Girl, the heroic daughter-in-law of the Trickster (Gangwa Matse), one particular recitation of which—collected by Biesele—was offered with a particularly dramatic flair.[23] Biesele sat with a group of friends: "Suddenly, from behind an anthill, popped the Ostrich Lady! She ran forward on skinny but elegant old legs, shouting 'Wanh, wanh, wanh,' and scattered the children." Thereupon, she pointed "her lips like an ostrich's beak" and scratched "one toe in the sand as if it were a big claw," saying, "It's me, the old Ostrich Lady." Then, flapping "her bent arms, pretending they were wings," she asked who was asking about Beautiful Python Girl? "Here I am come to tell you." Beautiful Python Girl, as the Ostrich Lady and others related to Biesele, was not only the daughter-in-law of Gangwa Matse but also the daughter of Elephant, the encampment's headman. She lived in the encampment along with her husband, Kori Bustard, and her sister, Jackal, who had wanted Kori Bustard—with his wonderful feather crest which he would vainly toss to and fro as he ran about the bush—for herself.

One day, Jackal, feeling hungry, suggested that she and her sister travel to the bush to gather the fruit of the Nah Tree which grew hard by the spring and was just then in season. Arriving at the Nah Tree, Jackal convinced her sister—who was a python, after all—to climb out onto a branch, heavy with Nah fruit, which dangled directly over the spring. Thus, as her sister egged her on to slither further and further, the branch broke, sending Beautiful Python Girl to the spring's bottom. Thereupon, Jackal disguised herself as her sister and returned alone to the encampment. But Kori Bustard, returning from the hunt, suspected a trick. He took a wildebeest tail whisk, dipped it in a bowl of fat, and whisked it across his supposed wife's face. Rather than displaying a beautiful, glistening face, however, the greedy jackal immediately went to licking the fat from her own whiskers. Thus, Kori Bustard knew beyond suspicion what had happened. He placed poisoned arrows under his wife's sleeping mat and, in the morning, Jackal was dead. All the animals traveled together to the spring and, there in the depths, they could just barely make out the dim shadow of Beautiful Python Girl. Gemsbok dipped his hind leg in the spring but couldn't reach down deep enough to rescue Beautiful Python Girl. Then, Kudu tried with the same poor results. Then came Ostrich. "With the very tip of one claw he was able to scratch the python." Finally, Giraffe, standing shyly by the side of the spring, was convinced to try and, when he dipped his hind leg into the waterhole and fished around a bit, he "grasped the python and shook the mud off her while she was still down there. Then he opened his mouth and laughed! He began bringing her up and up and up toward the surface. It was a very deep spring! As the python came near the surface, the other animals saw her and hugged each other. They fell to the ground laughing. The giraffe brought her up, and lifted her to the surface. At last he laid her on the ground. She lay there and vomited up water." And dipping his leg into the depths once again, he drew something else from the spring and, laying it gently at the side of Beautiful Python Girl, all saw what had happened. "The python had given birth in the bottom of the spring!" The animals "were so delighted that they embraced each other and rolled on their backs on the ground," saying, "Here's our beautiful girl again." And they said, "Yes, this is a very good thing the giraffe has done for us."

The story profoundly reflects the manner in which the San view their environment: both the physical environment which provides them their resources and the social environment which allows them to manage those resources efficiently. Physically, San well-being is dependent upon the existence of water, and particularly permanent waterholes, as well as the game animals— whose provision of their own flesh is complemented by their sponsorship of medicinal songs and dances. Thus, it is not surprising that a spring and game animals—particularly large game animals—figure so prominently in this story. Socially, the San depend upon an economy based in sharing. People give freely of the food they have obtained and, likewise, freely receive gifts of food from the other members of their group. There is no expectation of an immediate or like return on a gift but rather a sense that everything evens itself out in the end. Indeed, such an economic strategy is imperative in a foraging ecology inasmuch as no one can ever be confident of getting everything he or she needs every day. Further, San social relations are largely egalitarian and based in coop-eration. This egalitarianism seems to help keep sharing relatively equitable. In other words, as is illustrated in the custom of insulting the meat, if someone had greater status than another, he or she might feel a right to a greater share of the essential goods upon which society depends. The greatest danger to a social design based in reciprocity and egalitarianism is discord—based perhaps in jealousy, greed, or envy—and this danger is underscored by the language in which the myth is cast.

In fact, an essential element of the story hinges on its attention to language, an attention which creates a kind of mythic rhetoric: a mythic means, that is, of establishing meaning. As Biesele explains, when narrating the story of Beautiful Python Girl, storytellers employ particularly evocative verbs to differentiate the heroine from her sister. "The python walks-and-shimmers, walks very slowly, sparkles like the sun, glides like a grand person," or "undulates slowly along." But the jackal "wobbles" and "bounces." She "laughs harshly" and "speaks in a rough voice." Even the whisk, when brushed across the Python's smooth face, makes an elegant sound but it makes a grating sound when it is brushed across "jackal's dry and hairy" face. While it could be supposed that the verbiage simply represents a naturalistic description of the python and the jackal, in reality there is something more: a sociological differentiation between a positive assessment of the cooperative member of the group as opposed to a negative assessment of a selfish member. In other words, the disparity in language does not simply illustrate different animal natures but rather serves to illustrate how different animal natures can be used to symbolize different "types" in San society. Discordant sounds are indicative of uncooperative or otherwise disagreeable individuals. Sweet sounds on the other hand are indicative of those who behave in accord with San precepts and display a generous spirit.

This distinction seems to be extended through the modulation of the storyteller's tone: When discussing what the San themselves see as the sometimes ridiculous antics of the "old people," the storytellers will liberally employ puns and scatological humor, bringing a kind of bawdy sensibility to the telling. But, then again, the story's tone can become almost reverential. For instance, San storytellers might employ the use of specialized respect terms which "can enhance the politeness, prudence, or delicacy of any utterance," and which "form what is almost a second language." Respect words are especially metaphorically charged: the lion, for instance, can be called Moonless Night, Cries in the Night, or Calf Muscles of Nightfall. At times the special nature of these respect words is enhanced by embedding them in "a kind of litany form" which, according to Biesele, is also used when enumerating even the everyday names of the large game animals: When the San "enumerate the animals, especially the large meat animals, whether in folktales or in ordinary conversation or in answer to questions, they do so in a highly stylized, almost rhapsodic fashion. They count graphically and visually, putting successive fingers up to their lips as each animal's name is called. There is a certain way of stressing the syllables that appears in no other context." As the recitation proceeds, it takes on a "singsong" quality. The eyes nearly "glaze over" as the first syllable goes down in tone and the "second, the pluralization, goes up high and then comes down again, trailing off from near-singing into silence. People love to do it, and they count off the animals at every opportunity. The effect it conveys is of a dream landscape dotted with an impossible plenty of kudus, buffaloes, eland, giraffes."[24]

In fact, San myth is polyphonic, consisting of linguistic variations that correspond to different mythic realms: the one of the Trickster—living in his encampment in the West and coming to the San in the company of the Gang-wasi; the other of the Creator—living in his encampment in the East and surrounded by all the large game animals. Lorna Marshall suggests that the San "tell tales" of Gangwa Matse's "doings without restraint." They "say his name aloud," and "howl and roll on the ground with laughter at his humiliations." But "when they speak of the great one of the east," Gangwanana, "they whisper and avoid his name." And Richard Katz observes that when the San speak of the gods, they "speak in a quiet tone, implying a respect for the gods' power." Yet, when they speak to the Trickster and the Spirits of the West (who, Biesele reports, themselves speak in a quavering tone along with a lisp), they "yell out insulting and profane phrases."[25] Biesele points out that the great distinction in the San approach to these two gods has led some analysts to view them as representing two different religious systems: one indigenous to the San; the other borrowed from neighboring Bantu traditions. But, Biesele suspects, rather than arising from two distinct traditions, the two deities represent different manifestations of a single deity—and a number of San report that the Trickster eventually left the earth and *became* the Creator. Others conversely report that, because the Trickster is named for the Creator, the two gods maintain what the San call a Kuna (Elder Namesake)/Kuma (Younger Namesake) relationship with one another and this is the reason that they enjoy a joking relationship between themselves.

Biesele suggests that the lineaments of everyday San language inevitably find their way into San storytelling. Perhaps, then, the relationship between the Creator and the Trickster is best worked out on the basis of the differential language usage employed in describing and talking to them. It seems, in fact, that the balance which defines San society on the basis of respect and joking relations—and the lineaments of everyday San speech which adheres to that balance—extends to spiritual matters as well. Relations between the San and the Creator, Gangwanana, are—like those between individuals who maintain a respect relationship with one another—freighted with respect and San linguistic usage—for instance, the use of a reverent tone and the practice of name avoidance through the deployment of respect terms—reflects that. Likewise, relations between the San and the Trickster are easy and familiar and San linguistic usage—for instance, sexual joking and the unfettered use of the god's name—reflects that as well.[26] Thus the delicate balance that maintains the integrity of San society, keeping a safe social distance in potentially disruptive relationships but solidifying those relationships where cooperation is particularly beneficial, is reflected and sanctified in myth. We will revisit this introjection of everyday speech patterns into myth, as well as the social significance of such an introjection, when we later turn to an explication of the rhetorical function of myth.

Yet another intriguing feature of the Beautiful Python Girl story involves a folkloric motif which we encountered in the *Epic of Gilgamesh*: the Earth-Diver and/or Post-Diluvian Bird motif in which an animal dives to the bottom of the sea in search of earth or a bird is sent out from a boat in search of dry land. Whereas in the San Creation, Gemsbok, Kudu, Ostrich, and Giraffe each dip one of their hind legs deep into the spring to bring forth Beautiful Python Girl and her newly born daughter, Guinea Fowl, in *Gilgamesh* we find Utnapish-tim releasing the Dove, the Swallow, and the Raven in order to seek out dry, habitable land. We will shortly encounter the Iroquois Creation in which Pick-erel, Comerant, and Muskrat successively dive to the bottom of the sea for a bit of mud with which to create our world, Turtle Island, on the back of the Sea Turtle but other versions of the motif abound: In Siberia, Old Man and Old Woman, alone on a hill in the midst of the primal sea, send out Iron Loon, Horned Grebe, and Red Throat Loon to collect mud from the bottom of the sea with which to create the world on the sea's surface. Once earth is created, they send out White Raven to ascertain if it is yet habitable. Two times, White Raven returns unsuccessfully, but on its third trip he pecks at a dead body float-ing upon the waters and turns black as a result. Old Man thereupon curses Black Raven to the life of a carrion eater. Among the Ojibwa, the fate of the Old World raven is transferred to the New World crow. In this version of the story, Nenebuc, the Ojibwa Trickster God, kills Lynx who, dying, inundates the world with a flood. Nenebuc, seeing that "the end of the world" is upon him, builds a raft and invites all the animals who swim toward him aboard. When the flood subsides, Nenebuc first sends Beaver and next Muskrat to the bottom of the sea for dirt—which Muskrat succeeds in obtaining. Like Old Man before him, Nenebuc places the dirt on the sea and, thereafter, sends out White Crow who, feeding on some dead fish, turns black. He then sends out Gull who eats only a mouthful of dead fish. The black tips of his wing are indica-tive of his ancient fault. Finally, Owl goes out and, seeing that the earth is ready, doesn't return to the raft. "Then Nenebuc let all the animals go from the raft," and departed for the west. He "is there yet, lying on his back, singing and ham-mering at his wigwam poles, in place of drumming, all the time. He will stay there until he gets up again three years before the end of the world, when he will travel all over the world to see the animals and the Ojibwa again. He will not die until the end of the world." Fascinatingly, in Slavic flood myths God sends the Devil to the bottom of the sea in search of earth. Succeeding, the Devil collects a bit of mud in his mouth—rather than using the more obvious manner (for an anthropomorphic entity) of catching up a bit of earth in his hands. He thus aptly reveals his ancient avian origins: the fact that he is simultaneously an Earth-Diver and Post-Diluvian Bird.[27]

Elephant and the Branding of Animals

Notable, in this Earth-Diver motif, is the fact that creation is often precedential to destruction and such is certainly the case with Beautiful Python Girl. Biesele reports that in one version of the tale, an intriguing conclusion is offered by the storyteller. When Beautiful Python Girl is brought back to the encampment, her father, Elephant, the encampment headman, becomes grave, asking what Jackal has done to his "beautiful daughter" who "no longer sparkles as before." Then, Elephant, "got all his medicines" and washed his daughter. And he "blew in her eyes and blew in her ears to erase the awful memories of the evil that she suffered at the hands of Jackal in the cold darkness of the well." Then, calling "everyone together," he made a pronouncement. Since Kori Bustard had failed to protect his wife, he would from that time forward "just be a bird who flies around and eats gum off the bark of trees." Then, turning to his daughter, he said, "And you, my daughter Python, who used to be so beautiful, you will just be a snake and lie around coiled in the shadows. And I too, will just be an elephant tearing up trees looking for food to eat. Let this camp be split up forever. Let us all live separately. We are no longer related." Thus, it was that the encampment "split up" and its members all "went their separate ways and became the animals they are today."

In apocalyptic terms, the golden age—when humans and animals were not so distinct from one another but rather lived together in a single encampment with Elephant as their headman, speaking a single language and cooperating for one another's benefit—was violently upended. And though trouble had come into the world, humans, now going it alone, gained that which they needed in order to survive: the game animals with their medicinal powers. When the moment of the dispersal arrived, Kori Bustard used "his strong wings to fan the fire of creation," proclaiming that from "today people will no longer be people but will have markings and be animals." Thereupon, the Old People—activating their potent medicine (*num*)—began to "write the name of all the animals on their hide," branding them by giving them their distinctive markings. They gave Zebra his stripes, Giraffe his spots; they branded Kudu, Wildebeest, Springbok, Gemsbok, Duiker, Kori Bustard, and Python. But when Hyena came to receive his markings, they mercilessly burned his anus and chased him away. Thus ended "the magical time when animal and human identities were merged."

Biesele views the myth of Beautiful Python Girl and that of the Branding of Animals as female- and male-centered creation stories. If the female centered creation, in which Gemsbok, Kudu, Ostrich, and Giraffe attempt to extricate Beautiful Python Girl from the "Spring of Creation," inevitably calls to mind the Earth-Diver motif, the male-centered creation, in which the "Fire of Creation" is fanned in order to brand the animals, brings to mind another common folkloric motif, the Differentiation of Animals. In the Iroquois Creation, for instance, we will witness the miraculous appearance of an oil pit into which animals will swim in order to get their fat and become thereby distinct from one another. But, beyond the correspondence of San folkloric themes with those of other societies, these two San tales—the first centering on the Spring of Creation, the second on the Fire of Creation—seem to refer obliquely to San initiation rituals. In the Spring of Creation, jackal seems to be unsuccessfully undergoing a girl's first menstrual (menarcheal) seclusion. In the Fire of Creation, hyena seems to be unsuccessfully undergoing a boy's first-kill initiation.

In a number of versions of the first story, Jackal's grandmother asks if Jackal, taken to be in her menarcheal seclusion, is in need of a pubic apron. The seclusion in a hut, the lack of speaking, the anointing with fat, and the provision of a pubic apron are all indicative of a girl's first menstruation rite. Beautiful Python Girl, on the other hand, successfully makes the transition from a girl to a woman: the animals encircling the spring is evocative of the San women dancing the Eland Dance around the menarcheal seclusion hut; the heroine's seclusion culminates in the birth of a child; and Beautiful Python Girl, like her sister, is anointed with fat—though she does not indecorously attempt to lick it up. In analogous tales, the heroine is "washed, rubbed with ochre, dressed freshly, hung with ornaments, and placed upon a skin mat as would be a girl freshly emerged from her first menstrual seclusion." Further she is escorted back to the encampment in honor, with mats placed all along the route and the animals rejoicing at her triumphal return. And, as some versions of the Branding of Animals make clear, Hyena is punished for not providing an appropriate game animal to share with the encampment in the context of a boy's first-kill rite. In bringing in a steenbok, a smaller animal which contains no *nao*, the magical essence present in large game animals such as the "giraffe, gemsbok, kudu, hartebeest, and wildebeest," he has failed the first-kill ceremony that San boys undergo in preparation for manhood. In this initiation, males from the age of 15 to 20 set up their own hunting camp, make their first kill, and undergo ritual scarification: all in preparation for the taking of wives.

Hyena, failing to achieve a proper first kill, cannot receive his markings. The other animals, conversely, are able to make their first kill and receive their markings which, in the San language, are described with the same words used to describe the scars a boy receives when he successfully kills his first animal. Inasmuch as male scarification is linguistically equivalent to animal branding upon creation, scarification seems to be a remembrance of the ancient kinship between animals and people, a kinship that was broken only when animals first received their marks.

There is still more: Once married, a San man must, living in the encampment of his new wife's family, provide his in-laws bride-service through provisioning them with meat: often "long enough for the boy's youth to have turned to manhood." Under these circumstances, resentment can occur along predictable fault lines in San society: between a man and his in-laws and, as a result, between a husband and his wife. In some stories, Beautiful Python Girl's mother, upon seeing some ripening bulbs—which look a bit like testicles—on the ground where her son-in-law had been hunting, vulgarly jokes that her son-in-law has 'lost his balls.' Clearly this is inappropriate language for a mother-in-law who should be following the strict protocols of an avoidance relationship with her son-in-law. Guinea Fowl reports her grandmother's outrageous behavior to her father who, in response, kills his mother-in-law. That night, Beautiful Python Girl—to avenge the death of her mother—kills her husband as he sleeps. She soon, thereafter, has to flee his brothers' vengeance. As they pursue her with their bows drawn, Guinea Fowl warns Beautiful Python Girl each time the brothers get close. The heroine then throws magical objects in their pathway: first, morningstar thorns so that her pursuers become hopelessly entangled in a magical briar patch; then, devil's claw thorns with the same effect; finally, she sends a cloud against them which rains so mightily that it breaks "their bows and arrows and the stings of their loincloths" so that they helplessly stand there "wearing only their penises." Having given up their pursuit and retreated to their encampment, they are—in an episode which cannot help but bring to mind that of Jericho—destroyed when the heroine takes out her magical gemsbok horn and, blowing upon it, kills her dead husband's family and demolishes their encampment.[28]

In much the same manner, Merrywise escaped a witch in an Appalachian folktale, Epomata eluded a wicked sorceress in a Sicilian fairy tale, and Beatrice escaped the Devil in an African American folktale. As the witch almost overtook Merrywise and his two brothers, Merrywise had Tom throw out a stone which turned into an insurmountable wall; next, his brother Bill threw down an egg which was transformed into a great lake. And then Merrywise himself threw out his magical acorn which sprang into a fully grown oak tree up which the boys escaped.[29] And Epomata, fleeing her mother with Federico (whose father, not unlike the youthful Buddha's father, sequestered his son in a tower to prevent an intolerable fate), instructed her lover to keep a lookout inasmuch as she had to manage their horse. And, when Federico warned that the sorceress was gaining on them, Epomata turned herself into a garden and Federico into its gardener. Then, in danger of being overtaken once more, she transformed herself into a church and Federico into its sacristan. And when the sorceress was about to overtake them a third time, Epomata transformed herself into a pond and Federico into an eel who kept slipping through the sorceress's wicked fingers.[30] Finally, Beatrice, the devil's daughter, escaped her father's wrath in the tale Zora Neale Hurston collected in her own hometown of Eatonville, Florida. As Beatrice fled in her father's buckboard, she had Jack keep watch for the devil who pursued them. With three magical ruses—the first two kicking up sand to slow down the devil and the third transforming herself and her father's horses into grazing goats (Jack, too strong for transformation, hiding in a hollow log)—they eluded their nemesis.[31]

Why the persistence of such themes as animals reaching, or diving, through water to obtain what lies at its bottom—whether a recently birthed python or a bit of earth? Why the persistence of the frantic flight with a companion warning each time the enemy approaches and magical items thrown behind the fugitives to become such significant obstacles? Is it a matter of diffusion—the passing of a folkloric motif from one society to another? And, if so, what society is the source of the motif? Or is it a matter of psychology—the fact that the motif, like some recurrent feature of our dream life, satisfies some longing within our psyche? Perhaps it is some admixture of both. But with an inability to answer such questions adequately, I will simply point out that at the end of one version of the San story of Beautiful Python Girl's flight, the heroine miraculously transforms herself into the first game animal: steenbok (curiously, the same game animal for which Hyena was so cruelly humiliated). Thus, that particular iteration of the magical flight tale becomes an origin story for the San hunting ecology.[32]

San Ritual: The Medicine Dance

The San, as we have seen, depend on the principle of sharing in order to manage their resources in a sometimes undependable environment. But sharing without rancor is not always easy. People, after all, are quite often motivated by self-interest and the San share in our common human failing. So how do the San accomplish the difficult task at hand? Religion seems to come to their aid, bolstering the sharing ethos. The major San ritual activity is the medicine dance—not undertaken in a scheduled manner but rather when a member of the encampment falls ill or the encampment as a whole is suffering from some general, and perhaps even social, malaise. When a dance is held, the women—in a circle about a fire—sing, while the men—in a circle about the women—dance. And in typical San fashion (the San always giving credit to the next person), the men claim that the women's singing is going to accomplish the good that they are looking forward to. It is their singing, after all, that activates the *num* (medicine) which Gangwanana placed in everyone's belly upon creation. As the men—and particularly those men who are reputed to be *num kausi*, "medicine holders," or shamans—continue to dance, the *num* heats up and begins to boil, traveling up their spinal column and exploding in their head, upon which they enter *kia*, or trance, state.

Upon entering *kia*, the world is spinning and the people around the fire start to disappear or begin to appear as small and immaterial birds, their singing little more than a thin and muddled chirping. And from their midst appear the Gangwasi, the ghosts of the recently departed San. They appear like smoke, perhaps floating, maybe on one leg only. And, indeed, it is one of them, perhaps envious of the living, or perhaps again missing a loved one, who has sent the sickness (*twe*) against the patient. A *num kausi* may go into shamanic battle with one of these ghosts, perhaps attempting to chase it away, or shooting spiritual arrows—the immaterial alter ego of the poisoned arrows that the San use in the hunt—against the ghost. He may as well begin to suck on the patient's body and perhaps even produce the outward manifestation of the sickness that the ghost has set upon the patient: a sliver, a broken arrowhead. He, and others among the *num kausi* who have entered *kia*, will then begin to massage the body of the patient, using their own sweat as a medicinal potion. Tellingly, the outward manifestation of *num* is the hot, wet perspiration which the men use to massage the body of the afflicted.[33]

As Richard Katz points out, "sweat (*cho*) is the most important phenomenon in healing." The San "equate sweat with the steam rising from boiling water" and believe *num* is "exposed on the surface of the healer's body in the form of sweat," especially the sweat which breaks out on the healer's forehead, the small of his back, his chest and armpits. The medicinal qualities of this sweat are best summed up in the words of one healer, who mumbles as he is about to enter *kia*, "My sweats are hot, my sweats are wet."[34] This hot, wet "sweat is rubbed onto the body of the person being healed, focused on the area of illness when it is specified," as if those with a surfeit of *num* share their excess with those who have a deficit. In fact, everyone has num. It resides in each person's belly where Gangwanana himself placed it. It is cold and dry when dormant.

But when *num* boils, "it scatters throughout the dance like the sparks that shower from a roughly stirred fire."[35] And when one's *num* is boiling, he can play with the fire around which he dances without being burned. Thus, treating a patient with *num*—which has been heated up to its boiling point—activates the dormant *num* within the patient, rendering that which was cold and dry to a substance that is now hot, wet, and active. It seems, then, that just as the San share their meat when they have been successful in the hunt, equalizing that essential physical resource, they too share their *num*—restoring their fellow encampment member's cold, dry deficit with their own hot, wet surfeit and bringing him or her, thereby, back into equilibrium: neither too hot nor too cold but rather—as the San themselves describe it—cool and restored. In essence, religious behavior becomes an idiom—or metaphor—for the essential San sharing ethos. And, interestingly, the San do not boast about healing abilities any more than they do about hunting prowess. Rather, they say that healing is simply "something we do to help others."[36]

But there is something more. The restorative properties of *num* depend not only on the particular qualities of the San social environment (that is, the willingness of fellow encampment members to share their healthful well-being) but also upon the specific properties of the physical environment. For instance, the San depend upon the help of the animals that populate the Kalihari (they whom the San consider to be their ancient relatives) not only for their nutritional needs but also for the medicinal songs and dances with which they activate, or heat up, their latent *num*. The songs and dances are named for and provided by the animals (and perhaps especially by a special class of medicinally potent animals): gemsbok, eland, and giraffe. Biesele reports on the origin of the Giraffe Dance: "One story goes that a woman named Beh was alone one day in the bush. She saw a herd of giraffes running before an approaching thunderstorm. The rolling beat of their hooves grew louder and mingled in her head with the sound of the sudden rain." It was then that "a song she had never heard before came to her, and she began to sing." Gangwanana "told her it was a medicine song." Beh returned home and "taught the song to her husband," whereupon the two "sang it and danced together. It was indeed a song for trancing, a medicine song."

In fact, while *num* is ever-present, having been placed in the Sans' bellies by Gangwanana, it is most effectively activated with the gift of the ancestral animals: the medicine songs and dances. Perhaps this is why Gangwanana is said to live in the sky as a kind of "Lord of the Animals," surrounded by "leopards, zebras, locusts, lions, jackals, dogs, pythons, mambas, eland, giraffes, gemsbok, and kudus." And perhaps this is why spirit-animals figure so prominently in San myth. Biesele reports that two aspects "of the trance dance, the circular dance path and the central fire," hearken back to "two fundamental structures" regularly seen in San mythology. The "diverse animals clustered about the central spring of creation," into which Beautiful Python Girl fell, and the "central fire of creation," with which the animals were branded before their dispersal, "appear to be symbolically linked to the form of the all-important curing dance." In other words, in the resuscitation of Beautiful Python Girl and the branding of animals, we are witnessing the primal medicine dance. Thus myth, which in the San universe centers on the ancient doings of the spirit-animals, undergirds ritual—as performed in the omnipresent medicine dance—which, in its turn, serves to undergird the San economic ideal of reciprocity through the sharing out of medicine.

Further, beyond the spirit-animals, there is a suggestion that the Kalihari itself is inscribed in the medicine dance. When the rains and warm weather of summer come to the Kalihari, it is a benevolent season of plenty. And this season extends well into the autumn when the weather begins to cool and the rains have ceased but there is still a surfeit of good summer foods. During this period, it is neither too hot and dry nor too cold and dry. And the San have plenty of food available relatively close at hand. But as the rains end and temperatures begin to drop with the approach of winter, the encampment—having to be well stocked with wood to keep the fire going throughout the night and having, as well, to be kept close to a permanent waterhole for a greater length of time—begins to run short of the preferred food and greater distances have to be traversed in order to obtain it. These conditions become exacerbated with the arrival of spring, but previous to the coming of the spring rains, when the Kalihari becomes scorched and dry. In Biesele's words, "the wet season is life, the dry one death and deprivation."[37]

Little wonder then that the premier San medicine (*num*), or at least its outward manifestation (*cho*, sweat), is perceived as hot and wet and is sometimes described as a ripe pod ready to burst: in one instance a San healer saying that his fellow healer "comes and bursts *num* open so that we both can have some."[38] In this, *num* partakes of the nature of a benevolent Kalihari, the Kalihari when it is at its most beneficent: when "atmospheric conditions, men's hunting, women's childbirth, and the great meat animals," all collude to create for the San a season of plenty or, as Biesele so eloquently describes it, "a dream landscape dotted with an impossible plenty of kudus, buffaloes, eland, giraffes."[39] In fact, the San are explicit in this: the mysterious *nao* complex, that same complex which inscribes animals with their magical essence, suggests that the Kalihari's climactic conditions have a controlling influence on hunting success, childbirth, and the activation of *num*. But activating *num*, hunting, and giving birth, likewise, have a controlling influence on the Kalihari's weather. This mutual influence may give rise to a bad *nao*—in which the Kalihari is cold and dry, hunting is difficult, childbirth is troubled, and medicine suffers a deficit— or it may give rise to a good *nao* in which the Kalihari is warm and well-watered, hunting is successful, parturition is assured, and medicine "scatters throughout the dance like the sparks that shower from a roughly stirred fire."[40] Perhaps it is in the mysterious workings of the *nao* complex that we may understand why Beautiful Python Girl, liberated by the animals' primal medicine dance, is not pulled singly from the spring into which she has fallen. Rather, in the deep recesses of this permanent water source, she has miraculously given birth. Fertility acts very much as the token—the symbolic signifier—of the Kalihari in its benevolent season of fruitful parturition.

3. The Social Environment and Sociological Metaphors

Family, Community, Nation

But it is not simply our ecological adaptations that provide us the metaphors with which we construct our mythologies. It is likewise our sociological adaptations. In fact, society—the network of social relations that define a group—is inextricably linked with ecology because it is society's function to facilitate the collection, processing, and equitable distribution of resources as well as to minimize the disruptions that self-interest might bring to an equitable distribution. Still, there is more to society than mere ecology. Understanding a social network—its extent, its various functions, the rules that sustain it, its uncanny ability to engender affiliation and minimize internal conflict—allows us to understand the manner in which cultural transmission and group identity, both functions of the social network, are facilitated. Further, understanding the real, flesh-and-blood, social relations that define a society—say, that between a San father and his children—allows us to understand the sociological metaphors that are embedded in and sanctified by our mythologies: say, that which views Gangwanana as the Father and the San as his Children. Central to mythology's sociological metaphors are the intersecting arenas of family, community, and nation.

The family serves as a means of maintaining the basic integers of the division of labor that characterize a society in a small, manageable unit: the household. That is to say, it serves as a kind of collective of related people by which the tasks that it takes to support a subgroup of society (given the means by which the society exploits its environment) are accomplished. Families are globally constructed on the basis of a number of kinship relations including both consaguineal (blood) and affinal (marital) relations. Among consaguineal kin, at least a mother, a father, and their children are almost always present. But this nuclear family, while an extremely common organizational principle for the household, is by no means universal. Households may include siblings of either the wife or husband (an expanded family) or grandparents and grandchildren (an extended family). Affinal kin (kin defined by marriage) are created according a number of patterns. Marriage may be based in monogamy, serial monogamy, or polygamy. Polygamy may entail polygyny, where one husband may have two or more wives, or polyandry, where one wife may have two or more husbands. Polyandry, a rare marital model found especially in the Himalayas, will figure prominently in our discussion of the Indian epic, the *Mahabharata*, later in this study. Some societies prefer marriages to be arranged. Other societies allow what in India are sometimes called "love marriages" solely involving the choice of the husband and wife to be. And, interestingly, same-sex marriage has not been an uncommon feature of human marital designs. Not only have we historically had female husbands in a number of West African societies—Dahomean, for instance—where a woman might take a wife to do her household tasks so that she might concentrate on economic activities— maintaining her own compound, farm, and palm-groves—but we also have male wives among the Lakota and other Plains nations. For instance, a vision-quest or dream might lead a Lakota man to live as a woman (or, more properly, *winkte*) and marry a man, and—among these—a few might even maintain warrior status. Whereas the Dahomean female-husbands did not necessarily have sexual relations with their female wives, Lakota male wives did apparently have sex with their male husbands, likely taking the passive role.[1]

The rules of kinship not only define the nature of the family. They also serve to align a number of families into a community. For instance, the San kinship system, including its delineation of respect and joking relations, creates of the encampment a kind of extended family and serves as well to strengthen relationships among encampments. Moreover, the custom of namesakes can extend those kinship relations to individuals who share no true consaguineal or affinal relationships, creating a second—fictive—kinship system. Richard Lee experienced the San fictive kinship tradition firsthand when he was given a San name by a woman who, feeling a bit sorry for him inasmuch as he had no relatives about, named him Tontah after her dead uncle. Since she had named him, she instructed him that he should call her mother. Soon thereafter other people instructed him as to the nature of the relationship that Lee's new name, and new mother, created between them. Over time, Lee found that he had relatives scattered throughout the Kalihari.[2] Kinship traditions, then, can easily serve as the basis for alliances among communities: whether independent foraging encampments or interdependent agricultural villages.

Another example of a fictive kinship network is represented by the concept of *comparatico*, or co-parenthood, in Sicily. When a man or woman stands up as godfather (*patrino*) or godmother (*madrina*) to a child at baptism, he or she becomes co-father (*compare*; Sicilian *cumpari*) or co-mother (*comare*; Sicilian, *cummari*) to that child's parents. In actuality, this long string of *cumpari* and *cummari* relationships extends well beyond the limited set of individuals who stand up as godfather or godmother to a child to include any individual of the adult population on whom one can depend. As a Sicilian American woman from Brooklyn put it: "Oh, everybody was *cummari!*" The terms *cumpari* and *cummari* can draw just about anyone—including relatives, friends, and neighbors—into the system of fictive kinship and the system of mutual obligation (a kind of impromptu mutual aid society) that kinship (actual or fictive) implies. Shepherds will watch out for one another's sheep. Farmers, whether sharecroppers or small landholders, will cooperate in the harvest or threshing. The *cumpari* who is also the *padrone*, or boss, can be expected to select his godson for day labor in either the urban or rural context. While the explicit Sicilian kinship system functions like the typical American—or what anthropologists call Inuit—kinship system, privileging the nuclear family through having separate terms for mother, father, sister, and brother, but lumping aunts (whether mother's sister or father's sister), uncles (whether mother's brother or father's brother), and cousins (whether on the mother's or father's side) each under a single term, *comparatico* functions more like the classic Hawaiian kinship system in which everyone in the parental generation is called by the same terms used to refer to mother and father and indeed take on many of the parental functions to all children in the group. It essentially says that one has kin everywhere and anywhere upon whom he or she can count in times of extremity.

The ties forged by kinship are often expanded by such institutions as clans, lineages, or sodalities. These institutions are likely the mechanisms by which the independent encampments of foragers developed into the alliances characteristic of agricultural villages. Clans group together families by stipulating a common descent. That is to say, it is believed that clan members are related through some distant ancestor. For instance, the Seneca, one of the five nations of the Iroquoian Confederacy, maintain eight clans: the Bear, Wolf, Beaver, Turtle, Deer, Hawk, Heron, and Snipe. Every member of the Seneca nation belongs to one of these eight clans—the membership in which is inherited from one's mother. Inasmuch as the Seneca maintain a rule of clan exogamy (i.e., a person must marry outside his or her own clan), one's father, though a member of the communal Seneca household (i.e., the bark longhouse), is not a member of his wife's and children's clan but maintains throughout his life membership in his mother's clan. Lineages group together families by demonstrating common descent. Ancient Hebraic society, for example, was comprised of lineages reckoned through the male line and the names of each lineage's generations were scrupulously maintained. *The Gospel According to Matthew* begins by recounting such a lineage in a series of famous begats: "The book of the generation of Jesus Christ, the son of David, the son of Abraham. Abraham begat Isaac; and Isaac begat Jacob; and Jacob begat Judas and his brethren." The passage continues to catch up among a number of progenitors the kings, David and Solomon, before culminating with "Joseph the husband of Mary, of whom was born Jesus, who is called Christ. So all the generations," the Gospel recounts, "from Abraham to David are fourteen generations; and from David until the carrying away into Babylon are fourteen generations; and from the carrying away into Babylon unto Christ are fourteen generations."[3]

Sodalities, rather than postulating ancestral ties, are associations requiring their members to come to one another's aid. They often include, among their various organizational devises, age sets and age grades. Age sets, comprised of individuals who are born during a determined period (perhaps a single year or perhaps again a period lasting 4 or 5 years), share a number of predetermined activities with one another. Age grades move an age set through various defined ranks (for instance, juvenile, warrior, chief, elder) within a society. Not surprisingly, age sets and grades generally intersect one another so that the set is initiated as a group when it passes from one grade to another. American society maintains both age sets and grades in its educational system: all boys and girls born in a single year go through each successive grade together. Sodalities famously include the military associations which characterized Native American bison hunters of the Great Plains. The Lakota, for instance, maintained a political structure centered on sodalities. At its apex was the Chief's Society, instituted by its Guardian Spirit, the Buffalo, and comprised of the older men—or Big Bellies—who advised the chief. Allied with the Chief's Society were the somewhat younger men of the Mandan Society, instituted by the Owl and comprised of all those entitled to wear the Owl Feather Headdress and tasked with conserving the fire whenever the group moved. Alongside these two paramount sodalities existed four military sodalities, responsible for defense, policing duties, and scouting: the Stout Hearts, instituted by Prairie Chicken; the Fox, who had both the Fox and his companion, the Jack Rabbit, as its Guardian Spirits, the Keepers of the Crow, who had the Skunk as its Guardian Spirit; and the Badger, instituted by its Guardian Spirit, Badger himself.[4] Such a structure, tasked as it was with both the governance and defense of Lakota society, brings us directly to another essential aspect of society: the nation.

The nation encompasses an entire society with a single governing structure: that is, a polity. Though in the past, the term tribe was often applied to the concept of the nation, that term has taken on unhelpful connotations over time and it doesn't very well signify the fact that though these societies may not exist as independent states (such as Haiti) or semiautonomous regions (such as Sicily), they are—even if incorporated by a single state (such as Nigeria)—still nations. Thus, for example, the Yoruba nation exists (among many others) within the borders of the modern state of Nigeria and Yoruba people, whom I have queried, generally view themselves as both Yoruba and Nigerian. Various types of nations have been isolated by anthropologists: The band is a polity characteristic of foragers. It does not extend beyond the local encampment and has headmen, characterized by prestige (influence based in respect) but not privilege (special rights incumbent upon their office) or power (ability to coerce others). The alliance is a coalition of agricultural villages overseen by chiefs with both prestige and privilege but still no power. The state is a stratified polity with a hierarchy of settlements (cities, villages, and hamlets) overseen by a king with prestige, privilege, and power. Today, the modern (or constitutional) state—which differs from the traditional state mainly in the fact that its leader (often an elected president or prime minister) functions more or less as a constitutionally constrained king—predominates the world's nations.

The Emergence of Class

One of the hallmarks of society, and one that is inextricably intertwined with the nation, is the stratification system which may be heavily subdued and circumscribed—as it is with the San—or nearly flagrant in its inequitable distribution of authority and resources. Stratification levels within a society are strongly correlated to ecologies. Foraging societies are largely egalitarian. That is to say, there is very little authority within foraging groups. Adult men may have some limited authority over adult women and adults may have some limited authority over younger people, but in most cases these differential levels of authority are minimized. Egalitarianism makes sense in the foraging context where the group's well-being and perhaps even survival depends upon reciprocity. Egalitarianism seems to avoid any rational means of undermining sharing inasmuch as its maintenance offers no justification (i.e., differential status) for the inequitable distribution of resources that, more often than not, characterize mercantile societies. When we move toward agriculture, there is often a group of individuals, chiefs, in charge of collecting and redistributing excess agricultural produce. The redistribution may be more or less equitable or inequitable but nonetheless there are individuals in charge. The term used to describe this sort of stratification is rank. Here, the society is divided into chiefs (and chiefly families) and commoners. The commoners, not surprisingly, comprise the great mass of society. Mercantile societies, with their complex division of labor and numerous occupations (each of which is always subject to more or less prestige) are characterized by class: marked distinctions between occupational categories often correlated with a markedly inequitable distribution of resources. Not surprisingly, class is freighted with attendant problems. Beyond access to resources, one's position in society offers him or her access to power: the ability to control others. As Ward Goodenough notes, "the inequalities of real power tend to find expression in social rules, whose shape is inevitably influenced more heavily by the interests of those who enjoy the greater real power. It follows that in some societies some categories of person enjoy far fewer rights and privileges than other categories." Not surprisingly, "persons who are most deprived by the rules have less incentive to honor them," and have, at times, been prevailed upon to overturn them.[5]

Subsistence Pattern	Residence Pattern	Economic Mode	Political Leadership	Political Level	Authority Order	Social Order
Foraging	Encampment	Reciprocity	Band	Headman	Prestige	Egalitarian
Agriculture	Village	Redistribution	Alliance	Chief	Privilege	Rank
Mercantilism	City	Exchange	State	King	Power	Class

Table One: Ecology and Society[6]

Many anthropologists speak of closed class systems, where individuals can never move outside their class, as caste systems. But class versus caste may not be such a useful distinction. Class is seen in more industrialized states while caste is more characteristic of pre-industrial states. In essence the lack of movement between classes in preindustrial mercantile states is descriptive rather than proscriptive (though, certainly, religious dictum can render such movement difficult to imagine). In general, it's not that one cannot move. Rather, one has a body of knowledge and tools pertinent to the class into which he or she is born. Thus, it is not unexpected that he or she participates in the same class (i.e., follows the same occupation) of his or her parents. Such is the case for Indian society which—particularly in agricultural villages—centers on the intersecting concepts of household, village, and caste.

Governing the formation of the family is the rule of caste endogamy—marrying within one's caste—but village exogamy: marrying outside one's natal village. As a result of these rules, when a new family is formed, both the bride and the groom have grown up with the technology that is pertinent to their caste occupation, *jāti*, but the bride must go to live with her groom's family, fellow villagers, and (not unusually in the early years of marriage) her groom's father's household. Thus, the Indian family exists as an extended patriarchal structure in which the wife (living as she does with her husband's people) some-times enjoys a small share of authority: until, at least, she has her own grown sons to represent her interests. At the same time, the Indian family exists as a repository of knowledge and tools with which to continue a traditional occu-pation, a number of which are necessary to the functioning of the typical village. And though cooperative with one another, these *jātis* are organized hierarchi-cally into a number of castes (*varnas*) according to their relative value. The sanctity of this system is affirmed by none other than Krishna: the human avatar (or incarnation) of Vishnu (the god of preservation). When the Great War that is at the center of India's sweeping epic, the *Mahabharata* finally arrives, Arjuna, the greatest archer known to mankind, balks at going to war and killing family members and onetime friends. But Krishna, who is acting as Arjuna's charioteer, offers a discourse on the caste system. After enumerating its parts—Brahmas (priests), Kshatriya (royal warriors), Vaisyas (honored laborers such as farmers and merchants), and Shudras (lower order laborers) but notably making no mention of Dalits (outcastes or untouchables to whom were relegated unclean occupations such as working leather and cleaning latrines)—Krishna tells Arjuna that death has no reality to the man who safeguards Dharma (order or the law) by accomplishing the duty of his caste without desire: without a wish to gain profit, for instance, or win a war. With this teaching in hand, Arjuna is able to resume his military duties without hesitation but not before Krishna reveals to his mortal friend his divine form:

> Having said this, O monarch, Krishna, the mighty Lord of mystic power, then revealed to Arjuna his Supreme sovereign form, with many mouths and eyes, many wondrous aspects, many celestial ornaments, many celestial weapons uplifted, wearing celestial garlands and robes, and with unguents of celestial fragrance, full of every wonder, resplendent, infinite, with faces turned on all sides. If the splendor of a thousand suns were to burst forth at once in the sky, then that would be like the splendor of that Mighty One. Arjuna then beheld there in the body of that God of gods the entire universe divided and sub-divided into many parts, all collected together. Then Arjuna, filled with amazement, and with hair stand-ing on end, bowing with his head, with joined hands addressed the God.[7]

It is as if, after speaking forth the caste system, and embedding it in the concept of Dharma, or sacred duty, Krishna's act of revealing himself in his eternal and infinite form creates of the caste system an unassailable essence of the cosmos: and one unlikely to be thwarted without consequence.

Though the caste system was abolished by the Indian constitution of 1950, Dalits—numbering perhaps 250 million people—suffer notorious abuse to this day. But it is not only India that retains vestiges of a caste system despite its illegality. And it is not only India which sanctified its caste structure myth-ically. Though institutional segregation—America's one-time infamous racial caste system—was outlawed by the Civil Rights Act of 1964, integration often had to be enforced: at times by the National Guard. And some of segregation's lingering after-effects seem not yet overcome. Part of the difficulty in combatting segregation, particularly in the American Southeast, was the fact that the "sanctity" of first slavery and later segregation had been preached from Southern pulpits even into the 20th century. Anyone who has read Frederick Douglass's *Narrative of an American Slave* has encountered the peculiar use of the mythic "Curse of Ham" that was made by white Southern churches to justify the enslavement of Africans and African Americans:

> And the sons of Noah, that went forth of the ark, were Shem, and Ham, and Japheth: and Ham is the father of Canaan. These are the three sons of Noah: and of them was the whole earth overspread. And Noah began to be an husbandman, and he planted a vineyard: And he drank of the wine, and was drunken; and he was uncovered within his tent. And Ham, the father of Canaan, saw the nakedness of his father, and told his two brethren without. And Shem and Japheth took a garment, and laid it upon both their shoulders, and went backward, and covered the nakedness of their father; and their faces were backward, and they saw not their father's nakedness. And Noah awoke from his wine, and knew what his younger son had done unto him. And he said, Cursed be Canaan; a servant of servants shall he be unto his brethren. And he said, Blessed be the Lord God of Shem; and Canaan shall be his servant. God shall enlarge Japheth, and he shall dwell in the tents of Shem; and Canaan shall be his servant.[8]

Despite the obvious reference to Canaan, the mythic patriarch of the traditional enemy of the Hebraic peoples, the Canaanites, white Southern churches continuously preached that Ham was the progenitor of Africans—going so far as claiming that Ham's skin was turned black by Noah's pronouncement.

A curiosity arises from the fact that, in a number of extra–Biblical versions of the Flood Myth, the Raven which is sent forth from the ark is, upon eating carrion, cursed by Noah and turned from white to black. We witnessed the same transformation visited upon Raven in the Siberian Flood Myth and Crow in the New World Ojibwa version. The non–Biblical transformation of Ham's skin from white to black is an ancient one and could, in fact, represent a transference of the Raven's metamorphosis to Ham.[9] But however it came to be, the racial overtones of such a transformation, once established, became particularly attractive to white Southern churches which continuously cited the re-scripted myth, not only through the slaveholding but also the Jim Crow era, in order to justify the continued abuse of African Americans. Illustrative of the power of this mythic misreading is the rupture that occurred between Southern and Northern congregations of a number of Christian denominations—Methodism, Presbyterianism, and, of course, Baptism—as the American Civil War approached. Douglass's *Narrative* came out in 1845, the year in which Abolitionists gained control of the Baptist National Convention and wrote into church by-laws that no slaveholder would be supported with missionary monies by the Baptist Church. As a result of that rule, the Southern Baptist Church—the largest Protestant denomination in the U.S. today—was born as a slaveholding religion. It proclaimed that Southern Baptist Church monies would indeed be provided for the missionary activities of slaveholders. The Southern Baptist Church did, though, apologize for its pro-slavery origins and support of seg- regationist policies in 1995: 150 years after its birth.

The fact that the "Curse of Ham" was used in such an infamous manner draws attention to the fact that where myths, which for most of human history have been transmitted orally, have become ossified by the written word and fundamentalist interpretations, they are no longer subject to the transforma- tions that keep myths relevant given changing sociological concerns. In such cases, the sermon—in which the written myth is kept alive through the mech- anism of a new sort of oral tradition—becomes the major source of the myth for most adherents to the faith. I have been told, when querying Evangelical Christians about the story of Cain's unacceptable sacrifice, that the reason Cain's offering was disdained by god was that Cain was lazy while Abel was a diligent worker. It almost goes without saying that no such implication exists in the Bible—any more than does an implication of Ham's skin turning black. It seems then that the alterations which occur in the translation of a written version of an ancient myth to a contemporary sermon must be steeped in current, rather than ancient, social relations in order to keep the myth socially relevant.

Gender and Sexuality

We earlier considered the inculcation of male and female gender identities in San rites of passage: the girl's menarcheal seclusion and the boy's first-kill ceremony. We will momentarily consider analogous gender identities incul- cated in remarkably similar rites among the foraging Euahlayi of Australia. And, as we proceed through this study, we will witness numerous attempts to incul- cate gender identity and establish the parameters of acceptable gender behavior in a wide array of rites of passage. But we will also witness—along with the emer- gence of hierarchy and its attendant ills—an almost unbroken diminution in the status of women as we move from foraging, through agricultural, to mercan- tile ecologies. Among the foraging San, the authority of an encampment's elder women is notable enough to allow some to be spoken of as headwomen, while among the foraging Euahlayi of Australia, elder women, though not as privileged as San women, do manifest a significant store of authority and respect. And, in fact, there is a Euahlayi word—*innerah*—for "a woman with a camp of her own."[10] Though the life of women may seem difficult among New Guinea's agricultural Dani, most of whom have lost a portion of some of their fingers in commemoration for a dead kinsman, among the agricultural Iroquois, women maintain so much authority within their communities that the Iroquois have at times been described not only as matrilineal (charting descent through the female line) and matrilocal (taking up residence with the family's mother's kin) but even matriarchal (maintaining political authority in the hands of women). Within the context of mercantile societies, we find that a woman in India (living in her husband's native village and perhaps even his parents' home) often has to depend on her grown sons in order to exert her own authority—even while India has experienced a female head of state in the person of Indira Gandhi. Conversely, in the United Sates, though we do find that a woman expects a significant level of authority in her own home, the idea of a woman in the presidency seems difficult for many to imagine and the thought of fixing pay disparities between men and women remains controversial.

Perhaps most emblematic of the diminution of women's authority is the attempt to control female sexuality, including the usurpation of reproductive control by men. This usurpation, having as much to do with men's concern for ensuring paternity in hyper-patriarchal societies as with issues of morality, include one of the more troubling cultural traditions with which anthropologists (who attempt to maintain a policy of cultural sensitivity) have had to contend: female circumcision or female genital mutilation (FGM). Invariably supported by indigenous religious traditions, FGM at times has led to the death of girls who have undergone clitoridectomy (removal of the clitoris) and perhaps even more radical surgeries. The tradition is particularly prevalent in the Nile River Valley, where both Muslim and Christian communities are involved in the practice, as well as West Africa and portions of the Arabian Peninsula. Yet another chilling example of the consequences of attempts to control women's reproductive health arises from the studies of Nancy Scheper-Hughes in the Northeastern Brazilian shantytown of Alto do Cruzeiro.

Here, Scheper-Hughes found that of 579 live births over a period of 25 years, 308 infants survived until five years of age. In seeking an explanation for such a high infant mortality rate, Scheper-Hughes found that in the impoverished environment of Alto do Cruzeiro women had to depend upon men for a livelihood and sex was the most likely means of keeping a man in the household. Birth control and abortion were not options in this fervently Catholic society, and the lack of employment often called men away from their homes. Perhaps remittances would be sent for a time to the mother of a man's child but, almost inevitably, the remittances would end, perhaps as the result of the man finding another woman in his new locale. If—under these circumstances—a child became listless and ill, the mother would interpret the symptoms as expressing the child's desire to die. Having other infants to care for, and lacking the most basic commodities, the mother would begin to ration both the household food and her own personal affection. In Marvin Harris' words, "If people are deprived of the means of preventing unwanted conceptions and births, this does not mean that they will support the unwanted child after it is born." Easing the pain of the "indirect infanticide" that plagued the shantytown was "the belief that after babies and infants die, they become angels. The little corpses are placed in cardboard coffins and escorted to shallow graves by a smiling and laughing throng of children." And, of course, "mothers do not weep," for the little ones who have, after all, joined the host of the other diminutive angels from Alto do Cruzeiro.[11]

That said, gender is not simply a matter of female and male roles as promulgated in rites of passage or gender disparity measured out in inequitable distributions of authority, resources, and reproductive control. It also impacts each society's ideals of sexuality and sexual identity. And, not surprisingly, myth plays an essential role in legitimizing or—as the case may be—delegitimizing certain gender identities and forms of sexuality. For example, the Nayar—members of a *jāti* (subcaste) in Kerala State, India—historically lived in matrilineal households comprised of related women, a brother or father of the women, and the women's children. There was no permanent husband present in the Nayar household. A group of perhaps four to eight Nayar households comprised a single, exogamous (out-marrying) lineage which maintained links "with two or three other lineages," a kind of ritual "neighborhood." Each lineage sponsored, "every few years," a

> grand ceremony at which all its girls who had not attained puberty, aged about seven to twelve, were on one day ritually married by men drawn from their linked lineages. The ritual bride-grooms were selected in advance on the advice of the village astrologer at a meeting of the neighborhood assembly. On the day fixed, they came in procession to the oldest ancestral house of the host lineage. There, after various ceremonies, each tied a gold ornament (talī) round the neck of his ritual bride. The girls had for three days previously been secluded in an inner room of the house and caused to observe taboos as if they had menstruated. After the talī-tying each couple was secluded in private for three days.

Kathleen Gough, who undertook the study of this Nayar group-marriage ritual, "was told that traditionally, if the girl was nearing puberty, sexual relations might take place," at that time. But, after that, "the ritual husbands left the house and had no further obligations to their brides." Rather, the bride was free to undertake sexual relations with any man of the neighborhood—or others who might be visiting the neighborhood—as long as he was not a member of her own lineage. Any resulting children belonged to their mother's lineage.[12]

Conversely, the Sambia, of New Guinea, do not believe that men produce their own semen. Thus, in order to eventually marry and impregnate a wife, prepubescent Sambia boys must collect semen through performing fellatio on postpubescent youths. The signal that they are about to embark on this process comes when "a piercing, melodious" cry arises from the forest. Then a small group of boys from allied hamlets, an age grade of seven- to ten-year-olds, are told that the voice is that of Aatmwogwambu: the female hamlet spirit. Her voice is created by a pair of bamboo flutes. Thereupon, the "novices" are removed from their mothers' houses—where they have been brought up in a manner no different than that of their young sisters—to the cult house, newly constructed for the ritual initiation. There, "bachelors," another age grade comprised of thirteen- to sixteen-year-olds, begin the process of remaking boys into warriors through orally inseminating their young charges. In so doing, they allow the novices to gain the store of semen they will need to become men and warriors as well as husbands and fathers.[13]

Among the most fascinating discussions on the intersection of gender and sexuality are those which center on variable definitions of gender. In fact, when considering gender from a global perspective, one finds that dividing the world into male and female is insufficient in understanding the complex roles gender offers to various societies and the sexual expectations that such roles occasion. Globally, anthropologists have found up to five culturally recognized genders: female, male, male-female, female-male, and neuter. In the context of such multiple genders, the understanding of sexuality becomes more complex than is sometimes suspected. In India, for instance, hijras—male to female transgender individuals—belong to yet another jāti of Indian society and are responsible for a very specific set of religious duties: particularly blessing newborns and newlyweds. We will encounter them when we turn to a consideration of Hindu tradition. The Polynesian term fa'afafine likewise refers to an individual who, though born male, lives as a woman. While in Samoa, adolescent males might sometimes have sex with one another even as they protect their sisters from the sexual overtures of their fellow villagers, and there is likewise some amount of sex between post-adolescent males (referred to by the obsolete term *tauatane*, a term also used to describe dancing and fighting between men who maintain masculine gender identities), fa'afafine sexuality is defined quite distinctly from these instances. A boy's propensity to develop into a fa'afafine was noted at an early age if he showed an inclination for feminine rather than masculine tasks around the house. Not characteristically thought to be indicative of homosexuality, one's status as a fa'afafine nonetheless tends to be associated with maintaining sexual relations with masculine men—even if, as has been reported in the past, some fa'afafine would marry women and have children.

Though fa'afafine status seems not to be idealized in Samoan culture (a fa'afafine's brother perhaps expressing the same embarrassment that he would in the case of a promiscuous sister), it is neither proscribed. Christianity having nearly displaced traditional Samoan religion, it may be the case that the traditional status of fa'afafines has suffered some diminution. Further, Western concepts of gay identity have intruded on the fa'afafine tradition, redefining both the fa'afafine and the sexual expectations that such status implies.[14]

But there are some indications that the fa'afafine's position in the past may have carried spiritual significance. When Tagaloa, the Samoan creator god, created a rock in the sea as a resting place, and then split the rock into pieces, each of which became one of the Polynesian islands, he set upon each island a man and a woman. These two became the progenitors of each of the island's population. Later still, Tagaloa established chiefs for each of the islands and, finally, a chief among chiefs—that is, a king—on the island of Greater Manu'a: the first island he created. Royal personages in Samoa were, from that time forth, spoken to in respect terms, not unlike those which were used by the San when speaking of Gangwanana or the large game animals, while an everyday vocabulary was employed when speaking to commoners.[15] It may be that bipartite gender identity is, like the distinction between nobles and commoners, such an essential element of traditional Samoan mythology that those who are attracted to the same sex still conform to the socially sanctioned gender identities of *fafine* (woman) and *tane* (man). As the "mixed blood Samoan" fa'afafine Dan Taulapapa McMullin expresses it: "Without relationship there is no identity." In other words, an individual's identity is an expression of his or her network of social relationships. Inasmuch as McMullin was recognized by his grandmother as a fa'afafine at an early age, it was accepted—especially by more traditional Samoans—that his sexual relations would be with masculine men. Chillingly, upon moving to the mainland from American Samoa, McMullin's non–Samoan "U.S. Army drill sergeant father" instructed his Samoan wife to tell their son "to act like a boy because we were not in Samoa anymore." But when he returned to Samoa and accepted his first lover, who wore the traditional lavalava clinched at the waist and oiled his bare shoulders and hair with coconut oil, his choice was accepted by the traditional villagers among whom he lived, one old woman teasingly waving a banana in front of his face while the other village women laughed good-naturedly at the joke.

Though there seems to be no knowledge of a religious signification for the fa'afafine tradition, McMullin reports a telling episode from Samoan mythology: Nafanua, binding and covering her breasts, made of herself "the greatest warrior of Samoan history." But one day, in the course of a furious battle, her breasts were exposed and she "retired from fighting." From then on, she became—in a situation remarkably similar to one that we will shortly witness among the Iroquois—an advocate for peaceful discourse, influencing the manner in which Samoan governance, communal and decentralized, was undertaken in the community's meetinghouse.[16] As such, she became a goddess. McMullin seems to view this deity as especially significant in the context of his own fa'afafine identity, perhaps intuiting that if a female-to-male transgender deity exists, it is not unlikely that its converse, a male-to-female transgender deity existed, perhaps before the advent of Christianity in Samoa. A possibility would be presented by a deity named Satia who would become male or female before slipping into the bed of a mortal of the opposite sex.[17] Interestingly, though the phenomenon is not described, the word fa'atane, a woman who exhibits masculine behavior, is listed in George Pratt's 1862 Samoan dictionary, suggesting that the converse of the fa'afafine was once to be found in Samoan society.

Native American two-spirits, like hijras and fa'afafines, are born male but live out their lives as women, generally taking a husband and carrying out all the activities which the women of their nation would normally undertake—though some might also participate in warfare and other male-centered activities. Perhaps the most famous two-spirit was Wewha of Zuni Pueblo. Befriended by the anthropologist Matilda Coxe Stevenson in the late 19th century, Wewha was said by some Zuni to be a hermaphrodite but was described by Stevenson as a biological man who lived as a woman. In fact, Stevenson, when describing Wewha's death, said—almost apologetically—that she always used the pronoun she to describe Wewha as she "could not think of the deceased, who was a good friend, as anything but a woman." Wewha was further described as "the tallest person in Zuni; certainly the strongest, both mentally and physically. She had a good memory not only for the lore of her people, but for all that she heard of the outside world. She spoke only a few words of English before coming to Washington, but," during her six months' stay there, she "acquired the language with remarkable rapidity, and was soon able to join in conversation. She possessed an indomitable will and an insatiable thirst for knowledge. Her likes and dislikes were intense. She would risk anything to serve those she loved, but toward those who crossed her path she was vindictive." Still, if occasionally "severe she was considered just."[18]

Similar traditions exist for female to male transgender individuals but—for some unexplained reason—they seem rarer, not as extensively studied, and subject to stricter sexual regulation. Sadhin are female ascetics in India who live as men and, as is the case with male ascetics, are expected to remain celibate.[19] Sumatran Tombois explicitly adopt masculine identities and seek out sexual relations with women—whom they will support financially and expect to cook and clean for them.[20] Sworn Virgins in Albania took on the role of men, particularly if there was no man in the family to avenge the death of a father or brother killed in a blood feud. Still, they too were expected to remain celibate—even if they did, like Pashe Keqi, one of Albania's last Sworn Virgins, carry a hunting rifle, sit with "legs wide open," and down "shots of raki" with the men at the village tavern. Keqi tellingly suggested that he might have been content to remain living as a woman had there been someone to avenge the death of his father some 60 years ago. But, as things stood, he had little choice. And, besides, "Back then, it was better to be a man," Keqi asserted, "because a woman and an animal were the same thing. Now, Albanian women have equal rights with men, and are even more powerful. I think today it would be fun to be a woman."[21]

Of Dreamings, Songlines and Walkabouts

Let us take a moment to explore the network of social relations as it impinges on the Euahlayi, an Australian Aboriginal nation in New South Wales, and

Wewha (**National Archives and Records Administration, through Wikipedia, photograph by John Hillers**).

Euahlayi mythology. Among the more intriguing descriptions of Aboriginal culture is that provided by Katie Langloh Parker who, born perhaps of the fact that as a child she was saved from drowning by an Aboriginal girl, presented an empathetic view of the Aboriginal Euahlayi nation. Her description of

Euahlayi culture, and particularly her collection of Euahlayi myths, offers some of the best concrete evidence to fill out a set of Aboriginal concepts that are far too often offered in the abstract—the Dreaming, Songlines, and Walka-bouts—concepts which speak in a most direct manner to our ability to understand Aboriginal culture.

The Euahlayi, like other Australian Aboriginal people, made a wide use of their resources in western New South Wales. And like other foraging societies, men took care of the bulk of hunting duties while women were responsible for the gathering of vegetal food. Likewise in consonance with other foragers, Euahlayi society was characterized by relative egalitarianism—with apparently low-level gender and age status differentiation—promoting a generalized reciprocity in the distribution of resources. The primary game animals of Euahlayi hunters were kangaroo and emu but a wide variety of other animals were exploited: iguana, opossum, piggiebillah, paddy melon, and bandicoot, among others. Likewise, a variety of fowl, fish, and shellfish were exploited. Other animal foods included ant larvae and frogs as well as several animal products: notably honey and emu eggs. Hunting techniques included the use of "nets, snares, fish traps, spears, boomerangs, and hunting dogs." Driving both kangaroo and emu into nets was a collective activity, entailing the use of either hunting dogs or spears, but snares could be used—particularly near water-holes—to catch these animals as well. Boomerangs seemed to be used particularly to catch waterfowl and expertise with boomerangs was a source of pride for hunters who, unlike San hunters, were apparently free to brag about their hunting prowess. Fish, and particularly Murray Cod, being an important food source, Parker goes into some detail in describing Euahlayi fishing techniques: "To catch fish," the Euahlayi "make small weirs and dams of stones, with narrow stone passages leading to them. The fish are swept by the current into these yards," where they are either speared or caught up with the bare hands. "The most celebrated of these stone fish-traps is at Brewarrina on the Barwon River. It is said to have been made by Byamee," the Euahlayi's supreme god and culture hero, along with "his giant sons." Byamee not only built the Brewarrina fish-trap. It was he "who established the rule that there should be a camping-ground in common for the various tribes where, during the fishing festival, peace should be strictly kept, all meeting to enjoy the fish and to do their share towards preserving the fisheries."

"Common vegetal foods," Parker states, "include the yam and a number of other roots obtained with the digging stick." Further, "seeds of Dheal and Noongah trees are made into cakes as well as those of barley grass." In a description reminiscent of our earlier discussion of Natufian culture, Parker reports that when "the doonburr, or seed, was thick on the yarmmara, or barley-grass," the stalks were collected in great quantities whereupon a spot was cleared, creating a great "brush-yard" of barley grass stalks. "Each fresh supply of yarmmara, as it was brought in by the harvesters, was put in this yard. When enough was gathered, the brush-yard was thrown on one side, and fire set to the grass, which was in full ear though yet green." As the grass burned, the harvesters turned it over with sticks, knocking the seeds from the stalks. They then threshed and winnowed the seeds, putting away the clean grain "in skin bags to be used as required." The grain was "then ground on large flat dayoorl-stones, with a smaller flat stone held in both hands." Once readied, the flour "was made into little flat cakes" which were baked, "first on pieces of bark beside the fire to harden them," then directly in the ashes. Of the dayoorl-stones, Parker reports, these "grinding-stones are handed down from generation to generation, being kept each in the family to whom it had first belonged. Should a member of any other use it without permission, a fight would ensue. Some of these stones are said to have spirits in them; those are self-moving, and at times have the power of speech."

The environmental resources upon which the Euahlayi depend find their way most exactingly into Euahlayi social structure—particularly in the context of the nation's system of moieties, clans, and totems. Every Euahlayi belongs to one of two moieties: the Gwaigulleeah (light-blooded) or the Gwaimudthen (dark-blooded). "The origin of this division is said to be the fact that the original ancestors were, on the one side, a red race coming from the west, the Gwaigulleeah; on the other, a dark race coming from the east," the Gwaimudthen. Besides belonging to one of the two moieties, all Euahlayi belong as well to an animal clan: some of these clans belonging to the Gwaigulleeah moiety, others to the Gwaimudthen. Well-represented clans include the Iguana, Opossum, Bandicoot, and Paddy Melon among the Qwaigulleeah and the Emu, Kangaroo, Bilby, and Black Snake among the Gwaimudthen. "Upon arrival in the Narran River region of New South Wales," Parker reports, Gwaigulleeah and Gwaimudthen alike must have been in their original animal forms for the animals were only given their human form by Byamee when he first ventured into the Narran River basin with his two wives. Byamee, thereupon, created of the animal nations human clans and gave each clan a number of subtotems which were its special inheritance and to which it maintained special rights and duties: animals, plants, celestial bodies, items of human manufacture, winds, rains, clouds, the body parts of both Byamee and his principal wife, Birrahgnooloo. In myth, these subtotems would sometimes come to the aid of a member of the clan to which the subtotem belonged. For instance, when two of the Seven Sisters—the Pleides, who are subtotems of the Iguana clan—were abducted and brought to earth, they were saved by the Pine Tree, another of Iguana's subtotems, which, growing miraculously, delivered them back to their home in the sky.

Essential rules govern the relationships of moiety to moiety and clan to clan and the dispersal of subtotems among clan members. For instance, children belong to their mother's moiety and clan and strict rules of exogamy govern moiety and clan alike. "A Gwaigulleeah may under no circumstances marry a Gwaigulleeah; he or she must mate with a Gwaimudthen." And if a Euahlayi were to marry a member of his or her own clan (even if this clan were from a distant nation), the results would be catastrophic. Parker reports: "One old man here said, when I asked him what harm it would do for, say, a Beewee man," a member of the Iguana clan, "to come from the Gulf country, where his tribe had never had any communication with ours, and marry a girl here," that "all Beewees were originally changed from the Beewee form into human shape. The Beewee of the Gulf, originally, like the Beewee here, had the same animal shape, and should two of this same blood mate the offspring would throw back, as they say of horses, to the original strain, and partake of Iguana (Beewee) attributes either in nature or form." As serious as the rule against incest (marrying within the clan) is the rule against miscegenation: marrying with Euro-Australians. Among the lore taught initiates in the two-month seclusion of the Boorah, the male puberty ceremony sponsored by Byamee, was the fact that "the oldest shamans could see in their sacred crystals pictures of the past, pictures of what was happening at a distance in the present, and pictures of the future; some of which last filled their minds with dread," for, it was claimed, that "as time went on" the color of the Euahlayi people, "as seen in these magical stones, seemed to grow paler and paler, until at last only the white faces of the Wundah, or spirits of the dead," were to be seen. "The reason of this," the shamans were convinced, "must surely be that the tribes fell away from the Boorah rites, and in his wrath Byamee stirred from his crystal seat in Bullimah." He had promised that so long as the Euahlayi "kept his sacred laws, so long should he" remain at Bullimah, and the Euahlayi nation would prosper. But if, on the other hand, the Euahlayi "failed to keep up the Boorah rites as he had taught them, then he would move and their end would come, and only Wundah, or white devils," would be seen "in their country."[22] Thus, at one end of the spectrum, marriage between clan members leads back to the times preceding the ordering of the earth by Byamee; equilibrium involves the regular maintenance of the rule of law (as sponsored by Byamee) in which Gwaigulleeah (light-blooded) people marry Gwaimudthen (dark-blooded) people and the Euahlayi prevail; at the other end of the spectrum, miscegenation between the Euahlayi and Euro-Australians leads to an apocalyptic world in which the Euahlayi are no more and the Narran River region is populated solely by howling ghosts.

Euahlayi Mythology

This last concern brings us to religion. The Euahlayi, like other Australian Aborigines, practice a religion which anthropologists call totemism. In brief, totemism entails a belief in a spiritual, as well as a material, existence for all essential elements of the environment. Animals, plants, items of human manufacture, topographical features, even celestial bodies can all be totems. The spiritual totem, say Kangaroo, is related to the people as an ancestor. Each totem in a given society may be ancestral to (1) the entire society, (2) various subsegments of the society such as moieties or clans, or (3) individual members of the society. The Euahlayi, like other Aborigines, maintain, through totemism, a sense of spiritual kinship with everything in their environment which they consider essential to their well-being: in Parker's words, they are all related through a belief in a "golden age when man, birds, beasts, trees, and elements spoke a common language." This ancient mythic time is referred to as the Dreaming. When, in the ancient times of the Dreaming, Byamee came into the Narran River region, he was accompanied by his two wives: his principle wife, Birrahg-nooloo, and his secondary wife, Cunnumbeillee. And he—as his wives struck the parched ground with their digging sticks bringing forth springs, rivers, and lakes—transformed the resident animals into the various clans that exist among the Euahlayi today. Any individual member of the Euahlayi nation honors his or her clan's totem through upholding its law—though, notably, among the Euahlayi, that law does not include a "taboo against eating one's totem animal as is often the case in other Aboriginal nations." Parker suggests that "it might not be feasible to deny one clan an important food source, the kangaroo, for instance, or emu, because it happens to be that clan's totem." But, as we will momentarily see, a ritual enactment of the taboo finds its way into the Euahlayi first-kill initiation.

Essential to an understanding of the Dreaming are the concepts of Songlines and Walkabouts. Songlines are literally songs but also a totem's tracks left on the land in visible form such as an outcropping of rock, a woodland copse, a waterhole, just about any topographical feature imaginable. Thus, Songlines are visible. But they are also songs that are preserved by men and women for whom the totem, who left his or her tracks on the landscape that is Australia, is important. Perhaps the totem in question is a person's clan totem—the totem that represents the clan as a whole—or perhaps again it is his or her individual totem (subtotem): that is, one of the totems that his or her clan preserves and uses as a personal name for a member of the clan. Each clan, which historically numbered about 50 people, had to have enough individual totems to cover each clan member and when a clan member died his or her totem was recycled to a newly born clan member. If one were an adherent to a particular totem through clan affiliation, he or she had a right to that totem's songs, ceremonies, and sacred designs and an obligation to uphold his or her law. Each song relates to a significant track of the totem and to know an entire Songline is to know the entire history of the movement of that totem in the ancient Dreamtime when the land was still soft, when the totems' movements left deep footprints upon the earth, and the very landscape that is Australia was being thereby created. Further, it allows one to strike out into the wilderness and follow that totem's Songlines on a Walkabout. Though primarily conceived of as an element of the rite of passage that carried a boy into manhood, a rite which we will momentarily visit, the Walkabout can be undertaken by anybody at any time. Notably, during the course of the Walkabout, one finds himself or herself not only in the present but also the mythic past. And, further, one may gain insights into the future through such a pilgrimage. Past, present, and future are, therefore, intimately united in the Walkabout—offering the experience a timelessness which is its own special sort of ASC.

The intertwined concepts of the Dreaming, Songlines, and the Walkabout—the philosophy, that is, which maintains that there is an ancient, mythic world (the Dreaming) which we may, through esoteric knowledge (Songlines) not only enter but actually experience (Walkabout)—underscore the kinship which Australian Aborigines almost universally maintain with their environment. But in order to understand that philosophy—and its sociological ramifications—more fully, one must consider it as concretely expressed in Aboriginal mythology. Let us then consider the Euahlayi story of Bahloo, the Moon:

> Bahloo, the Moon, looked down at the earth one night, when his light was shining brightly, to see if anyone was moving. When the people were all asleep was the time he chose for playing with his three dogs. He called them dogs, but the people called them snakes: the death adder, the black snake, and the tiger snake. As he looked down on the earth, with his three dogs beside him, Bahloo saw a small group of Euahlayi crossing a creek. He called out to them saying, "Stop, I want you to carry my dogs across that creek." But the Euahlayi, though they liked Bahloo well, did not like his dogs, for sometimes when he had brought these dogs down from the sky to play upon the earth, they had bitten not only the earth dogs but also their masters; and the poison left by the bites had killed those bitten. So the people said, "No, Bahloo, we are too frightened; your dogs might bite us. They are not like our dogs, whose bite does not kill us."
>
> Bahloo said, "If you do what I ask you, when you die you shall come to life again. See this piece of bark. I throw it into the water." And he threw a piece of bark into the creek. "See how it comes to the top again and floats. That is what would happen to you if you would do what I ask you: first under when you die, then up again at once. But if you will not take my dogs over you will die like this," and he threw a stone into the creek, which sank to the bottom. "You will sink like that stone and never rise again!"
>
> But the people said, "We cannot do it, Bahloo. We are too frightened of your dogs."

"I will come down and carry them over myself to show you that they are quite safe and harmless." And down he came, the black snake coiled round one arm, the tiger snake round the other, and the death adder on his shoulder, coiled towards his neck. He carried them over. When he had crossed the creek he picked up a big stone, and he threw it into the water, saying, "Now, you cowardly people, since you would not do what I asked of you, forever you have lost the chance of rising again after you die. You will just stay where you are put, like that stone does under the water, and grow, as it does, to be a part of the earth. If you had done what I asked you, you could have died as often as I die and have come to life again as often as I do. But now you will only be men while you live and bones when you are dead."

Bahloo looked so cross, and the three snakes hissed so fiercely, that the Euahlayi were very glad to see them disappear from their sight behind the trees. The people had always been frightened of Bahloo's dogs, and now they hated them, and they said, "If we could get them away from Bahloo, we would kill them." And thenceforth, whenever they saw a snake alone they killed it. But Bahloo only sent more, for he said, "As long as there are people, there shall be snakes to remind them that they would not do what I asked."

The myth of Bahloo, on one level, explores the amorphous and psychologically fraught ideas of mortality and immortality through a comparison of snakes (the visible symbols of immortality since they slough their skins) and dogs (the visible symbols of mortality since they don't). Snakes are the dogs of Bahloo, who is the patron of female initiation and immortality since he passes through his regularly recurrent phases (a feature that, from the Euahlayi perspective, is analogous to the snake's shedding its skin). But just plain old dogs are the dogs of the people who are emblematic of mortality since we people, after all, do die. Yet, on another level, the distinction between the moon and his dogs (snakes) and the people and their dogs (dingoes) becomes more trenchant from the Euahlayi point of view because, as we earlier saw, the Euahlayi have an ancient prophecy that says they are—once so decimated by white people (i.e., Euro-Australians)—destined to disappear entirely from the world. In other words, death is not only the individual but also the collective destiny of the Euahlayi: at least during the period of unfettered Euro-Australian encroachment on Euahlayi existence. What the myth does, then, is work out not only the psychologically perplexing issues of life and death but also the troubled relations between Australian Aborigines and Euro-Australians.

Of course, not only the Euahlayi have myths that work out the complex issues of life and death and their sociological ramifications. It is probably worth remembering that in Judeo-Christian mythology, it is a snake that robs humans of immortality through tricking them into eating from the Tree of the Knowledge of Good and Evil and, in doing so, brings about different fates for men and women. Other societies, as well, allow the snake such symbolic import: for instance, Mesopotamian, in which the snake robs us of eternal youth, and Dani, in which the snake wins a race with the bird for sovereignty over human beings and thereby brings us death. Thus, the symbolic value of Bahloo's dogs—that is, snakes—is a familiar one. But what about the Euahlayi's dogs: dingoes? The Euahlayi story would probably not propose the conceptual juxtaposition of snakes and dogs if the two integers did not share some integral characteristic. For the Euahlayi, that characteristic is found in another myth which speaks of Bougoodoogahdah, a cannibal who lived apart from human society with her 400 dingoes. She would trick Euahlayi hunters into going to a secluded ridge where, she claimed, they would be able to hunt paddy melons. Once there, she would sic her dingoes upon them. Then, she and her dingoes would feast upon their flesh. Yet, the Euahlayi, discovering her ploy, killed both her and her dingoes. Bougoodoogahdah's heart became a bird whose cry— Bougoodoogahdah—brings on the rain. And, in times of drought, the Euahlayi will steal the bird's eggs from her nest in order to induce her cry. But the dingoes became all manner of poisonous snakes—except for two who had never set their teeth to human flesh. They became harmless, non-venomous snakes. Still, many Euahlayi died before Bougoodoogahdah and her 400 dingoes were subdued and their fates are memorialized by "heaps of white stones," fossilized human bones, which lay to this day upon the gruesome ridge where they fell. Notably, when Byamee created the various Euahlayi clans from the animals resident in the Narran River basin, he refused to allow dingoes to become the ancestral totem of any of the clans. Rather, he took away their ability to speak. From that moment on, dingoes could only "bark and howl" and communicate with their onetime fellow animals, now human beings, with a "look of yearning and dumb entreaty" in their eyes.

Rites of Passage

One further image is at play in the Euahlayi myth of Bahloo: the distinction between a stone which drops forever to the bottom of the stream as opposed to a piece of wood which drops temporarily but rises again. The image echoes one that involves a sacred item essential to male initiation, the bullroarer whose construction was attributed to Byamee: he who wandered into the Narran River basin with his two wives, created the various Euahlayi clans from the animals that inhabited the region, instituted the Boorah initiation ritual in order to induct Euahlayi boys into his own mysteries, and then left the river basin to his human creations. He constructed the first bullroarer of stone but— as he whirled it over his head by its cord—it failed to call out to the people in the proper spirit-voice of the Gayandi. But one day, as "he was chopping a big Coolabah tree," a tree which Parker notes was cruelly burnt down without concern for its sacred nature, "out flew a big chip. Byamee heard the whizzing sound it made, gave another chop, and out flew another; again the whizzing sound. 'That is what I want,' he said. 'I'll make a Gayandi of wood.'" He took a wooden chip, whittled it down into an oval with sharp points at either end, and bored a hole through one of the points. Then, attaching a piece of twine to the hole, he whirled the bullroarer overhead and the proper sound, a kind of whirring hum, occurred. Thus, was born the Gayandi, the voice of the spirit of male initiation. With the Bullroarer created, Byamee held the first Boorah ceremony in order to initiate his own sons—bestowing on them the status of men, hunters, and warriors—and only then did he take up his exalted place on his crystal seat at Bullimah, his encampment in the eastern sky, to which the spirits of deceased men go. The Milky Way is the pathway that they take to Byamee's sky camp. The stars are their campfires and "the dusky haze" is created by their campfires' smoke. Another sky camp exists in the west where the spirits of deceased women busy themselves with the manufacture of war weapons.

The myth of Bahloo, the Moon, and that of Byamee and the Gayandi both refer to Euahlayi initiation and thus allow us to consider another set of sociological metaphors which enter upon Euahayi mythic thought. If Euahlayi mythology depends upon moiety and clan as well as Aboriginal and Euro-Australian relations in order to communicate its message, Euahlayi ritual depends upon gendered relations in order to become legible. For instance, Bahloo is the patron of female initiation inasmuch as menstruation is considered the periodic analogue to the Moon's phases while Byamee is the patron of male initiation inasmuch as his provision of the living bullroarer offers Boorah initiation its spiritual essence. Intriguingly, female and male initiation—because a token of divinity resides at the center of each—are charged with a spark of immortality. One here thinks of the notion of liminality: a moment "betwixt and between" what one has been and what one is to become, a moment wherein the initiate is imbued with a special spiritual—and perhaps even dangerous—power.

Girl's initiation displays a number of parallels to the initiation of San girls which we explored in the context of Beautiful Python Girl. The Euahlayi girl is taken "into the scrub" by an older woman, most often her grandmother, who has constructed a small hut of brush. There, the woman covers the girl's limbs with mud, sets fire to a "thick heap of Budtha leaves," the smoke of which the girl has to swallow, and makes the girl lie down in a hollow scooped out from the earth. Here, begins a two-month seclusion during which the girl will be instructed on her life as a woman, starting with the fact that she will no longer be able "to run about as she pleases" but will have to assume the duties and decorum of womanhood. For the duration of her seclusion, the girl is not to sleep during the day or, indeed, before the encampment, close at hand, beds down for the night. She is not to eat honey. And that food which she can eat, daily set out by her sponsor, should be eaten at "the first streak of day." With the close of the two month's seclusion, the girl—happy to be nearing the end of such a lonely period—will move to a second hut, nearer to the main encampment, which has been prepared for her by the encampment's women. Now the girl's sponsor "rubs off the mud with which she plastered the girl's limbs when first they went away" from the encampment and which she periodically renewed. She then paints the girl "in different designs with red ochre and white gypsum, principally in spots." She places a forehead band plaited with white Kurrajong fiber over the girl's brow and adorns the band with "sprays of white flowers." She likewise adorns the girl with "goomils—opossum hair armlets—into which she places sprays of flowers matching those in the girl's hair." Then, scattering "a handful of white swan's down over the girl's head" and tying round her a girdle woven from opossum sinew and hair, a garment that defines her as a woman, she places "a sacred sprig of the Dheal tree through the hole in the septum of the girl's nose" and sets a bouquet "of smoking Budtha leaves" in the girl's hand. Then the girl, to the accompaniment of the encampment women's singing, returns to her home. There, she will be taken to her future husband who will be seated "on a log, with his back towards her." He is not yet permitted to "look on her face." She will retreat to yet another temporary camp, this one even closer to the main encampment, where she will pass the next month. And, in this fashion, she will be accompanied, step-by-step, and camp-by-camp, to the moment when she takes up residence with her new husband at his own fire.

    Boy's initiation likewise brings to mind the initiation of San boys. "Up to a certain age," Parker reports, our boys are brought up "as our girls—charms are sung over them to make them generous, honest, good swimmers, and the rest; but after that they are taken into the Weedegah, or bachelors' camp, and developed along manly lines." They will learn, for instance, the ancient art of making fire (which only initiated men dare undertake) and begin to be trained up in the various Euahlayi hunting strategies. When the requisite number of boys was deemed to be ready for initiation, there would arise one night "a whizzing, whirling boom" far out "in the scrub. As the first echo of it reached the camp, the women, such as were still young enough to bear children, stopped their ears, for should any such hear the Gurraymi," the women's name for the Gayandi (the Boorah spirit's voice), that spirit would surely kill them. Then, the old women would begin "to sing a Boorah song." And a headman would hold aloft a spear with the *waywah*, the "emblematic belt of manhood," affixed to it. This *waywah*, "the principal article of a man's dress," consisted of "a belt, about six inches wide," woven from opossum sinews," from which hung—at the belt's back, front, and sides—short pelts woven from strips of kangaroo rat and paddy melon skin. The song, the display of the *waywah*, and the sound of the bullroarer would all serve to reveal to the boys "that the hour of their initiation" was finally at hand.

A Boorah ring was then cleared and surrounded with earthen mounds and a smaller Bunbul (or little Boorah) ring was constructed. Around the Boorah ring, the trees were stripped of a patch of bark and effigies of the various clan totems and subtotems were carved into the living wood while around the Bunbul were sculpted earthen effigies of Byamee with a war club in each hand, Birrahgnooloo (Byamee's principal wife) with a spear in each hand, and the various Euahlayi clan totems, along with one of a mysterious deity who, according to some, was Byamee's brother, he who was "not born of woman, having lived before the human race existed, and before Byamee traveled as Creator and culture hero through Australia." These sculptures were plastered over and then painted with sacred designs while, at the center of the Bunbul "a large heap of wood was placed" in readiness for the lighting of the "Yungawee, or sacred fire." Finally, with the sound of bullroarers coming from every direction out in the bush, the people gathered around the big Boorah ring, the initiates as well as "the Munthdeeguns, or men in charge of them." The Munthdeeguns were painted "and had leafy twigs tied round their wrists and ankles, as had the boys also, and all carried in their hands small branches of green." Again, the *waywah* was held aloft on its spear. The women gathered about the ring "were singing Boorah songs. Some held their breasts as a sign they had sons among the initiates; others put their hands on their shoulders, which showed they had brothers going to be made young men. All the women had leafy twigs tied round their wrists and ankles as the men had." The Boorah song over, the men marched off, "closely behind them the two oldest men with their tufted spears; the Boorah boys closely after them. The women followed, carrying bunches of leafy twigs with which they pelted the boys."

Finally, the boys, "painted red," were called into the Bunbul, the little Boorah ring, where the sacred fire was lit and "where their respective Munthdeeguns" began to "daub them with white. Thereupon, the boys found themselves abashed, with their hands clasping their thighs and their "heads abased," in the midst of the chanting throng. "With the Boorah spirits whistling and whizzing all round them," and hemmed about by the warriors' spears, the boys suffered their skins to be "scratched with stone knives and mussel shells." And he who did not display fear during this ordeal was told, "'You are brave; you shall be *boorahbayyi*," an initiate, "first and afterwards *yelgidyi*," one initiated, "and carry the marks that all may know." Then, a hole—the first of many that would eventually mark his back, shoulders, and arms—was bored into his shoulder with a stone burin, sucked upon to remove any traces of uncleanliness, and filled "with powdered charcoal." It might even happen that one of his front teeth were knocked out. That done, each man" took hold of his charge, hoisted him onto his shoulder, and began to dance "round the ring with him. Then the old women" were instructed "to bid the boys good-bye," and the boys along with their sponsors disappeared into the bush.

During his period of seclusion in the bush, a boy is under the special patronage of Gayandi, the spirit of the Boorah, carved from the living wood by Byamee. But, as we have seen, Byamee first attempted to create a Gayandi from stone. This first Gayandi becomes a sort of "disobedient deputy" to Byamee. Darramulun—also called, like the voice of the Bullroarer, Gayandi—exists as a kind of alternate spirit of Boorah initiation. Rather than simply knock out a front tooth of an initiate to show that he has successfully undertaken his first Boorah, Darramulum—too powerful to function as the true patron of initiation—will attempt to eat the initiate's face. And, though the initiate is protected by the wood Gayandi, he is in danger from the excesses of the stone Gayandi. He is, in fact, both subject to and the source of mysterious and dangerous powers. But as his seclusion progresses, he will be successively removed from such an anomalous condition. He will eventually be taken upon his first hunt where he is expected to take an emu. With the emu killed, he will be made to lie down upon the dead bird and, after the bird is cooked, he will suffer its fat to be rubbed on the joints of his arms and legs. Then he will be made to eat a bit of the emu's flesh—feigning disgust as he does so—after which the flesh of the emu, which has been forbidden him for the length of his seclusion, is no longer considered taboo. In this, we see a ritual memory of the ancient prohibition against eating the totem that is so common in Australian Aboriginal society. Finally, after passing a number of months in the bush, the boys, "painted principally white," return to the Boorah ring, where the *waywah*—the belt which signifies one's entrance into manhood—is "put on them." And the boys' mothers come "up behind them, and put their hands on their sons' shoulders," whereupon they rub "all the paint off their sons' bodies." With his first Boorah accomplished, the onetime boy is now a warrior who can carry weapons. And upon completing his fifth, he can take his rank among the *dorrunmai*, the headmen, who maintain "few privileges beyond being accepted authorities as to war and hunting."

When considering the major movements of the Boorah, Victor Turner's analysis of rites of passage, those rituals that serve to usher us from one social status to another, becomes especially trenchant. Turner maintains that all such rites consist in a movement from separation, in which a previous status is left behind, through transition (or limen), in which one is infused with imagery of his or her previous and coming statuses simultaneously, to incorporation, in which one is brought into his or her new status. In the light of such a formulation, one cannot help but note that the Boorah boys enter the Bunbul (little Boorah ring) painted in red. As the Boorah begins, and the boys embark upon their career as initiates (*boorahbayyi*), they are daubed with white paint. Finally, upon achieving the status of *yelgidyi* (initiated ones), they are painted mainly in white. It seems likely that the alteration of colors from red, through red and white, to white serves as one of the many demarcations of the sociological alteration to which the boys are being subjected. Fascinatingly, when they are painted in red and daubed with white, markings that they carry with themselves when they enter the bachelor's camp, they answer almost exactingly to Mary Douglas's observations on liminal—or threshold—personae: those who exist "betwixt and between" defined social categories and who, as such, are both spiritually dangerous and vulnerable. "Where the social system explicitly recognizes positions of authority," Douglas suggests, "those holding such positions are endowed with explicit spiritual power, controlled, conscious, external and approved—powers to bless or curse." Conversely, Douglas points out, "where the social system requires people to hold dangerously ambiguous roles, these persons are credited with uncontrolled, unconscious, dangerous, disapproved powers—such as witchcraft and evil eye. In other words, where the social system is well-articulated, I look for articulate powers vested in the points of authority; where the social system is ill-articulated, I look for inarticulate powers vested in those who are a source of disorder."[23] Little wonder, then, that when Katie Langloh Parker encountered boys in the bush during their Boorah seclusion, they fled as if she "were a devil in petticoats." And little wonder, as well, that when the boy's metamorphosis was complete, the last vestiges of paint—not unlike the last vestiges of mud that adorned a female initiate's body during her seclusion—were removed from his body.

4. Religion as Indigenous Philosophy

Ideology

Other animals, and certainly all complex mammals, share with humans the dependence on a particular ecological adaptation and a functional social order but it is not altogether clear that they share with us the existence of an ideology: a worldview that hinges upon group affiliation. Our possible singularity in this regard rests upon the fact that ideology—while the result of a particular history, a unique set of ecological concerns, and a distinctive social configuration—is preeminently a function of language, not only as it emerges in everyday conversation and gossip but especially as it is deployed in verbal folklore: the folktale, the legend, and—most profoundly—the myth. Claude Lévi-Strauss developed the idea of a structural anthropology, a theoretical approach to unlocking the secrets of a society's ideology. It postulated the existence of an "underlying structure" for any cultural phenomenon: including, most famously, mythology. Structuralism claims that, in language, abstract ideas are given substance by symbols borrowed directly from the environment (both the physical and social) and that these concrete symbols allow members of society to make sense of the abstract ideas that the symbols represent.

Lévi-Strauss borrowed an image from geology to explain the phenomenon: he points out that when the geological layers, or strata, of a glen or gorge or canyon become disrupted through some erosional factor so that one cannot determine where one stratum ends and another begins, one will sometimes find two plants growing cheek-by-jowl, so close together that they seem to be sprouting from the same soil or environment. But, in fact, the one plant may demand a slightly more alkaline, the other perhaps a mildly acidic, soil. The invisible strata of the two different plants' environments—that is, the very soils from which they spring forth—are rendered visible by the nature of the plants that these different soils allow to thrive. The geological strata are like the abstract

114

ideas that myth serves to explore while the plants are like the concrete symbols that myth uses to render abstract ideas tangible, legible, comprehensible. The symbols—if interpreted correctly—allow one to uncover the deep, structural, or ideological, meaning of the myth.[1]

In the same way that two plants growing cheek-by-jowl reveal the scrambled geology beneath them, the Australian Euahlayi myth of Bahloo explores the amorphous and psychologically fraught ideas of mortality and immortality (ideas hidden in the story like disturbed geological layers) through a comparison of snakes—the outward (or visible) symbols of immortality since they slough their skins—and dogs—the outward (or visible) symbols of mortality since they don't. Likewise, the intersecting concepts of the Dreaming, Songlines, and Walkabouts are essential elements of Euahlayi ideology fleshed out in Euahlayi myth. The concept of the Dreaming is given substance by the totems themselves, the animals that inhabit the Dreamtime. The concept of the Songline, so similar to our own concept of history, would have no meaning without an intimate knowledge of the topography of the Narran River basin that so centers Euahlayi myth. And the concept of the Walkabout is continuously exemplified by the mythic peregrinations of the totems themselves. What one notices when engaging in a structural analysis is that mythology offers a kind of communal—or, perhaps better, indigenous—philosophy with which each of us, in our own particular manner, distills the essence of our society's ideological basis, and then, with that essence in hand, casts our own elongated shadows upon that society's culture.[2]

The Iroquois Creation

Let us then look at the manner in which ecological and sociological concerns are *ideologically* wedded from the perspective of a most singular society: the Iroquois Confederacy, an alliance of Native American nations that, for most of its history, stretched across what is today western New York from the Genesee to the Mohawk Rivers. The Confederacy, founded anywhere from the 13th to the 15th century, conceived of its territory as a great longhouse—modeled after the communal bark lodgings of the Iroquois—comprised of five nations: the Seneca, Cayuga, Onondaga, Oneida, and Mohawk. The longhouse proper was a rectangular structure constructed in posts made of young trees, its walls and roof covered over with sheets of bark. It had doors on each of its ends and smoke holes in its roof to let out the smoke from the several hearths which were aligned along the long axis running down the middle of the house. The people slept and stored their possessions in bunks that ran along the long walls of the house. The Iroquois were historically matrilineal, reckoning clan descent through their mothers, and matrilocal, taking up residency in the wife's house. Therefore, the longhouse lodged related women, their husbands, and their children. All women and children in the household belonged to the same clan. The men of the household—because of the rule of clan exogamy (i.e., that one must marry outside his or her clan)—belonged to the various others. This house became the metaphor for the interrelationships of the original nations of the league. The Seneca were the Keepers of the Western Door of the longhouse, the Mohawk the Keepers of the Eastern Door. The Onondaga, who inhabited the central territory of the league, were the Keepers of the Central Fire and from their nation was selected the paramount Iroquoian chief: the Adodarho. Together these three nations were considered the Elder Brothers of the League. Two other nations, the Cayuga, residing between the Seneca and the Onondaga, and the Oneida, residing between the Onondaga and the Mohawk, were considered the Younger Brothers of the League. Thus, these nations, residing side-by-side across their homeland just as families resided side-by-side in the compartments that ran the length of the longhouse, became collectively known as the Hodenosaunee, or Longhouse People.

The origins of the Iroquois—and the agricultural practices that sustained them—are most fully described, and thus sanctified, in the Creation which speaks of one of the Iroquois's preeminent gods, Sky Woman or Grandmother, falling to earth from the Sky World above. The Sky World—an ancient paradise where all the humans and animals lived together, sharing a longhouse and speaking a single language, under the amiable leadership of their chief, Grandfather—is presided over by the Celestial Tree which provides all the foods upon which the gods in the Sky World live. It also houses the Celestial Orb which bathes the Sky World in its light. One day, Grandfather, embracing his new wife, Sky Woman, unknowingly impregnates her with his breath. Yet, angered at discovering her condition, he uproots the Celestial Tree—creating a bottomless pit in doing so—and pushes Sky Woman out of the primal Sky World through that pit. Sky Woman, attempting to break her fall, catches the seeds that are scattered about the roots of the Celestial Tree under her fingernails. But fall she must and the earth itself, created to catch her, is formed on the back of a turtle who comes up from the primordial sea. Sky woman is gently wafted onto the Turtle's back upon the interknit wings of the various sea fowl. Once safe on the Turtle's back, a number of animals—the pervasive Earth-Divers whom we earlier encountered—dive to the bottom of the sea to make the back of the Turtle habitable. Pickerel and Cormorant die in their attempts but the lowly Muskrat (who fretted aloud over his ability in one version of the Creation that I heard) achieves the task, bringing up a tiny bit of mud beneath one claw and setting it upon the back of the Turtle. Thus, with the addition of wet earth, our world—Turtle Island—is born. Once settled upon Turtle Island, Sky Woman gives birth to a daughter. Then, when her daughter comes of age, she—in turn—is impregnated by the West Wind and bears him twin sons: Elder Brother (or Good Mind) who comes out normally through the birth canal and Younger Brother (or Evil Mind) whose frenetic birth through her armpit kills his mother. Still, in doing so he provides Turtle Island with its agricultural bounty for when Grandmother and Elder Brother bury their daughter and mother, corn springs from her breasts, beans from her fingers, and squash from her belly. Further, the holy plant tobacco springs from her forehead and string potatoes from her toes. Her spirit returns to its source, the Sky World, creating the path, the Ash Way (the Milky Way) that all spirits tread after departing their body.

Shortly after the death of his mother, Elder Brother goes off in search of his father who, after cruelly testing his son's mettle, presents him with three wriggling bags. The first falling from Elder Brother's grasp spills into the sea, filling it with all the fish and swimming creatures. The second, also slipping from Elder Brother's grasp, opens to the expanse of the sky, filling it with all the birds and flying creatures. The last, Elder Brother brings unopened to Sky Woman who instructs her grandson to shoot an arrow in the ground. Where his arrow strikes, a pool of oil bubbles forth and Grandmother Sky Woman instructs Elder Brother to open the sack just a bit and allow the animals inside to come out one-by-one. Out comes bear, and deer, and all the other animals that walk on land. Grandmother and Elder Brother have them wallow in the pit and soak up as much fat as they can bear, causing them to be healthy and good to eat. But some of the animals, like mink and fox, they fish out of the pit and wring the oil from their lanky bodies for these animals, fatless, will never be good to eat. After witnessing his brother's act of creation, Younger Brother becomes envious and attempts to destroy Elder Brother in shamanic battle. But Elder Brother prevails, imprisoning his evil twin in a cave beneath Turtle Island. He then casts his Grandmother back into the Sky where she becomes the moon, watching over the seasons and women in their menses.[3] Finally, he creates humans from the wet clay of a riverbank and mounts the Ash Way to reside in the Sky World whence he rains down the beneficent power, *orenda*, to his entire creation, inundating Turtle Island with the blessings of peace, good health, and healing medicines. Yet his evil brother, howling in anguish in the cave beneath the world, inundates his brother's creation with a malevolent power, *otgont*, continuously threatening Turtle Island with all that is evil: incessant tides of war, illness, and witchcraft.

The ecological metaphors which find their way into the Iroquois Creation are especially based in agricultural practices—particularly those centered on the *Diohekon*, the Three Sisters: Corn, Beans, and Squash.[4] The three maintain a sacred relationship with one another and the people whose very survival is dependent upon them. Luckily, the region that the Iroquois inhabit is a fertile one where the success of the crop is virtually assured and thus the three become benevolent, nurturing, deities. Witness the Iroquois prophet, Handsome Lake, reporting on the munificence of corn, in his *Gaiwiio,* or *Good Tidings,* which is the basis of Iroquois religious thought today:

> The day was bright when I went into the planted field and alone I wandered. It was the time of the second hoeing. Suddenly a damsel appeared and threw her arms about my neck and, as she clasped me, she spoke, saying, "When you leave this earth for the new world above, it is our wish to follow you." I looked for the damsel but saw only the long leaves of corn twining round my shoulders. And then I understood that it was the Spirit of the Corn who had spoken: She, the Sustainer of Life. So I replied, "O Spirit of the Corn, follow me not but abide still upon the earth and be strong and be faithful to your purpose. Ever endure and do not fail the children of women. It is not time for you to follow for *Gaiwiio* is only in its beginning."[5]

It is as intimate a relationship between Handsome Lake and the Spirit of the Corn as that which we witnessed between Odysseus and Athena. In Handsome Lake's inevitable journey to the Sky World, Corn desires not to be left on Earth. But as Hamlet admonished Horatio, "If thou didst ever hold me in thy heart, absent thee from felicity awhile, and in this harsh world draw thy breath in pain to tell my story," Handsome Lake is clear that, even with his death, it will still be the duty of Corn—along with her constant companions, Beans and Squash— to nourish Iroquois mothers and their children as long as the earth endures and thus ready them for the New World to come.

The collective representation of Corn, Beans, and Squash is indicative of Iroquois gardening practices. Of primary importance is the fact that gardening is in the hands of women and communal: the produce of Iroquois gardens belonging not to the family but the clan, that group of women and their dependents who work the garden collectively and reside together in a longhouse. The women's gardening procedure is based in slash-and-burn technology. First, a stretch of forest is slashed. Large trees and brush are cut down (the men undertaking this heavy task) and left to dry. After several weeks, the dry brush is set on fire and the resultant charcoal and ash is mixed with the soil using a heavy digging stick: a large, stout pole which simultaneously breaks the soil and mixes the ashes with it. Now, the garden is ready for planting. The Iroquois women classically did not plant their seeds in rows as, under European domination, they would later come to do, but instead in mounds, representative of Sky Woman's daughter's breasts. And into each of these mounds they would place corn, beans, and squash seeds together. This method of planting had two advantages. First, it would save labor. Rather than stringing the beans, the Iroquois women would allow them to climb up the cornstalk. And rather than continuously weeding the garden, the squash leaves, spreading over the ground around the base of the cornstalk, would keep weed growth in check. Second, it would conserve the soil. Corn is notoriously harsh on the soil, draining it of nitrogen, but beans replenish the soil, providing it with the nitrogen that corn consumes.

Inasmuch as women preside over agricultural production, Sky Woman and her daughter center much of the agricultural imagery that finds its way into the Creation. But in the hunting of animal food, a necessity inasmuch as the Iroquois had no domestic animals besides the dog, men take precedence. Thus, the metaphors which append to hunting strategies center on Elder Brother who, under the tutelage of Sky Woman, gave animals their fat. Like the branding of animals in the San Creation, it is the provision of fat in the Iroquois Creation which not only differentiates animals but also makes them edible. Animals without fat pertain to the cave beneath the world, the place where Elder Brother imprisoned Younger Brother, and are dangerous. Animals with fat pertain to the beneficent power of the Sky World and are medicine: the medicinal quality residing in the fat itself. This is the significance of the oil bath and a friend, upon reciting the story to me, mentioned that the animals were not easily differentiated until they gained their fat: "Oh, they were all sort of gray and dull and you couldn't really tell the difference of one from another until they had their fat. Then their fur became bushy and shiny and colorful! Oh, it was something to see!"

Existing in tandem with the concept of food, then, is that of medicine. Animal fat is medicinal as are, for instance, the first sap of the maple and early strawberries. But the premier Iroquois medicine is tobacco. Tobacco comes into play early on in the story with the discussion of the Celestial Tree in the Sky World. From its roots sprout fragrant leaves of tobacco and Grandmother Sky Woman clutched some of these as she fell from the Sky World. Later still we see tobacco spring from the forehead of Sky Woman's daughter when she is buried and the importance of that incident, happening precisely when the Three Sisters enter Turtle Island, cannot be overstated. When my friend told me the story she said quietly and reverentially, "and from her dear forehead sprang ... tobacco." She paused before the word tobacco and spoke it even more softly than the rest of the sentence. It is tobacco, after all, which allows us to speak to the gods for its smoke carries our words up to the Sky World where our prayers can be heard and answered. But two very different medicinal principles are alluded to in the story: the first, a beneficent spiritual power established by Elder Brother's placing of fat in food animals, is called *orenda*;

the second, a malevolent spiritual power characterized by scavenging animals without fat and unhealthy to eat, is called *otgont*.[6]

As important as the creation of plants and animals—and the various medicines—is the creation of humans who will simultaneously exploit and live in continuum with these seminal resources. And inasmuch as Elder Brother undertook that final creative act, he is often referred to as the Creator. In one version of the Creation recited to me, a striking element was added to the episode which speaks of the creation of humanity. Here, Elder Brother not only created man, but he created him from the red clay of a riverbank, he created the "red man" and placed him deliberately on Turtle Island (i.e., North America). This modern addition warrants comment. Many Iroquois dispute the assertion that Native Americans came to North America over the Bering land bridge. Their point, then, is that the Creator, Elder Brother, prepared Turtle Island specifically for the Native American whom he placed within its protective confines. The only immigrants from the Native perspective then are those whom the Iroquois (sometimes disparagingly but usually just matter-of-factly) call Anglos and to whom I have heard some Iroquois teasingly refer as "the original boat people."

Thus, beyond a sanctification of subsistence strategies, depending on a wide array of ecological metaphors, the Iroquois Creation elaborates an ideal configuration of cosmic order through the deployment of a number of sociological metaphors—expressing male and female spheres of activity, for instance, or Iroquois/Anglo interaction. The elaboration starts with the impregnation of Sky Woman's daughter, something that Sky Woman looks at with foreboding. In fact, this pregnancy brings death into the world through Younger Brother's unnatural birth through his mother's armpit and his triumphant act—reported in some versions of the Creation—of standing on his mother's dead body. And then Sky Woman's daughter's ascent to the Sky World offers a first pathway between Turtle Island and that primordial place of power: Sky World. That path, the Ash Way, is the conduit which carries Elder Brother's beneficent power, *orenda*, to Turtle Island. But there is another path that exists between Turtle Island and the cave beneath the world where Younger Brother is imprisoned. It was along this path, according to some versions of the Creation, that Younger Brother secured his bag of loathsome and poisonous animals: rattlesnakes, harmful insects, and flesh-eating worms. And though imprisoned in this cave, along with all manner of dangerous animals, Younger Brother still seeks to emerge, "and his voice is heard giving orders" in that gruesome place. And along with that awful voice arises the malevolent power *otgont*.[7]

Accordingly, Elder Brother, the Creator, resides in the Sky World as the Sun whence he reigns down blessings on his human creatures for as long as they propitiate him with tobacco. Grandmother too resides in the Sky World as the moon and watches over her grandson's creation. Younger Brother resides in the cave beneath the world, a continuous source of disorder ready to break out and overwhelm the Earth—herself a god, Grandmother's daughter and the Twins' Mother—from whom springs forth that other set of seminal deities, the *Diohekon*. The aged Grandmother, Sky Woman, mediates the struggle between her two grandsons: the one representing order, *orenda*, emanating from the Sky World; the other representing chaos, *otgont*, emanating from the cave beneath the world. Further, Elder Brother's *orenda* not only animates the medicinal quality of animal fat—and the healthful animals (deer, bear, and beaver, for instance) which are differentiated one from the other by it. It also animates the state of peace, medicine societies, the emblematic medicine, tobacco, and by extension the holders of that medicine, the Iroquois themselves. Younger Brother's *otgont* conversely animates proscribed animals (such as the loon, fox, mink, and weasel), war, witches, the primary medicine of the Anglos, alcohol, and by extension, the holders of that medicine, Anglos themselves. The aged Grandmother represents the confluence of the two and, notably, she makes no attempt to convert the poorer to the better cause. In fact, as some versions of the Creation make clear, she prefers Younger Brother to Elder Brother. This preference on a general level corresponds to the Native American's penchant for championing the underdog—something we witnessed in the story of the No Account Boy—but it also underscores the essential nature of disorder in Iroquois cosmology, expressing the fact that order cannot be rendered meaningful without is troublesome complement.

The cosmic order espoused in the Creation is solidified in Iroquois ritual life. Iroquois calendrical ritual corresponds directly to the Iroquois Creation by propitiating, through reenactment, the acts of the major deities and thus insuring that their blessings are always at hand. Since the time of the Iroquois prophet, Handsome Lake, around 1800, Iroquois calendrical ritual has been codified in six major ceremonies. The year opens and closes with the Midwinter or New Year Ceremony in late January or early February in which all deities are propitiated and medicines renewed. It proceeds through the Maple Sap (late March, early April), Corn Planting (early May), Green Corn (late May), Strawberry (May), and Corn Harvest (August) Ceremonies, to return finally to the Midwinter Ceremony once more. In each of these ceremonies, a special element of the Iroquois agricultural calendar is propitiated through prayers, songs, dances, and a feast highlighting whichever element (perhaps wild strawberries) that is being propitiated. The year ends and begins with the Midwinter ceremony, when the Sun (Elder Brother, the Creator) enters his solstice, and the Moon (Grandmother) has begun to wax once more, and the Pleides constellation (seven brothers whose intensely spiritualized dancing caused them to rise into the sky) appears. During this ceremony, the Creator and all his creation are emphatically worshipped and nearly every ritual that accompanies the five other calendrical holidays is performed. Thus, the year opens and closes with an undertaking of Iroquois ritual life in its entirety.

Iroquoian Political Structure

The sociological metaphors at the center of the Creation arise especially from the unique political structure of the Iroquois Confederacy. But in order to thoroughly unpack these metaphors, we must consider one more story. As singular within the Iroquois narrative repertoire as is the Creation, this story deals with the bringing of the Great Peace to the originally unallied Iroquoian nations which had, up until that point, been in a state of constant warfare against one another. As the story goes, a baby was born immaculately to a Huron maiden whose mother, in shame, attempted to kill it. But despite her many attempts—setting it in a roaring flame and placing it beneath the sheet of ice that covered James Bay—she would each night find the child suckling at his mother's breast, the two safely wrapped in a warm bearskin blanket. The child, growing into manhood, was rejected by the Huron so he traveled by a stone canoe across Lake Ontario until he set foot in the territory of the Onondaga Nation. In the meantime, the Mohawk, Hiawatha, had lost his five daughters to the malicious magic of the sorcerer Osinoh. Disconsolate, he set out for the wilderness until he arrived in the Onondaga territory. There, he encountered the Huron prophet: Peacemaker. The prophet soothed Hiawatha's seemingly unbearable grief whereupon the two, Peacemaker and Hiawatha, went to subdue the monster Adodarho. This deformed man floated upon a nest of snakes within a desolate swamp. His hair was a mass of writhing snakes and he howled in unbearable anguish. Peacemaker sent Hiawatha forward to comb the snakes from Adodarho's hair, an act we earlier encountered when we considered Inuit culture, and to massage the seven crooks out of his debilitated frame. So consoled, Adodarho became peaceable and the *otgont*—the malevolent power that emanated from him in the form of witchcraft, illness, and warfare—was instantly replaced with *orenda*: the beneficent power which washed the world in medicinal dances, healthfulness, and peaceful alliance. Peacemaker established Adodarho as the first of fifty Peace Chiefs and Hiawatha as the second and, from then on, the Seneca, Cayuga, Onondaga, Oneida, and Mohawk— all of whom provided Peace Chiefs to the Iroquoian council house—never went to war against one another again.

Yet, to this story one must add a little-known episode referred to as the Mother of Nations. I have never actually heard this story recited in its entirety. Nor have I read a version of it in any book. Rather, I have been told what it's about in bits and pieces from various sources. The Mother of Nations was said to be from the Onondaga Nation, though I have also heard that she was a member of the Neutral Nations that lived just to the east of the Iroquois Confederacy in what is today Pennsylvania, Ontario, and Ohio. And one woman told me that she was Sky Woman's daughter, the first woman to be born on Turtle Island. This Mother of Nations seemed to glory in accounts of warfare and she would parlay the gossip she received from visiting warriors into further intelligence: egging the warriors on through offering bits of information and flattery and, thereby, stoking the conflict. That was until she one day encountered Peacemaker on his mission to pacify the Iroquois. He commanded her to cease her warmongering: to henceforth urge men towards peace rather than feats of war. And he gave her the title, Mother of Nations, which she carries to this day. Reminiscent of the onetime warrior woman, Nafanua, who became the sponsor of Samoa's governing assemblies, it would be the Mother of Nation's duty, from then on, to arbitrate grievances and to render a binding accord between warring parties.

The story of Peacemaker and the Mother of Nations relates in a most direct manner to the Iroquoian political system. In this system, Peace Chiefs, War Chiefs, and Clan Mothers function very much like three branches of government: A set of 50 Peace Chiefs, each representing a single clan of a single nation, legislates. A set of War Chiefs, selected from the various villages of the five allied nations, is responsible for the alliance's defense but also listens to the Peace Chiefs' councils. The War Chiefs are regularly described as the eyes and ears of the Clan Mothers, reporting on the Peace Chiefs' various councils to these women who have watched the Peace Chiefs since they were boys. It is on the basis of these lifelong observations that the Clan Mothers nominate the Peace Chiefs. The Clan Mothers, representing (like the Peace Chiefs) the various clans of the various nations, nominate and impeach the Peace Chiefs. If a Peace Chief (contrary to the character traits that allowed the Clan Mothers to nominate him in the first place) counsels out of self-interest or personal antagonism, the Clan Mothers are within their rights to impeach him. In essence then, the Clan Mothers wield the power of ratification (by not taking any action after receiving an account of the Peace Chiefs' council from the War Chiefs) as well as veto (by impeaching the Peace Chiefs after the War Chief's report). From the Iroquois perspective, no one is more qualified to impeach a Peace Chief than the Clan Mothers. As one woman put it: "We women are the ones who know who should be a Peace Chief or a War Chief. We've watched the men since they were little boys. If they take things too personal, try to get back at others, they may make good War Chiefs but not Peace Chiefs. But if they don't take things personal, let it slide like water off a duck's back, now that boy will make a good Peace Chief." As if this unique plan of checks and balances alone were not enough to uphold the democratic ideal characteristic of the Iroquois, the Confederacy historically took democracy a step further than most governmental systems would be willing to go. The Peace Chiefs were unable to legislate without unanimity of opinion. Thus, a majority could never undermine the rights of a minority.

Notice how exactingly the story of Peacemaker and the Mother of Nations reflects the constellation of characters that populate the Iroquois Creation. Standing in the place of Sky Woman is the Mother of Nations. Standing in the place of Elder Brother is Hiawatha. And standing in the place of Younger Brother is Adodarho. But notice as well how the story of Peacemaker and the Mother of Nations reflects Iroquoian political structure. Just as the Mother of Nations animates the spirit of the Clan Mothers, Hiawatha (before Adodarho's conversion and elevation) animates the spirit of Iroquoian Peace Chiefs, and Adodarho (before Peacemaker subdued him, converting the worse to the better cause) animates the spirit of Iroquoian War Chiefs. It is as if the spirit of the gods (Sky Woman, Elder Brother, and Younger Brother) is transferred via the heroes (the Mother of Nations, Hiawatha, and Adodarho) to the three branches of the Iroquoian polity (Clan Mothers, Peace Chiefs, and War Chiefs). Thus, a political system is sanctified by its likeness in the Sky World and the gods are rendered all the more meaningful by carrying the stamp of the human institutions which they sponsor. Sociological metaphors aptly create a cosmic order which is to be found reflected throughout Iroquoian culture. If we think back to the No Account Boy, for instance, this order is manifested in the figures of the No Account Boy's Grandmother, the No Account Boy himself, and the Naked Bear. It is, in the final analysis, this ideal cosmic order—triadic in nature and fleshed out with such ecological metaphors as the Three Sisters and sociological metaphors as the Clan Mothers, Peace Chiefs, and War Chiefs—that form the nucleus of Iroquoian ideology. And this cosmic order—comprehending so much of Iroquoian culture—allows us to make sense of such abstractions as alliance and peace or enmity and war; beneficent *orenda* or destructive *otgont*; healthfulness and life or disease and death. Ideology, then, consists of a universe of concepts rendered meaningful by the various ecological and sociological metaphors which give it shape, substance, and meaning.

The role of ideology in Iroquoian culture may be most intriguingly expressed by the ascendancy of woman in Iroquoian political thought, an ascendancy that captures the imagination of contemporary Iroquois and Anglos alike and has given rise to speculation as to the level of uniqueness of the Iroquoian polity. Is it unlike any human political structure known to date? That is to say, do women gain the preeminent position in the balance of powers among Clan Mothers, Peace Chiefs, and War Chiefs, creating of the political structure a veritable matriarchy? Many Iroquois today believe so and have told me as much. Yet this is but one of the distinctive features of the Iroquoian Confederacy's political structure: a structure which has been variously credited (sometimes controversially) with the inspiration for the American government, communism, and the women's suffrage movement. A number of Iroquois point out that Benjamin Franklin explicitly credited the Iroquois as the source of some of his ideas—particularly that of Federalism—when contemplating the structure of an American political system. In fact, one woman bluntly told me, "Now I'm going to tell you how you robbed our system of government." The three branches of government, the system of checks and balances, and the rotation of speakers in the legislative process, all point to this theft in her view. The only thing the U.S. missed in her estimation was the importance of the feminine voice in its constitution. As she expressed it, "You left out the women!" Other Iroquois speak of Karl Marx and Friedrich Engels' borrowing of the Iroquoian concept of communalism in order to construct their notion of Communism. Indeed, Marx and Engels had read Lewis Henry Morgan's account of the Iroquois in *Ancient Society*, one of the earliest works of anthropology. Still others are aware that Elizabeth Cady Stanton, the New York suffrage and women's rights activist, explicitly cited her female Iroquois neighbors' political autonomy, ability to buy and sell property, and right to divorce (all of which were denied to Euro-American women) as inspirations to her movement. Lucretia Mott, who organized along with Stanton the 1848 Seneca Falls Convention for women's rights, had earlier that same year visited the Iroquois Cattaraugus Reservation even as a Euro-American style political structure (which would largely disenfranchise Iroquois women) was being discussed by the community.[8] It seems little wonder that the American suffrage movement began in the territories that once belonged to the Iroquois and that the famed Declaration of Sentiments which came out of the Convention was signed by Elizabeth Cady Stanton, Frederick Douglass, and Susan B. Anthony in the town of Seneca Falls, New York. Yet, despite the debt that Americans most likely owe the Iroquois, treatment of the later by the former has sometimes been, simply put, abominable.

The Code of Handsome Lake

Perhaps nothing better expresses the essential nature of ideology to culture than the role it plays when society enters one of its inevitable periods of culture crisis. In fact, there came a time when the Iroquois were destined to lose the well-balanced ecological, sociological, and (indeed) ideological system that was enshrined in the Iroquois Creation, reenacted in Iroquois ritual life, and exemplified in the structure of the Iroquois Confederacy. Defeated in war and relegated to small outposts of their once extensive hunting territories in what is today western New York, the Iroquois became, for a time, a broken people. As reported in the *Gaiwiio*, the "Good Tidings" of the Iroquois prophet Handsome Lake, a group of Iroquois hunters sets out from their reservation, Cornplanter Village, in southwestern New York. As the pack ice melts, they push down the Allegany River in their canoes until they come to Pittsburg, "a little village of white people," or—as the Code literally calls them—Our Younger Brothers.

> Here they barter their skins, dried meat and fresh game for strong drink. They put a barrel of it in their canoes. Now all the canoes are lashed together like a raft. Now all the men become filled with strong drink. The yell and sing like demented people. Those who are in the middle canoes do this. Now they are homeward bound. Now, when they come to where they had left their wives and children, they embark to return home. They go up Cornplanter Creek. Now that the party is home the men revel in strong drink and are very quarrelsome. Because of this the families become frightened and move away for safety. So from many places in the bushlands camp fires send up their smoke. Now the drunken men run yelling through the village and there is no one there except the drunken men. Now they are beastlike and run about without clothing and all have weapons to injure those whom they meet. Now there are no doors left in the houses for they have all been kicked off. So, also, there are no fires in the village and have not been for many days. Now the men full of strong drink have trodden in the fireplaces. They alone track there and there are no fires and their footprints are in all the fireplaces. Now the dogs yelp and cry in all the houses for they are hungry.

Still, rather than succumbing to such desolation, the Iroquois, under the tutelage of Handsome Lake, set about the unenviable task of accommodating themselves to a new agricultural and social order.

In 1797, his nation a smoldering ruin, Handsome Lake lay dying in his family's longhouse, the victim of the latest of a series of evils that had beset the Iroquois: alcohol. Near death, or perhaps just beyond its threshold, he witnessed himself rise out of his body and leave the protective confines of the longhouse and his circle of mourning relatives, enter the clearing before the door of the longhouse, and there witness the Messengers: "three men clothed in fine clean raiment." He describes them as follows: "Their cheeks were painted red and only a few feathers were in their bonnets. All three were alike—middle aged, handsome, commanding men—and they had in one hand bows and arrows while in their other were huckleberry bushes and the berries were of every color." They gave him the medicinal berries to eat, whereupon he began his long and arduous recovery. Over a number of successive visitations, the Messengers instructed Handsome Lake as to the Creator's desires for the Iroquois people, teachings which Handsome Lake transmitted to the Iroquois by means of his Code. Among the most essential teachings was the institution of four preeminent taboos: witchcraft, love magic, abortion, and—most emphatically—alcohol. With the recitation of these four taboos, the *Code* moved on to codify a number of Iroquois social regulations governing marriage, child-rearing, treatment of the elderly, reciprocity, community life, and reverence for the *Diohekon*.

While all these regulations were in keeping with traditional Iroquois ideals, certain accommodations to the Euro-American conquest were inevitable. From here on, the Messengers instructed, the Iroquois would give up their communal longhouses and adopt the Euro-American log cabin. Likewise, communal farming, in the hands of the Clan Mothers, would be replaced with family farming under the auspices of the family's husband and father. In other words, a communal and largely matriarchal ecological adaptation would give way to private property and an explicitly patriarchal system. Since the animals that the Iroquois had heretofore depended upon—particularly deer and black bear—were no longer readily available, Euro-American domestic animals would be raised: primarily cattle, pigs, and chickens. And, further, Euro-American models of education would be (if not explicitly accepted) tentatively explored.

Handsome Lake, upon the completion of the Messengers' instructions, was offered a number of apocalyptic visions. Among them is the Messengers' command to look upon "a house with a spire and a path leading into" it but "none out."

> There was no door, neither were there any windows in the house. Within was a great noise, wailing and crying, and the house was hot. Then the Messengers asked him what he saw. He answered, "I saw a house with a spire and a path leading to the house. There was no door; neither were there any windows in the house. Within was a great noise, wailing and crying, and the house was hot." Then they replied, "You have truly seen. It is a hard matter for Indians to embrace these conditions, that is, to embrace the belief of Bible believers."

The implications are clear. Whereas the new Euro-American ecological order is inescapable, there is a way to remain essentially Iroquois despite it all and that way entails maintaining fidelity to the old gods and the ceremonies they have ordained. Further, the proper place to serve the ancient Iroquois religion is the Longhouse with a door on both its eastern and western ends and its hearth properly situated in the center of the building. To worship in a building without windows and doors, a building with a spire, a building that can be entered but never exited—to worship, that is, in a church—is the very essence of damnation to the Iroquois who remain true at heart. And, if there was still any doubt as to whether the Iroquois should honor their old religion or rather cleave to the new, Handsome Lake offers this final vision:

> So they proceeded on their journey and it happened that a vision appeared unto them. They seemed to be advancing toward an approaching man. Soon they met him and passed. Now when they were a distance apart they turned and he was facing them. So they greeted each other. Then said the man, "Handsome Lake, I must ask you a question. Did you ever hear your grandfathers say that once there was a certain man upon the earth across the great waters who was slain by his own people?" That is what he said when he spoke. Then answered Handsome Lake, "It is true. I have heard my grandparents say this." Then answered the man, "I am he, Seganhedus (He Who Resurrects)." And he turned his palms upward and they were scarred and his feet were likewise and his breast was pierced by a spear wound. It appeared that his hands and his feet were torn by iron nails. All this was true. It could be seen and blood was fresh upon him. Then said the man, "They slew me because of their independence and unbelief. So I have gone home and shut the doors of heaven that they may not see me again until the earth passes away."[9]

Then, Jesus declared that Handsome Lake as well would most likely suffer the people's rejection of his vision, a declaration that proved largely untrue.

Prophets and Revitalization

When a society suffers some sort of stress—drought, disease, rampant crime and antisocial behavior, tyranny, missionary activity, conquest and colonization—it is rife for the emergence of a prophet who can spontaneously enact a revitalization movement: a transformation of society through a reconfiguration of its religion. Prophets, Anthony Wallace suggested in his explication of revitalization movements, emerge under similar historical circumstances: a period of cultural stress gives rise to an individual's visionary reconfiguration of society. Whether the individual gains disciples or not depends largely upon the prophet's ability to communicate and promote his vision of society: that is, on his personal charisma. Where the charisma of the prophet is sufficient to promote his reformulation, we see the revitalization of the society's religious structures—if not the birth of a new religion. Where it is not, the prophet and his vision are forgotten to history. Ecological and sociological changes, if they come at all, will follow only once the prophet's revisioning of his or society's religion is institutionalized. All religions, Wallace expansively claims, are likely the result of successful revitalization movements.[10]

There is the intriguing suggestion in the regularity with which the revitalization process unfolds that without a reconfiguration of a society's ideology, there is little possibility of a transformation of its ecological basis or social structure. The necessary conclusion to such an observation is that ideology is as essential a component to culture as is ecology and society. This does not mean that technological innovations aren't adopted for their own sake or that social relations aren't realigned in the natural course of human affairs. Rather, it means that ideology, as the confluence of ecological and sociological concerns, is the most malleable component of culture and, therefore, the ideal arena for a wholesale reformulation of society. If such were not the case, we would not find revitalization—and the prophets who act as its ambassadors— at the center of so many societal histories.

Of course, one such prophet is Jesus himself. Handsome Lake is yet another. Still, a third, Joseph Smith, created a uniquely Euro-American faith in Western New York: perhaps as a result of the experience of Handsome Lake given the fact that his vision occurred in the ancient Iroquois territory. A fourth, Wovoka, of the Paiute Nation, created a movement which extended well beyond the borders of his own nation and found adherents in a number of Native American nations—including the Lakota. And yet one more, Black Elk, instituted a vision that not only revitalized his own Lakota Nation but also invigorated the budding American Indian Movement (AIM) and its pan–Indian ideology. Still others who find themselves among the ranks of prophets are the Buddha, Nat Turner, and Muhammad. Each of these prophets experienced a mystical state— often, if not always, subject to the parameters of ASC—during which they experienced a vision and, not unusually, a command to preach the nature of their vision to humanity.

Jesus's vision occurred when he went alone into the wilderness and was subjected to the three famous temptations. The Buddha's—also characterized by cruel temptations—occurred under the fated Bodhi Tree. Muhammad's occurred in the cave on Mount Hira wherein—during a period of intense meditation—he was instructed in the Qur'an by the angel Jibril, known in the West as Gabriel. Though often condemned, Nat Turner manifests a history that reads like that of other prophets. While hiding from his master in a lonely wood, Turner witnessed "white spirits and black spirits engaged in battle" as the sun fled away into darkness. "The thunder rolled in the Heavens," and blood flowed in mighty streams. When he finally gathered a small band of slaves about himself and, filled with the Holy Ghost, unleashed god's command, he and his followers left 55 dead—many of them women and children—among the class of slaveholders in Southampton County, Virginia, and the reverberations of the largest slave revolt in U.S. history were such that Harriet Jacobs, in *Incidents in the Life of a Slave Girl*, noted that the whites in her town of Edmonton, North Carolina, redoubled their vigilance lest their slaves, like those of Southampton County, rise up and murder them in their beds. Joseph Smith, while praying in the solitary forests of western New York, was—like Moses before him—presented with the miraculous writings that would form the basis of Mormonism. Wovoka, during a solar eclipse, saw a rejuvenated earth—with all the generations of dead Indians returned as well as the game which they would once again be able to live by—brought on by leading a good, clean life and undertaking the hand-in-hand (or circle) dance. Black Elk, in the course of a childhood illness, received from his six grandfathers in a flaming tepee in the sky the secret of a great medicine which would restore the Lakota people. The medicine was contained in a number of gifts presented by the grandfathers: a bowl which held within it the sky, a bow-and-arrow, a sacred pipe with a spotted eagle feather attached to its stem, and a mysterious herb with blossoms of blue, yellow, red, and white. Fascinatingly, he used that medicine just as Indra used his thunderbolt: to destroy a demon who had swallowed up all the earth's waters. Though the prophet is not characteristically divine, it is not unusually the case that divinity resides within him. Thus, of Muhammad, we are told "that Muhammad is a man. But the Muslim response to the traditional saying that Muhammad is a man is, 'Yes, but like a ruby among stones,' which is to say Muhammad is a man, but he's a very unusual sort of man. He's not divine, but he has the divine in him, in the sense that he is divinely inspired. His character is luminous. His ability to intercede on behalf of Muslims has historically been a very important part of his persona. He is the beloved of God."[11]

The Lakota

Almost one hundred years to the date after the Iroquois experienced the profound teachings of Handsome Lake, the Lakota experienced a cultural upheaval that reverberates throughout Native America to this day. Historically, the Lakota undertook a remarkable ecological adaptation to the North American Great Plains in the mid–17th century. Originally agricultural villagers who had been encountered in what was to become Minnesota by Jesuit missionaries in the mid–1600s, they—with the advent of horses from Spanish Mexico in the early 1700s—dramatically altered their subsistence pattern to become nomadic hunters of buffalo (or, more properly, bison) centering especially on what was to become South Dakota. They maintained this adaptation well into the late 19th century when their life as roving buffalo hunters was no longer tenable.

Throughout their history as nomadic hunters, the Lakota exploited an environment dominated by rolling prairie supporting an abundance of buffalo, antelope, deer, and elk. The prairie was interspersed with ponderosa pine ridges—the pine providing the Lakota with poles for their tepees—and streams along which grew stands of cottonwood: the bark providing them fodder for their horses; the tree itself providing them their famous Sun Dance pole. Further, the cottonwood groves provided the Lakota a good protected place in which to camp. Horses, essential to this new ecology, came to the Lakota along two routes: passing along the eastern edge of the Rockies through Nez Perce and Shoshone territories and from the southern plains trading through a network of Comanche, Cheyenne, and Arapahoe partners. The dog, which the Lakota had long used as a beast of burden and adjunct to the hunt, was quickly displaced as the Lakota's prize domestic animal by the horse. And the name applied to the horse, *šunka wakan*, or sacred dog, linguistically captured the essential nature of this new addition to Lakota technology. Hunting, and particularly the hunting of buffalo, became the mainstay of Lakota ecology but wild vegetal foods such as wild plums and chokecherries with which to make *wozhapi*, a thick berry pudding, were exploited as well. Likewise, the prairie provided various roots, such as wild turnips and onions, which would be collected, braided, and hung to dry. But the Lakota, having long been agriculturalists growing the classic Native American crops—corn, beans, and squash—before giving up their sedentary village life in favor of nomadic hunting did not give up these agricultural products entirely when they adopted a foraging lifestyle. Rather, they would extract corn from farming peoples, sometimes by force.

Comprising the largest division of the *Očeti Šakowin*, or Seven Council Fires, an alliance of Sioux nations forged before the western migration to the Great Plains, the Lakota were, in turn, comprised of an alliance of seven bands, an alliance within an alliance, including the Oglala, the Sičangu, the Hukpapa, the Sihasapa, the Itazipčo, the Oohenopa, and the Miniconjou. But even the bands were subdivided. The encampment, or *tiyošpaye*, is described by Elizabeth Grobsmith as the "basic unit of social life" for the Lakota. It consisted of the thirty or so families—generally a group of brothers and male cousins along with their wives and children—who lived, traveled, and hunted together and, in many cases, became the nucleus for the settled communities that characterize Lakota reservation life to this day.[12] But even the encampment could be looked at as an alliance of families, each living within its own tepee. Thus, the Lakota, previous to the conquest of their land by the *Wasichus* (as they called Euro-Americans) and the replacement of their round tepee by the pioneer's square log cabin, viewed their alliance of nations, bands, encampments, and families through the metaphor of the sacred Hoop of the Nation. In the Oglala shaman Black Elk's words:

> You have noticed that everything an Indian does is in a circle, and that is because the Power of the World always works in circles, and everything tries to be round. In the old days when we were a strong and happy people, all our power came to us from the sacred hoop of the

nation, and so long as the hoop was unbroken, the people flourished. The flowering tree was the living center of the hoop, and the circle of the four quarters nourished it. The east gave peace and light, the south gave warmth, the west gave rain, and the north with its cold and mighty wind gave strength and endurance. This knowledge came to us from the outer world with our religion. Everything the Power of the World does is done in a circle. The sky is round, and I have heard that the earth is round like a ball. And so are all the stars. The wind, in its greatest power, whirls. Birds make their nests in circles, for theirs is the same religion as ours. The sun comes forth and goes down again in a circle. The moon does the same, and both always come back again to where they were. The life of a man is a circle from childhood to childhood, and so it is in everything where power moves. Our tepees were round like the nests of birds, and these were always set in a circle, the nation's hoop, a nest of many nests, where the Great Spirit meant for us to hatch our children. But the Wasichus have put us in these square boxes. Our power is gone and we are dying, for the power is not in us anymore.[13]

Notice how thoroughly spirituality pervades something as seemingly ordinary and practical as social organization for the Lakota. While it seems natural to view Lakota society as a nesting of social units such as the family, the encampment, the band, the nation, and the alliance, alternatively viewing that nesting in the light of the metaphor of the sacred hoop of the nation—circles within circles, all deriving their spiritual energy from the world of nature of which they form an integral part—adds a spiritual aura to Lakota social order that makes of it something more, something richer, than simply a network of social relations. Then, when adding to such a conception, the notion of the utterly foreign square—without indigenous significance, devoid of spiritual power, disconnected from the world of nature, an unwelcome symptom of conquest—the notion of the spirituality of the conception of the nation's sacred hoop is thrown, if at all possible, into even bolder relief. One could certainly describe Lakota social order as it appears through various behavioral manifestations, such as settlement patterns, or conversely as it is perceived through a rich array of spiritually charged metaphors. But it isn't altogether clear that the description would be complete without a consideration of both.

Lakota Spirituality

Although the Lakota suffered a brutal military conquest, the repeated theft of their lands through callous disregard of treaties, and crushing levels of prejudicial behavior exhibited to this day among some of their non–Native American neighbors, they have managed to maintain a delicate balance between a Lakota worldview, an ideology in which they could still envision themselves as belonging to the sacred Hoop of the Nation, and the inevitabilities of western ecologies in which the buffalo hunt and life in the *tiyošpaye* were no longer possible. Grobsmith describes this singular accommodation: "Although assimilation had occurred on one level—in the use of western technology and so forth—it had not occurred at a deeper level. What was the result of the adoption of a western style of life while personal goals and motivations derived their meaning from a different—a native—set of precepts? What adjustments did (and do) Lakota make to accommodate the dominant society's rules? And to what extent were contemporary problems such as alcoholism a result of this juxtaposition of two rather radically different traditions?"[14] The fact that Lakota ideology retains its relevancy, despite dramatic alterations to the Lakota ecology and social structure, suggests that there is something of intrinsic value to its universe of indigenous metaphors, something which allows the Lakota people to continuously adjust to the twists and turns of a sometimes tumultuous history.

And, in fact, one can sometimes catch a glimmer of that adjustment in the conceptualization of that most essential Lakota metaphor: the buffalo. The Lakota made their onetime dependence upon and appreciation for the buffalo explicit in an intriguing story collected by the Native American anthropologist, Ella Deloria. *The Buffalo People* speaks of a young man who found himself married to both a corn and buffalo maiden by each of whom he had a young son: a *ziwinla*, a pale boy with a yellow complexion and hair light and fine like corn silk, and a little buffalo calf boy with large brown eyes and luxurious black hair. While the corn maiden was gentle and full of helpful magic, the buffalo maiden was somewhat capricious, unpredictable, and easily took offense at an even unintended slight. One day, resuming her buffalo form, she took the little buffalo calf boy away from his father and returned to her tribe of buffalo people. But, happily, with her own magic tassels, the corn maiden gave her husband the means of retrieving his little buffalo calf son. Still, each time he caught up with his fleeing buffalo wife and child, the irate buffalo maiden set forth a test to confound her unhappy husband. At one point, when she and her son had resumed their place in the buffalo herd, she demanded that her husband be able to distinguish their son from the other buffalo boys but the buffalo calf boy came to his father's rescue, frantically twitching his ear to ensure that his father would be able to pick him out of the teeming herd of buffalo calves. With the finding of his son and the soothing of his buffalo wife's injured feelings, the young man was integrated into the tribe of the buffalo people. The little buffalo calf boy became thereby the progenitor of the Lakota people but the corn maiden was not forgotten. Due to her magical aid, she—and her son by the young man—became the progenitors of the Arikara, agricultural people who grew corn, beans, and squash and who—on the basis of their ancient kinship ties with the buffalo people—would provide them with stores of dried corn to carry them through the harsh winters of the Great Plains.[15]

Yet, the ecological adaptation made by the Lakota with the advent of horses and which resides at the center of *The Buffalo People* was destined to fall apart. The plains would be taken from them and the teeming herds of buffalo would, sometimes purposefully, be decimated by an encroaching population of *Wasichus*. The Lakota would need a new means of surviving and a new metaphor to sanctify it. Consider then the words of the Lakota shaman, Black Elk: "There is a story about the way the pipe first came to us. A very long time ago, two scouts were out looking for bison. When they came to the top of a hill and looked north," they saw someone approaching. As the figure drew near, they saw that it was that of a woman, "young and very beautiful," wearing "a fine white buckskin dress." And "one of the scouts, being foolish, had bad thoughts and spoke them; but the other said: 'This is a sacred woman; throw away all bad thoughts.'" The woman, understanding the foolish scout's intentions, spoke, saying: "If you wish to do as you think, you may come." And as the foolish scout went to her, he became enveloped in a white cloud which, upon dissipating, revealed what he had become: "a skeleton covered with worms." Then the woman instructed the righteous scout saying, "You shall go home and tell your people that I am coming and that a big tepee shall be built for me in the center of the nation." This the man did. And as the people awaited the sacred woman around the newly built teepee, they saw her coming, "very beautiful and singing." And as she sang, "there came from her mouth a white cloud," fragrant and holy. Within the teepee, she presented "the chief a pipe with a bison calf carved on one side to mean the earth that bears and feeds us, and with twelve eagle feathers hanging from the stem to mean the sky and the twelve moons." And, of this pipe, she said, "Behold! With this you shall multiply and be a good nation. Nothing but good shall come from it." Then, still singing, she left the tepee. And, "as the people watched her going," she became "a white bison galloping away and snorting, and soon she was gone."[16]

The significance of this pipe, the gift of White Buffalo Calf Woman, to a people whose very existence depended upon the bison is underscored in the ritual life of the Lakota for whom every religious ritual is centered upon its use. And its provisor, White Buffalo Calf Woman herself, figures prominently in this ritual life: her impersonator, for instance, landing the last stroke of the axe on the cottonwood tree selected for the Sun Dance.[17] In fact, with the visitation of White Buffalo Calf Woman, Lakota ritual became more firmly centered upon the Seven Sacred Rites. For the young man, the most important of these is the spectacular sequence which opens with a purifying Sweat Lodge Bath, proceeds through a solitary Vision Quest undertaken out upon the open plains, and culminates in the brutally ecstatic Sun Dance. During the Vision Quest, the initiate would take himself off to a secluded locale, perhaps among the sacred Black Hills, and—while praying and fasting—literally cry aloud to be visited upon by a vision. The vision would provide him not only with a spiritual ally upon whom he could call in time of need but also a series of songs and a set of ritual paraphernalia with which he might bestow honor upon his spirit ally. During the four-day Sun Dance, the initiate would gaze persistently at the sun while dancing about a Sun Dance pole to which he was affixed by rawhide thongs attached to a skewer which was run under the skin of his chest, piercing not only the skin but also the pectoral muscle just beneath it. With a violent charge, he would tear himself free from the Sun Dance pole, ripping open his chest, and emerging simultaneously into manhood and warrior status.

Likewise, a Lakota girl could undertake a ritual initiation into womanhood upon the advent of her first menstruation with the Buffalo Ceremony: "At the onset of the menstrual flow the girl was secluded in a special hut." There, for the three-day seclusion period, she worked at decorative porcupine quill work. "At the end of this time she was purified in a sweat bath. Then her father's respect relatives brought many fine things as presents: horses, beautifully worked gowns, bags, pouches," to be distributed in the most important Lakota social ritual, the Giveaway. In the Giveaway, held not only in honor of a girl's passage to womanhood but also at the birth of a child, a wedding, or a funeral, goods were generously distributed throughout the *tiyošpaye*. The Giveaway, in fact, was the means by which the Lakota maintained reciprocal economic relations—not unlike what we earlier witnessed among the San. As the Buffalo Ceremony proceeded, "a woman of outstanding character—chaste, gentle, and quiet—was chosen to wash the girl ceremonially, and then she was dressed in lovely new clothes and escorted to the ceremonial tepee."

> A man who had dreamed the Buffalo Spirit was chosen to officiate, for such a man knew the proper ceremony and could also endow the girl with the blessings and aid of his spirit. Anyone could look on at the ceremony, but only those who had previously had the ceremony performed for them could take their places as honored guests. The ceremony was to insure for the girl supernatural aid from the Buffalo Spirit in obtaining virtues which she would have for life. At the conclusion of the ceremony the gifts were given away in the girl's name and, since she was the cause for such a Giveaway, those who had received gifts thanked the girl. A girl who had been so distinguished was supposed to be generous and hospitable, kind and chaste. In adult life if such a woman were stingy, lewd, or unkind she had obviously repudiated her prestige, and of her the people would say, "A mere fragment of one who has been sung over in buffalo style. A fine buffalo woman she turned out to be!"[18]

Beyond these ceremonies, White Buffalo Calf Woman authorized the Keeping of the Soul for one year after death, the Making of Relatives, instituted when those ancient relatives—the Lakota (i.e., the Buffalo People) and the Arikara (i.e., the People of the Corn)—were reunited in friendship, and the Throwing of the Ball—in which a sacred ball was thrown by a young girl in the four cardinal directions and, finally, into the sky in celebration of Wakan Tanka, the Lakota Creator who, it is sometimes said, contains all other gods within his person and whose most visible manifestation is the Sun.

It seems likely that the story of White Buffalo Calf Woman may have gained greater immediacy for the Lakota at a time when both the herds of buffalo on which they lived and the Lakota themselves were in decline as a result of the Euro-American conquest. If so, it is as if the declining buffalo, the one-time strength of the Lakota people, provided for their replacement in the form of a medicinal ceremony: the offering of sacred tobacco to the one God, Wakan Tanka, of whom all other gods are manifestations. It is as if, though the Lakota would no longer exist as buffalo hunters, they would nonetheless maintain their identity as the Lakota people born, at once, of the abundance and subsequent degeneration of the teeming herds of the Great Plains. If such is the case, it would seem that ideology—and particularly its religious dimension—is the arena where adjustments to altered environmental and sociological conditions are most readily accommodated and where the dissonance between an indigenous worldview and a western technology alluded to by Grobsmith might be minimized.

Ghost Dance and Wounded Knee

Along with the ascension of White Buffalo Calf Woman—and the Seven Sacred Rites—came a trend in which Lakota identity was augmented by a kind of pan–Indian identity: an identity centering on Native American as well as national identity. In other words, one was simultaneously Native American—or Indian, as most of my Native American friends tended to say—and Lakota. This pan–Indian identity often arose out of the worst abuses perpetrated against Native Americans, as if a commonality of mistreatment of various Native American nations forged a new cultural identity which did not replace but rather augmented the old. The Iroquois were among the earliest Native Americans who—having become entangled in the colonial rivalries of first Britain and France, then Britain and America—had to radically adjust to their transformation from essential and equal participants in the French and Indian Wars to a conquered and dispossessed people on the heels of the American Revolution. The Lakota as well had to contend with a dehumanizing conquest. A century later than the Iroquois, the Lakota were facing strikingly similar circumstances, circumstances culminating in the Ghost Dance movement and the massacre at Wounded Knee Creek on the Pine Ridge Reservation: home to the Oglala Band of the Lakota of which Black Elk was a member.

In the late 19th century, the Lakota, as the result of the American conquest of their nation and the resultant depletion of their resources, experienced a profound cultural collapse. Not being able to adjust to a Euro-American farming strategy (as was demanded of them by the U.S. government) because their land was unsuited to such an ecology, they turned to a prophet, the Paiute healer Wovoka (known also by his English name, Jack Wilson) who preached of a revival of Indian spirituality and well-being as well as a return of Native American sovereignty and the abundant game which sustained it. Wovoka had experienced a vision in which he was told that by undertaking a circular hand-in-hand dance and living a good, clean life, all the dead members of his nation and, in fact, all Indian nations, would return to life along with the basis of their subsistence: the game which had year-by-year diminished to such an extent that Native Americans could no longer survive without adopting Euro-American agro-pastoral strategies.[19] He explained his vision in a letter:

> All Indians must dance, everywhere, keep on dancing. Pretty soon in next spring Great Spirit come. He bring back all game of every kind. The game be thick everywhere. All dead Indians come back and old blind Indian see again and get young and have fine time. When Great Spirit comes this way, then all Indians go to mountains, high up away from whites. Whites can't hurt Indians then. Then while Indians way up high, big flood comes like water and all white people die, get drowned. After that, water go way and then nobody but Indians everywhere and game all kinds thick. Then medicine-man tell Indians to send word to all Indians to keep up dancing and the good time will come.[20]

Wovoka's vision was carried back to the Pine Ridge reservation. The Lakota at Pine Ridge were almost completely demoralized by the time Wovoka's Ghost Dance arrived at their reservation. Not only had they been brutally suppressed by the United States, probably at least partly to avenge their unexpected victory at Greasy Grass (or Little Big Horn) against George Armstrong Custer, but also treaty after treaty which they negotiated with the United States was rescinded. The last blow to the Lakota was the discovery of gold, "that yellow metal," as Black Elk described it, "that makes the Wasichus crazy," in their sacred Black Hills: a discovery which they knew spelled their loss of this last vestige of their once expansive territory. In such precarious circumstances, the Lakota people turned to the Ghost Dance religion in the hope of a return to their pre-conquest conditions. No less a dignitary than the leader of the Hunkpapa Band of Lakota, Sitting Bull, was consulted by the U.S. agent James McLaughlin to put a stop to what was mistakenly considered by the American forces to be a preparation for war (i.e., a war dance). But when Sitting Bull sensibly suggested to McLaughlin that the two of them travel to Nevada together to meet with

Wovoka and decide for themselves whether the Dance was nonsense or not, McLaughlin ordered Sitting Bull's arrest: during the perpetration of which Sitting Bull was shot and killed by agents of the American government.[21]

And in this climate of fear and misunderstanding, not to mention intrigue and deception, a tragedy unfolded: American forces fired upon Ghost Dancers. As the dancers—including many women and children—fled up a dry gulch, the bullets from the American Gatling guns mowed them down. Here is Black Elk's description of the aftermath of the massacre at Wounded Knee:

> Men and women and children were heaped and scattered all over the flat at the bottom of the little hill where the soldiers had their wagon-guns, and westward up the dry gulch all the way to the high ridge, the dead women and children and babies were scattered. When I saw this I wished that I had died too, but I was not sorry for the women and children. It was better for them to be happy in the other world. It was a good winter day when all this happened. The sun was shining. But after the soldiers marched away from their dirty work, a heavy snow began to fall. The wind came up in the night. There was a big blizzard, and it grew very cold. The snow drifted deep in the crooked gulch, and it was one long grave of butchered women and children and babies, who had never done any harm and were only trying to run away.[22]

Black Elk, as Alice Kehoe has cogently argued, may have—disheartened and perhaps even partly broken by the events he witnessed—nonetheless found the means for a revitalized Lakota identity arising out of the ashes of Wounded Knee. He elevated the likely traditional tale of White Buffalo Calf Women to a place of new spiritual prominence: celebrating her role as provisor and patron of the sacred Chanunpa (pipe) in which tobacco would be used as a medicinal curative during the Seven Sacred Rites of the Lakota people. Through participation in these rites—and especially today the Sweat Lodge, Vision Quest, Sun Dance sequence—Lakota identity has emerged as a major vehicle of not simply Lakota but in fact Native American identity in the United States.

In fact, the shared memory of Wounded Knee, more than any other single instance in the long and troublesome history of Anglo-Indian relations, has offered a singular focus to the political arm of pan–Indianism, the American Indian Movement, or AIM, for when AIM decided to take its stand in defense of not simply the Lakota but, in fact, of all Indian people, it went to the Pine Ridge Reservation. It went, in fact, to Wounded Knee Creek. There, members of AIM assented to the pleas of local Oglala women who, using the traditional rhetorical device of weeping aloud as they pled for help, asked members of AIM if they were willing to fight for their people. In 1973, when two Lakota women, Helen Moves Camp and Gladys Bissonette, approached AIM members during a dinner at a Pine Ridge reservation community center, weeping aloud and pleading that the activists, including Dennis Banks, be willing "to fight for Indian people," and fight specifically at Wounded Knee, they were linguistically casting modern political activists in the mold of traditional Lakota warriors, such as those who fell before the gunfire of U.S. forces at Wounded Knee Creek in 1890. In Kehoe's words, they "not only spoke in terms of nineteenth-century Lakota values, but they used traditional Lakota formal oratorical discourse, including crying as a sign of sincerity in their pleas," calling upon the Lakota practice of *hanbleceya,* or "crying for a vision."[23] A neutral interpretation of the event would simply be that the women were asking for the help of political activists in the face of political oppression. But understanding the rhetorical heft of Moves Camp's and Bissonette's oration allows us to understand that the women were asking the AIM activists to restore the traditional Lakota warrior's ethos which they believed had been lost in the face of continuing affronts to Native American sovereignty. It was in this environment that, under the tutelage of Leonard Crow Dog who told them the story of White Buffalo Calf Woman and tutored them in the Seven Sacred Rites of the Lakota people, members of AIM reoccupied the mass grave of their ancestors, only to be once more shot upon by the American authorities. As is the case with the massacre at Wounded Knee Creek nearly a century earlier, it is not easy to get a handle on how the shooting actually broke out but, once it did, the memories of the earlier incident become indelibly entangled with those of the latter.

As a result of this second conflagration, AIM activist Leonard Peltier— despite requests for clemency on the part of Amnesty International, the Southern Christian Leadership Conference, and numerous other human rights organizations—remains in federal prison. As a result of a shoot-out on the Oglala Pine Ridge reservation in which two FBI agents and one Native American were killed, Peltier was brought up on charges in the 39th Circuit Court in Milwaukee. As his defense attorney Stephen Glynn recounts, the Milwaukee jury was apparently deadlocked, Judge Christ Seraphim was prepared to declare a mistrial, and the prosecutor did not intend to retry the case. Then, Leonard Crow Dog, "who carried the sacred peace pipe of Sitting Bull," instructed Glynn to allow the trial to proceed and let the jury announce its verdict. Glynn, not surprisingly, remonstrated. Leonard Crow Dog, Glynn reports, said "Look, I don't think you understand. I know what is going to happen here. There will be two or three electrical storms, with lightning, and then the jury will come back with a not-guilty verdict." Glynn was, of course, apprehensive: "I walked back to the courthouse and I thought, 'This is going to turn on how many times lightning strikes?' That night, in the depth of winter, Glynn stood on his apartment balcony and watched 'a lightning storm like I have never seen before.' A few hours later, the jury was back with a not-guilty verdict after deliberating 11 hours." Yet, the acquittal "was little more than an academic exercise," for Peltier had already been convicted "in federal court in Fargo, N.D., of killing" the agents eight months earlier."[24]

5. Anthropomorphic Metaphors and Identification

Mythic Identification

Though the world's mythologies depend so heavily upon ecological and sociological metaphors, there is yet another set of metaphors that finds its way into our religious life. Encapsulated in the human form itself, it catches up a wide array of symbols expressed through the human body and body image, human actions and gestures, even characteristic attributes and utterances. These anthropomorphic metaphors are—like their ecological and sociological cousins— found globally and many cross-cultural boundaries: the right and the left hand; the head, the breast and arms, the belly and thighs, the legs and feet; the Eye of Providence; Horus' Eye; the beating heart of a sacrificial victim lifted up to receive the embrace of the Sun; Waterbug's heart gingerly balanced over the spot where Zuni Pueblo will be raised up. Rosy-Fingered Dawn creeps over the horizon. Zeus nods his head and vast Olympus reels. Thor knits his brow and mankind quakes in fear. In such imagery, spirit itself—whether in the guise of a deity or a demigod, an ancestor or a ghost, an angel or a demon, a saint or a monster—becomes a metaphor which contains the ecological and sociological within its bounds.

In other words, spirit—existing at the apex of the ideological realm of culture—is the symbolic plane where culture's ecological and sociological realms intersect. Or, we might say, the ecological and sociological realms of culture are incorporated into the body of the spirit—simultaneously creating of spirit a metaphor which is necessarily anthropomorphic (human form) and reliably polyvalent (signifying multiple meanings simultaneously). To bring clarity to this suggestion, imagine the tormented body of a deity who, when he stretches out his right and left hands, is sociologically described as a lord or a king or a son but ecologically as a shepherd bringing his sheep and goats into their folds. Think of a deity who is called mother by an entire nation, who strikes the earth with her digging stick—the primary gathering implement of the nation's women as they search the parched earth for roots—in order to provide the nation with its water sources, and who—before leaving the earth—offers up a body part to each clan of her nation as one of its reservoirs of totems. The interrelationship of Hindu castes—precisely the locus where Indian ecological and sociological concerns intersect—is expressed in the context of the body of Brahma, the Creator: Brahmins are his head; Kshatriyas are his arms and shoulders; Vaisyas are his thighs and legs; Shudras are his feet. But Dalits—whose lives are marked by abuse and disdain—inhabit no part of the Creator's body. In myth, the human form is the precise site where our physical and social environments most fully coincide. Thus, anthropomorphic metaphors express a synthesis of these two environments. And, tellingly, such is as true in the case of spirit-animal deities—who continuously behave and look human-like—as it is of anthropomorphic deities who sometimes—as we have seen in the case San and Lakota spirits—retain both animal names and habits.

We earlier discussed the fact that culture is necessarily dialogic: arising out of the polyphony of voices that characterize society. Given the essential relationship of culture and language, one might fairly define culture as the sum total of signs—verbal, behavioral, and material cues—that are characteristically utilized in a society in order to foster communication and, to necessarily thereby, foster cultural affiliation: the principal of unity within a group. The process of using signs to foster affiliation is what we might call, following Kenneth Burke's lead, rhetoric.[1] Whereas we often think of the term rhetoric in the context of oration, and particularly political oration, it is clear from the earliest analyses of rhetoric, for example that undertaken by Aristotle, that rhetoric was historically viewed not simply as some august philosophical concept (and most certainly not as empty words) but rather as an organic part of indigenous culture: that part which doesn't simply seek to persuade but as well seeks to forge a sense of affiliation among a society's member. This affiliation is the result of social bonds solidified by the perception, among members of the group under question, of a commonality (or, as Burke would term it, consubstantiality) of worldview, a perception that is born of language. Nowhere, I think, do these principles become more obvious than in our myths which, first, rationalize our sense of affiliation by fostering—in mythic language—identifications with a group of deities held in common and, second, internalize that sense so thoroughly—through ritual reenactment of mythic episodes—that the myths themselves seem to inhabit every fiber of our being.

Thus divinity—whether in the guise of a spirit-animal ally, a ghost or ancestor, a spiritual force that emanates from a deity, a convocation of gods, a father or king of the gods, or a single god—always behaves (if not entirely looks like) a human. It is, in fact, the anthropomorphic nature of spirits that fosters our deep sense of identification with them—as well as our deep sense of affiliation with those with whom we share that sense of identification. Just as telling tales on one another (i.e., gossiping) orders, modulates, and solidifies the various bonds that exist within a community, the telling of tales on our anthropomorphic deities personalizes them by bringing them directly into the social life of the community. Thus, it should come as no surprise that mythology is, at its most basic, a set of beliefs about the various spirits that populate the universe. These spirits are multiform and include not only gods but also ancestors, ghosts, souls, demigods, monsters, and even amorphous spiritual forces. A specific society will have its own particularized set of spirits and, while religious specialists within the society may be the special adepts in mythology (the *stories* of the society's spirits) and ritual (the ceremonial reenactment of mythic episodes), the rank-and-file members of society all know, at the very least, the spirits themselves among whom they live and with whom they often interact on a very personal—or, perhaps better, in a very intimate—manner.

Gods are, of course, the major characters who populate our myths, but they are sometimes difficult to define. Often, theologians make a strong distinction between societies that are monotheistic, worshipping only one god, polytheistic, worshipping a number of gods, or monistic theistic, worshipping a number of deities that are actually one. Yet, when one attempts to apply these theologically sensible terms, they become a bit muddied. Really, what difference does it make that Christians allow three manifestations of their single deity and Hindus allow thousands? Does that really make the one monotheistic and the other polytheistic? To complicate matters further, it seems that some moderately monotheistic societies retain a number of godlike spiritual entities in their mythologies and simply disallow them to be called gods. For example, despite the fact that Judaism and Christianity are monotheistic religions, various Biblical heroes—Noah comes immediately to mind—often stand in for the gods and goddesses of other societies. In fact, a major source for Noah— Utnapishtim, the Faraway, he who survived the flood and repopulated the world not only with men but also with the animals that he brought aboard his ark— is a Mesopotamian god. Perhaps a more useful observation with regard to the nature of gods is that the world's various pantheons of gods maintain strong correlations with its various social orders. For instance, one universally finds a hierarchy of gods in stratified societies. But where egalitarianism reigns among the members of society, it reigns among the gods as well: in such circumstances, we find that the gods make decisions collaboratively. Further, where there are no female gods (this only occurs with monotheism) or where the female gods are significantly less important than their male counterparts (this occurring in various polytheistic societies), we often see a weakened position for women both in the household and the society's political structure. As Zora Neale Hurston observed, perhaps too bluntly, "Gods always behave like the people who make them."[2] If they did not, I suppose we could add, the intense sense of identification a society must maintain with its gods would not be possible.

Hindu Deities

The gods of India offer a case in point. Though India is characterized by multiple religious traditions, the Hindu faith is as predominate there as is Christianity in the United States. But Hinduism is not monolithic. It can be characterized as multiple religious traditions pertaining to different epochs of India's history and different Indian regions. "Hinduism," Jonardon Ganeri maintains, "is a banyan tree, in the shade of whose canopy, supported by not one but many trunks, a great diversity of thought and action is sustained."[3] Yet a constant is found in the act of *puja*: the veneration of a deity represented perhaps in a statue placed upon an altar in a home, a simple roadside shrine, or an ornate temple. While performing *puja*, the worshippers may ring bells or clash cymbals. They may chant, sing, and perhaps even dance. Offering up fire, *ghee* (clarified butter), and the sweet scent of incense, they might request that food set at the deity's feet be consecrated as *prasad* which carries within itself the deity's blessing. In this, one of the most stunning spectacles of the Hindu faith, the worshippers are engaging in *darshan* (audience): the contemplation of an *ideal* visually *represented* in an image. At the same time, the worshipper is cognizant that the ideal—and the statue of the deity that represents it—are but parts of the larger concept of god: Brahman, the Absolute, which is all spirit and therefore nearly unrepresentable. In fact, though Hindu deities are almost innumerable, they are all part of Brahman, and the Hindu religion is therefore—like Judaism, Christianity, and Islam—best described as monotheistic. Further, Swamiji, a Hindu guru whom we will meet shortly, suggests that Brahman, the spiritual principle that governs the universe, is to be discovered within each of us and resides principally in the indestructible *ātman*, soul, which may one day experience *moksha*: permanently shuffling off its mortal coil to become reintegrated into Brahman.[4]

Among the various constituent parts of Brahman is a sort of trinity—or, more properly, Trimurti (Tri-form Deity)—including Brahma, the Creator, Vishnu, the Preserver (representing continuity in creation), and Shiva, the Destroyer (representing transformation in creation). Each constituent part of the Trimurti has a female counterpart that, like her male consort, is a manifestation of the ineffable Brahman. All are as well manifestations of Mahadevi, the Great Mother, who pervades feminine godhead. Sarasvati, goddess of poetry, is wife to Brahma. Lakshmi, goddess of prosperity, is the wife of Vishnu. And Parvati, goddess of power and warfare, is the wife of Shiva. But beyond such benevolent incarnations, Mahadevi has as one of her avatars Kali: naked and ornamented in human heads and limbs, her tongue protruding like a lion's from her lips, she incites Shiva on to his most destructive behavior. Creation, represented in the image of the Trimurti, depends on the delicate balancing of the principles of order (continuity) and disorder (transformation). Just as Grandmother Sky Woman balances the disparate energies of Elder Brother and Younger Brother, Brahma balances those of Vishnu and Shiva. At times, when the Shiva principle of transformation becomes too pronounced—for instance, once, when Shiva began the Dance of Death which signals the end of one age and the beginning of another, at an inappropriate time—the Vishnu principle of continuity must be reinforced. Then, Vishnu might descend to earth in one of his many avatars, or manifestations, the most famous of which are Rama and the blue-skinned trickster: Krishna. In yet another avatar, Vishnu manifests himself in the form of a turtle which, not unlike the Iroquois turtle, swims to the surface of the primordial sea in order to hold on its back the cosmic Mount Meru which sits at the center of creation.

We earlier encountered Vishnu stepping in when the world had gone awry. It was Vishnu, after all, in the guise of a blue-skinned boy, who made Indra realize that his glory in his own greatness was terribly misplaced. And though Shiva sometimes manifests a kind of majestic violence (for instance, when he cuts off the head of his own son, Ganesha, and only replaces it with the head of a passing elephant at Parvati's tearful pleas), he can as well be a remarkably benevolent deity. We will shortly encounter a tale of Shiva's largesse, and the lesson that it imparted, related by Swamiji. But if Vishnu and Shiva continuously order and disorder the world, Brahma busily safeguards his creation. One story in which he is seen to do so, the famous "Legend of the Fish," speaks to an earlier discussion we had: Manu, he who being warned of an impending flood by a fish to whom he had committed a kindness, built a boat with which to save humanity. The fish instructed Manu to "build a strong massive ark and have it furnished with a long rope. 'On that you must ascend, O great Ascetic, with the Seven Sages, and take with you all the different seeds which were enumerated by regenerate Brahmins in days of yore, and separately and carefully you must preserve them therein. And, whilst there, you shall wait for me, and I shall appear to you like a horned animal, and thus, O Ascetic, shall you recognize me!'" And Manu did the fish's bidding. Thus, when the flood descended, and Manu found himself on the "roaring and billow-beaten sea," his ark reeling "about like a drunken harlot," with "neither land nor the four cardinal points

Shiva dances over the body of Apasmāra, a demon symbolic of ignorance (author's photograph).

of the compass" visible, the fish came and towed him to the safety of Mount Himavat. "Then the fish, addressing Manu and the Seven Sages, told them these words, 'I am Brahma, the Lord of all creatures; there is none greater than myself. Assuming the shape of a fish, I have saved you from this cataclysm. Manu will create (again) all beings—gods, *Asuras* and men, all those divisions of creation

Ganesha (author's photograph).

which have the power of locomotion and which have it not.'" And, thereupon, Manu, First Man and He Who Survived the Flood, began repopulating the earth.[5]

While Brahma is not characteristically a focus of Hindu worship, Vishnu and his many avatars—for instance, Rama and Krishna—are. Those who maintain a special devotion to Vishnu are called Vaisnavs who include among their ranks the members of the "Hare Krishna" movement which gained so many western adherents. Likewise, Shiva, is widely worshipped and he too has his special devotees: Shaivites, among whom are found Lingayats, named for the stylized phallus (Lingam) which represents Shiva's nature as a fertility god. The Great Mother, in all her various manifestations, is also widely worshipped. But gods in India are diverse and extend well beyond the Trimurti and their many expansions. Some are as resplendent as was Krishna when he displayed his infinite and eternal form to a despairing Arjuna but others exist on a more humble plane. Some are worshipped throughout the subcontinent and others are known only at the local village level.

For instance, one god worshipped in the small village of Gopalpur in south central India is Shah Hussein, "the god of the Turks." He is somewhat distinct, when compared to the village's other principle gods, "in that he accepts offerings of meat and is worshipped by a nonvegetarian priesthood," and his "sacred ritual is conducted in the Urdu language rather than in Sanskrit." Shah Hussein was, in actuality, a Muslim resident of Gopalpur who died "within living memory" of his fellow villagers. "He was a saintly man, and after his death he agreed to stay in the village and protect it." By contrast, another major deity worshipped at Gopalpur, and one known throughout India, is Hanumantha, the warrior monkey god who aided Rama rescue his wife Sita from the ravaging demon Ravana in India's famed epic: *The Ramayana.* Together, "Hanumantha and Shah Hussein are Gopalpur's special gods. They stand ready to help in any emergency, but their assistance is always conditional upon the good behavior of people in Gopalpur." That said, their attributes are quite distinct from one another. At the festivities which attend each of the gods' annual celebrations before their respective shrines, their petitioners are apt to suffer possession. Once, a petitioner possessed by Hanumantha said, "If you don't worship with a good heart, you will be burned to ashes." Shah Hussein, on the other hand, said, in Urdu and through the vehicle of one of his petitioners, "Worship me when you feel happy." Yet another god especially venerated at Gopalpur is Bhima who, along with Hanumantha, is "specifically charged with protecting villages, arranging successful marriages, and ensuring that married couples bear children." Both Bhima and Hanumantha are avatars—or incarnations—of a single celestial deity, Vayu, the Wind, and as such partake in his warlike nature. While Hanumantha's martial skills are portrayed in *The Ramayana,* Bhima's are central to another of India's celebrated epics, *The Mahabharata,* wherein his unparalleled strength allows him to destroy the 100 Kaurava brothers one by one, bringing the Great War over the throne of Hastinapura to its inevitable conclusion. The essential nature of these three gods to the inhabitants of

Gopalpur is best expressed in the fact that most of the village boys are named "Hanumantha, Bhimarayya, or Saba (referring to Shah Hussein).["6]

When considering Bhima, a special order of gods emerges: human heroes who have undergone apotheosis, or exaltation to the level of deity: an organic outgrowth of the principle of reincarnation. Bhima was one of five brothers, the Pandavas, or sons of Pandu. The Pandavas had two mothers, the co-wives Kunti and Madri, and one earthly father: the onetime king of Hastinapura: Pandu. But they had as well celestial fathers which defined their heroic virtues. The first three sons were born to Kunti: Pandu's principal wife. Yudhisthira had as his father Dharma, the god of duty, law, and the virtuous path, which authorized him to serve as the rightful king of Hastinapura. Bhima had as his father Vayu, the wind, whose martial prowess imbued Bhima with such strength that he became the fiercest warrior known to mankind. Arjuna—son of Indra, king of the gods—was Krishna's favorite and the world's greatest archer. And the twins, Nakula and Sahadeva, born to Pandu's secondary wife, Madri, had as their fathers the Ashvins, the celestial twins who appear as the rising and setting sun and who imbued their sons with wisdom and resplendent beauty.

It was the fate of these brothers to participate in one of the marital designs that we earlier discussed, polyandry, or the marriage of one woman to two or more men. Though polyandry is not an acceptable marriage pattern in Indian culture, it is sometimes argued—on the basis of a passage in the *Rig Veda*, the oldest collection of Sanskrit scriptures—that, in ancient times, it was. Yet, it seems more likely that, inasmuch as the region where polyandry is most commonly found, the Himalayas, forms the northern frontier of the subcontinent and is numerously referred to in *The Mahabharata* as the roof of the world, some inkling of the singular Himalayan marital pattern must have surreptitiously slipped into Indian mythology to generate the conflict upon which *The Mahabharata* hinges. Two clans—the first comprised of the epic's heroes, the five Pandava brothers; the second, the Pandavas' wicked cousins, the hundred Kaurava brothers—went to war over the disputed throne of the kingdom of Hastinapura. The enmity between the two factions reached a head when the Kauravas insulted the Pandavas' irreproachably virtuous wife, the "slender-waisted" Draupadi: she "whose eyes are "like lotus-petals," whose "faultless features" are "endued with youth and intelligence," and whose body emits "a fragrance like unto that of the blue lotus." She was married to the five Pandavas by a trick of fate. The Pandava's mother, Kunti, believing her five sons—who, though kings by birth, were living as wandering ascetics—had been out collecting alms said, when they first brought Draupadi before her: "Enjoy ye all what hath been obtained." But her sons had not been out collecting alms. They had rather been participating in a tournament which had as its prize the hand of Draupadi in marriage. Kunti's inadvertent proclamation could not be taken back and would therefore extend to her son Arjuna's prize: Draupadi, whom he had won by stringing a bow which no other warrior could string. Thus, was Draupadi married to the five Pandava brothers. Still, the marriage was sanctified by none other than the god Krishna—the human avatar (or incarnation) of Vishnu, the god of preservation—who held Draupadi to be especially virtuous. Much later, when the wicked Kauravas won Draupadi at an infamous game of dice against their unlucky cousins, they attempted to undress her even though she was in her menstrual seclusion. Krishna miraculously caused Draupadi's sari to become endless and his holy charge's pristine modesty was thus preserved. But with such an outrage perpetrated against Draupadi, the death of the Kauravas—which was accomplished in a monstrous war between the Pandavas and the Kauravas—became inevitable.[7]

Hijras

All these heroes—Krishna, the Pandavas and Draupadi, even the vicious Kauravas—are deities in India. And these deities, like all others, have special devotees in particular regions, towns, sects, castes, and jatis. We have already seen how the residents of Gopalpur hold the second Pandava brother, Bhima, as one of their special patrons. Duryodhana—the worst of the Kauravas, he who ordered Draupadi to be stripped and who insolently showed her his thigh, as powerful as a lightning bolt and an elephant's trunk—is particularly revered in the northern state of Uttarakhand where he is considered an ancestral deity. Though he died in pain, receiving his deathblow—as an enraged Bhima had predicted—in the offending thigh, he ascended to heaven and took his place among the celestials. Further instances abound: Hijras, members of the male-to-female transgender community which constitutes its own subcaste (*jati*) within Indian society, are charged with a very specific set of religious duties and maintain their own special patrons, among whom are included Krishna and Arjuna.

"Hijras," according to Serena Nanda, "are culturally defined as 'neither man nor woman.' They are born as males and through a ritual surgical transformation become an alternative, third sex/gender category." They "worship Bahuchara Mata, a form of the Hindu Mother Goddess particularly associated with transgenderism." This Bahuchara Mata mutilated herself (a sacrifice we will see repeated in Italy's Saint Lucy) in order to repulse her would-be rapists. Hijras' "traditional employment," Nanda continues, "is to perform at marriages and after a child (especially a son) has been born. They sing and dance and bless the child and the family for increased fertility and prosperity in the name of the goddess. They then receive traditional payments of money, sweets, and cloth in return." Indeed, it was particularly important to my nephew's grandmother that the same hijra who blessed him and his twin brother at birth would perform the blessing at his marriage to my niece. Though much older now, this specific hijra was found and—despite some difficulties in arranging things properly—gave the new couple her benediction, dancing to the accompaniment of a young hijra's drum before offering her blessing. In fact, because of such duties—and the sometimes itinerant lives often circumscribed by poverty and social prejudice that hijras lead—Nanda views them as a special sort of wandering ascetic: ready to bless those who treat them with kindness and procure their services but as equally adept at curses—often bitter, pointed, and very public—hurled at those who mistreat them.[8] And hijras are characteristically treated with a good deal of ambivalence. One woman, for instance, told me that her father always admonished her to pay no attention to the "depraved" hijras who hung about the train station begging in her hometown. But my nephew was pointedly taught not to show any disrespect to hijras who, because they inhabit a body between the masculine and feminine, inhabit a realm between material and spiritual worlds. For this reason, he was taught, their pronouncements were uncannily accurate.

Arjuna is particularly revered by hijras because, previous to the outbreak of the Great War, he lived as a hijra for a year. This occurred as a result of the infamous game of dice. In losing the game, the Pandavas agreed to twelve years of exile from the kingdom followed by a year in disguise. Had they been discovered in the thirteenth year, they would have been punished with another twelve years of exile. Thus, the hijra disguise was a brilliant, and imperative, one. But it wasn't only a disguise. During the period, Arjuna *became* a hijra: dressing as a woman and offering blessings to newborns and newlyweds alike. Krishna likewise, became a hijra in order to seduce and kill a demon, Araka, who had never seen a woman, and who—in my nephew's telling—had been given the boon of not being subject to death at the hands of man or woman. During the struggle, Krishna loses his virginity and Nanda reports that in the hijras telling, a victorious Krishna pronounced: "There will be more like me, neither man nor woman, and whatever words come from the mouths of these people, whether good or bad, will come true."[9] In yet another story, Arjuna is transformed into a sacred Gopi—one of the female cowherds who adore Krishna—and taken by Krishna in this form into an enchanted forest where they make love. Afterward, Krishna transforms Arjuna back into his masculine form.

One episode from the *Mahabharata* that is particularly revered by hijras is celebrated at Koovagam, a small agricultural village in the south-western Indian state of Tamil Nadu that houses a shrine to Aravan. As Michael Edison Hayden reports, hijras flock to Koovagam to commemorate the sacrifice made by Aravan in the Great War between the Pandavas and Kauravas. Agreeing to fight to the death for the *Mahabharata*'s five heroes, he asks only one boon: that he be permitted to marry and know the love of a woman before he dies. Krishna himself honors Aravan's request, transforming himself into a woman and spending a night of love-making with Aravan before sending the valiant warrior to his death. Though the festival at Koovagam includes beauty pageants, dances, and—hijras from throughout India flocking to the festival—a nearly frenzied amount of socializing, its culmination surrounds a communal mourn-

Krishna (author's photograph).

ing over the death of Aravan. But this act of mourning extends well beyond the remembrance of things past. Despite their authorization in Hindu myth, hijras suffer significant prejudice in India. Further exacerbating the suffering they experience from social prejudice are the often crushing levels of poverty with which they live. And, because prostitution constitutes one of their economic mainstays, high rates of HIV infection affect the hijra community. Dr. Mohan Kumar, a psychiatrist who works with hijras and other transgender patients at Columbia Asia Hospital in Bangalore, suggests "that the cathartic release the festival provides is very real, and in some ways" essential to the hijras' sometimes precarious existence. "Most transgendered women in India," Dr. Kumar explains, "are getting sex, sex, sex—but rarely do they receive compassion or love. And the majority of Indians still believe that it is a vile curse, that these people are disgraced in the eyes of god." Dr. Kumar maintains that "the ritualized enactment of the feminized Krishna's love for Aravan is extremely powerful in hijra and Indian transgendered communities not only because of the cathartic healing the mourning ceremony provides through the release of tears but also because of a positive, aspirational element embedded in the story. The myth, ultimately, is about true love." Dr. Kumar suggests that "when Lord Krishna takes a female form for one night—he sleeps with Aravan. But it's romantic love. And so when Aravan dies, Krishna endures the sorrow of a devoted wife losing her lover."[10]

Swamiji

But hijras—living in communal houses, begging for a living, and offering blessings to both newborns and the newly married—are not the only community of sacred ascetics who maintain a unique approach to deity. In India an almost innumerable cast of ritual practitioners populate the landscape: shamans and *brahmins*; monks and nuns; healers, astrologers, and diviners; *sadhus* (wandering ascetics), *sannyasis* (those who have renounced materialism), *gurus* (teachers), *rishis* and *munis* (seers and sages). India's landscape is, in many ways, defined by the holy men and women who populate it and the sacred places they inhabit, tend, and wander. And it is their special prerogative to recite and interpret the doings of the gods. Kirin Narayan has charted the life and teachings of the *sadhu*, Swamiji, who was particularly devoted to the Mother Goddess, Saptashring Navasini Devi, "a large-eyed, coral-complexioned" goddess whose eighteen arms surrounded her "like the hood of a snake," and near whose "mountaintop temple" Swamiji had once lived.[11] Narayan has offered a fascinating explication of Swamiji's use of Indian folktales during the course of his spiritual teachings:

> In the early 1980s Swamiji lived in the upper story of an apartment building in Nasik Road, Western India. He usually met visitors in a front room with a green linoleum floor and an altar bright with Gods, Goddesses and Gurus at the far end. He tended to recline in an aluminum deck chair beside the altar, shoulders relaxed, legs stretched out towards his visitors who touched his bare feet for blessings. He wore faded orange cloth, sometimes wrapped around his neck and ending just below his knees, or else wrapped around his waist, with a second cloth around the shoulders for more formality. He was then in his sixties, and had gone through cataract surgery that left him wearing thick glasses with black frames. His round face and scalp were either clean shaven, or progressively shaggy with a white beard and wavy hair. During the hours that his doors were open to visitors, people from the town, the villages nearby, and other parts of India and abroad arrived in a nearly constant stream to seek his blessings and advice. Often, Swamiji told them stories.[12]

Among the many stories that Narayan relates is one in which Swamiji suggests that one must be open to the various vicissitudes of destiny, understood as the ineffable will of Brahman: or, as Swamiji calls the principle, Bhagavan (masculine) and Bhagavati (feminine), switching gender at will. A king has a minister who, inevitably, no matter what anyone says, replies, "That's good." When, one day, the king went off on the hunt and accidentally severed his toe, the minister's sole response was, not surprisingly, "That's very good," where-upon the king summarily dismissed the minister from his employ, to which the minster—once again and infuriatingly—could only reply, "That's good." Not long thereafter, however, the king—recuperated from his injury and hunt-ing once again—was captured by a forest-dwelling tribe who mistook him for a goat and intended to sacrifice him and, thereafter, each take a piece of his consecrated flesh (*prasad*). After fattening him up, the tribe's high priest was about to dispatch him but, noticing his injured foot, deemed him an unworthy sacrifice and released him back into the forest. Instantly realizing the sense in his minister's claim that having lost his toe was good—it saved his life, after all—he sent for the minister. "I now understand why you said it was good when I lost my toe," the king said, "but I fail to understand how it could have been good when I dismissed you from my service." To this the minister sensibly replied, "Your majesty, had I still been in your service, I—with my unsevered toe—would have been hunting at your side. Would I have not—uninjured as I was—serve as an apt sacrifice? Indeed, when you dismissed me from your service, it was very good."[13]

In yet another story, Swamiji touches on the nature of Shiva and Parvati. The story recounts the exploits of a pandit, a ritual specialist of the Brahmin caste, who has become disenchanted with his wife inasmuch as she is losing her youthful beauty. He elects to undertake *tapasya*—an ascetic discipline that involves meditation, often in the company of severe austerities—in order to find some remedy for his dilemma. But, somewhat out of keeping with the spirit of *tapasy*a, the pandit had his ever less desirable wife bake him a large stack of laddoos—sweet pastries fried in ghee (clarified butter) and stuffed with raisins and cashews. Settling himself in a lonely cave, the sadhu occupied himself with his "laddoo tapasya" until he attracted the notice of Shiva and Parvati travelling overhead in their celestial chariot. Despite Shiva's annoyance at such a luxurious form of *tapasya*, Parvati convinced her husband to offer the pandit a boon. Thus, Shiva gave the pandit three pebbles, each of which would grant him a wish. With the first pebble, he restored his wife's youth and beauty. Unfortunately, when she became beautiful, she attracted the attention of a ban-dit who abducted her and threatened the pandit with death if he tried to retrieve his wife. With the second pebble, the pandit transformed his wife into a tiger which killed the bandit. With only one pebble left, the pandit decided it would be easier for him to keep an aging wife than a beautiful one and he, thus, trans-formed his wife back to what she had originally been—an old woman to keep the company of an old holy man. Perhaps Shiva's boon was as flawed as the pandit's *tapasya*. Or, perhaps again, it functioned just as it was meant to![14]

Despite his veneration for all the aspects of Brahman, Swamiji's most fervent veneration is reserved for the Great Mother. Narayan speaks movingly of Swamiji's faith in his special deity as she, engrossed in her studies in India, faces the imminent death of her brother, Rahoul, himself a onetime disciple of Swamiji, back in the United States:

> My daily interactions with Swamiji were shadowed by the loss my family was facing and by the acute sense of being split, even in sorrow, across continents. Swamiji's attitude was of gentle concern. He asked me every day whether I had received any news. He enquired about the illness and all possible modes of treatment. He placed the entire issue in the hands of the Divine Mother. "If She wants to do something, She'll do it. He will recover. It's all up to Her." When I left India, Swamiji sent blessings to my brother, along with packets of *kumkum* from his worship of a silver *Shri Yantra*, symbolizing the Goddess. We placed this *kumkum* daily on my brother's forehead until we were placing it on a corpse in a hushed hospital room.[15]

Heroes and Tricksters

As is the case with Hindu deities, the nature of divinity is subject to great variation and, thus, the act of worshipping, venerating, or propitiating deities differs greatly from one religion to another. Further, our mythologies are not only populated by deities. Rather, our myths, legends, and folktales—taken as a whole—present a world teeming with spirits. Ancestors and ghosts represent the spirits of the deceased. Demigods may be minor gods, the offspring of gods and mortals, or flesh-and-blood humans who become the special friends of gods. Souls represent the spirit, or at least the spark of divinity, that resides within an earthly vehicle: the body. Even saints, shamans, priests, and—ominously—witches and sorcerers, though explicitly human, become the earthly vehicles for unearthly spiritual powers. Deities alone are never enough to contain the multitudes which comprise the world's teeming spirits. One could even make the argument that the initiate who, in the process of a rite of passage stands "betwixt and between" what he or she was and what he or she is to become, is—while suspended in that "liminal" space—as much spirit as matter. Thus, the Euahlayi girl in her menstrual seclusion and the Euahlayi boy in his seclusion in the bush are strictly avoided—both the menarcheal flow of blood and the nocturnal emission of semen being the outward indications of potent spiritual energy. It is, thus, that the initiate is hedged about with such stringent secrecy and taboo.

Still, within the context of such teeming spiritual diversity, there are two recurring figures found in our global mythologies: a god, spirit, or demigod who acts as a creator and culture founder, the Hero, and another who, following in the hero's footsteps, seemingly confounds all his creative work: the Trickster. Gilgamesh, Osiris, and Horus are exemplary heroes, as is Achilles. But Odysseus, while heroic in stature, is the Trojan Cycle's premier trickster. Other tricksters—sometimes gods, sometimes humans, sometimes spirit-animals— include the famous African American folk hero Brer Rabbit, the Native American spirit-animal allies Raven and Coyote, and the Hindu deity Krishna. Just as Joseph Campbell reminds us that the Hero has a thousand faces—that is, a thousand cultural manifestations of this single human archetype—so too does the antihero: Trickster. Further, the hero and the trickster are often paired: Elder Brother is the Iroquoian representative of the hero, involving himself, along with Grandmother Sky Woman, in the creation of the Three Sisters— corn, beans, and squash—and the healthful, fat-bearing animals. He is solely responsible for the creation of mankind and is associated with the creative power of the Sun and the Sky World. But we catch a glimpse of the trickster in the character of the Iroquois Younger Brother who goes about undoing his orderly Elder Brother's good works or—worse—appropriates his more productive sibling's creative work for himself. Surprisingly, Grandmother Sky Woman, in some versions of the Iroquois Creation, takes Younger Brother's part in his struggles with Elder Brother. But this seeming inconsistency should alert us to an important observation: the Trickster, whether Iroquoian, Hindu, or African American, has his own creative powers and is as sacred as the Hero.

The Lakota as well have their famous trickster, Iktomi. This first cousin to the better-known Winnebago trickster—with whom, in fact, he shares many of the exact same adventures—is conceived as anthropomorphic by the Lakota despite the fact that his name translates as Spider. While the Winnebago trickster is well known for his seemingly perverse antics, we no longer have any knowledge of such behaviors for the Lakota: Ella Deloria being loath to collect any stories which she considered immoral.[16] Of the Winnebago trickster we learn that he once fished his enormous penis across a lake to impregnate the bathing daughter of a chief on the other shore and only lost such abilities when he used his penis to chase a teasing chipmunk into a hole in a hollow tree. To his horror, when he finally gave up the chase and retracted his penis from the tree, the chipmunk had chewed off the penis almost entirely so that only a miserable stub was left. Thus, it is that today men have such short penises. Yet from the chewed off bits of penis, Trickster created for the benefit of mankind all the variety of edible water plants. Then, when Trickster—in the company of nit and raccoon—failed to hunt up any stores to carry them through the long Wisconsin winter, Trickster fashioned two breasts and a vulva from the liver and kidneys of an elk and married a chief's son who provided him and his companions with food. But when Trickster went to dancing too flamboyantly around a fire, the liver and kidneys, somewhat rotting as a result of their over-long use, dropped into the fire. And Trickster, so shamefully revealed, fled the wrath of his fellow villagers.[17] In other Native American versions, Trickster— while disguised as a woman—becomes pregnant and, in at least one, kills his husband after his disguise is revealed by a little girl who notices that when Trickster goes out to pee at night it sounds as if it is a man rather than a woman peeing. Like a cat chasing his own tail, the Winnebago trickster doesn't always seem to recognize his own body parts. Thus, he burns his anus with a burning brand from his campfire because it keeps farting at him. Though difficult for some—particularly those who have grown up in a Western Christian tradi-tion—to think of such stories as religious, for the Winnebago, the Lakota, and the Iroquois, there had to be a counter valence for the creative energy of the hero and this was always provided by the trickster.

Among the famous accounts of the Lakota trickster's misadventures is the following—exactly the same as an episode in the life of the Winnebago trickster—collected by Deloria. Iktomi, aimlessly traveling about, suddenly becomes aware of the unmistakable sounds of a dance—singing, drumming, and the percussive stamps of the dancers themselves—coming from within a dry buffalo skull. Peering in through one of the eye sockets, Iktomi discovers that the dance was being undertaken by the Mouse Nation and he begged his "Younger Brothers" to be admitted to the lovely lodge to participate in the fes-tivities. But as he thrust his head through the spinal aperture, the mice, crying, "Look out! It's Iktomi," fled the buffalo skull. And there was Iktomi, stumbling about blindly, a living man's body with a buffalo skull for its head, looking for a way to free himself.[18]

While the hero presides over the regular order of things—insuring that the child achieve adulthood and the soil produce its harvest—through spon-soring an orderly progression of rites of passage and calendrical ritual, the trick-ster presides over irregularity and even mayhem: sponsoring rites of reversal (where trickster may temporarily displace a chief or king from his throne) and bacchanalias (where the entire community is for a time allowed trickster's lax-ity). Lakota Heyokas and Zuni Koyemcis—both sacred clowns associated with their respective nations' tricksters—do everything in reverse and allow them-selves great latitude in behaviors which would not ordinarily be sanctioned: even lewd joking of the sort we witnessed in the context of San joking rela-tions. It is as if, wherever Trickster exists, the orderly, rule-burdened world would crack under the demands of normative behavior. Then Trickster comes along, releasing the pressure valve, and—setting his emissaries, our sacred clowns, in motion—the entire world, for at least a contained period, can go happily awry!

Progenitors and Scapegoats

But it is not only heroes and tricksters who frequent our mythologies. In a survey of the world's myths, legends, and tales, one cannot help but notice two rhetorical principles regularly at play: progenesis and scapegoating. Progenesis, accounting for the emergence of a people, hinges upon the elaboration of a singular archetype: the Progenitor, an ancestral genius of the family, the clan, the community, even the entire nation. The Egyptian Pharaoh was imbued by such a progenitor: Osiris. And Byamee, as well as his wives, Birrahgnooloo and Cunnumbeillee, were the progenitors of the Euahlayi people. Likewise, scapegoating, laying all the faults of the people on a lowly No Account Boy or Ash Girl, hinges upon the archetype of the Scapegoat: one who, despite the fact that he or she suffers social disdain, becomes the savior of a society. Not only the Iroquois No Account Boy is a manifestation of this archetype but also the Zuni girl who one day set out to hunt rabbits.

One of the world's most fascinating mythic entanglements involves the significance of progenesis in the Abrahamic religions—Judaism, Christianity, and Islam—in the personages of Isaac and Ishmael. The idea of Isaac as a progenitor of Hebraic society and Judaism is established in the Torah. The idea of Ishmael as an Arab progenitor and, by extension, a progenitor of Islam, extends back to a later Jewish tradition which passed into Arabic tradition during the early Islamic period.[19] In fact, while not truly an Arab progenitor in the Qur'an (which does not mention his name) but rather one of a number of prominent prophets, the Hebraic Ishmael is significantly reimagined in the Hadith (commentary on the Qur'an) and its reattribution of Isaac's sacrifice to Ishmael: a sacrifice celebrated in the Muslim holiday Eid al-Adha, the Festival of the Sacrifice. Christianity too is formulated partly on the basis of this view of Jewish and Islamic progenesis for (unfairly, we might add) some sects of the religion have come to view themselves as participating in the New Covenant: the transference of God's covenant from Israel to the Christian faith. Thus, Isaac becomes the Christian, rather than the Hebraic, progenitor, and Christianity—rather than Judaism—is set in opposition to Islam and its mythic progenitor. Such an ideology, it almost goes without saying, speaks not only to anti–Semitism but also a certain strain of Western Islamophobia: both of which we will later consider.

If progenesis is the mechanism by which myth renders itself a primal demarcation of societal affiliation, scapegoating is—chillingly—the mechanism by which myth completes the affiliative function that progenesis begins. In other words, if the sense of a common progenitor strengthens social bonds within a community, the sense of a common scapegoat helps to solidify those bonds. Certainly, the term scapegoating—and its western conceptualization— arises from a Hebraic Yom Kippur ritual in which a goat, upon whose head all the sins of Israel has been placed, is sent out into the wilderness. And, almost certainly, Christian ideas surrounding crucifixion are dependent upon this Hebraic ritual for its significance. But the actual practice of scapegoating extends far beyond these two religious traditions. Thus, the scapegoat archetype— whether in its manifestation as a No Account Boy or an Ash Girl—finds its way regularly into our global mythologies.

Perhaps the most famous No Account Boy—until, at least, Harry Potter emerged on the scene—was none other than the once and future king of England: Arthur. This apparent foundling was, unbeknownst to the English populace, placed in his lowly position by the machinations of the necromancer Merlin. Having been sent to Sir Ector to be "nourished" by his wife, Arthur was overshadowed by Ector's son Kay, only coming into his own when he proved himself by a singular trial: for there appeared "in the churchyard," of Saint Paul's, "against the high altar, a great stone four square, like marble, and therein was thrust a fair sword—naked—to the hilt, and letters were written in gold there about the sword that said whoso pulleth this sword out of this stone is rightwise king born of all England."

> So upon New Year's Day the barons rode unto the field, some to joust and some to tourney, and it happened that Sir Ector rode unto the jousts and with him rode Sir Kay, his son, and young Arthur that was Sir Kay's nourished brother; and Sir Kay was a knight and, he, having left his sword at his father's lodging, prayed young Arthur to ride for it. I will, said Arthur, and rode fast after the sword, but when he came home, the lady and all the household were out to see the jousting. Then was Arthur angry and he said to himself, I will ride to the churchyard and take the sword that was thrust in the stone, for my brother Sir Kay shall not be without a sword this day. So when he came to the churchyard, Arthur alighted and tied his horse to the stile, and went to the tent wherein stayed the men who guarded the sword, and found no knights there, for they were at the jousting. And so he grasped the sword by the handles and easily, if fiercely, pulled it out of the stone.

But when he presented the sword to his foster-brother, whose love for Arthur was of a less magnanimous hue than Arthur's for him, Kay immediately recognized the sword and, taking it to his father, proclaimed, "The sword from the churchyard stone is now mine wherefore I am rightfully king of this realm." Yet, failing to extricate the sword from the stone where his father had placed it once again, Kay admitted his lie and pledged himself to Arthur's service: becoming, with time, King Arthur's seneschal.

As we have seen in our earlier charting of the No Account Boy, the scape-goat often becomes the benefactor of his or her nation. The Iroquois No Account Boy becomes the model for the new order of Peace Chiefs. The Zuni Ash Girl becomes the vehicle through which the Zuni learn reciprocity. And Arthur is destined to, after a number of stumbles, rule over a Christianized Britain. This theme is especially well formulated in the story of the Holy Grail. Perhaps an invention of the poet Chretien de Troyes, though more likely bor-rowed from medieval folkloric tradition, the Grail was understood as the chalice of the Last Supper as well as that which caught Christ's blood when he was pierced with a lance at the crucifixion. Both items were said to have been trans-ported to Britain by Joseph of Arimathea, he—who in the Christian gospels—was said to have provided Christ with his own tomb. In Chretien's treatment of the legend, the well-being of a mysterious descendent of Joseph of Arima-thea, the Fisher King, as well as the spiritual health of Britain, falling—along with its king, Arthur—into ruin and desolation, hinges upon the curious ques-tion: "Whom does the Grail serve?" It was incumbent upon any good knight who visited the ailing Fisher King in his castle to ask, somewhat in the manner of a catechism, the question when the Grail mysteriously appeared before him. Yet Gawain, Lancelot, and Perceval, one after the other, failed to ask the essen-tial question. Had they asked, not only would the health of the Fisher King as well as Britain been restored but, moreover, an answer to the mysterious ques-tion might have been offered. The answer, never fully explicated, seems to likely have been that the Grail served Christ, the Fisher King, the Christian community, or all three. While the failure to ask the essential question by the perfect knight, Perceval, led to the death of the Fisher King, the various quests of Perceval thereafter to cleanse Britain of numerous heresies (characteristically thinly veiled references to Judaism and Islam in the anti–Semitic and anti–Islamic ideology of medieval Europe) and to collect various sacred objects (the lance that pierced Christ's side, Christ's crown of thorns, and the Grail itself) restored the debilitated court of Arthur to its initial splendor. And, of course, instituted the ritual of Holy Communion to ensure Britain's continued well-being.

Still, the Arthurian legend comes of age in medieval Europe. Thus, not surprisingly, it becomes hedged about with millenarian beliefs: beliefs in an apocalypse not unusually coinciding with the turn of the millennium. If Arthur prevails in the safeguarding of his kingdom, he is unable to safeguard his own legacy. An ancient fault—having unwittingly lay with his own half-sister, the fairy Morgan le Fay, and conceived with her a son, Mordred—festers within his psyche and his inability to expiate it continues to disorder humanity. In fact, in the cataclysmic battle between Arthur and Mordred, Arthur doesn't

The Roman ampitheater at Caerleon, Wales: a potential source for the round table legend (Wikipedia, photograph by Greenshed).

die. Rather, having received his mortal wound from his son (and nephew), he is spirited away on a mysterious barge to the mythical kingdom of Avalon. Having been carried to the seashore by Sir Bedivere, the king encounters a strange sight:

> At the shore, even fast by the bank, there came into view a small barge with many fair ladies on it, and among them all was a queen, and all they had black hoods, and all they wept when they saw King Arthur. Now put me into the barge, said the king. And so Bedivere did; and there received the king three queens with great mourning; and they set themselves down, and in one of their laps King Arthur laid his head. And then that queen said: Ah, dear brother, why have ye tarried so long from me? Alas, this wound to your head already becomes cold. And so then the barge moved away from the land, and Sir Bedivere beheld all those ladies go from him. Then Sir Bedivere cried: Ah my lord King Arthur, what shall become of me, now that you leave me alone among mine enemies? Comfort yourself, said the king, and do as well as you may, for in me there is no trust. I take myself into the vale of Avalon to heal me of my grievous wound: and if you hear never more of me, pray for my soul.[20]

It's hard to pinpoint what features give rise to the scapegoat—whether the Iroquois No Account Boy, the Zuni Ash Girl, or England's young Arthur—

beyond pointing out that whatever attributes are generally privileged in the society (and are therefore firmly situated in a mythic progenitor) are generally lacking—or, perhaps better, go unrecognized—in the scapegoat. Still, since the scapegoat seems to be a universal in human mythologies, the archetype must fulfill some murky function of the human psyche. It may be that it conjures psychic memories of youthful powerlessness: the sense of not being appreciated or of being unjustly punished. If so, the scapegoat's exaltation might represent a collective wish-fulfillment for vindication over ancient (and perhaps imagined) slights. But then again, the contiguity of the scapegoat archetype with that of the progenitor, the fact—that is—that the progenitor so often begins his or her history as a scapegoat, may express a psychic recognition of the essential nature of the sociological process by which a society expresses its commonality through sanctifying the progenitor at the expense of the scapegoat. If so, the vindication of the scapegoat—the fact that the scapegoat *becomes* the progenitor—serves as a warning to society of the perniciousness, the sheer meanspiritedness, and ultimately the potential social peril of scapegoating. That said, the fatal flaw that inevitably defines the scapegoat—the No Account Boy's bumbling mannerisms, the Ash Girl's reticence to marry, King Arthur's incestuous union with his fairy sister—may be the impetus for the apocalypse that so often accompanies the progenitor's history. Some inkling of this seems to be behind one of the most famous lines in world literature, "Call me Ishmael," wherein Melville explicitly recognizes the intersection of the scapegoat and progenitor archetypes and thereby creates of his protagonist the perfect symbol of humanity adrift—a symbol rife with apocalyptic possibilities.

Souls, Ancestors and Ghosts

Our consideration of progenesis—and its troubling counterpart—brings us to another category of spirits: that which exists within us, the soul, and its various manifestations when it departs its earthly vehicle: particularly ancestors and ghosts. Not unusually, the soul goes on—as we have seen even among our Neanderthal forebears—to another world: a spirit world, perhaps shorn of its physical deficiencies, perhaps not; perhaps in the West or the Sky, perhaps again beneath the Sea or the Earth's surface. This place may be paradisiacal, like Christianity's Heaven, or a place of torment, like Christianity's Hell. But it is not unusually conceived simply as a place of listless shades. Such was the conception of the Greek Underworld as one understands when Odysseus traveled to its very portal to speak with Tiresias, the onetime blind seer who had proclaimed to Oedipus his crime, and learn from him how he might finally find his way back home to Ithaca: "When I had prayed sufficiently to the dead," Odysseus' proclaimed, "I cut the throats of two sheep and let the blood run into the trench, whereon the ghosts came trooping up from Erebus—brides, young bachelors, old men worn out with toil, maids who had been crossed in love, and brave men who had been killed in battle, their armor still smirched with blood. They came from every quarter and flitted round the trench with a strange whining that made me turn pale with fear."[21] With a sip of blood, the indolent shades would gain some glimmer of their once living selves and find—if only for a moment—their tongues. While some among the world's spirits of the deceased move on to their afterlife to join the innumerable ranks of those who went before them, never to be seen or heard of again, others become the progenitors which we just considered. We may propitiate them from afar or we may invite them into our home, maintaining for them a household altar. Collectively, we may speak of these as Ancestors. Still others refuse to depart the earth they once tread and continue to lurk among their onetime fellows. Collectively, we may speak of these as ghosts.

Let us first consider the soul. Though encased within its earthly vehicle,

"Weighing the Fate of the Souls of the Deceased," Notre-Dame de Paris (Wikipedia, photograph by PHGCOM).

the human body, the soul is—in and of itself—spirit and may, if it does not travel to the abode of the dead, join the ranks of ancestors or ghosts once it shuffles off its mortal coil. In many traditions, Christian included, the soul is thought of as the spark of divinity within the human being. The Hindu tradition is explicit on this point: the soul (*ātman*) is indestructible (that is, subject to the process of reincarnation) and the part of Brahman—the infinite and eternal spiritual principle that pervades the universe—which exists within animate beings: animals, humans, and gods alike. Whereas in most traditions, the soul is allocated its specific place, in others it is amorphous and shifting. Christians may with some unease suggest that the soul is housed throughout the body or perhaps near the heart. The Dani of highland New Guinea, conversely, view the soul—which they call *edai-egan*, the seeds of singing—as situated in the solar plexus. And, as we will see, sickness is attributed to the soul's wandering from its rightful place to the small of the back. Then, while some societies maintain a belief in a single soul, others believe in multiple souls. The Euahlayi believe all people have three souls and shamans have four. The *yowee* is the personal spirit and much like the Christian soul in nature. The *doowee* is the dream spirit, active during one's sleep. The *mulloowil* is the shadow spirit: so subject to magical injury that the Euahlayi avoid stepping into another's shadows. The *yunbeai* is the spirit of the shaman's animal-familiar and provides him with many of his magical powers. Finally, while some societies believe that the soul is released at death, Americans come to mind, others—such as the Dani and Lakota—believe it is released during funerary rites.

Analogous to gods—in fact, perhaps their source in the evolution of our spiritual life—are ancestors and ghosts. Both are understood as spirits of the deceased but, whereas ancestors are beneficent and nurturing (in much the way that our heroes and progenitors are) and we may even enshrine them in household altars, ghosts are (not unlike our tricksters and scapegoats) wily and mischievous (if not out-and-out malicious) and we would rarely directly invite them into our lives. In fact, whereas ancestors aid and abet their descendants, ghosts generally envy the living and therefore cause us all sorts of undue harm. It may, in fact, be that the universality with which human societies recognize these two spiritual categories answers most exactly to E.B. Tylor's notion that the manner in which we imagine spirit has its origin in our dreams for it is in our dream life that we most regularly encounter the deceased: whether a reassuring relative or a predatory stranger. We will consider the veneration of ancestors when we turn back to Zuni Pueblo and move on to Sicily and Haiti, so let us momentarily consider the nature of ghosts.

Ghosts are a constant concern for the Dani—and figure prominently in the Dani's agricultural adaptation to the highland valleys of New Guinea's mountainous interior. While Dani men view themselves as farmers, tending their pig herds and sweet potato gardens, the actual division of labor is more complex than that view suggests. Since Dani society was characterized until the early 1960s by almost continuous war between alliances of neighboring villages, men would spend a good deal of their time either passively defending their alliance by manning watchtowers along their borders or actively engaging in battles or raids against enemy alliances—alliances which were always quite tenuous and subject to disintegration. Thus, Dani men tended to be responsible only for the heaviest farming activities: maintaining the irrigation ditches that surrounded their sweet potato gardens and breaking the gardens' soil with their single major agricultural tool, the digging stick: a stout post somewhat taller than a man. For the most part, then, women were the actual Dani farmers—planting, weeding, harvesting, and transporting their husbands' preeminent crop: sweet potatoes. Herding pigs, the almost single source of meat among the Dani, was an activity most regularly left to the children, both boys and girls.

For the Dani, ghosts are the spirits of the recently deceased members of the community which includes the entire membership of the alliance. Ghosts—particularly the spirits of those who have been killed in warfare against an enemy alliance—are especially malevolent and will cause the living members of their own alliance to suffer a kind of soul loss until their deaths have been avenged. Thus, after the funeral—which includes daubing the deceased's body with pig fat so the alliance's ghosts can participate in the funeral feast and sacrificing the upper digit of several fingers from girls closely related to the deceased with a blow from a blunt stone axe—the Dani find themselves back at war in an attempt to exchange one death for another. What happens is this: until the death of an alliance member is avenged, his (or sometimes her) ghost causes the souls—the *etai-eken* (seeds of singing)—of the living to migrate from their rightful place in the solar plexus to the small of the back. Thereupon, the living become ill. Only with the killing of an enemy can this sickness become remedied because, as a result of the death, the Dani undertake a celebratory dance called the *etai* (the singing) which calls the *etai-eken* back to their proper place (i.e., the solar plexus), thereby restoring the collective health of the alliance.

In a very real sense, Dani men were not marshaling their major resources, pigs and sweet potatoes, simply to feed themselves, their families, and—during celebratory feasts—their alliances. They were doing so as well to feed the ghosts because, along with the *etai*, the singing, a pig feast was undertaken when an enemy was killed—and (as the daubing of the body of the deceased with pig fat made clear) the feast was held for the sake of the ghosts as well as the deceased's many survivors. Little wonder then that the raising of pigs and the growing of sweet potatoes held such a strong incentive for Dani men: in sponsoring feasts comprised of the fruits of their labor, in actively avenging the deaths of their fellow alliance members in warfare, and—most importantly— in appeasing the rampant appetites of the ghosts, ambitious men became the bulwark of the alliance. They became, in a word, Big Men (as chiefs in New Guinea are commonly termed) with all the rights and obligations that that title entailed. The obligation of Dani Big Men to feed the ghosts—something that was expressed whenever an alliance member was born, wedded, or—most importantly—died, was nowhere expressed more succinctly than in the Dani ceremony called *Wonkonake*, Pig Treasure, a rare occasion in which the alliance itself was feted, for here a small ghost house was erected in the sponsoring village so that the ghosts could be explicitly included in the festivities but, at the same time, kept safely at bay.[22]

Fairies and the Æsir

Yet another class of spirits includes those which are not actively propitiated but nonetheless maintain an ethereal communion with their human hosts. Living in the wastes and sullen places beyond the confines of our farmsteads and villages or moving quietly and unseen among us, bringing luck or misfortune as the case may be, these spirits include Greece's Nymphs and Satyrs, Christianity's Angels and Demons, India's Gandharvas, Asuras, Rakshas and Nagas, the Islamic world's Djinns (Genies) and Native America's Little People. In those areas of Europe where ancient religious traditions lingered as Christianity slowly seeped into the collective conscious, the onetime gods often joined the ranks of such spirits: for instance, Celtic Europe's fairies and Nordic Europe's Æsir.

No society comes to mind in the consideration of fairy lore quicker than Ireland: particularly those areas of Ireland where the old Gaelic language lived on even into the 20th century. Of the belief in fairies in rural Ireland, Conrad Arensberg suggested that "in his daily life" the "Irish countryman" owed his allegiance first to the Church, but second to the ancient fairy beliefs of his nation:

One finds him, for instance, "blessing" himself on setting out for his day's work, or on beginning a trip or a new undertaking such as the potato-planting, with two purposes in mind. If you ask him, you learn, first, that he dedicates his day or his enterprise to God. He throws himself upon divine protection. Secondly, he seeks that protection to a definite end. He hopes to ward off thus the forces of evil and ill-luck. He hopes to assure himself the enterprise will prosper. He guards himself against molestation from "the good people." That does not mean he is motivated by fear even when "the good people" are concerned. His devotion springs from deeper and wider emotional sources than mere fear. Rather he makes his peace with the fairies; he pays them their due.[23]

For instance, as one man—a certain John Hanifin—discovered, one's charitable deeds to both men and fairies alike do not go unrewarded. Each morning the trough, into which his maids poured their buckets after the milking, was overturned and emptied of its content. Then, one morning, as Hanifin passed one of the ruined Fairy Raths—the ancient remnants of Neolithic fortifications that dot the Irish countryside—he heard a child's voice crying within for milk and its mother quieting him by saying that once John Hanifin's maids were done with their milking he would have his drink. Then Hanifin went into the Rath and announced aloud that he would reserve one cow's milk for the child each day. The next morning, and each thereafter, the one cow was always found to have been milked before the maids even set to their work and the trough was never again overturned. But then, when, a small time later, Hanifin's generosity to his neighbors—both fairy and otherwise alike—led to his own financial troubles, and the bailiffs came to confiscate his cows, the bailiffs were beaten unmercifully by unseen hands and John Hanifin's herd was left unmolested.[24]

As his household design made plain, the Irish countryman whose small farm "of four cows and a horse," a place that could provide grass enough for the animals and a small garden "of potatoes, cabbage, oats, and turnips" for the family, the fairies would always be treated with respect. The house, a two-room cottage with a sleeping loft beneath the eaves, was comprised of the kitchen to the east where the family cooked, ate, and—for the most part—lived and the west room nestled behind the hearth. This west room "was a sort of parlor into which none but distinguished guests were admitted. In it were kept pictures of the dead and emigrated members of the family, all 'fine' pieces of furniture, symbolic brass objects brought in by the bride at marriage; the sacramentals used when mass was celebrated in the house, in fact all religious objects, crucifixes, and so forth except the 'blessed lamp' and a 'holy picture' in the kitchen." To the west of this room, no outbuildings could be erected for it was there that the fairy paths passed and the fairies took their passage to and fro the land of the living and, Avalon, the mysterious abode of the dead beyond the setting sun.[25] These fairies are neither good nor evil but rather mischievous. Though if they are not treated respectfully or—perhaps worse—if a man behaves unsocially, they are known to become malicious. This was certainly the case with one John Connors.

Connors, from near Killarney in County Kerry, upset when his wife bore him his seventh daughter but never a son, refused to find a sponsor for the girl's christening. Yet, when she next bore him a son, he went off to Beaufort in search of a sponsor, claiming that there was none among the folk round about Killarney fit to stand sponsor for his newborn son. So, he bridled his horse and rode off toward Beaufort. But, as he went, "he met a stranger riding a white horse, a good-looking gentleman wearing red knee-breeches, a swallow-tailed coat," and a tall hat. The stranger asked Connors where he was going at such an hour. "To Beaufort," said Connors, "to find sponsors for my young son." But the man told Connors he had passed the road to Beaufort by a mile. So Connors turned back only to find the man once again. And the man told Connors he had passed the road a second time. Thus, turning back once more, he "rode on for an hour or so," until finding no side road, he encountered the stranger a third time. And, the stranger, saying that the night was too far gone to travel further, invited Connors to spend the night within his castle. But as Connors slept, the stranger took his clothing, put them on a corpse in the very likeness of Connors, and placed the corpse on Connor's horse, sending it—with a great slap to the thigh— back to Killarney. There, the body arriving, the whole neighborhood took to lamenting the death of John Connors, "for wasn't he a good man and the father of a large family?"

It was three weeks before Connors awoke, naked and shivering. Then covering himself in the single sheet which the stranger proffered him, he found himself alone in a barren field without a sign of the castle or the stranger or even the horse that had borne him hither. He made his way home on foot, keeping "to the fields for fear of being seen by somebody," until he approached some boys out looking for stray sheep who fled at the very sight of him. Then, as night fell, and "Connors' wife made her children get to their knees and offer up the rosary for the repose of their father's soul," Connors—still wrapped in his single sheet—rapped at his own window. "May the Almighty God and His Blessed Mother give rest to your soul," cried his wife when she saw him and, only when he summoned the parish priest, would she let her husband step over his own threshold. It was in fact the priest who, when Connors explained to him his disappearance, was able to clear up the mystery: "Oh, then, it's Daniel O'Donohue, King of Lochlein, that played the trick on you," said the priest. "Why didn't you get sponsors at home in this parish for your son as you did for your daughters? For the remainder of your life show no partiality to son or daughter among your children. It would be a just punishment if more trouble came to you. You were not content with the will of God, though it is the duty of every man to take what God gives him. Three weeks ago, your supposed body was buried and all thought you dead through your own pride and willfulness." And John Connors took the priest's good advice to heart. "No matter how large his family was in after years, John Connors never went from home to find sponsors."

The fairy chief, Daniel O'Donohue, mentioned in the tale was described as "King of Lochlein," Lochlein being "the old name of the upper lake of Killarney." He was, at times, "called O'Donohue of the Glen" and may have been the same fairy known as the Knight of the Glen—for both he and the Knight had a steed that was coveted by a certain Black Thief.[26] He is typical of the fairies that haunted the wild places of the Irish countryside and maintained the integrity of its inhabitants. In fact, O'Donohue and his kind are the same mysterious characters that haunt the ancient Arthurian tales from Britain, Wales, and Brittany. Just as a man of rural Ireland—to his seeming ill fortune but, in fact, to his great and unexpected luck—stumbles upon a mysterious assemblage of strange folk in the unbeaten pathways of the forest, field, or waste, so too do Arthur, Gawain, Lancelot, and—of course—Perceval. In one poignant episode of the *Quest for the Holy Grail*, Arthur's squire, Chaus, dreams in the depth of night that Arthur has left to pursue the quest without him. He thereupon rouses himself, shakes off his slumber, saddles his destrier, and sets off in pursuit of his liege. He follows Arthur's tracks until he comes upon a ruined chapel in the midst of a forested waste. Therein lies in state the corpse of a knight overseen by no other than four tapers in golden candlesticks. Chaus snuffs out one of the tapers and conceals its golden seat under his hose but, as he leaves the chapel, he is confronted by the dead knight's brother: "black and foul" and "taller afoot than the squire himself a-horseback." He "held a great, twin-edged knife in his hand," and demanded the return of the candlestick. But when Chaus refuses, claiming that he would present the candlestick to no other than his lord Arthur, the mysterious knight thrust his knife into Chaus' ribs right up to the hilt whereupon the squire awoke in his own bed crying, "Holy Mary! The priest! The priest! Help me for I am dead!" Upon administering the last rite, the priest found both the hilt of the fairy knight's blade protruding from Chaus' ribs and the golden candlestick secreted in the dead squire's hose.[27]

As the mandating of Christianity that began in 4th century Rome came to pervade all Europe, the displacement of indigenous religious traditions proceeded in a predictable manner, relegating one-time gods to the status of culture heroes or shrouding them in the guise of Christian saints. We will shortly see how the Greco-Roman patron of the city of Palermo, Saturn, is most likely lurking to this day in the visage of a peculiar personage referred to as the Genius of Palermo, and how the Greco-Roman virgin goddess, Artemis, finds expression in Palermo's treatment of the Immaculate Virgin. Likewise, the ancient Celtic deities of England, Ireland, and Wales were reconfigured in the Realm of Faerie. The fate of the Norse gods was much the same as that of their Greco-Roman and Celtic counterparts. Inasmuch as Christianity had come to Iceland by the time Snorri Sturleson wrote down a smattering of Norse myths in the early 13th century, he spoke of the various deities—the Æsir who inhabited the mythic realm of Asgard—as powerful magicians who had traveled to the north from their native Troy when their city was sacked by the Greeks. In this, he was following a time-honored tradition in which not only Virgil defined the lineage that came to dominate Rome as descending from a Trojan refugee, Aeneas, but also other poets postulated a number of Trojan ancestors for the various realms that came to be dominated by Rome. Felix Brutus was said to be the Trojan founder of Britain and the Elymians of western Sicily were said to have been led to their new stronghold by the Trojan Ancestes. The same process was at play when Christians and Muslims alike inscribed themselves into Hebraic myth: the first viewing themselves as the natural heirs to God's covenant with Abraham through the near sacrifice of Isaac; the second viewing themselves as the natural heir to God's covenant with Abraham through the near sacrifice of Ishmael. Among the essential Norse deities are Odin, the great All Father, Freyja, goddess of love, sacrifices, and magic, and Loki, the preeminent trickster who sometimes furthers but too often thwarts Odin's designs. Yet the most powerful of all the Æsir is Thor: Imagine a chariot drawn by two sturdy goats, Tanngnjostr and Tanngrisnir, careening across the sky in its descent from Asgard (the realm of the gods) to Midgard (the earth), its driver wielding his massive hammer, Mjolnir, which spawns lightning bolts and peels of thunder with each mighty blow against frost-giant, dwarf, or troll. One night, when Thor, accompanied by Loki, descended from his chariot to take refuge with a peasant family, he butchered his goats, stewed their meat, and shared the feast with his hosts, instructing them to throw the bones in the goatskins which lay stretched out upon the floor. The son, having a thigh, broke open the thigh bone to get at the marrow. Thus, when in the morning, Thor resuscitated his goats, one was found to have a limp brought on by a broken leg. "It is not necessary to dwell on this part of the story. All can understand how frightened" the host became when he saw Thor's "brows sink down over his eyes. Thor took hold of the handle of his hammer so hard that his knuckles grew white and, as might be expected," the peasant "and all his household cried aloud and sued for peace, offering him as an atonement all that they possessed. When he saw their fear, Thor's wrath left him and he took as a ransom the bondsman's children, Thjalfi and Roskva. They became his servants, and have always accompanied him since that time."

Of the All Father Odin, Snorri tells us that two ravens sit on his shoulders "and bring to his ears all that they hear and see. Their names are Huginn and Muninn. At dawn he sends them out to fly over the whole world, and they come back at breakfast time. Thus, he is called Rafnagud (Ravengod)." Further, he gathers half those who have fallen in battle, sending out the Valkyries as their escort, about himself in the great hall Valhalla to feast on the "flesh of the boar Sahrimner" who "is boiled every day and is whole again in the evening." Of Freyja, Snorri tells us that her chariot is drawn by sleek cats and the half of those fallen in battle that don't go to Valhalla are gathered up to her hall, Sesrynmer, seated within her own dwelling-place, Folkvang. For her are women of noble birth called *frú* (German *frau*) and, of course, that day we anxiously await throughout our work week called Freyja's Day (English Friday). Of Loki, Snorri tells us his own offspring, born of a giantess, will bring upon Midgard the apocalypse of Ragnarok: the ravenous but insatiable Fenris Wolf will swallow Odin whole but will be killed in turn by Odin's son, Vidarr, God of Vengeance; Hel, Queen of the Underworld, where those who die of natural causes drink their tepid mead within a cheerless hall, will unleash the hapless dead upon the world; and the Midgard Serpent, who dwells in the sea, will crack open the land, inundating its onetime cheerful halls with venomous draughts. Though Thor will vanquish the Midgard Serpent, he will die of its venom as he takes his ninth step away from his ill-fated victory.[28]

They may have been rendered cultural heroes rather than gods by the changing religious framework in which they moved. Still, the Æsir—like the mysterious fairies of the Celtic world—maintained much of their godly prerogatives. Further, they—again, like their Celtic counterparts—moved in a world alive with spiritual energies. Just as fairy raths, the broken remnants of Neolithic fortifications, were thought to be haunted by the "good folk" in Ireland, Nordic barrows—ancient burial mounds, sometimes stone-chambered, sometimes simply earthen knolls—were thought to be the haunts of the mysterious creatures we have come to know from fairy tales as well as the writings of J.R.R. Tolkien and J.K. Rowling: dragons, elves, goblins, trolls, and dwarves. The dragon sleeps harmlessly within the barrow, jealously guarding its treasure, perhaps the grave goods buried along with the hero for whom the barrow was erected, until molested by some errant treasure hunter.[29] Elves are, for the most part, indistinguishable from Celtic fairies. They look like us, though with a more ephemeral substance, and the best known among them are often representatives of ancient nobility. Trolls and dwarves are mysterious mountain dwellers, as squat and solid as the rocks and caves in which they dwell. Goblins are monsters with strange, inhuman, and not unusually animal-like faces. They are, sometimes, wicked and cruel, though sometimes simply mischievous and cunning.

Monsters

Dragons, trolls, dwarves, and goblins are but a few examples of a large and frightful class of spirits: monsters. These malevolent spirits, while often to be found in a society's myths—Satan, for instance, or the Hindu demon

Ravana—more often than not are found in a society's legends, harrying our heroes, and folktales, bewitching or otherwise terrorizing our good but vulnerable Ash Girls and No Account Boys. From the Anglo-Saxon Grendel to the Balkan Count Dracula to the almost innumerable cannibal-monsters that appear in Iroquois and Zuni myth—the Naked Bear, for instance, or Old Lady Granduncle—monsters seem to embody the inchoate fears of a society. Perhaps more than any other element of myth, they answer E.B. Tylor's suspicion that the origins of mythology are to be found in the dream or, in this case, the nightmare.

Among the most common malevolent spirits globally are sorcerers and witches. Sorcerers are usually described as being in control of their malevolent powers. They consciously manipulate ritual much as shamans and priests do. But whereas shamans and priests perform ritual for socially sanctioned purposes, sorcerers do it for socially proscribed, self-serving, and even nefarious reasons. In fact, a society's shamans—because the type of magic they practice is often called upon to combat sorcery and therefore demands knowledge of its methods—are not unusually suspected of being potential sorcerers. The San maintain such a belief. Richard Lee, while interviewing the powerful shaman Wa Na, was offered the following account of the sort of danger particularly powerful healers might present society: "The great healers were my husband and two other men, both of whom gave me *num*," she explained. "All are now dead. None were killed by god. All were killed by people. These great healers went hunting as lions, searching for people to kill. Then someone would shoot an arrow or throw a spear into these healers who were prowling around as lions. When these great healers tried to change back into their own human skins, they usually died. When a healer changes into a lion, only other healers can still see him. To ordinary people, he is invisible." These shamans, prowling about in the form of lions are said to bite or maul people who, as a result, can sicken and die.[30] Sorcerers are a bit different than the spiritual entities so far discussed because they demonstrably exist. That is to say, while at times they are simply believed in, at others, they are pointed out and some people will even claim to be sorcerers. Globally, accusations of sorcery seem to be more often leveled against men than women.

Conversely, witches are individuals who are animated by a malevolent power over which they have no control. Rather, their very presence brings harm on others. Some societies avoid accusing people of being witches, though a belief in witches may be used to help explain the various misfortunes that might afflict people. Others will accuse people of witchcraft and even punish them. The Iroquois prophet Handsome Lake suggested that witches publicly repent their witchcraft and receive no punishment thereafter. If it were too

hard for them to repent publicly, they might go alone into the forest and there repent. But such an empathetic approach is not always taken. Some societies rather embark on violent anti-witch campaigns, actually trying and executing suspected witches. These campaigns are often related to periods of cultural crisis during which accusations seem to fall disproportionally—as they did in Europe and colonial America—on the shoulders of women. Colonial America, infamously, was subject to a virulent "witch craze," a period of cultural turbulence that culminated in a number of witch trials and executions.

Not surprisingly given their European origins, American colonists heavily associated the practice of witchcraft with Satan worship and—in a period of colonial history characterized by fear of a sometimes harsh and forbidding environment combined with a virulent fear of the people who were native to such a forbidding land, Native Americans, the American witch craze took on a life of its own. Our major source for understanding the witch craze as it unfolded in colonial America is Cotton Mather's *The Wonders of the Invisible World*, written in 1693. Notably, Mather's working assumption is that America was the Chosen Nation—the recipient of the New Covenant to which we recently alluded—that had been ordained by God to be founded in the devil's own haunt. Thus it was, according to Mather and others, that the early colonists of the Massachusetts Bay Colony were so harried by witches. One of the accused witches, a certain Susanna Martin, was said to be foul-tempered and given to vicious harangues against anyone who crossed her. She was accused of sickening her enemies' cows so that they died, setting upon her detractors whom she would scratch, pinch, and bite, in a spectral form, and appearing within one's bedchamber as a succubus, laying so heavily upon her victim that he was immobilized in fear. When asked to explain why she caused such terror among her neighbors she was purported to have said: "I cannot tell; it may be that the Devil bears me more Malice than another."

One of the accusations laid upon Susanna Martin and a number of the other accused witches of Salem was—as we have just seen—that they would appear mysteriously in the dark of night within one's bedchamber, whereupon they would sit upon their victims' chests, immobilizing them with fear. This accusation answers a striking element of the dreamscape that has been analyzed by David Hufford in a study chillingly titled "The Terror That Comes in the Night." Here, Hufford considers the Newfoundland tradition of the Old Hag who comes in the dead of night, sits heavily upon one's chest, simultaneously

Opposite: **Gargoyles at Notre-Dame de Paris. A gargoyle is literally a waterspout but the term today generally includes all grotesqueries in medieval architecture (Wikipedia, photograph by John Cornellier [top], Florian Siebeck [center], Prosthetic Head [bottom]).**

immobilizing her victim and making him feel as if he is suffocating, as if his throat is constricting so menacingly that, should he attempt to cry out, no more than a pathetic squeak—alerting no one to his distress beyond the Old Hag herself—would escape. And, if he fails to awaken during the attack, he will die. According to Hufford's respondents, one can summon the Old Hag against another through reciting the Lord's Prayer backward and in the name of the devil and one can ward her off her attack by drawing her blood with a pocket knife or praying. Hufford characterizes the Old Hag tradition as a culturally inscribed explanation of a universal physiological phenomenon: the night terror—and its symptomatic sleep paralysis—that occasionally arises in the nightmare experience.[31]

It is likely, in fact, that the vast array of monsters which haunt our global mythologies have their source in our nightmares' worst phantoms. One particularly chilling monster is the Romanian vampire: said to be the corpse of one who—usually as the result of some sort of peculiarity, perhaps a reputation for witchcraft, perhaps a disability, perhaps a belief that his death was brought about by suicide—retained his soul after death. He was, as a result, thought to bring about the death of relatives and fellow villagers. Further, he was said to be in communion with the devil (*dracul*), witches, and those afflicted with the evil eye, and—like these other nefarious entities—he would scrupulously avoid houses protected with garlic. If an inexplicable series of deaths afflicted a family after his demise, the suspected vampire would be disinterred and, if his corpse lacked the usual signs of decomposition, was red and bloated with the vital source that he nightly imbibed, or found to be sitting up, "like a Turk," in his casket, a stake would be driven through his heart or his heart would be removed, burned in hot cinders, and drunk in a potion of water and ashes by potential victims. Thereby further catastrophes could be averted. He was not unusually thought to be animated by a kind of unholy and obsessive love, the knowledge of which seems to have—along with newly emergent scientific descriptions of blood-sucking bats from South America—made its way into Bram Stoker's novel *Dracula*.[32]

Wherever they exist, there is a suggestion that monsters such as the sorcerer, witch, or vampire, the Naked Bear or Old Lady Granduncle, become more perilous to the individual who does not honor societal rules. Thus, the Christian devil—and by extension his realm, hell—are clearly within the functional traditions of monsters globally. But there are monsters who seem to attack out of a sense of envy. Grendel, for instance, seems unable to endure the revelry of the castle Heorot and thus subjects Hrothgar's stronghold and its inhabitants with his cannibalistic rampages. But, whether these monsters are motivated by breeches of social conduct on the part of their victims or envy of the living on the part of the living dead, they have at least one thing in common: they seem to always inhabit the interstices between life and death, between health and disease, and thus they tenant the very places that cause us the greatest inchoate terror. Emblematic of their propensities are the Mayan lords of Xibalba, the Underworld, whom—as we earlier witnessed—Blow Gun Hunter and Little Jaguar subdued: Xiquiripat (Flying Pack Saddle) and Cuchumaquic (Gathered Blood) who caused men to bleed to death; Ahalganá (Edema) and Ahalpuh (Pus Maker) who caused men to swell, ooze pus, and become jaundiced; Chamibac (Lord of the Bone Staff) and Chamiaholom (Lord of the Skull Staff) who caused men to "waste away until they were nothing but skin and bone," as well as Ahalmez (Filth Maker) and Ahaltocob (Misery) who would send disasters upon men "as they were going home," so that "they would be found wounded, stretched out, face up, on the ground, dead." But it is not only the Lords of Xibalba who exist as incarnations of our greatest fears. Both vampires and zombies are revenants, ghouls that rise from the grave to terrorize the living: the first in order to create more of themselves, the second to endure unending labor as the slave of a sorcerer. The werewolf wreaks its deadly havoc when night, the abode of the dead, is invaded by day, the abode of the living, in the guise of the full moon: then the quick and the dead come into consonance with one another with catastrophic results. Adodarho, Old Lady Granduncle, Grendel, and any number of cannibal-monsters threaten to make of men beasts of prey, turning the hunter into the hunted, and rendering us into nothing more than quivering masses of fear that feed upon ourselves.

Mythic Semiotics: The Signifier, the Signified and the Sign

Culture, as we have seen, consists of the system of beliefs and behaviors acknowledged by a society in order to sustain itself: to sustain itself, that is, with regard to its various material needs but also to sustain its integrity as a social group—whether that group is as small as a family or as large as a nation. Significantly, any single individual—because each of us maintains multiple affiliations—participates in multiple, and often conflicting, cultures. For instance, one's familial culture may come into conflict with the culture that emerges in one's group of friends; likewise, the culture of a minority group— perhaps a sexual, religious, or ethnic minority—may come into conflict with the culture of a dominant, or majority, group within a single society. And these conflicts may become exacerbated in the cultures of various political groupings—conservatives, for instance, or liberals—within the society. Read simplistically, the definition of culture would suggest that we could predict a person's thoughts or behaviors on the basis of his or her societal affiliations. But as Ward Goodenough aptly points out, a person does not believe and practice every- thing everyone else in his or her society believes and practices. Rather, he or she is "competent" in the set of beliefs and behaviors characteristically acknowl- edged by his or her society.[33] In other words, one doesn't have to be a Christian to be conversant with the concept of Trinity. It is likely that being a member of a society dominated by Christianity, one would become competent in some of the basic precepts of Christianity: the belief in the Trinity, for instance.

For this reason, culture is best understood not as an *essential aspect of being* but rather as a *variable process of communication*, not necessarily expressing who one is but rather where one is coming from. Put another way, one could say that culture is a semiotic system, a system of signification. Semiotics, in this context, is the study of the signifier, the signified, and especially the sign: that which unites the signifier and the signified. Further, it extends the explo- ration of the intersection of language and meaning beyond the study of verbal artifacts to include behavioral and material artifacts as well. In Roland Barthes' famous exemplification of the method, the rose is the signifier; passion is the signified; and the rose as a symbol of passion is the sign.[34] Yet, this passion- laden rose doesn't exist in a vacuum. Its semiotic impact is expanded when Anne Brontë admonishes, "he that dares not grasp the thorn should never crave the rose," or William Blake laments, "O rose thou art sick," or William Shake- speare exclaims, "A rose by any other name would smell as sweet," or Gertrude Stein chides, "A rose is a rose is a rose." Barthes, of course, limits his discussion to secular, and particularly political, mythologies. But if we extend his analysis to actual—rather than secular or political—mythologies, we may begin to real- ize that the spirit as a sign which contains within the geography of the body such trenchant ecological and sociological metaphors would offer the perfect vehicle for human devotion. Not only would such a sign allow the faithful to formulate, on the basis of its anthropomorphic nature, a sense of identification with it but also to experience, through ritual propitiation, a sense of control over the ecological and sociological exigencies contained within its confines.

6. Ritual Enactment and Affiliation

The Myth-Ritual Complex

Religion is most productively viewed as the necessary outcome of the myth-ritual complex. Myth is the vehicle which allows us the opportunity to learn about the gods. But ritual, through mythic reenactment, is the vehicle which allows us to incorporate their essence into our very being. Thus, while myth fosters identification with the body of the gods, ritual solidifies affiliation within the body of the faithful. Think for a moment of Christian communion. By reenacting the myth of the Last Supper, participants become, in a way, temporarily like the deity. This act of becoming like Christ, the famed *imitatio Christi*, is reinforced in Christian communion through the act of ingesting symbols of the deity's body and blood: bread and wine. It may, in fact, be its ability to affect such an incorporation that defines ritual as one of the primary vehicles in which a society's group identity is forged. Think here of the name of the central Christian ritual: Communion. The name, rather than emphasizing the reenactment of the Last Supper, or the incorporation of Christ into the body of the faithful, emphasizes the incorporation of the communicants into a single, unified, community.

This is what, it seems to me, Émile Durkheim was attempting to get at in his discussion of religion: the manner in which ritual knits together the communicative power of verbal, behavioral, and material culture to engender the "shock and awe" factor that most dramatically fosters affiliation. In the words of C. Scott Littleton, "Durkheim pointed out that religion and society everywhere are inextricably bound together, and that the former is necessarily a 'collective representation'—a projection, if you will—of the later."[1] Perhaps it is the ability of ritual to engender community that has inspired some political regimes to depend so heavily on secular ritual in order to instill a sense of nationalistic fervor in its citizenry—so much so that some analysts have described the creeds which employ such tactics as religious in tenor. It is likely that Melville was thinking of such instances when he had Ahab nail the storied doubloon to the Pequod's mast, promising the gold piece to that sailor who first spotted the White Whale and, thereby, whipping his crew into such a frenzy that it became entirely invested in his mad scheme.

Just as Communion serves to solidify the Christian community, perhaps even globally, the ritual life of Islam may be that aspect of the faith most responsible for forging a pan–Islamic identity in the Maghreb, Islamic North Africa, the Mashriq, Islamic Southwest Asia, and beyond. The sense of affiliation engendered in Islam's rich ritual life can even, at times, supersede distinctions between Sunnis, who view Abu Bukr, Muhammad's father-in-law, as the prophet's rightful successor, and tend to seek authority in the person of a Caliph, and Shias, who view Ali, Muhammad's son-in-law, as the prophet's rightful successor, and tend to seek authority in the person of an Imam—for wherever they reside and whatever sect they recognize, Muslims adhere to Idabat, the Five Pillars of Islam: (1) Shahada, the profession of belief in the one God, Allah, and the sanctity of the teachings of his prophet, Muhammad; (2) Salat, five daily prayers toward the Holy City of Mecca; (3) Sawm, fasting during the month of Ramadan; (4) Sakat, charity to those who are less fortunate than oneself; and (5) Hajj, at least one pilgrimage to Mecca. Perhaps the Hajj, more than anything else, transcends national boundaries to unite all Islam's adherents into a single body. For in the Hajj, the great pilgrimage to the birthplace of Islam, Muslims nearly universally see the culmination of the Five Pillars. All who are financially and physically able descend on Mecca in the *Dhul-Hijjah*, the month of the Hajj, to the oft repeated refrain, "There is no god but Allah and Muhammad is his Messenger." Uniformly dressed in white, the pilgrims enter the Great Mosque. Here, they encounter the Kaaba, a black cubical shrine built of unmortared granite and adorned with the sacred names of God. It is said to house the spot where the first man, Adam, worshipped and to have been built by Ibrahim (Abraham) and his firstborn son, Ishmael. It is on those counts that Muslims specifically face the Kaaba, rather than Mecca itself, during their five daily prayers. The Kaaba is circled seven times by the pilgrims who, from there, travel to various spots where the Angel Jibril (Gabriel) revealed the teachings of the Qur'an to Muhammad or where Muhammad, in his turn, revealed the teachings to his followers. Before their return to Mecca, they encounter the three pillars of the Jamraat, representative of the three temptations that Satan used to dissuade Ibrahim from honoring God's request to sacrifice Ishmael. Like Ibrahim before them, the pilgrims defy Satan and drive him away with stones, but whereas Ibrahim launched his stones at Satan himself, the pilgrims symbolically reenact his fury through casting their stones at the three pillars of the Jamraat. Beyond the Five Pillars, Islam celebrates a feast in honor of the close of Ramadan and another in honor of Ibrahim's near sacrifice of Ishmael. And there is as well veneration of saints, holy men or good *djinns* (genies), which center on shrines in both villages and urban neighborhoods. Likewise, adherents regularly attend mosque where they learn the lessons imparted by the Qur'an which reports the Revelations received by Muhammad from Allah via visitations from the angel Jibril while in a meditative trance in a cave on Mount Hira (not far from Mecca), the Hadith which reports upon Muhammad's ministry and the Sharia, writings which develop a code of conduct based on the Qur'an and Hadith.[2]

Ritual will often make use of specialized language, perhaps containing archaic words not understood by all (or sometimes any) of the ritual's participants. Catholicism historically made use of Latin in order to maintain continuity with its historical roots in Roman society but also because it functioned as a *lingua franca* among the various societies that adopted Christianity. Perhaps Latin was retained as well because it maintained religious authority firmly within the hands of the clergy. Such was the claim of Protestant Reformationists—though today, some Protestants insist on the spiritual purity of the King James translation of the Bible. Hebrew centers the recitations of Jewish Shabbats (Sabbaths) and archaic African terms are employed in the Vodou (Voodoo) Service. Many Muslims feel that any translation of the Qur'an does not contain the sacred essence of its revelation which only resides in the original Arabic. But beyond specialized language, ritual depends on sacred spaces, from simple household altars and roadside shrines to ornate cathedrals, temples, synagogues, and mosques. And these ritual spaces are demarcated with any number of sacred items. Such items may include the ornate altars that adorn Christian churches, Zuni Kivas, and Hindu temples, not to mention the sacred sculptures and items that these altars house. So striking is the body of material culture that pertains to ritual that it, in many ways, forms the basis of a society's artistic production. Think, for instance, of the façade of Notre Dame du Paris with its striking assembly of saints, sinners, angels and demons, all arrayed about its magnificent Rose Window, a portal to heaven itself. But despite its diversity of ritual language and its rich array of material culture, ritual is characterized by a number of common forms: rites of passage, in which an initiate or a set of initiates moves from one social status to another; rites of intensification, in which a group—often at a moment of stress caused by illness, environmental hardship, or political turmoil—attempts to ameliorate its condition; festivals, calendrical ceremonies insuring the proper progression of the agricultural cycle or great feasts feting the gods themselves; and pilgrimages, during the course of which the pilgrims follow in the footsteps of their gods or particularly revered saints.

Essential to establishing the various social statuses that create society, ushering—as they do—each individual from one status to another, are rites of passage. We earlier considered Victor Turner's explication of the manner in which the rite of passage allows an initiate to emotionally experience his or her change of status through a tripartite formulation: (1) separation, whereby the initiate is symbolically shorn of his or her previous status; (2) transition (or *limen*), which is characterized by the merging of symbols from both the status one is leaving behind as well as the status one is attempting to attain; and (3) incorporation, whereby the symbols of the new status are bestowed upon the initiate. Most interesting is the interstitial phase: transition. Turner characterizes it by the term liminality (from the Latin, *limen*, or threshold). Here, in Turner's view, the initiate is in an ambiguous but spiritually powerful state "betwixt and between" two articulate integers in the society's social order: perhaps girl and woman; perhaps boy and man. Indeed, the entire ritual is geared toward allowing the initiate (as well as those who participate in the ritual as mere spectators or active sponsors) to feel the liminal moment. But, notably, Turner sees this same process, and particularly the moment of liminality, as being in play not only in rites of passage but also in rites of intensification, which have as their specific focus the forging of a group's communal identity—especially at moments of particular need. In the San medicine dance, for instance, the liminal moment is achieved when the women's singing and the men's dancing have reached such a crescendo that the recognized shamans start to enter *kia*, trance, and the ghosts themselves enter the thronging dance circle. It is only then that the group's store of *num*, medicine, begins to flow reciprocally throughout the body of worshippers. Perhaps with the advent of agriculture, for which the scrupulous maintenance of a ritual calendar ensures the fertility of the crops and animals upon which the people depend, calendrical festivals begin to overshadow foragers' periodicalized medicine dances. But, here again, liminality is fostered in the ubiquitous feast, the sharing forth of the central foodstuffs, particularly the society's staples, those "staffs of life" that signify the society's well-being. And this feast, with its liminal energy, is carried forth into the festivals of preindustrial mercantile societies wherein the bulk of the populace is still in touch with agricultural production. Liminality likewise animates the pivotal moments of the pilgrimage. As the pilgrims enter the Great Mosque during their Hajj, for instance, the uniform white clothing that they wear is an apt expression of their liminal state, "betwixt and between" all social categories, neither what they were before nor yet what they will soon become, equal in all measures. Though, despite the moment of ritual egalitarianism, with their completion of the Hajj and their return home, the pilgrims characteristically gain significant position within their various communities.[3]

Judaism

Judaism provides a particularly apt illustration of the role of ritual in forging group identity. Though characterized by a number of subdivisions which emerged during the formation and spread of the diaspora, the scattering of the Jewish people throughout the world, Judaism is as well characterized by a marked degree of shared identity born of a common mythology and ritual calendar. Whether approaching Judaism from an Orthodox (literal), Conservative (ritually conservative but theologically moderate), Reform (theologically liberal) or Hasidic (ultra-orthodox and charismatic) perspective, the Torah's account of the bondage of the Children of Israel in Egypt—commemorated, as we will shortly see, in Sukkot, Passover, and Shavuot—serves to give meaning to the notion of the diaspora as a whole. Having been removed from the land promised, according to the biblical account in Genesis, to their progenitor Abraham, first by the Assyrian (8th century BCE) and next by Nebuchadnezzar's Babylonian invasion (6th century BCE)—in which the First, or Solomon's, Temple was razed—the Jewish diaspora found its origins. But it was during the Roman campaign of the 1st century CE—in which the Second Temple was raised and Jerusalem became, under the name Ælia Capitolina, a Roman colony into which Jews were forbidden entrance upon pain of death—that the diaspora was finalized. From that time forward, Jewish identity was forged in the crucible of a diasporic European history. Though there were always Jewish communities in Israel—as well as in other southwest Asian localities such as Syria, Iraq, Iran, and Egypt—after the Roman campaign, the descendants of which are collectively known as the Mizrahim, the majority of Jews, from then on, lived in Europe where they split—in the early Middle Ages—into two great communities. The Ashkenazim, historically *shetl* (small village) dwellers, speakers of Yiddish, and characteristically small-scale farmers with some craftsmen and merchants among them, based in central and eastern Europe represent the decisive bulk of today's Jewish population: some 70 percent though upwards of 90 percent previous to the Holocaust. The Sephardim, speakers of Ladino, historically settled in Iberia (Spain and Portugal) and (after Ferdinand and Isabella expelled Jews from Spain in 1492) Italy, North Africa, Turkey, and the eastern Mediterranean, represent perhaps 20 percent of the global Jewish population. Other, smaller populations exist. For instance, Italkim, Jews who lived in Italy from Roman times, may represent the remnants of the root population that gave rise to both the Ashkenazic and Sephardic communities.[4] Despite such a scattering of Jews throughout the world, the Torah's account of the Egyptian captivity (as recounted in the Exodus) and its ritual commemorations (particularly in the context of Passover) not only give form to the Jewish community in the diaspora but offer as well the promise of a return to the homeland: a return that is continuously underscored in the ritual calendar by the Aliyah, the "coming up" or "ascending" to the lectern to read from the Torah, which suggests to the participants the ineffable hope of a return—in spirit or in actuality—to a restored (or, today, secure) Israel.

In his memoir *The Garden of the Finzi-Contini*, Giorgio Bassani gets to the heart of this sense of belonging to a singular community—and, ominously, not belonging to the wider community among which it moves—as he charts the creeping effects of anti–Semitism on the Jewish community of Ferrara at a time when Italian Fascism and German Nazism were becoming more firmly entrenched in one another's ideologies. Indeed, as the Jews of Ferrara fell more and more under the sway of a nationalistic frenzy constructed largely on their backs, so much so that they were banned from the city's tennis club, the significance of what it meant to be a Jew in pre-war Europe became more pressing: "For it's a fact that Jews—Sephardic and Ashkenazic, western and Levantine, Tunisian, Berber, Yemenite, and even Ethiopian, under whatever sky History scattered them, are and always will be Jews, that is to say, close relatives," Bassani's father claims. And Bassani himself, thinking over the significance of his father's observation in the charged environment in which Ferrara's Jews find themselves, attempts to work out the significance of his community's identity and the even more singular identity his own family shares with the somewhat eccentric Finzi-Contini family: "That we were Jews, nevertheless, and inscribed in the ledgers of the same Jewish community, still counted fairly little in our case. For what on earth did the word 'Jew' mean," beyond that particular "intimacy—secret, its value calculable only by those who shared it—derived from the fact that our two families, not through choice, but thanks to a tradition older than any possible memory, belonged to the same religious rite, or rather to the same *school*?"

When we met at the threshold of the entrance to the temple, as a rule at dusk, after the embarrassed formalities exchanged by our parents in the gloom of the porch, in the end we almost always climbed, still a group, the steep stairs that led to the third floor, where, crowded with a mixed throng, wide, echoing with sounds of organ and singing like a church—and so high, among the rooftops, that on some May evenings, with the big side windows flung open towards the setting sun, at a certain point we found ourselves bathed in a kind of golden mist—that was the Italian synagogue. So only we, Jews, to be sure, but also brought up in the observance of the same rite, could realize actually what it meant to have the same family bench in the Italian synagogue, up there on the third floor, instead of on the second, in the German one, so different in its severe, almost Lutheran assemblage of wealthy, bourgeois bowler hats. And this was not all; because, even taking for granted, outside the strictly Jewish world, an Italian synagogue's being different from a German one; with everything in particular that such distinction involved on the social and the psychological planes, who, besides us, would have been able to provide specific information about "the Via Vittoria people," just to give one example? This expression regularly referred to members of the four or five families who had the right to attend the separate little Levantine synagogue, also known as the Fano synagogue, situated on the fourth floor of an old house on Via Vittoria: the Da Fano family of Via Scienze, in fact, the Cohens of Via Gioco del Pallone, the Levis of Piazza Ariostea, the Levi-Minzis of Viale Cavour, and I forget what other isolated family groups: all slightly odd people in any case, characters always a bit ambiguous and elusive, for whom religion in the Italian school had taken on too popular, theatrical a form, almost Catholic, with evident effect also on the character of the people, open and optimistic, for the most part, very "Po Valley," whereas religion for those others had remained essentially worship to be performed in a small group, in semiclandestine chapels to which it was best to go at night, slipping along the darkest and most infamous alleyways of the ghetto. No, no; only we, born and brought up intra muros, so to speak, could know, could really understand these things.[5]

In other words, whether Italkim (Italian, in Bassani's terms), Ashkenazim (German), or Mizrahim (Levantine), the Jews of Ferrara—at least in Bassani's estimation—most thoroughly felt their affinity to one another and difference from the outside world—in their weekly celebration of Shabbat (Sabbath): until, that is, the Holocaust cast its dark pall over its remembrance.

Among a number of people who kindly allowed me to interview them on the subject of Jewish culture and identity was Bobbi. Both her maternal and paternal grandparents emigrated from the Ukraine and grew up not terribly far from Kiev. Bobbi grew up in a New England community then dominated by Orthodox Jews congregating together because of the presence of the Orthodox synagogue which centered so much of the community's life and, of course, because Jews were not always welcome in nearby Christian neighborhoods. Her mother's father was a Kohen (Priest) but her father's family were not particularly devout, some opting not to undergo Bar or Bat Mitvah—the boy's and girl's initiation respectively. Bobbi sees this lack of strict participation in religious duties, including observing Shabbat, as an economic necessity. And this reality is significant enough for the existence of a particular classification, that of "*shomer Shabbat*," to refer to someone who conscientiously observes the rules that govern the Shabbat. In fact, many Jewish businesses in Bobbi's community stayed open during Shabbat—starting at sundown on Friday evening and continuing until sundown Saturday—simply because they did not have the resources to close. Bobbi strongly associated strict religious observance with relative affluence: affluent women, for instance, having the time to participate in the Women's Sisterhood of the Temple, a luxury her own working mother could ill afford. That said, her mother maintained a Kosher household, a tradition that Bobbi continues, and actively celebrated the major Jewish holidays.

The essential rites of passage for a boy are Brit Milah, the Covenant of Circumcision, creating of him a member of the Jewish nation, and Bar Mitvah, the Boy's Commandment, obligating him as a full participant in the Jewish faith. Brit (or Simchat) Bat, the Girl's Covenant, and Bat Mitvah, the Girl's Commandment, function similarly to the boy's more firmly established rites. Governing Brit Milah is the concept of the covenant, or *brit*, for circumcision not only admits a boy into the Jewish community. It also, as a covenant between God and the Jewish people, creates the Jewish nation. It was instituted, at God's command, by Abraham at the birth of Isaac. But an especially interesting feature of the ritual, undertaken eight days after the boy's birth (remembering that, in Judaism, the day begins with the advent of the evening rather than at midnight) alludes to another epoch of Jewish history: a chair is set aside in remembrance of Elijah who protested Queen Jezebel's attempt, in the reign of King Ahab, to institute the worship of Baal. It is sometimes said that Jezebel also attempted to end circumcision and thus God's covenant with Israel. Elijah stands—perhaps because of his intercession on behalf of the rite—as the protector of infants, shielding them against the predations of Lilith: Adam's first, disobedient, wife—she who being created, like her husband, from the dust of the earth, refused to abide by his commands, and sends various ills against infants to this day.[6] The Sandek (Godfather), generally an older male relative, occupying a chair just to the left of Elijah's chair, holds his little charge on his knees as the Mohel—generally a rabbi trained in circumcision—performs the procedure. Today, a baby girl, too, has her ceremony, Brit Bat, sometimes held, like the Brit Milah, on the eighth day after her birth—during which her father is called to the temple lectern to read from the Torah and perhaps, as well, to announce her Hebrew name. Then, on the 31st day after birth, the boy—if he is his mother's firstborn—undergoes the Redemption of the Firstborn Son. Since the firstborn Jewish boys (unlike the firstborn Egyptian boys) were not killed at the Passover, they were consecrated to God and destined for temple service. Nevertheless, they could be redeemed from that duty through the payment of five shekels—today, in the United States, often five silver dollars—to a Kohen (Priest). Bar Mitvah (Boy's Commandment) and Bat Mitvah (Girl's Commandment) are the rites of passage in which a boy, at thirteen, or a girl, at twelve or thirteen, take on the responsibility (formerly in the hands of their parents) for remaining faithful to Jewish law. The ceremonies are often marked (today, usually for both boys and girls, at least in Conservative and Reform temples) by being called to the lectern to read from the Torah: a moment which caused both nervousness over one's facility with Hebrew but pride at taking one's place within the faith in more than one of my respondents. Both Bar and Bat Mitvah signify the child's passage to adulthood but, as well, given the sometimes virulent strains of anti–Semitism that have shaped the diaspora, serve as an opportunity to ponder what it means to be a part of the Jewish community. The taking on the responsibilities of the rabbi, if only for one day, at the altar in front of the congregation and before the ark which houses the Torah underscores this new obligation.

While Bar and Bat Mitvah establish the individual's place in the community, Jewish holidays, arranged calendrically, exemplify the essence of Jewish cultural history and identity. Though organized around an ancient agricultural cycle in which the opening of the yearly round marks the transition between a dry and rainy season with its autumn planting (Rosh Hashanah) as well as the barley (Passover), wheat (Shavuot), and autumn (Sukkot) harvests, the cycle notably hinges upon seminal moments of biblical history which provocatively speak one to another as well as to extra-biblical historical moments. The Egyptian captivity speaks to the Holocaust and the Babylonian captivity, in which Solomon's temple was razed, speaks to the Roman conquest, in which the Second Temple fell and Europe became the home for the vast bulk of the Jewish populace. The foods which adorn the Passover table speak not only to exile in Egypt but also to the diaspora in Europe and perhaps even the United States— where today a full third of the world's Jews, as many as in Israel, reside. And ceremonies that evoke Elijah, who fought the religious suppression of Ahab and Jezebel, allude to the Persian and Seleucid (Syrian-Greek) conquests (both of which were marked by religious persecution) and—through them—to the modern state of Israel wherein religious practice can be carried on without fear or censure. Underscoring the intersection of the agricultural cycle and the historical oscillation of dispersal and return is the fact that an entire cycle of Torah readings—accomplished in the continuous act of the Aliyah—is completed by the Shabbat of Sukkot, whereupon the reading is started anew. So much history is here evoked that it could perhaps be claimed that as central to Jewish identity as the shared history that we so briefly glossed is the rich tapestry of the calendrical holidays which imparts so much a sense of self and community—but simultaneously, at times, a profound sense of otherness—to the participants, even for those who are not necessarily strict adherents of the Jewish faith.

Acting as the lynchpin of the ritual calendar, Shabbat commemorates God's day of rest after accomplishing his Creation. Each week at sundown on Friday evening, the family ends the week by lighting candles, asking God's blessing on the household, and sharing a simple meal opened with wine and two loaves of bread: characteristically, the braided challah. Shabbat generally entails attending synagogue, usually on Friday evening or Saturday morning, where a recitation will, over the yearly cycle of Shabbats, lead to a complete reading of the Torah. Bobbi describes her synagogue—which she refers to with the Yiddish word, Shul (literally, School)—as a rectangular building made of stone, adorned with a stained-glass window, and entered via a staircase that traversed the entire front of the building—and would occasionally serve as a place to set an unruly child for a short "time out." The ground floor of Bobbi's synagogue consisted of the vestry where the breaking of the fast—a simple feast consisting of bread and wine following the close of holy days—was held and the chapel: approached via a second, short, staircase carpeted in deep burgundy. The chapel consisted of a central aisle which ran between two rows of pews, perhaps 40 or so rows altogether. At the front was a lectern, raised upon a podium, behind which was the Ark (closed to view by means of drawn curtains which were elaborately embroidered with a depiction of the Ten Commandments) that contained the Torah scrolls. During services, one man would open the curtains, and another reverently remove the Torah from the Ark. In doing so, each of these men was performing an Aliyah, that is participating in a covenant that entailed being called up (literally, ascending) to the lectern in order to offer a reading from the Torah.

Once the Torah was placed upon the lectern and unrolled, the rabbi began his devotional reading, never touching the Torah itself but using a silver stylus to keep his place. One by one, other men were then called to perform an Aliyah—or offer a Torah reading—until all requisite Aliyahs (or, more properly, Aliyot) were accomplished. Each of these men might be called by the rabbi himself or—and Bobbi associated this with the stricter rabbis ("Old Country" as she says) who only prayed—the cantor (or singer) might call the men to perform the Aliyot. Following the Torah reading, the sermon, based on the reading, which could last anywhere from an hour to two or even more was preached by the rabbi. There had to be a quorum of ten men, a minyan, altogether to fulfill the requirements for a worship service and, as is the norm in an Orthodox synagogue (though not necessarily in Conservative and unlikely in Reform temples), the men sat downstairs, in the chapel proper, while the women sat upstairs in a balcony. Here, according to Bobbi, the Women of the Sisterhood members insured that girls—and particularly teenage girls—maintained proper decorum throughout the service. After Friday services, Bobbi's family would have a Shabbat dinner which consisted of chicken, some kind of potatoes, several vegetables, rolls and butter, and—though it might not seem extravagant by today's standards—this was the special dinner of the week entailing both more preparation and more courses than the regular daily fare: perhaps of meatloaf and a vegetable or two. The meal began with the traditional lighting of candles, undertaken regularly but informally by Bobbi's mother, and the recitation of a Kiddush: a ceremonial prayer sanctifying the wine and challah that graced the table and reminding the family that Shabbat commemorated God's day of respite upon completing the Creation. If the dinner were held at her maternal grandmother's house, the meal would be a bit more formal and include her grandmother's special chicken soup with Matzo balls: three varieties running from fluffy to crisp in order to satisfy each of her grandchildren's particular tastes.

Rosh Hashanah, generally falling in September or very early October, opens the Jewish New Year. It is the first of the High Holy Days, ushering in the ten-day period of repentance culminating in Yom Kippur. During this period, observant Jews examine their lives—where they have behaved well and where they may have behaved sinfully—and seek atonement. Inasmuch as the start of the year necessarily commemorates God's creation of the world, Rosh Hashanah entails the remembrance of Adam and Eve—as well as their primal sin and their repentance thereof. Rosh Hashanah services, at least at Bobbi's Orthodox synagogue, lasted all day, children occasionally being allowed breaks in the Hebrew school where they might receive some instruction on the topics of the service. It opens with the blowing of the shofar, or ram's horn, in the synagogue as a call to worship as well as to the self-examination that characterizes Rosh Hashanah and memorably includes the eating of apples dipped in honey and other sweets in order to express a symbolic wish for a sweet year to come.

On the eve of Yom Kippur, candles are lit and a pre-fast meal is eaten, for when, at nightfall, Yom Kippur—the Day of Atonement, the most solemn day of the Jewish year—opens, a day of fasting and communal prayers for forgiveness of sins at the synagogue commences. It is customary to wear white, symbolic of purity, on Yom Kippur and leather shoes are avoided: apparently an ancient remembrance of a time when going barefoot was an expression of self-abasement. The entire day may be spent in the synagogue, sometimes with a short break in the afternoon, reciting prayers from morning to evening and reading the Book of Jonah with its emphasis on the inevitability of the hand of God but also God's forgiveness. The final prayer service ends with a long blast of the shofar. Thereupon, at Bobbi's synagogue, the fast would be broken with a light repast in the synagogue's vestry.

Sukkot, following soon after the High Holy Days and falling generally in October, simultaneously celebrates the autumn fruit harvest, which closes the agricultural cycle, and commemorates the Israelites' forty years of wandering through the desert on their way back to the Promised Land from the Egyptian captivity. It is celebrated through the construction of temporary booths called sukkot (sing. sukkah) that represent the temporary shelters of the Israelites during their wandering. Some celebrants may eat in sukkot for the entire seven days and nights during which the journey is commemorated. Historically,

Sukkot was one of the three holidays that entailed a pilgrimage to the temple of Jerusalem where offerings from the harvest were given. Sukkot concludes with Shemini Atzeret, during which celebrants begin to pray for rain and Simchat Torah, Rejoicing in the Torah, which marks the end of the Torah reading cycle and beginning it all over again. The occasion is celebrated with singing and dancing with the Torah scrolls.

Hanukkah, literally the Dedication but often called the Festival of Lights, falling in early December and lasting for eight days, commemorates the defeat in 165 BCE of the Seleucid (Syrian-Greek) dynasty, ending its occupation of Israel and squelching the attempt by the Seleucid emperor Antiochus IV to replace the Jewish faith with worship of the Olympian deities. Remembrance of the rebellion—led by the small band of Maccabees, a priestly family dedicated to the maintenance of Jewish religious practice—serves as a moment in the calendrical cycle when Jewish identity itself is commemorated. The festival is observed through the lighting of candles on a nine-branched Menorah. From a flame on the central branch, each of the eight side branches are lit, one for each of the festival's eight nights. The holiday is called Hanukkah, Dedication, because it marks the rededication of the Temple after its desecration by Antiochus IV. Spiritually, Hanukkah commemorates the Miracle of the Oil. According to the Talmud, at the rededication of the Temple, there was only enough consecrated oil—pressed from olives and sanctified by the High Priest—to fuel the eternal flame in the Temple for one day. Miraculously, the oil burned for eight days—which was the length of time it took to press, prepare and consecrate new oil. Latkes, or potato pancakes, originally fried in schmaltz, rendered chicken fat, a remembrance of the miraculous temple oil, centers the Hanukkah meal. Though Hanukkah was never considered a major holiday in Judaism, not being authorized in the Torah, it has become much more visible and widely celebrated in modern times, mainly because it falls around the same time as Christmas but also because it has national overtones that have become particularly evocative since the establishment of the State of Israel.

While Hanukkah speaks of conquest and desecration, Purim speaks of conquest and dispersal, for Purim commemorates the rescue of the Persian Jews—remnants of the first diaspora resulting probably from a raid on the northern kingdom of Israel by Assyrians in 722 BCE—from an attempt by the Persian King Ahasuerus's councilor, Haman, to destroy them. As recounted in the Book of Esther, Haman advised the king to exterminate his Jewish subjects but Esther, hiding her Jewish ethnicity, became Ahasuerus's queen. When Haman's plan became clear, Esther's uncle, Mordecai, advised his niece to reveal her true identity and to beg the king for her people's lives. When she did so, the king had Haman executed and placed Mordecai in his stead. Of the foods which grace the Purim table, the most famous is the one named, after Ahasuerus's wicked councilor, Hamantashen: triangular pastries filled with sweet pastes of poppy seed, dried fruits, or preserves. Purim generally falls in February or March.

Passover is the week-long holiday falling in April that commemorates the liberation from bondage in Egypt through the Exodus. In ancient times, it coincided with the barley harvest. It centers on family worship and the Seder: the Passover meal. Leavened products, chametz, are removed from the house prior to the holiday and are not eaten during the Passover celebration. Homes are searched (historically with a candle though today as often with a flashlight) in order to discover pieces of chametz that have been placed around the house, cleaned (to insure no chametz remains), and a symbolic burning of the chametz discovered, gathered in a small paper bag, is conducted on the morning of the Seder. The Seder table—often ornately set and adorned with candles and a plate of Matzo, unleavened bread, at its center—provides the opportunity to impart the lessons of the Egyptian captivity and the return to Israel. The meal itself—served not on the set of dishes reserved for meat, or the set reserved for dairy, that characterize a Kosher home, but rather on a special set of Passover dishes—includes, of course, matzo, representing the fact that Jews had no time to let their bread rise before they wrapped it and fled Egypt. Not unusually, someone—perhaps a grandfather—hides a piece of matzo from the table and sends out one of his grandchildren to find the matzo before the dinner begins.

Beyond matzo, bitter herbs—such as horseradish or romaine lettuce—represent the bitterness of slavery. But charoset, a sweet mixture of chopped nuts, apples, and cinnamon soaked in a bit of wine, while expressing hope for a sweet future represents as well the mortar Jews used to construct the buildings of ancient Egypt: perhaps even the pyramids according to some Seder participants. A roasted egg symbolizes the springtime renewal of god's covenant with the Jewish people as do sweet greens such as parsley or watercress. These last however are dipped in saltwater, symbolic of the bitter tears shed by the enslaved. Present on the carefully laid out Seder plate is the roasted shankbone of a lamb in commemoration of the lamb which was sacrificed and whose blood was placed on the doorposts of Jewish houses so that the angel which passed over Egypt would know not to kill the firstborn male of the household.

Four cups of wine must be drunk, each relating to a portion of the Passover recitation of God's fourfold promise of redemption: to bring the people out of Egypt, to deliver them from their bondage, to redeem them with outstretched hand, and to renew his covenant with them. A fifth cup of wine is set aside for

Elijah, for whom the home's front door has been opened and a place at the table reserved. Elijah, in this instance, seems to represent a remembrance of the survival of Israel's firstborn sons, the circumcised, but he also carries a hope for another ingathering of the diaspora, another return to Israel. As Bobbi expressed it, "Passover is a very hopeful time. And the coming of Elijah represents the goodness and the hope of the future." During the Seder a number of readings, each associated with one of the foods on the Seder plate and contemplating the significance of the Exodus, are read. Fascinatingly, while the celebration refers, as does much of the ritual calendar, to historical moments of oppression at the hands of enemies, celebrants take a moment to remember the suffering of Egyptians as a result of the plagues sent against them, sympathetically spilling a bit of wine for their sake.

Following upon the heels of Passover is Shavuot, celebrated in late May or early June and commemorating the revelation of the Torah on Mount Sinai. Also known as the Festival of Bikurim, or First Fruits, Shavuot anciently coincided with an early wheat harvest. Shavuot customs—particularly decorating homes and synagogues with greenery and wearing white clothing, symbolic once again of purity—do in fact suggest a First Fruits ceremony with an emphasis on continued fertility of the crops and livestock as the agricultural cycle proceeds. Further customs include eating dairy foods (for instance, cheesecake and blintzes), perhaps because—Shavuot also coinciding with periods of birthing and weaning—the stock was heavy with milk at this juncture of the year, and meditation on the life of Ruth, a Moabite whose devotion to Naomi leads her to adopt the Hebrew god as her own. Thereupon she earns a meager living for herself and Naomi by gleaning Boaz's harvested field—asserting this postharvest right of the poor. Eventually, Ruth and Boaz marry, providing Israel with the lineage of King David. Passover and Shavuot, coinciding with the barley and early wheat harvests, were historically the occasions of the second and third yearly pilgrimages to the temple of Jerusalem and likewise entailed offerings from one's agricultural bounty.

In essence, the entire calendrical cycle, opening with the High Holy Days and returning to them once again, while stamping the individual with a rich tapestry of memories and thus providing a fertile soil for the nurturance of cultural identity, simultaneously—because Jewish culture emerges so often in the diaspora—stamps the individual with a profound sense of otherness, and this sense of otherness may, at times, have a palpable influence on a group's construction of identity. Perhaps nowhere is this otherness more visible than in the Hanukkah season as celebrated in predominately Christian countries. There, it becomes a sometimes troubling dilemma to decide whether to celebrate Christmas and Hanukkah, keeping the former secular and the later religious, or treating Hanukkah as a kind of Jewish alternative to Christmas (something it never was), or to ignore Christmas and treat Hanukkah in the manner in which it customarily was: a minor Jewish holiday. Yet, we would be remiss if we here failed to mention another potent factor in the construction of Jewish identity. While such identity in the diaspora was undoubtedly fostered by Jewish tradition, including the maintenance of essential rites of passage and a vibrant ritual calendar, it was as well sustained by a sometimes virulent anti–Semitism, especially in a world lurching toward the Holocaust. In the same period that Giorgio Bassani experienced the closing of the city tennis club to Ferrara's Jews, Bobbi and her group of teenage friends were subjected to an American lifeguard's angry outburst. As they were about to leave the public beach and cross a stretch of beach that fronted a private club, the lifeguard stood up on his high perch and shouted: "No Jews on the beach." One doesn't need to wonder at how crushing such an experience—coming, as it did, in the midst of an otherwise happy outing—could be. Yet, regrouping themselves, Bobbi and her friends revisited the beach the following weekend. As the lifeguard readied himself to repeat his performance, the teens—prepared this time, wearing necklaces adorned with a mezuzah or a Star of David—calmly stepped off the beach, into the surf, and continued their stroll, even offering a sociable wave to the lifeguard as they passed his station by.

Ritual Authority: The Case of Zuni Pueblo

Our ritual life, whether Hindu tradition as expressed in the teachings of a guru or Jewish tradition as offered up in the instruction of a rabbi, is characteristically in the hands of ritual specialists. In foraging bands or simple agricultural alliances (practicing slash-and-burn gardening), overseeing ritual is the responsibility of part-time specialists: shamans. In intensive agricultural alliances (employing the plow, fertilization and irrigation) as well as mercantile states, ritual life is in the hands of full-time religious specialists: priests. Thus, ritual authority mirrors and reinforces the social structure that characterizes a group. If shamans are prevalent in egalitarian societies where authority is not in the hands of a few and priests reflect the hierarchical concerns of mercantile societies where a complex division of labor and full-time specialization give rise to feelings of authority—in both the interpretation of myth and the enactment of ritual—on the part of religious authorities, what of the intermediate category: one who is "betwixt and between" the shaman and the priest? A particularly cogent example of just this instance is demonstrated in the religion of Zuni Pueblo where the religious specialists are part-time but nonetheless begin to manifest the authority of a full-time priesthood: so much so that priests are not only the religious but also the political authorities within Zuni society.

A very special altar, adorned with sacred objects, is said to be secreted in a Kiva, or sacred chamber, four rooms deep at Zuni Pueblo in New Mexico.[7] In order to understand this altar, the sacred objects it holds, its architectural positioning, and its significance to the various priesthoods that govern Zuni society, the Zuni Creation—and the cultural realities to which it refers—must be considered. Zuni is a Pueblo: a village constructed of flat-roofed adobe houses that were historically entered and exited via a hole in the roof: not unlike what we witnessed at the Neolithic village of Çatal Hüyük. Some houses were multistoried so one would enter lower rooms through a hole in the floor of an upper room. And six of these houses contained a sacred Kiva, sometimes housed beneath an upper story. Ladders, not surprisingly, were ubiquitous at Zuni though today many houses have doors. Ecologically, the Zuni relied on light rainfall and irrigation from springs and the Zuni River in order to sustain the classic Native American agricultural complex—corn, beans, squash—in a sometimes precariously arid environment. And while they did historically maintain flocks of domestic turkeys, almost all animal food was obtained through hunting: deer and bear being particularly prized game animals though a number of small animals were also regularly hunted: for instance, as we witnessed in the story of the Zuni Ash Girl, rabbits. Sociologically, Zuni clans and families were matrilineal. Thus, one belonged to his or her mother's clan and family. Clans were exogamous, a woman marrying someone from outside her clan, and families were matrifocal, her husband coming to live in her household. But Zuni political life was primarily in the hands of men. It was, in fact, overseen by a large number of priests, each of whom was related in one way or another to a character from the most essential story to come to us from Zuni Pueblo: the Emergence.

In that story, the Sun Father, raining down upon the Earth in the form of a waterfall, engendered two sons, the Ahayuuta, or Twin War Gods, born from the suds and foam that welled up where the waterfall struck the parched soil.[8] But the world was still very lonely: "Always the Sun came up; always he went in. No one in the morning gave him sacred meal; no one gave him prayer sticks." Thus, he said to the Ahayuuta, "You will go down into the fourth womb." And he told them that, arriving there, they were to bring the Ancestors of the Zuni people out into the daylight of their Sun Father. Thus, "laying their lightning arrow across their rainbow bow, they drew it." And, shooting an arrow into the earth, they followed it down first through one room, then a second, then a third, and finally into a fourth. These rooms were situated, like the houses of Zuni Pueblo itself, one under the other.

Zuni Pueblo (National Archives and Records Administration, through Wikimedia, photograph by Timothy O'Sullivan).

When they entered the fourth womb it was dark inside. They could not distinguish anything. They said, 'Which way will it be best to go?' They went toward the west. There they met a youth face-to-face.

"You have come," he said.

"Yes, we have come. How have you lived these many days?"

"Here, where you have entered upon my road, I live happily. Sit down."

When they were seated, he questioned them. "Now speak. I think there is something you wish to say. It should not be too long a talk."

"Yes, indeed, it is so. In order that you may go out standing into the daylight of your Sun Father, we have entered upon your road. However you decide, so shall it be."

"Yes, indeed, now that you have entered upon my road here where we live thus wretchedly, far be it from me to talk against what you propose. Now that you have come to us here inside where we just trample on one another, where we just spit on one another, where we just urinate on one another, where we just befoul one another, where we just follow one another about in darkness, how should I speak against it?"

And the Ahayuuta kindled a fire whereby they could see the youth more clearly but when the light flared up, the youth fell down crouching. He had a slimy horn, a slimy tail, he was slimy all over, with webbed hands. The Elder Ahayuuta said," Poor thing! Put out

the light." His Elder Brother saying thus, the Younger Ahayuuta put out the light. The youth then said, "Oh dear, what have you there?"
    "Why, we have fire," they said.[9]

In fact, in the fourth room down under, the Ancestors lived miserably. They were slimy and had horns and tails, webbed hands and feet. They trampled on one another, urinating and defecating on their fellow human beings. And they had no fire to offer them warmth or light. Worse yet, their foodstuffs were merely the wild grasses that grew in the fourth room down under. Thus, arduously and with their magical art, ascending one room at a time, the Ahayuuta brought forth the Ancestors into the daylight of their Sun Father. Thereupon began the search for Itiwanna, the Center, where the Ancestors would found their village: Zuni Pueblo.

During the many years of their pilgrimage, they encountered a number of obstacles. First, they had to cleanse themselves of their amphibious features which they did upon arriving as Moss Spring. There, the Ahayuuta washed away the Ancestors' slimy horns and tails, the webbing between their fingers and toes. Then, when one boy mated with his sister, the mysterious Koyemci, sacred clowns who do everything in reverse, were born. And when a baby was found to have disappeared, its spirit was seen playing near the place of emergence. Thus, the Ahayuuta realized that witchcraft and death had surreptitiously come into the world but, happily, so too did—fast upon the heels of these twin catastrophes—corn and the various Beast Societies that combat illness. And as the Zuni attempted to cross a river to get to their predestined homeland, the children whom they carried on their backs as they swam were turned into biting turtles, frogs, and water snakes and were thus dropped into the river. When the Ahayuuta went to the bottom of the river to investigate, they learned that the children had not drowned but become the Kachinas who continuously danced there at the bottom of the river in Kachina Village for the well-being of the Zuni and the yearly return of the waters that would insure their crops. Finally, Waterbug, an insect that skirts along the surface of bodies of water, stretched out his legs in the cardinal directions and upon the spot that his heart sheltered, Zuni Pueblo was constructed.

While the Emergence authorizes the worship of the Ancestors, they who were brought forth into the light of their Sun Father, on the part of every Zuni man, woman, and child, it authorizes as well a dizzying array of priests, each of which is tasked with the governance of Zuni society. Among priestly duties is the management of the great rituals which center Zuni spiritual life: particularly the celebrations of the summer and winter solstices, the latter including the spectacular Shalako ceremony during which the Ancestors themselves— in the guise of towering, multicolored figures with rolling eyes, snapping beaks, and extravagant swaths of feathers—visit Zuni Pueblo. Not surprisingly, it is the job of the Sun Priest as the earthly representative of the Sun, to establish the timing of each year's ritual calendar: "He sets the dates for the solstices, from which all other ceremonies are dated. His calculations are based on observation of the sunrise in winter and the sunset in summer. These observations are made at shrines outside of the village. When the sun rises (or sets) behind certain landmarks, the date for the solstice is at hand. However, the calendar is disarranged by the desire to have the celebration of the solstice coincide with the full moon, and the Sun Priest is the subject of bitter criticism when the sun fails to oblige in this matter."

This Sun Priest is too sacred a personage to concern himself with the secular concerns of Zuni so, in order to manage those, he delegates some of his authority to the two Bow Priests: the earthly representatives of the Ahayuuta. In their hands is the management of the defensive and policing affairs at Zuni Pueblo. These, they accomplish through the auspices of the Bow Priesthood, which includes all men who have killed an enemy, and its Bow Priesthood Society Chief, who manages the affairs of war, along the Bow Priesthood Society Scalp Chief, who maintains the Scalp House—a visible reminder of the Mayan skull racks—and manages the Scalp Dance. Particular elements within the body of Ancestors are propitiated by a number of Rain Priesthoods which— along with the Kachina Society (consisting of all Zuni men) and the Koyemci (sacred clowns)—are tasked with insuring the timely return of the rains to Zuni Pueblo. Likewise, a number of medicine society priesthoods are responsible for combatting the illnesses which entered the world, along with witches who are said to be the source of illness, shortly after the emergence. The Rain Priesthoods notably include the North, West, South, East, Zenith, and Nadir Priesthoods. They propitiate the spirits who "live in all the waters of the earth," whose houses are the towering cumulus clouds, and who are heard in the singing of frogs "from every puddle after the drenching summer rains." The Medicine Priesthoods are dominated by the Spirit-Beasts who, like the Rains, are associated with the Six Cardinal Directions: the Mountain Lion (North), the Bear (West), the Badger (South), the Wolf (East), the Eagle (Zenith), and the Mole (Nadir).[10] In a fascinating tale collected by Dennis Tedlock, it was the lowly Mole who—after the failure of the more powerful Medicine Society Spirit-Beasts—thwarted the designs of a band of witches when they attempted to destroy the Ancestor, Payatamu, he who insured that his Sun Father rose and set each day.[11] As one can imagine, with so many priestly offices in such a small society (numbering fewer than 2,000 people in the 1930s), authority is widely diffused throughout the Zuni body politic—so much so that officiating as a priest is almost egalitarian in its formulation.

The altar secreted in the most sacred Kiva at Zuni Pueblo consists of a number of feathered prayer sticks, including two that are described as male and female and are said to represent the "life of the people." Prayer sticks— painted in various colors and decorated with the feathers of different species in accord with their various religious functions—are particularly sacred at Zuni and one of the items which the Sun Father was said to desire as part of his worship when he sent the Ahayuuta to retrieve the Ancestors from the fourth room down under. The altar contains two rock columns as well: the one of crystal, the other of turquoise. Finally, it contains a heart-shaped rock said to be the "heart of the world." This last item is said to contain four arteries reaching out to the four cardinal directions and is believed to be situated at the Middle Place, the very center of the world, that was discovered when Waterbug stretched forth his legs and selected for the Zuni their homeland. So sacred is this altar, the visual symbol of the Emergence that establishes how it came to be that the Zuni today live at Zuni Pueblo, that only the Zuni high priest—that is, the Sun Priest, he who is the earthly representative of the Sun Father himself—may access it.[12]

Women's Spirituality: My Grandmother's Kitchen

As a priesthood emerges and solidifies its religious authority, the masses tend to become less actively invested in ritual participation and are not unusually relegated to the role of passive spectators. Under such circumstances, the priestly class increasingly becomes responsible for interpreting not only the correct meaning of the societies' mythologies but also the intricacies of their ritual reenactments. Yet, shamans are not simply replaced by the newly emergent priesthood. They are rather displaced. While the duty of priests becomes encumbered with the apparatus of the state and its political hierarchy, shamans remain to service the community at the local—indigenous—level as healers, mediums, and diviners. Likewise, as the official state offices of the priestly elite are more regularly allocated to men, the offices of the local, indigenous, healers, mediums, and diviners fall increasingly to the lot of women.[13] And perhaps not surprisingly, these localized, indigenous, community-based practitioners increasingly become the victims of priestly attacks: accused, not unusually, of witchcraft.

The historic antagonism between the priestly class and indigenous, female, healers was highlighted in my own family by the uneasy relationship my grandmother, Lucia, who immigrated to the United States from a small farming village near Naples shortly after the turn of the previous century, had with her parish priest. His refusal of my grandmother's plea for help in feeding her six children—when my grandfather, tubercular and unable to work, was institutionalized—was but one of a long string of events that eventually led her to leave the Catholic Church. But even when she did finally make the break, the memory of "that stingy priest" could not preclude her veneration of the pope who (in the visage of Paul the 23rd) always looked out beneficently upon her kitchen: the constant setting of my grandmother's healing practice. In fact, there was more to the priest's cold-heartedness than the stinginess which my grandmother ever after his rebuff imputed to him. He had, in fact, caught wind of my grandmother's role as a healer. I suspect that a certain level of suspicion on the part of male religious authorities when women infringe upon their hallowed duties is inevitable. And I suspect that a certain level of resentment on the part of women who might view priestly attempts to curtail their religious independence as indicative of flawed spirituality is inevitable as well. Thus, it seems almost inescapable that women might compartmentalize gendered spheres of religiosity: allowing the priest his public spiritual arena while maintaining for themselves a secret women's space for religious expression. Certainly, my grandmother did as much.

In Southern Italian and Italian American society, the belief in *malocchio* (evil eye) pitted two spiritual forces, *invidia* (envy) and *grazia* (grace), against one another. If a *strega* (witch) or a *jettatore* (sorcerer) afflicted with the evil eye looked upon a victim with envy, the victim would fall ill: perhaps a nagging headache, perhaps impotence or debilitating menstrual cramps, perhaps again a persistent fever or an infection that wouldn't heal. In the worst scenarios, ravaging diseases and even death could result. The individual called upon to create of grace a palpable tool with which to combat envy in the Italian American community was a *cummari* (godmother), she who existed at the center of an extensive fictive kinship network created by the custom of *comparatico* (co-parenthood) and who, likewise, took on the responsibility of an infant's spiritual well-being when she stood up with him or her at baptism. Godmother is not a title, in this instance.[14] Nor is it the term for one who heals the evil eye. In fact, there was no term for an evil eye healer in my grandmother's community—and I have never encountered one in the course of field investigations or readings. Rather, the term expresses the social reality that the evil eye healer exists as one among the many in a social/spiritual network which is primarily in the hands of the community's women. In the context of the evil eye cure, a *cummari* borrowed the priest's baptismal imagery in order to mobilize grace and do combat against the insidious power of envy. But the ritual which she used to cure the evil eye, though replete with baptismal imagery, underscored her role as godmother not to a single individual but rather to an entire community.

My grandmother had already been in the United States nearly ten years before she learned how to cure the evil eye but she may have had a special right to the curing ritual. Her personal patron saint was Santa Lucia, bestowed upon her because she was born on Saint Lucy's Day (December 13). When about to be raped by her wicked brother, San Aniello, Santa Lucia tore her own eyes— the source of her irresistible beauty—from her head. She was instantly presented with a new pair of glorified eyes by an angel along with the gift of curing the evil eye. As for her brother, it was often said that he was the ultimate source of evil eye. For instance, if a pregnant woman or her husband worked on December 14, Saint Aniello's Day, their child might be born with the evil eye which would be denoted by a unibrow, a hairy bridge between the eyebrows, a notable feature of San Aniello's. Grandma would cleanse the evil eye in much the same manner as a San shaman would cleanse his or her patient: by drawing envy out of her patient's body and replacing it with the spiritual power of grace. She did this by means of a purifying ritual which symbolically reenacted that which, in many ways, was the most important rite of passage in the Italian American community, the patient's baptism into the Roman Catholic Church. Holy Water, borrowed directly from the church, was employed. Olive oil, used to trace a cross on the forehead, was evocative of the church's use of chrism for the same purpose. Salt—baptism's *salis sapientis*, pressed upon the infant's lips—was sprinkled about the kitchen to keep the invidious gaze at bay. And the prayers employed, particularly the *Hail Mary* and *Our Father*, likewise spoke to the healing ceremony's baptismal source.

My grandmother would begin her curing ritual by tracing a cross in olive oil on the foreheads of both her patient and herself. She would again dip her finger into the tin of oil and carefully shake three drops into a dishpan of water. For each drop she would offer the Trinitarian Formula: "In the name of the Father, the Son, and the Holy Spirit." If the oil (normatively) beaded the illness was of the mundane sort but if it (ominously) slicked the illness was the result of envy and a cure would have to be affected. Nine times my grandmother would recite the *Hail Mary*. With each recitation she would shake a drop of oil into the water. With the ninth recitation she would add an incantation, the purpose of which was to chase away the envy. I do not know my grandmother's incantation. To reveal an evil eye incantation without the proper intent is to ruin its efficacy. It may only be revealed to two women during the healer's lifetime and then only at midnight on Christmas Eve. Due to the priest's interference, and perhaps also due to the fact that the tradition was slowly waning, my grandmother's incantation died with her. With the incantation uttered, the divination would again be undertaken to determine whether the cure had been effective. This time, if the oil beaded, the water would be thrown outside the house in a spot where it will pose no danger. But if it slicked, the water would be poured down the kitchen sink and the cure repeated. The implication is that if the cure is effective, the envy is contained in the water. If not, it remains within the patient—and, ominously, the *cummari* can unload the curse on an unaware passerby if she chooses to pour out the water at a place where two paths cross. This odd turnabout—where the healer becomes the bewitcher—sheds light upon the nature of the spiritual powers of grace and envy. They are not so much two different things as they are two extremes of the same thing. And, indeed, the *cummari* is commonly perceived to be as able in the use of envy as she is in the use of grace.

When the priest caught wind of my grandmother's practice, his perennially irate nature was displaced with fury. He told my grandmother that curing the evil eye was an act of devil worship and that if she did not give it up forthwith she would surely burn in hell for eternity. It almost goes without saying that my grandmother—in her appropriation of Catholic ritual—was, as one of her *cummari* wryly noted, "cutting in" on the priest's territory. Sadly, shortly after the priest's admonition, a neighbor's goat—a beautiful goat, the pride of the neighborhood, named Nina—fell ill and its owner, Mr. Campagna, turned to my grandmother for a cure. When she refused to undertake the ritual, the goat's *owner* accused grandma of giving the goat the evil eye in the first place. Perhaps this is why my grandmother never failed to display a mischievous grin whenever the word *strega*, witch, arose in conversations. Still, she always maintained that she was sorry for the death of Nina but didn't have any other option than that which she took: "I couldn't risk going to hell," she blandly stated, "and, anyway, I didn't do animals." That was that.

Perhaps not surprisingly, the complex of belief and behavior subsumed under the amorphous term *malocchio*, like all other complexes that characterize immigrant communities, was destined to be lost. Shortly before my grandmother's death, our conversation happened to fall upon the old clients who used to come by the kitchen for the evil eye cure. Suddenly, one of my aunts exclaimed, "Ma, you don't really believe all that stuff, do you?" But all my grandmother could muster—not ready to reject her own ancient beliefs out of hand but not ready either to embrace what seemed more and more a quaint archaism—was a wan, "*Non lo so.*" That is, "I don't know." It was a sad moment and we all, for a time, fell silent.

My grandmother's ambivalence with regard to her spiritual proclivities brings us directly to our next topic: who, precisely, is in control of our spiritual life? In those cases where a priesthood maintains exclusive rights to an authoritative, or orthodox, interpretation of our mythology, a bit of the essence of the myth-ritual complex is lost: that portion that brings together our ecological and sociological concerns and makes of them a whole. Thus, other traditions have to be elaborated in order to fulfill that essential function. Women's spirituality is one such tradition. But it is not only women's spirituality which reintegrates ecological and sociological concerns in the case of priestly stultification. Other mechanisms as well accomplish that function. We have already encountered one: the reliance on the sermon rather than the sacred text itself. We will now turn to two more: in the first instance, the transference of the sociological function of myth to legend; in the second instance, the maintenance of an entirely separate religious tradition side-by-side the prescribed religion. These explorations will occur in the context of two seminal, and curiously analogous, societies: Sicily and Haiti. These two islands—existing at the crossroads of two tumultuous seas and two brutal historical movements—will offer a primer in the inevitability of religions' ecological and sociological functions even in those environments where religious officialdom seems to thwart such functions.

7. Mythic Rhetoric: Allegories, Ancestors and Apocalypses

Palermo

On the Feast of the Immaculate Conception I stepped out onto the street to be greeted by an unusual calm. The route of that evening's procession had been laid out in arcs of incandescent lights suspended over the streets and the continuous rush of economic development, marked most notably in Palermo by an endless crunch of traffic, was momentarily halted. There are times when a low-lying blanket of wintry Mediterranean cloud—threatening to drench the city and turn its grand boulevards into torrents—enshrouds Palermo, when all movement is suspended, when all colors become saturated, when each detail of a particular landscape becomes indelibly impressed upon the memory. Such was that morning in Palermo.[1]

Palermitans view their city's history as a series of foreign occupations: Carthaginian, Greek, Roman, Byzantine, Arabic, Norman, Swabian, French, Aragonese, Spanish, Bourbon, Italian, each leaving behind its indelible trace. And, indeed, that view made sense of what might have otherwise seemed a great jumble of architectural features as I wandered about the city that day. Palermo rises from the *Conca d'Oro*, the Golden Shell, an alluvial plain drenched in hot white sunshine and wedged between the sharp limestone peaks of Sicily's northern coast and the shimmering Tyrrhenian Sea. It is centered upon a low ridge that descends northward from the hills ringing the city to Palermo's harbor, la Cala.[2] Its historic center—at places still bounded by the city's ancient Carthaginian walls and extravagant Spanish gates—is divided into four somewhat irregular quarters by two boulevards: the Corso Vittorio Emanuele, running down the ridge from hill to harbor and presided over by the looming Cathedral, remnant of Palermo's most glorious Norman epoch, and the Via Maqueda which crosscuts the ridge just a short walk down Vittorio Emanuele from the cathedral. Where the two intersect, demarcating the four adjacent quarters of the city's historic center, four ornate facades stand. These together form Palermo's famed *Quattro Canti* (Four Corners). At ground level, four elegant fountains, caught in the facades' curving arcades and representative of the four rolling seasons, fill the *Quattro Canti* with the sound of splashing waters. Above the fountains, grand niches contain statues of four of Palermo's Spanish kings: Phillip I, II, and III, and the Emperor Charles V, under whose crown Palermo regained a slight glimmer of its old Norman grandeur. And above the kings, presiding over that square that Palermitans consider the very heart of their city, are the patron saints of the city's four adjacent quarters: Cristina, Agatha, Ninfa, and Olive.

Scattered throughout this landscape are the numerous relics of a tumultuous past: Arabo-Norman architecture—its fortified palaces graced by the cracked casements of keyhole arches, geometric inlays of colored stone, and soaring magenta domes—defines the city's Golden Age to inhabitants and guests alike. But it gives way over the turbulent centuries to a number of Gothic styles patronized by the Normans' Aragonese successors. The clusters of magenta domes that seem to almost float over a languid city and the stark crenellations beneath them are methodically hidden by rose windows, slender colonnades, and delicate spires as the sumptuous Catalonian Gothic style wraps the city in its ornate mantle. Yet, this too gives way to the Plateresque facades

Palermo's Quatro Canti (Wikipedia, photograph by Bengt Nyman).

of Imperial Spain. In the profuse statuary and reliefs that grace these facades, angry prophets raise their fists at the city while the gentle patrons shed quiet tears over it. With a single blast of Gabriel's horn, plump cherubs fall from the clouds and angels supplicate the Immaculate Virgin with hands extended in mournful prayer. Here, Emperor Charles V strides into the city in the guise of a beggar, ferreting out corruption in Palermo's judiciary; there, he presides over the city in all his imperial majesty, the corrupt judges flayed and their skin upholstering the seats of the new judiciary. This last depiction—which sets the hopes of the Palermitan populace on the shoulders of a benevolent foreign ruler—underscores a constant of Palermitan history. Inasmuch as rule always came from abroad, and Sicily existed as a kind of internal European colony, Palermitans were forced into developing institutions which could effectively combat oppressive regimes: most notably, violent urban riots which periodically swept through the city and secret societies such as the ancient Beati Paoli or the 19th century Mafia whose *public* function was to avenge injustices— even as they capitalized themselves with other, decidedly more nefarious, activities.

Aside from its architectural splendors, Palermo seems, at first blush, like any bustling mercantile port. It is frenetic with the labor of many classes of men and women, each going about its own particular act of production and feverishly trading one item for another. During my stay, those trades involving the provision of food, shelter, and clothing, and the tools to either process or outfit those three commodities, still seemed to predominate in the Sicilian economy—at least for those lucky enough to have work, unemployment then likely hovering at an unhealthy 50 percent.[3] Some trades, at least to my senses, seemed to be more omnipresent and evocative of the culture than others. I was always enthralled to see the bakers bustle through the streets in their white shorts and T-shirts in the midst of winter, a tray of freshly baked loaves held aloft to escape the dangers of the jostling crowd, or the chestnut vendors who would take a small handful of steaming nuts from their roasters and press them upon a homeless beggar. One could peek into the open shop doorways to see cabinet and furniture makers hammering away at the fixtures and furnishings that would outfit the interiors of Palermitan apartments. The laundresses too could be seen at their work, the doors of their establishments always flung open to let out the heat of their irons and presses.

Nowhere is the freneticism and intense productivity that so defines Palermo more apparent than in the city's major markets, particularly the *Vucciria*. It takes its name from the French *boucherie*, the butcher's quarter, and is the oldest of the city's markets. Here, one finds a varied collection of booths bordered by shop fronts and presided over by long tables buckling under the weight of eels, squid, octopus, and sardines. Palermo's shepherds provide mutton, pork, beef, and cheese to the market. Its fishermen provide all the various species that the Tyrrhenian Sea affords. Fruit from the orchards (Sicily being a major producer of citrus since Arabic times) and a rich array of vegetables (squashes and legumes, tomatoes and innumerable greens) from the gardens of the small agricultural villages that surround the city are always plentiful, and it seemed that in Palermo one supped often enough on a plate of pasta smothered in whatever fresh vegetables the market had to offer that day topped off perhaps with a pan of grilled sardines. The merchants ply their wares feverishly, and though a modern market economy with weights and prices prominently displayed, generally chalked on small pieces of wood, prevails, each transaction is based on a number of variables: how much you shop at the booth, how much you are just then buying, what wares or services you might provide the merchant in turn, and, perhaps just as important, how much the merchant likes you. In the *Vucciria*, as in the other markets of Palermo, imports and manufactured goods were ever-present. Perhaps they are even more so today; the great freighters that transport them to and fro are only a short walk away in Palermo's industrial port. But during my stay in Palermo, the *Vuccciria* was predominantly a market of local produce, patronized by local artisans and workers: barbers, hoteliers, barkeeps; monks, priests, nuns; shoemakers and tailors; Mafiosi, bankers, and soldiers; civil servants, teachers, and police.

Still, there was a dirty underbelly to Palermo's feverish economy. It is encapsulated in the term *miseria* (misery): a term which, in Sicily, refers to a life characterized by hardship and a constant scramble to eke out a meager existence. No less astute an observer than Booker T. Washington commented on this condition at the particularly acute juncture of the early 20th century: "I have been more than once through the slums and poor quarters of the colored people of New Orleans, Atlanta, Philadelphia, and New York," Washington notes, "and my personal observation convinces me that the colored population of these cities is in every way many percent better off than the corresponding classes in Naples, Catania, and Palermo." And when Washington turned his attention to rural Sicily, his assessment of the people's suffering was even bleaker:

> I have described at length the condition of farm laborers in Italy because it seems to me that it is important that those who are inclined to be discouraged about the Negro in the South should know that his case is by no means as hopeless as that of some others. The Negro is not the man farthest down. The condition of the colored farmer in the most backward parts of the Southern States in America, even where he has the least education and the least encouragement, is incomparably better than the condition and opportunities of the agricultural population in Sicily.

Further, Washington aptly ascertains the cause of rural Sicily's misery: "In Sicily a few capitalists and descendants of the old feudal lords own practically all the soil and, under the crude and expensive system of agriculture which they employ, there is not enough land to employ the surplus population. The result is the farm laborers are competing for the privilege of working the land." In contrast, he points out that "if a Negro tenant does not like the way he is treated he can go to the neighboring farm; he can go to the mines or to the public works, where his labor is in demand. But the only way the poor Italian can get free is by going to America, and that is why thousands sail from Palermo each year for this country." Perhaps, given the nature of his program for the economic betterment of African Americans in the Southeastern United States, Washington's assessment of the benevolence of American farmers, local governments, and mine owners was overstated, but his deep empathy with the Sicilian populace was a gift they rarely received: "I went to Italy," he concludes, "with the notion that the Sicilians were a race of brigands, a sullen and irritable people who were disposed at any moment to be swept off their feet by violent and murderous passions. I came away with the feeling that, whatever might be the faults of the masses of the people, they were, at the very least, more sinned against than sinning, and that they deserve the sympathy rather than the condemnation of the world."[4]

Sicily's Folkloric Repertoire

Still, Palermo's history and socioeconomy are best viewed not in the city's vibrant architecture or bustling streets but rather in the rich tapestry of stories that comprise its folkloric repertoire. Sicily, after all, is the place where the sea routes of Africa, Asia, and Europe converge. It is a land which accrues legends. And its landscape is every bit as scoured and pocked by the exploits of its heroes as ever was Australia's by the ancient peregrinations of its totems. It was on Sicily's rugged coast that Odysseus, tired and hungry, incautiously entered the cave of the Cyclops Polyphemus. Luckily, he had the foresight to introduce himself to the cannibal not as Odysseus but rather as Oudeis: Nobody. Thus, when Odysseus and his men had tricked the Cyclops into tasting too much of their undiluted wine and blinded his single eye, Polyphemus, barricaded along with his intended victims in his cave, shouted out crazily to his fellow Cyclops that Nobody had poked out his eye and they ignored his mad ravings. Yet, upon escaping the monster, Odysseus couldn't resist taking credit for his trickery: "If anyone should ask who blinded you, Cyclops," he yelled as his ship set sail, "Tell him it was Odysseus!" Thus, Polyphemus, bombarding Odysseus's ship with the jagged boulders that still jut out of the churning waters off Sicily's eastern coast to this day, was able to beg his father, Poseidon, to block Odysseus' passage home. And then on the flower-strewn plain before Pergusa, a lake in the Sicilian interior which because it is without visible inlet or outlet is said to be the entrance to the Underworld, Hades—burning with desire—swept down to abduct Persephone, wandering distractedly as she gathered the beautiful wildflowers. Zeus, at the urging of Demeter, Persephone's mother, ordered his brother to release Persephone from his underground kingdom. Yet Hades prevailed upon Persephone to eat but a single pomegranate seed before leaving his side and, on tasting the rare fruit, Persephone was obliged to remain with her husband and lord for a third of each year. She issues forth from her husband's lair in the spring with the first of Sicily's preeminent crop, wheat, to spend the other two-thirds of the year with her mother, but, with the harvest over and the dreary winter settling upon the land, she retires once again to her husband's dusky kingdom.[5]

Then again, with Camelot in disarray and the knights of the Round Table dispersed, King Arthur, gravely wounded in mortal combat against his rebellious son, Mordred, was spirited by his sister, Morgan le Fay, to Sicily. The halcyon days of Camelot were there recreated in Avalon: Morgan's fairy kingdom at the foot of a belching Mount Etna. Yet, the fire and brimstone and the noxious flows of lava that the mountain daily emit are the constant reminders that this land of ghostly lords and ladies, of opulent palaces and marvelous gardens, is not Camelot but its pale counterfeit. Still, Morgan did what she could to render her magic kingdom an abode more suitable to a Christian king such as Arthur. When the Norman Count Roger first contemplated the enterprise of wresting Sicily from its Muslim overlords, he balked at the sight of the perilous Strait of Messina: that same strait which the Greeks populated with the shipwrecking monsters Scylla and Charybdis. Yet Morgan overcame Roger's hesitancy by placing a mirage in the shimmering waters between Italy and Sicily, a mirage of a city—replete with palaces, monasteries, fortifications, great gates, and sumptuous gardens—so close that one could almost touch it. The mirage, which appears in the strait to this day and was well known enough in the 19th century to be mentioned by the seafarer Herman Melville in his novel *Moby Dick*, is called, after Morgan le Fay, *La Fata Morgana*. It convinced Roger to set sail in 1061 and create of Sicily a Norman kingdom. Now, in a crypt which Morgan prepared for her languishing brother in a mountain cleft, Arthur sleeps, his wounds slowly healing, until that day he awakens, rejuvenated, to reclaim his earthly kingdom. Yet, he has been seen now and again in his mountain hideaway, once in the time of the Norman King William II by a groom to the bishop of Catania who, chasing a runaway palfrey into a crevice of the mountain, was led by a "mysterious youth" to Arthur himself reclining on a sumptuous couch and displaying the wounds that open anew each year.[6]

But beyond ancient legends left by its Greek and Norman invaders, Palermo's folkloric repertoire includes indigenous fairy tales, a local tradition of both saints' and bandits' lives, and a number of vibrant city legends. A particularly telling fairy tale is that of Cola Pesce: Niccolò the Fish. Cursed by his mother for spending all the hours of the day playing in the surf, he developed scales, gills, webbed feet and hands, and was comfortable only in his beloved sea, gasping for air at those times that he had to venture onto dry land. One day Frederick the II, King of Sicily and Emperor of the West, he whom the world applauds but whom Sicilian popular tradition holds a petulant tyrant, sent Cola Pesce to sound the perilous depths merely to satisfy his princely whims, throwing the half-fish, half-man baubles to retrieve when he demurred. How could Cola refuse Frederick's requests? He was a king, after all. And even if he could refuse, the glittering baubles sinking beneath the waves were more than he could bear. Nothing that Cola Pesce described—mountains and valleys beneath the waves, horrible monsters, even the fact that Sicily sat on three stone columns, one intact, another in ruins, and a third crumbling—satisfied the king who kept sending Cola deeper and deeper until a trail of lentils streaming to the water's surface let the onlookers know that Cola Pesce had succumbed to the unknown perils of the depths, perhaps being caught in the vortex of Charybdis herself. Now, whenever the earth trembles, the people think of the third crumbling column which only Cola has seen and whose demise will spell the end of Sicily and all her inhabitants.

Among Palermo's notable saint's lives is one which treats of Palermo's own patron, Santa Rosalia, Not only is she said to be a descendant of Charlemagne but also the niece of William the Good, fourth Norman king of Palermo. She, curiously enough, seems to represent a synthesis of the two medieval claimants to Sicily: the papacy, which claimed Sicily as its gift first from Constantine and then again from Charlemagne's Carolingian dynasty,[7] and the Swabian Holy Roman Empire, which claimed Sicily as its inheritance from the Norman kings. She fled the luxury of the court in preference to a life of quiet penitence and contemplation in a grotto on Monte Pellegrino, a limestone promontory which rises on the western fringe of Palermo. In 1624, as a plague ravaged the city, she appeared to a lone hunter on the mountain and instructed him to retrieve her bones which had been encased in translucent stone by the calciferous water which dripped from the roof of her grotto. The hunter carried her bones into the city, whereupon the plague ceased. Rosalia was declared the city's patron and a shrine was built around her grotto on Monte Pellegrino.

Quite the opposite of Palermo's devotional saints' lives are the adventurous tales of Palermo's bandit-heroes, the most famous of which is Salvatore Giuliano. A son of Montelepre, in the Province of Palermo, Giuliano was just 20 years old when he was accused of smuggling two sacks of wheat in order to augment his family's post–World War II grain ration. The *carabinieri*, the national police, confiscated both his mule and his wheat. But, taking advantage of a momentary distraction, Giuliano attempted to flee, whereupon the *carabinieri* shot him, wounding him gravely. One of the *carabinieri*, Giuseppe Mancino, was ordered to finish him off, but Salvatore, hearing the order, struck first, critically wounding Mancino with a pistol that he had hidden in his boot. Mancino died the following day in Palermo while Salvatore, wavering between life and death for a month, healed completely and took refuge in the hills around Montelepre. It was then that the Italian government set a force of 800 *carabinieri* to exact their retribution upon Giuliano. Failing in their attempt, they set about exacting their vengeance instead upon the helpless citizens of Montelepre, arresting 125 of them. Giuliano's father, who was among the arrested, was beaten bloody by one of the *carabinieri*. Salvatore witnessed the entire scene from a hiding place and his wrath became uncontainable. He attacked the *carabinieri*'s convey waiting in the town square. One of the officers died and another was seriously injured. From then on, the *carabinieri* hunted him without rest and without mercy, but he always managed to escape until he was finally denounced by his most devoted friend and lieutenant, Gaspare Pisciotta. He was slain on July 5, 1950, and—as the story is told—his body was dragged out into the street so that it appeared as if he had died in a gunfight with the *carabinieri*. Four years later, Pisciotta was poisoned by a seemingly innocuous morning coffee in Palermo's infamous Ucciardone prison.[8]

Among the most famous of Palermo's city legends is the tale of *The Sicilian Vespers*:

In Palermo, the French governed and there was a master shoemaker who had a wife as beautiful as the sun. The king had her called before him on a pretext and afterwards he married her. The Palermitans mocked her, saying: *Prima cuncupina, e ora riggina*; First a concubine, now a queen. The king was angered and to spite the houses of the Palermitans he decreed that every girl who married had to sleep with a soldier on the night of the wedding. Giovanni Procida had a daughter who was promised, but, on hearing the cast of this law, he was afraid to let her marry. There was a captain living with him, posted as an orderly for the neighborhood. Giovanni said, "How can I allow my daughter to marry when she will carry the stigma (along with all the others) of having a soldier the first night? I won't permit her to marry." But he did, and when she returned from the church, the captain wanted her. The girl fled and, throwing herself from a window, was killed. Her father could bear no more and feigned madness. He went about murmuring through a deaf horn into the ears of everyone. To the Palermitans he was saying, "On the Feast of the Holy Spirit," and he told them what day that was, "we will kill the French." Before the French he feigned madness. And in this manner he traveled about all the towns and villages and the French left him alone. They mocked him believing he was truly mad. When the hour arrived, I don't know how the fighting began, but the slaughter broke out at the Church of the Holy Spirit and from there spread everywhere. Not one Frenchman survived. The terrible thing is that even the pregnant French women were massacred and that was unjust. In order to know if someone were French, he was told to say čiči, chick pea, and if he said çeçi he was killed because the French don't know how to say čiči.[9]

The legend provocatively transects history. On Easter Monday, in the year 1282, before the vesper service at the Church of the Holy Spirit, Palermo, a French sergeant harassed a young Sicilian woman, and her husband killed him. When the sergeant's comrades attempted to avenge him, they were likewise slaughtered. The carnage spread throughout Palermo where "the rioters broke into the Dominican and Franciscan convents; and all the foreign friars were dragged out and told to pronounce the word čirčiri, chick pea, whose sound the French tongue could never accurately reproduce. Anyone who failed the test was slain. By the next morning some two thousand French men and women lay dead; and the rebels were in complete control of Palermo." Perhaps most intriguing is the legend's retention of the name Giovanni Procida. Though it has never been definitively established to what extent it was he who fomented the discontent against France, historically Procida was an integral member of the Aragonese government which took the reins of power in Sicily in the rebellion's aftermath.[10]

If *The Sicilian Vespers* underlines Palermo's penchant to rebel in the face of tyranny, another of Palermo's notable city legends, that of *The Beati Paoli*, speaks to Palermo's dependence on secret societies—rather than rebellions—in order to combat the continuous presence of foreign authorities. The innocent orphan Costanza, secretly married to the noble but penniless Corrado, is accosted by a certain Prospero, a vagrant who in the ensuing scuffle is wounded in the cheek by Corrado's sword. That evening as Corrado flies to Costanza's home disguised in the cape and beret of his manservant, he too is accosted. He gains the better of his assailant and chases him without the walls of the city. He finds himself in an open field where a group of men—dressed, like himself, in capes and berets—is gathering. He is herded along with the others into a secret chamber and thus by an accident of fate (and costume) finds himself in the midst of the Beati Paoli: a nocturnal convocation of men of the people whose sole intent is to avenge the injustices of the Spanish aristocracy and to curb the excesses of that aristocracy's iniquitous arm: the Inquisition. Among the petitions that Corrado witnesses that evening is one against a prince who is keeping the young son of a peasant locked up in his dungeon and administering daily beatings, another against a minister of the Inquisition who is attempting to ruin the reputation of a good family through pressing too insistently on

a young daughter, and finally Prospero's petition against Corrado himself. The
Beati Paoli grant Prospero his petition, the death of Corrado. But when the
attempted execution is carried out, Costanza (hidden in the same cape and
beret that had earlier allowed Corrado to be mistaken as a member of the Beati
Paoli) is mistaken for Corrado and killed. The retribution is swift and spells
the end of the Beati Paoli—whose sole duty, retribution on behalf of a beleaguered populace, was so terribly abused. Implicit in the tale is the message that
secret societies carry within themselves an inherent weakness: the society's
own function can go horribly awry and justice in the face of oppression can
easily become its own terrible injustice. Then, the populace—which the secret
society is sworn to protect—becomes the society's unhappy victim. It is a message which resonates with clarity in present-day Sicily.[11]

Still, despite the continuous ebb and flow of stories which washed Sicily's
shores, it was epic—the legends of knights and ladies, of distant lands and mysterious kingdoms, of ferocious battles and fantastic journeys—which came to
dominate Sicily's folkloric repertoire. Designated by the term *cuntu*, a term
which suggests the telling of historical tales, epic notably included recitations
of both the Trojan and Arthurian Cycles. But it was the Carolingian Cycle
which became the mainstay of *cuntu* and the foremost expression of Sicilian
folklore. The cycle consists of the stories of Charlemagne and his hand-picked
knights, the Paladins: preeminent among them Roland and his illustrious cousin Renaud. Just as the Normans carried the cycle to Anglo-Saxon England,
where its seminal episode, celebrated in the *Song of Roland*, was reputedly sung
to rally the troops at the Battle of Hastings (1066 CE), so too did they (according to my interlocutors) carry it to Sicily in their conquest of the island (1061
CE), at the time a Muslim emirate. Since the days of the Norman invasion,
Sicily's landscape has contained memories of the Paladins. The town Capo
d'Orlando (Cape Roland) and the promontory Monte Oliviero (Mount Oliver)
commemorate the sojourn of their namesakes: Paladins who, legend has it, visited the island along with Charlemagne on their return from a crusade to
Jerusalem.[12] Though not indigenous, once the Carolingian Cycle found its way
to Sicily, it completely revitalized the island's folkloric repertoire, offering it
the singular focus which endures to this day.

While rare to know the historical antecedents of medieval tales, here (as
with the legend of the Sicilian Vespers) we do. On August 15, 778 CE, Charlemagne's army suffered a humiliating defeat described perhaps 50 years later by
Einhard the Frank, a member of Charlemagne's court. While leaving off its
Spanish campaign, the rearguard of Charlemagne's army was ambushed in a
pass of the Pyrenees by a horde of Basques. Whereas the Franks were hindered
by their unfamiliarity with the rough terrain and their heavy armor, the Basques

were at home in the mountains and rendered the fleeter by their light armaments. It was recounted that a number of important personages were killed in this skirmish, notably including Roland, Lord of the Breton Marches. But within 200 years, this tale had been substantially reformulated in the crucible of oral transmission and millenarian fears. By then, Europe had lost territory in Spain, Sardinia, and southern Italy—including all of Sicily—to Muslims whose courts were reputed to be grander and more splendid than any of Europe's Christian courts, more splendid even than Rome itself. And European Christians began to fear further encroachment on that which they considered "Christian soil." In the climate of fear and frustration that took hold as the year 1,000 CE approached, European Christians began to believe, almost universally, that Charlemagne was not dead but rather asleep in his chapel as Aix-au-Chapelle and that, when Christ returned for his thousand year reign, the last great Holy Roman Emperor would awake, "shake off his slumber," and, at the head of his legion of hand-picked knights, the Paladins, drive the "Saracens" (the medieval European term for Muslims) from the "threshold of France."[13]

In *The Song of Roland*, Charlemagne has captured all the cities of Spain except for Saragossa, which is under the rule of the Saracen king, Marsilius. He holds a council where he accepts Ganelon's advice to permit Marsilius the option of converting from Islam to Christianity rather than suffering a siege under the walls of Saragossa. Roland, nephew to Charlemagne and stepson to Ganelon, having hoped to gain the Spanish crown for himself, angrily nominates his stepfather as ambassador to Marsilius and Ganelon accepts the nomination but vows to avenge himself upon his stepson for the nomination means almost certain death. At the court of Marsilius, Ganelon betrays Roland, suggesting that Marsilius might get the better of the Christian forces if he pays tribute to Charlemagne, then attacks the rearguard of the army as it heads back to Charlemagne's court at Aix in France. Ganelon will arrange that the twelve Peers (Charlemagne's finest knights), including Roland (the best of the Peers), will be in the rear guard. At Roncevaux, a pass in the Pyrenean Mountains, the rearguard of Charlemagne's army is ambushed by Marsilius' forces. The odds are overwhelmingly against the Peers and despite Oliver's plea that Roland blow his Oliphant and alert Charlemagne to the treachery, Roland vows to fight to the death. Only when Roncevaux becomes littered with the corpses of Christians and Saracens alike does Roland deign to blow his Oliphant, knowing that Marsilius' forces have been broken. Arriving at Roncevaux, Charlemagne sees the result of Ganelon's treachery: Roland and the Peers are dead. Back at Aix, Ganelon is tried. He claims that he has justly avenged himself upon his stepson, but it is deemed that he has also betrayed his sovereign, Charlemagne, in the process. He is condemned to be quartered by four war-horses.

We find in the *Song of Roland* an oral tradition that has infused history with myth, transforming Charlemagne's rearguard's assailants from Basques into Saracens and, thus, reconfiguring a skirmish between Christian forces into a Holy War between the forces of Christendom and Islam. *Old* and *New Testaments* have been here conflated to recreate Charlemagne's war in the image of that between the Hebraic tribes and the enemies of Israel as well as that between Christ and the Beast of the Apocalypse. Further, God the Father and God the Son have been recreated in the characters of Charlemagne and Roland. The Peers now number twelve, as do the tribes of Israel and Christ's apostles, and a traitor cut in the mold of Judas Iscariot has been added to their ranks. Moreover, we find the special patronage that the angel Gabriel offers Roland, who, as his mythic counterpart does at doomsday, sounds his horn in the earthly apocalypse of Roncevaux. Note that the re-imagination of the historical catastrophe suffered by Charlemagne's army at Roncevaux is couched in all the anxieties of a Europe under siege from the growing might of Islam and in fear that its very existence is threatened. Not surprisingly, given the emotionally charged environment that produced such a tale, all medieval Europe became enthralled by the feats of the Carolingian heroes—even as Sicily became especially invested in their exploits.

In fact, around the year 1200, the poet Jean Bodel set forth the three subjects most suitable to courtly treatment: the matters of Rome, Britain, and France. The matter of Rome centered upon the Trojan Cycle: the fall of Troy, the subsequent peopling of Europe, and the consolidation of the Roman Empire. As we earlier noted, not only Aeneas went forth to father Rome but a number of Roman territories in Italy, France, and England were reputed to have Trojan ancestors as well. We read *in Sir Gawain and the Green Knight*, for example, that Felix Brutus left Troy to found Britain and in the Icelandic *Prose Edda* the Norse gods are said to have been magicians who fled a burning Troy. Sicily, like much of Europe, willingly inscribed itself into the matter of Rome, postulating Trojan ancestors for a number of its towns: Thucydides, for instance, reporting that an early Sicilian people, the Elymians, believed themselves to be descendants of the Trojan Ancestes. The matter of Britain dealt with the Arthurian Cycle in which the knights of the Round Table witnessed the passage of spiritual authority (symbolized by the Holy Grail) from the descendants of Troy's Felix Brutus (Arthur, Gawain, and Gareth, among others) to the descendants of Jerusalem's Joseph of Arimathea (notably, Lancelot, Galahad, and Perceval). Once again, a Sicilian connection was postulated for the matter of England. Arthur—as we noted a moment ago—was said to be trapped beneath Mount Etna, the belching volcano a palpable symbol of his eternally festering wounds. The matter of France centered upon the Carolingian Cycle in which

Charlemagne and his Paladins pursued the purified (that is to say, Holy) Roman Empire. To the matter of France, Sicilians always felt their greatest connection.

In fact, as I learned during the many conversations I had on the cycle, Palermitans (more so in the past, ever less readily today) considered themselves the heirs of the Carolingian dynasty by means of their 11th century Norman rulers, one of whom, Roger II, made the correspondence between himself and Charlemagne explicit. Just as Charlemagne was crowned Holy Roman Emperor in Rome's St. Peter's Basilica on Christmas Day, 800 CE, Roger was crowned king of Sicily in Palermo's Cathedral on Christmas Day, 1130 CE. And Roger's grandson, the Emperor Frederick II, allowed the correspondence between the Carolingian and Norman dynasties more immediacy when he gained not only the crown of Sicily (1197 CE) but also the Holy Roman Empire (1220 CE), and declared Palermo to be the imperial capital. His body is ostentatiously entombed in Palermo's cathedral. I suspect it was its apocalyptic themes—along with the fact that Sicily had been wrested from its Muslim overlords by Roger's Christian forces to become the seat of the Holy Roman Empire just as *The Song of Roland* was coming of age—which rendered the Carolingian Cycle so amenable to Sicilian society and allowed it to be knit so seamlessly into the fabric of the Sicilian folkloric repertoire.

It was the Carolingian Cycle that brought me to Palermo. Here, the stories of Charlemagne and his Paladins were available to me from four sources: the Sicilian popular press, the recitation of storytellers, the city's general populace (among which an extremely wide knowledge of the cycle was diffused) and the marionette theater (which presented the Carolingian Cycle in some 270 hour-long episodes). It was undoubtedly the fact that the Carolingian Cycle became, over time, the preeminent matter of Sicilian puppetry that epic still remained active in the oral tradition where I was able to study it. Over and again, during my sojourn in Palermo, I would enter the marionette theater— its dim interior adorned with hand-painted posters depicting the scenes that were just then to be performed and presided over by the gaily painted and heavily festooned stage—amidst the maddening clash of the cylinder piano. And there I would—along with an ever-shrinking slice of the Palermitan populace and, ever more common today, a scattering of tourists—take my seat on one of the theater's spare benches. I was lucky enough to bear witness to a tradition which was rapidly giving way first to the cinema and next to television and, probably as much as anything else, to a reputation for being the entertainment of the *popolino*: that is, the working poor.

Central to this immense story, as it emerged at Palermo, are the exploits of two heroes: Roland and Renaud. Roland is the perfect knight, always maintaining fealty to his sovereign, Charlemagne, even when that sovereign's judgment has been clouded by the dissembling of that arch-traitor, Ganelon. For his unwavering loyalty, Roland suffers death at the hands of the Saracens in a pass in the Pyrenean Mountains at Roncevaux, a death that has been prearranged by the traitor Ganelon with the Saracen King Marsilius of Saragossa. But Roland dies valiantly. He refuses to blow his Oliphant and alert the main host of Charlemagne's army to the disastrous battle until he has broken the might of the Saracen host. When he finally blows the Oliphant—ushering in the final apocalyptic battle between the forces of Christendom and Islam—the vein in his temple bursts. His cousin, the noble rebel, Renaud, having been banished from Charlemagne's court as a result of Ganelon's wicked machinations and resorted to banditry in order to survive, returns just in time to fight valiantly with the French at Roncevaux and hear the dying confession of his good cousin Roland:

> Bishop Turpin, I repent having killed don Chiaro, a Christian. I repent having challenged my uncle Charlemagne with a glove. And lastly I repent having left my wife a virgin. Good Lord in heaven, I can barely see with my eyes! Where are you? Renaud? Ricciardetto? Bishop Turpin? I believe that I am dying. But at least I will die with my right hand towards Spain. Then, when my uncle Charlemagne finds me, he will know that I died as a hero and not as a coward!"[14]

Renaud is the mirror image of Roland: a valiant knight but inverted. Instead of fealty, his troubled relationship with his sovereign is characterized by rebellion. And whereas Roland will quit the incessant battle against Saracen knights if he believes he can convert his erstwhile enemy to Christianity, Renaud inevitably fights to the bitter end. Roland's penchant for forgiveness (and its concomitant value, obedience) and Renaud's for vengeance (and its concomitant value, rebellion) speak to a most strikingly important difference between the two premier Paladins, a difference to which we will momentarily turn.

The Carolingian Cycle

On the morning of the procession, I took my coffee at a small café not far from my room, a place where I had stopped a few times before. The café was quiet, the day being a holiday, and the owner less harried than usual. He gave me a free coffee and asked what brought me to Palermo. "It's the only place where the Carolingian Cycle is still being told," I said. He thought for a moment and said, "The Normans brought the Carolingian Cycle here, you know." He then added somewhat solemnly, "But they didn't take it back with them." He was intimating that the stories of Charlemagne and his Paladins somehow belonged to Palermo now, that they had somehow *become* Palermitan, though I was unsure at the time of the significance of his statement. Luckily, however,

I had come, at some point during my stay in Palermo, to comprehend that some of my most important understandings of the significance of epic to the Palermitan people were to be had in some of my most casual conversations. Thus, I learned to toss my notebooks aside periodically and spend the day just hanging about and chatting with people. I learned, in fact, that hearing *about* the stories was just as important as *hearing* the stories.

One of the early conversations I had about the Carolingian Cycle was with a shopkeeper on my street named Maria. She was probably well into her seventies and concerned herself with the welfare of everyone (particularly the young men whom elderly women in Palermo often simultaneously extol and keep in check) in the neighborhood. She insisted that I take milk with my coffee as it was winter.

"And have you had your coffee this morning?" she asked.

"Yes, Signora," I dutifully answered. "Just a moment ago."

"And did you take a little milk with your coffee?" she persisted.

"No, Signora."

"*Mio Dio,*" she exclaimed to her daughter-in-law, who was just then taking inventory in the back of the shop, "Here is a good boy who studies and studies, who never causes his mother any trouble; up and down the street he goes, always with his notebook in hand, and he can't even afford a little milk with his coffee. Rosaria, make the boy a cup of coffee; be sure to put a little milk in it."

As I sipped my coffee, I explained to Maria that I was not a student at the university, but that I was in Palermo studying the Carolingian Cycle. She immediately told me whom I should champion and whom I should disdain. "Don't pay any attention to Roland," she told me. "He's no good. There he had a perfectly good wife at home, Alda the Beautiful, and he ran around starting fights over Angelica, even with his own cousin, Renaud de Montauban. Renaud is the good one. Pay attention to him. He always acts honorably." Maria's privileging of Renaud over Roland is, as I was slowly coming to learn, standard procedure in Palermo. But what was most striking about Maria's comments to me at the time was the fact that her interpretation of epic centered so entirely upon characters and their attributes. As a friend from a small, inland village who knew epic mainly from her village festival told me, "That's because these old people think those characters are real." Perhaps a better way to explain Maria's approach to epic is to say that epic in the not so distant past was understood as history: history with marvelous elements added but history nonetheless. We could fairly call it legendary history: history which allegorically imbues its heroes with a spark of divinity.

The penchant for allegory that typifies the Carolingian Cycle in Palermo—

but was already discernible in the *Song of Roland*—was pointed out to me by a woman who, upon seeing a marionette of the infant Rolandin (diminutive for Roland) wrapped in swaddling clothes, said, "See? The swaddling clothes! See? He's born in a cave!" The traditional setting of Christ's birth in Sicilian nativities is a cave, or grotto, a place (as we witnessed in the tale of Santa Rosalia) laden with spiritual significance. "A shepherd is there," she merrily continued. "You understand? It's one of the puppeteers' tricks!" In fact, Roland was continuously being offered up as an allegorical representative of Christ. He was born in a manger. He was delivered up to his enemies (in this case, Saracens rather than Romans) by epic's answer to Judas Iscariot: Ganelon of Maiance. His act of self-sacrifice for his lord Charlemagne (epic's allegorical representative of God) was understood to be the exact equivalent of Christ's sacrifice on Golgotha. Even the act of blowing his Oliphant furthered the allegory for the angel Gabriel (who blows his horn at the apocalypse) is, in medieval iconography, a Christ surrogate. But, surprisingly, Roland's self-sacrifice was not entirely lauded by epic's working-class audience. It was rather harshly judged as emblematic of a blind obedience to Charlemagne's dictates. And his nickname, Cross Eyes, a name underscored by the fact that Roland is always depicted with eyes looking somewhat crossed and even a bit stunned, seemed to encapsulate that critique.

Renaud, on the other hand, was epic's allegorical representative of Christ's mythic progenitor: the biblical David. But this David would barely be recognizable to a society without a tradition of social banditry. A phenomenon in which a child of the community (like England's Robin Hood and Sicily's Salvatore Giuliano) runs afoul of the law and is forced to take to the hills and rob for his livelihood, social banditry is a commonality to both ancient Israel and premodern Sicily. In fact, David's youthful history is exactly that of the social bandit. He was banished from the court of King Saul and took refuge with his band of 600 outlaws in the caves of the Judean Hills. He solaced himself in laments over the unjust treatment he received from the hands of his sovereign. And he resorted to comic thefts—such as cutting the hem of Saul's robe while the king, by a happy coincidence, was relieving himself in David's mountain hideaway. Even when David, in the course of a notable lament, displayed the hem of Saul's robe to the sovereign—as proof that he might have killed the king had he been disloyal to the crown—Saul was unrelenting. There is even the suggestion that David carried a bit of his lawless behavior to the throne: his affair with Bathsheba displays all the earmarks of abduction. Renaud's history follows the same trajectory. Banned from Charlemagne's court, he gathers up a band of 600 outlaws. He, like David, founds a citadel in a mountain hideaway from which he harries the countryside. And laments over his unfair treatment, invariably declaring that his acts of outlawry amount to just retribution, mark his career. Further, he—again like David—resorts to comic thefts and impromptu abductions. A notable episode of the Carolingian Cycle involves Renaud abducting his future wife, Clarice, amidst a declaration that his behavior is justified inasmuch as Charlemagne planned to marry Clarice off to a Saracen. In fact, Renaud's nickname, the Mafioso, is a direct nod to the character's bandit nature: the Mafioso being, in the context of Palermitan society, the very model of the urban social bandit. And, as if to confirm such a nefarious affiliation, Renaud's eyes— direct and perhaps a bit impenetrable—speak to a mechanism that Mafiosi commonly employ to maintain their reputation for toughness. Tellingly, if Roland's self-sacrifice is rarely applauded, Renaud's banditry is deemed to be ennobling inasmuch as it expresses the knight's rebellious nature.[15]

Maria often commented on the adventures of Charlemagne, Roland, Renaud, Ganelon, and Angelica to me and I once made the mistake, not having been long in Palermo and not yet knowing much about the traditional composition of epic's audiences, of asking her where she would go to see the plays. She was taken aback and said, "I've never been to one of those places!" I found out later that epic's audiences consisted not only of the *popolino* but exclusively of men and boys from that beleaguered class of society. Maria had learned all the stories from her brothers. And luckily, her offense at my inadvertent affront to her womanly modesty was momentarily shrugged off with the recognition that I was just another untutored, not to say dumb, foreigner. Still, despite my miscomprehensions, she had clued me into something essential: the epic hero, Roland, was not actually the hero of the Palermitan version of the Carolingian Cycle: at least not to the working-class men and boys who were its patrons. In fact, he was rather scorned—and sometimes pitied. Renaud was, in actuality, the very image of the hero to Palermitans. As one man explained it to me, Roland was not completely disliked. "When he's rescuing damsels or killing Saracens everyone cheers for him. It's just that Roland tends to be a little flat, too one-sided, always doing what he's supposed to. There are more sides to Renaud's nature." But why, I came to wonder, would Palermitan storytellers create a hero—and everybody I talked to (Maria included) considered Roland the hero of the Carolingian Cycle—only to heap upon him the worst sort of abuse?

But even as I pondered this question, a glitch intruded upon my studies. A continuous theme of the Carolingian Cycle, both in its medieval formulations and its current Palermitan iteration, is that of marshaling the forces of Christendom against the intrusion of Islam upon "Christian soil" (i.e., Europe). The fact that the tradition I was studying was tinged with an Islamophobic animus (of a sort that even today has found its way into both European and American political discourse) would have been little more than a background concern for me had it not been for an unexpected set of circumstances that began on my first day in Sicily. After trundling out of the rail station, my bags in hand, I was confronted with the uncomfortable fact that I couldn't find a room I could afford. Luckily, the entrepreneurial proprietress of a modest *pensione* that I checked suggested that, though the *pensione* was full, I might share a room with *"un bravo ragazzo"* ("a great fellow") and, after I stowed my bags, my new room-mate, Faisal, took me out onto the balcony to show me the view. Our room looked out onto the famed Via Maqueda which crosses Palermo's historic center and empties, as fate would have it, just below the balcony, onto a frenzied piazza fronting the train station. Just as we stepped out onto the balcony, a horse, drawing a cart down Via Maqueda, became spooked and refused to enter the treacherous stream of traffic crushing its way through the piazza. I looked down at his terrified eyes, sheltered by blinders but fully visible from above, as Palermo erupted into a frenzy of honking horns, racing engines, and cursing motorists. I laughed aloud at this, my first image of the city before me, and Faisal affectionately pressed his cheek against my arm. We were friends from there on in.

Thus, it was natural that I bring him along one night to see a performance of the marionette theater. Unfortunately, I didn't think about it at the time I issued the invitation but, as I just mentioned, a mainstay of the Carolingian Cycle is the battle of the forces of Christendom—championed by Charlemagne, Roland, Renaud, Oliver, Astolphe—against the infidel, Islam, championed by an array of Saracen knights: Marsilius, Falseron, Bulogant, Ferraù, Agrican. Even in the very first episode, *The Death of King Pepin*, Charlemagne's father, the episode's namesake, announces his success in annihilating the Saracens who dared to attempt a conquest of France, proclaiming: "I am content that peace reigns in our land, after the many wars that we have withstood against these vile Saracens who wanted to conquer France, who wanted to aggrandize the false faith of Muhammad. We have destroyed them, causing them to repent having ever set foot on Christian soil." The evening's fare was sprinkled with the usual battles, culminating in a spectacular beheading of a Saracen knight, but Faisal took everything in stride and my embarrassment was quickly quelled when he—who assimilated so easily to "Christian soil" that he took the name which Sicilian friends had offered him, Fabbio, without a complaint—said, "It's just a story." It was Faisal who (when the stock market crashed—Black Monday, October 19, 1987—and I lost in a day twenty dollars to every hundred I exchanged) took me to the set of rooms rented out, for the most part, to a group of Tunisians—working for a while before returning home to perhaps buy a house or a shop or set up a business—and thus rescued my faltering budget. Beyond the Tunisians living in this set of rooms, and me, an American, there was Mohammed, a fellow from Togo. The Tunisians, Mohammed, and I, shared one bath, with a toilet that could only be flushed by lugging in a bucket of water from the communal sink in the hallway and a tub that could only be supplied by a couple of buckets of water heated by a gas plate, also in the hallway. There was no glass in the rooms' window casings but there were shutters which had to be closed in the daytime or one would come home to find that the cats who prowled the nearby rooftops had taken up temporary residency on his bed.

Tunisians had a long history in Sicily beginning in the ninth century when the Byzantine admiral Euphemius invited the Aghlabid emir of Tunisia to aid him in his bid to become Sicily's governor and offered the island as an Arab tributary: "The response came immediately. An elite army of more than 10,000 men—Arabs, Berbers and Spanish Moslems—landed at Mazara, and another conquest of Sicily had begun."[16] The conquest lasted from 827 to 965, Palermo falling early on in 831. And as Christianity yielded to Islam and the Greek language of the Byzantine Empire to Arabic, Palermo (now called Balerm) became the premier city of Sicily and its court is said to have rivaled those of Cairo and Baghdad. But the monuments—including, by some counts, 300 mosques— of Arab Sicily in that city that were not destroyed in the succeeding Norman invasion have been so heavily built over by subsequent generations that they are barely recognizable for what they were.[17] Still, the stonework on the inner wall of the church of St. John of the Lepers is the original Arab construction of a fort seized by the Norman, Roger I, in his invasion of Palermo.[18] And *Il Cassaro*, the original name of the Old City's major thoroughfare, the Corso Vittorio Emanuele, is a cogent memorial to the Arabic fortification that once stood at its head: *Al Kasr*. Arab Sicily might have endured longer than it did had it not been for the fact that the Aghlabid dynasty which ruled Sicily from its Tunisian stronghold was weakened by a tenth century civil war, "complicated by the advance of the heretic Shiites," which pushed the Muslim capital east to Cairo, leaving Muslim Sicily both more independent and increasingly vulnerable to Christian invasion.[19] Still, the reminders of Arab Sicily were ubiquitous. For instance, the Churches of Saint John of the Hermits, Saint John of the Lepers, and Saint Cataldo seem, at first glance, to be more in the nature of mosques than churches. Soaring above the heavy stone crenelation in each of these sanctuaries, striking magenta domes speak directly to the Arabic occupation which broke Sicily's long era of Byzantine rule and was broken in its turn with the Norman invasion. In my mind, these Arabo-Norman domes signify Palermo, perhaps because of the inability to determine precisely whether they represent the Byzantine, Arab, or Norman occupations of the island.

As they became more comfortable with me, my Tunisian flatmates would occasionally attempt to convert me to Islam. I characteristically staved off these attempts, suggesting that I was not particularly spiritually inclined, but one day—thinking, as I recall, that having some religion would probably be deemed better than having none—I said to my closest friend among the Tunisians that I basically felt all religions were equally valid. *"Michele, hai sbagliato,"* he said without hesitation. "Michael, you are mistaken. There is only one true religion and you will know whether it is Judaism, Christianity, or Islam by the actions of its adherents!" ("Good God," I thought to myself. "We're all going to hell in a hand wagon!") But, in actuality, I appreciated the attempts at conversion as they were not particularly aggressive, and they represented my new friends' concern with my well-being, not to mention the fact that my anomalous appearance among them was no longer viewed as so anomalous.

Saint John of the Hermits (Wikipedia, photograph by Bernhard J. Scheuvens).

In fact, there could have been good reason to resent me for the Tunisians were sometimes not treated so well in Palermo. And I know our landlady was taking merciless advantage of them. Yet, I remember one time, when a Palermitan man was speaking poorly of Tunisians, another stepped in to criticize him, saying, "No, the Tunisians are good people. As long as they assimilate to Sicilian society." I know that, mainly, the Tunisians managed to adapt enough to meet their goals but must have suffered terribly in a world where the word for barbarian is

Turk, a term resulting from the long years in which Sicily was the bulwark against the expansion of the Ottoman Empire and even served as the jumping off point for the famed maritime battle of Lepanto between the forces of European Christendom and Ottoman Islam, but a word which as well seemed to sometimes be used as a synonym for Muslim (just as is Arab, too often, in the United States today). Likewise, the term Christian was not unusually used as a synonym for human being. And I also remember a particularly poignant moment the night a *coup d'etat* was occurring in Tunisia (one which brought to power the man who fled the country with the outbreak of the Arab Spring) and we were watching the reports from Tunis coming fuzzily over the television, so near to Palermo is Africa. The events of the night inevitably led to discussions of the way things were back home and here in Sicily. Most of the Tunisians I lived with were fundamentalist Muslims and didn't empathize with the secular Tunisian government, but one man did. He was sweeping the common area, not much more than a widened hallway, and he said he didn't care if Sicilians looked at him with disdain. "My shoes may be broken," he said, "but my pride is intact. Do you know what my pride is?" he asked. "No," I answered. "Wait a minute," he said, and he went to his room and emerged with the Tunisian flag: the new moon and morning star on a field of red. He held it to the end of the broomstick and began waving it. "This is my pride," he proclaimed. "You know what your pride is good for?" one of the women asked. "Cleaning your broken shoes!" Thereupon, the man retreated to his lonely room.

Dialogism and Rhetoric

After dawdling about the streets on the morning of the procession, waiting for the evening's festivities to begin, I popped back up to my room for a moment where a singular tragedy was unfolding. Mohammed, having the day off from work, had bought a chicken at the market, and, just as he was preparing to butcher it in our communal sink, the bird flew out the window. "That stupid beast," Mohammed swore as I was coming up the stairs. "It has the mind of an animal." And, indeed, it looked pretty stupid standing out on the roof unaware that stray cats lived there, and no doubt fed at times on incautious birds. Mohammed and I clambered out onto the roof of ancient and precariously slanted tile and began chasing the chicken. I was gaining more respect for this stupid beast which would let us come within inches of her and then flutter off, gobbling and clucking, to a point just beyond our reach. She was teasing us. As we hauled ourselves back into the window, I going first and having to catch all 270 pounds of Mohammed as he lunged headlong over the sink, Mohammed swore again, "That stupid beast! I was trying to save its life!" (In fact, he wanted to eat it.) The chicken clucked and strutted off, oblivious to the dangers which awaited her. As I was running back down the stairs, the woman who teased our flatmate about his flag came in and, as her son and husband were still at work, she desperately needed someone to run to the market for her. She had learned all the possible complaints in Italian and decided to use them against me that day. "Good morning, *Signora*," I said as I raced down the stairs. "Oh, what a life full of misery! My stomach hurts and my tooth still aches. These Christians are so bad here. They take advantage of us and don't care if we live well or die. Only the French Christians are good. I wish we could go back there, or to Tunisia. Muslims are always good people. They take care of one another." As she was winding down, she slapped some money in my hand and asked me to go to the market and pick up some bread.

Perhaps due to my living arrangements, perhaps due to fact of being in Sicily itself, I was coming to realize something essential that day. Mohammed, the Tunisians, and I were not always communicating through words alone but quite often through what linguists call speech acts. Mohammed's speech act, I think, was syncretic, as much African as Palermitan, and I am unsure exactly as to why he claimed to be saving the chicken's life, unless it was a kind of appeal, a means of reasoning with the chicken itself or perhaps the universe at large. The point is that his speech act was part of his attempt (unsuccessful as it was) to get the chicken back. The Signora's speech act on the other hand was Palermitan, or, more properly, Mediterranean, and immediately recognizable to me. It was the lament, the cry of the *popolino*, the working poor who formed the great bulk of Palermitan society. As such it existed as the spoken symbol of *miseria:* the unending scramble to make a hard living. What—very fuzzily at first but later with greater clarity—came into focus for me that particular day was this: culture gives us a very particular language with which we not only express *what we think* but also *who we are*.

This language, which we may refer to as the rhetoric of identity, consists of a number of verbal artifacts: notably tropes, speech acts, and tones. Tropes are symbolic equivalencies. They include such disparate strategies as metaphor (implicit comparison), simile (explicit comparison), metonymy (referring to something by an attribute), synecdoche (referring to something by one of its parts), antonomasia (employing a name as an epithet or an epithet as a name), and—one of my favorites—the cryptonym, a metaphor which seeks to reveal through concealment.[20] Speech acts are almost innumerable but famously include hyperbole (overstatement), litotes (understatement), apostrophe (exclamatory address), consolation, threat, promise, lie, prayer, joke, and supplication, not to mention the Signora's lament or Mohammed's appeal. Tones, essentially genres of speech, include sarcasm, irony, teasing, joking, reservation, solemnity, boisterousness, boastfulness, and gravitas among numerous others. Significantly, these tropes, speech acts, and tones are necessarily contextualized by both behavioral and material artifacts—expressions, gestures, actions, clothing, accoutrements, physical settings—without which the information verbally conveyed could become amorphous or, worse yet, misconstrued. What's more, these behavioral and material artifacts—like their verbal counterparts—behave as signs: cues which signify in contiguity, apposition, or juxtaposition to the verbal artifacts they accompany.

Think for a moment of a minister approaching the altar within the sanctuary to offer the Lord's Prayer to his or her parishioners. In the repertoire of the minister, this very specific speech act, the recitation of the Lord's Prayer, signifies the minister's religious authority even as the same speech act, the recitation of the Lord's Prayer by the congregation, signifies submission to religious authority. A major sociological metaphor—that of god as the congregation's father—centers the speech act and an appropriate tone, reverence, modulates both the minister's and the parishioners' voices as the speech act is undertaken. Further, a set of behavioral traditions encumber the recitation as well: heads are bowed, eyes are closed, hands are folded. And the recitation is undertaken in the context of a rich array of material culture: the altar containing the chalice, wine and host; the sanctuary which is defined by the dais, which contains the altar and where the minister presides, as well as the pews where the parishioners' devotion is centered upon the altar and the ministerial duties toward it.

Behavioral Artifacts	*Verbal Artifacts*	*Material Artifacts*
(1) Expression (2) Gesture (3) Action	(1) Trope (2) Speech Act (3) Tone	(1) Clothing (2) Accoutrements (3) Setting
(1) Eyes Closed (2) Head Bowed (3) Approaching Altar	(1) Father, Kingdom (2) Prayer (3) Reverence	(1) Vestments (2) Altar, Chalice (3) Sanctuary, Dias, Pews

Table Two: Verbal, behavioral, and material artifacts are listed in the top row; examples of each in the context of a recitation of the Lord's Prayer are offered in the bottom row.

These tropes, speech acts, and tones are formulated through the mobilization or redeployment of normative linguistic processes—a kind of playing with language—in order to imply something more than the mere denotative value of an utterance. Phonetics can be used to suggest different class affiliation: in the early history of the Massachusetts Bay Colony, for instance, omitting the final *r* in words allowed colonists to emulate the privileged accent of the home country. The artful use of morphemes (roots, prefixes, or suffixes) can offer an utterance various suggestive qualities: for instance, the morphological form, -er can be added to the name of a political group in order to suggest a degree of fringe ideology (John Bircher, Teabagger, Birther) or the Spanish suffix -ero can be added to the ethnic term Maya in order to rhetorically transform an ethnic label into an occupational label (i.e., *Mayero*, or Yucatecan agricultural worker).[21] Altering the grammatical environment of a word can give that word a connotative rather than denotative value: "I see the light," for instance, rather than "Turn on the light." There can even be gestural cues or specific social settings that might alter the normative understanding of a communication. Think about the significance of the statement, "You look gorgeous in that outfit," if the speaker rolls his or her eyes while saying it. When language—and, importantly, the nonverbal communication that surrounds it— is rhetorically charged, communication moves beyond that which is merely informative to that which communicates identity.

In this, tropes, speech acts, and tones—embedded in their behavioral and material context—artfully conspire to create a distinctive voice. And it is this distinctive voice, really, which serves to communicate identity: to communicate, that is, the worldview that arises out of one's sense of affiliation. But affiliation, like voice, is a complex affair, growing—as it does—out of one's cultural context, personal experience, and individual personality. Culture, as it impacts one's network of affiliation, is partly a matter of fate: where one is born, where one comes to live, among whom one moves. But it is likewise a matter of social imperatives: for instance, one's status in the context of his or her social system and the dictates that such status implies. Then, quite distinct from cultural context, one's personal experience consists of the innumerable episodes that mark one's individual history. These episodes—sorted, emphasized or minimized, and stored away in one's memory bank—allow an individual to flesh out the social schemes that culture provides us. Personality, is largely the product of the interplay of one's cultural context and personal experience, but it is likewise effected by biopsychological orientation (involving individualized behaviors that are at least partially genetically inscribed) and other almost innumerable and extremely individualistic factors: say, overseas travel, an interest in Russian literature, educational opportunities, personal appearance, a love of opera, everything and anything which demarcates one's own particular individuality. Born in the cauldron of culture and experience, and tempered by personality, one's sense of affiliation imparts to the individual a worldview as singular and rarified as one's fingerprint: but a worldview that can (indeed must) be communicated in order to negotiate its significance. And, therein, lies the rub: not only does each of us learn our voice from those with whom we most closely affiliate but we also, in turn, use that voice (so learned) in order to communicate our sense of affiliation to others: a kind of eternal feedback loop is thus engendered in which we communicate our own affiliation even as we comprehend the complex set of affiliations that others continuously communicate to us. And it is in the constant negotiation of our place within that feedback loop that identity is formulated.

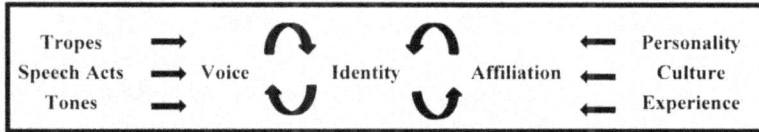

Tropes →				← Personality
Speech Acts →	Voice	Identity	Affiliation ←	Culture
Tones →				← Experience

Table Three: Just as Tropes, Speech Acts, and Tones conspire to create Voice, Culture, Personal Experience, and Personality Conspire to Engender Affiliation. Further, whereas Identity is a Function of Affiliation, it can only be expressed through Voice.

This brings us back to an earlier discussion. Though the fact that we are dreaming animals elucidates our religious life, the fact that we are both social and speaking animals elucidates the intersection of affiliation and voice that is at the center of identity. In fact, so critical is that intersection to identity formation that, as Deborah Tannen has recently pointed out, we not only speak but also interpret the words of others in a manner consonant with our network of affiliations.[22] Such being the case, culture seems to work very much like a wiki: everyone in the society has an editorial role, an ability to participate in the dialogue that is ultimately culture, but the dialogue itself—the culture proper—resides in no one. It is supra-individual. At the same time, however, it informs the individual for it gives voice to what would otherwise be inchoate information and allows it to express not simply *itself* but also *the self*. Put another way, we could say that culture is not something which resides in a society or, for that matter, in any individual member of a society. Rather, culture should be viewed as a process of communication—certainly verbal but also behavioral and even material—which allows members of a group to "speak" or, better, to represent themselves both to one another as well as outsiders. Culture then is a thing that is—very literally—spoken, performed, and crafted.

Thus, one cannot honestly say when speaking of Sicilian culture that Sicilians do this or that. Rightly speaking, nothing can be truly predictable about a Sicilian simply on the basis of the fact that he or she is a member of Sicilian society. Rather, one can say that a Sicilian who wishes to manifest affiliation with a Mafia style subculture—a subculture that has, for Sicilians at least, historically been denoted by a manner of speech, behavior, and dress as much as group affiliation—may do so through the affectation of a recognizable rhetorical repertoire that includes a number of verbal, behavioral, and material cues which collectively speak to his toughness. Likewise, a Sicilian who wishes to manifest affiliation with the church has at his disposal a number of verbal, behavioral, and material cues which collectively speak to his piety. A priest will, after all, rarely resort to the sarcasm which so often marks the Mafioso's speech. And, while the Mafioso certainly might make recourse to the priest's invocation of the Holy Trinity, he is as likely to do so in a curse as a blessing. Rhetoric then serves to interject identity (read, in this context, as the recognition and communication of group affiliation) directly into the cultural arena. It functions as a kind of communicative "grouping up," a linguistic mechanism for picking one's team.

And such is most certainly the case with the Carolingian Cycle. In fact, dialogism—the use of socially distinctive voices in the characterization of its heroes—is continuously at play in Sicilian epic. It was easy to spot the linguistic distinction between Christian knights and Saracens: Christians, in battle, employ a clear, resounding diction and they tend to use hortatory address—a bit like a Shakespearian soliloquy. But Saracens are given to gory oaths—and the oaths of the Saracen giants are exceptional: the bequest of Goliath who swore that he would throw David's flesh "to the birds of the sky and the beasts of the earth."[23] Agrican, a particularly vicious Saracen who abducted Roland's beloved Angelica, follows in like tradition, saying, at one point, "Agrican of Tartary swears that I won't call myself by name if I don't skin you like the dog that you are!" And to Roland's rejoinder, "Listen, Agrican, I have advised you once, and it is not my habit to repeat things a second time, leave Angelica in peace! Angelica is mine and no one is going to take her away," Agrican continues his blustering oaths, crying, "Vile, Roland, I'll eat your heart right out of your chest as well as that of this disgrace, Angelica!"

Not surprisingly, when Roland and Renaud were found in battle, they sounded indistinguishable from one another. They spoke in clear Italian—rather than Sicilian—and, moreover, they spoke in the resounding, hortatory address characteristic of Christian knights. But when they were found in other—and very specific contexts—they almost seemed to be speaking different languages. Snatches and phrases from Church liturgy, of the sort that I heard in the homilies preceding and following the procession of the Immaculate Virgin, kept surfacing in epic. And almost invariably from the lips of Roland: that perfect knight. In fact, Roland sounded startlingly like a Sicilian priest—making liberal use of liturgy and prayer, even the Apostles' Creed, in a highly sincere tone—when he was at his most obedient self. For instance, when Roland had delivered the deathblow to his adversary Agrican, he immediately set about an attempt to convert him to Christianity: "Oh, my Good Lord! Here I am at your feet! I beg of you, permit me to baptize and save the soul of this innocent." But Renaud too, when involved in his most audacious rebellions against Charlemagne, spoke in a remarkably distinct manner. He sounded alarmingly like a Mafioso: making liberal use of threat and slipping regularly into a sarcastic tone. I obviously wasn't cavorting with Mafiosi during my time in Sicily but I did, in a happenstance manner, learn something of their speech patterns. During a robbery which I had the unfortunate opportunity to witness, a friend of mine (like me, a foreigner to the city) was about to intervene. One of the men—who were carting furniture out of the storeroom which they had, in full daylight, broken into—stopped his activity. He did not take his eyes from mine. He smiled steadily and noncommittally, but his message was very clear: 'Get her out of here.' Further, the Maxiproceso, a group trial of 500 Mafiosi, was underway in Palermo's Ucciardone Prison during my stay in the city. Thus, I had ample opportunity to witness the peculiar locutions of those who sought—unsuccessfully, as it turned out—to defend themselves. Renaud made regular recourse to the threat (often veiled) and sarcasm when he was perpetrating a robbery or abduction and I once heard him, his voice dripping with sarcasm, say to his brother who was urging him to make haste to the battle at Roncevaux: "Brother, Ricciardetto, *perhaps* you have *forgotten* that I left my arms in Paris when I rendered myself subject to Charlemagne. Yet *if* you remember well, after the death of my wife, Clarice, I swore that I would no longer carry arms, that I would no longer do combat, that I would no longer kill people! And now, *what is it* that you ask of me, brother?" The Mafioso survives on a perception of calm toughness and the effective management of others' fear. Sarcasm regularly colors his speech as well as the use of veiled threats. But these threats are always mitigated. They are most often not meant to harm; they are rather meant to keep one in check.

The disparate characterization of these two heroes, effected most fully by their disparate speech patterns, points to a peculiarity of class structure in Sicily. Historically, Sicilian priests were allied with the aristocracy who were—inasmuch as appointment to priestly offices in Sicily was a royal prerogative—their sons, brothers, uncles, and cousins. Moreover, the aristocracy—as well as its priestly corollary—was, because of Sicily's long history of colonial occupation, invariably foreign. Conversely, Mafiosi were necessarily allied to the *popolino* inasmuch as the men (and boys) who filled their ranks were precisely the sons of the *popolino* who had run afoul of the alien authorities. If the priestly class was invariably foreign, the Mafia was necessarily indigenous. Thus, an ambivalent allegiance that Palermitans manifested towards their priests was likewise directed towards Roland—with his priestly diction. And the protective net that the Palermitan *popolino* threw around the Mafia (and that was manifested in the famed code of *omertà*, secrecy) governed the loyalty that working-class men and boys (not to mention their wives, mothers, and sisters) directed toward Renaud—with his lawless diction. But even here, a marked ambivalence could be discerned. Inasmuch as the Mafia demanded tribute (i.e., extortion) for hedging the authority of an overbearing aristocracy, it existed as a kind of alternate, and often belligerent, authority.

Outsiders can never understand how an institution as nefarious as the Mafia can be treated with anything other than disdain. But outsiders are characteristically unaware of the long history of secret societies at Palermo—not to mention their function as a sort of indigenous authority. In fact, I only came to the realization that the Mafia was understood as the latest iteration of a long line of secret societies when a woman, exasperated, once exclaimed to me in response to a foreigner's complaint about the high crime rate in Palermo, "Up north there are terrorists. Here we have the Mafia. The terrorists will kill anybody. The Mafia will only kill you if you do something wrong. Which is the more honorable? Excuse me. I think the Mafia." But, to be sure that I understood that she was not supportive of today's Mafia, she quickly added, "I'm talking about the true Mafia, the Mafia when it was more like the Beati Paoli." For Palermitans, then, the Mafia is but one more of those necessary inconveniences that one endures in a life too often characterized by *miseria*. If it capitalizes itself at the expense of the people, it still is—or more properly was—perceived as an institution which grew organically out of the plight of the *popolino*. Thus, the preference for Renaud among Palermo's working poor expressed a cogent social reality. It was Renaud, after all, rather than Roland, who was thought of as the true son on the people. Little wonder then that he earned the infamous nickname: the Mafioso.

Still, I should here note that the aristocracy is no longer a social force in Sicily and the ruling class (politicians and businessmen; some titled, most not) that replaced it is predominately indigenous. Likewise, the priestly class is now almost entirely culled from the ranks of the Sicilian populace. And the Mafia has, probably due to the drug trade and globalization, become indistinguishable from other criminal cartels, with very few of the ennobling characteristics that defined secret societies to the Palermitan populace in the past. Further, the *popolino*, while still viewing itself as Sicilian, more and more often (since Italy's 1860 Unification) views itself as Italian and (with the further integration of EU policies into Sicilian life) European as well. Perhaps it is the changing social realities, then, as well as the cinema, television, and a reputation as the entertainment of the masses that has spelled the demise of Sicilian epic. That said, the modern state of Italy—of which Sicily is most decisively a part—has had the misfortune to be at times defined by Sicily's long history of foreign occupation, something I learned when, on my first visit to a marionette theater, a young boy, his face brightening with surprise, said to me, "But you speak like a soldier!" He then turned to his friends and reiterated, "But he speaks like a soldier!" Though I did not entirely understand it at the time, he was telling me that my Italian was like that of an outsider, like that of someone *not* from Palermo. And it seemed peculiar to me that the Italian soldier could be the very model of the foreigner, at least in the mind of my young interlocutor.

The Genius of Palermo and the Immaculate Virgin

I wandered here and there throughout the afternoon, just having a look around, until it was time for the procession. It began at the church of Saint Francis, home of the Immaculate Virgin, with a benediction, a release of white doves, and the ringing of bells. Bits of blue and yellow paper were dropped from the balconies above. They fluttered in a syncopated tumble, catching the light of the sun on each half turn, blanching and blushing as they fell. Hands stretched up to catch them for they were prayers. They read *Viva Maria Immacolata*! Long live Mary the Immaculate! A bell rang once. The penitents caught hold of the bier. It rang again. The bier was shouldered. It rang once more, and the penitents lumbered along the Via Paternostro. Each locked one arm around the bier, another around the man ahead of him. Though the men beneath her stumbled and collapsed into one another, stopped to wipe the sweat from their brows, then moved haltingly along once again, the silver Virgin moved in a smooth, effortless progression, directing her gaze here and there about the adulatory crowd as a band of flutes and drums, trumpets and violins began to sound.

As she crossed the Corso Vittorio Emanuele, I ran ahead of the procession in order to catch a glimpse of the procession entering the square before the Church of Saint Dominick, but as I cut through the Vucciria, Palermo's ancient market, I caught my first glimpse of the oddest statue tucked into a niche of a wall. I thought it was a man being attacked by a serpent and I momentarily lost interest in the procession. I asked some other people cutting through the market what the statue depicted but they didn't know, so I trailed along to Saint Dominick's and rejoined the procession. There the procession stopped before a tall column supporting another Immaculate Virgin. Here, with the aid of a fire truck's hydraulic ladder, a bouquet of poinsettias was presented to the Virgin on the column. And with that presentation, I realized that this Virgin was the same as the one down on the square, Immaculate, and that it was not any Virgin who could be honored on this day, but only the Immaculate Virgin. In this case, Mary's attribute was not Intercession, Motherhood, nor Pity, but only Immaculacy. Those other attributes belonged to other Marys and could only be addressed on other days, under different contexts. And it was not without a certain sense of irony that I realized that each of these various Marys, though all one person, had various Greco-Roman goddesses, deities dating from Palermo's earliest epochs, lurking behind them: Hera, Artemis, Persephone, Demeter, even (a bit notoriously) Aphrodite. And with that realization, another followed fast upon its heels. Roland and Renaud were governed by the same narrative logic as the Immaculate Virgin. Why couldn't Roland be a knight in one context, a priest in another? Likewise, why shouldn't Renaud trade in his knightly attributes for those of the Mafioso? The transformations were only natural in their narrative contexts.

The Genius of Palermo (Wikipedia, photograph by Fabrice de Nola).

The procession left Saint Dominick's and streamed into the Quattro Canti, there resting under the watchful eyes of the four quarters' patron saints. The night air was chill, and the crowd hovered all the more closely about the Virgin, dark shadows flitting about the piazza, soft murmurs merging with the tumbling waters of the nearby fountains. It was here in this very same chill night air of the Quattro Canti during this same procession of the Immaculate Virgin that the legend of the *Beati Paoli* opens with Prospero's affront to Constance's modesty. And it was as if the spirits of Constance, Corrado, and Prospero slipped silently among the crowd in the thick night air. The bells rang once, and the bier was shouldered; they rang once again, and the procession continued along the Corso Vittorio Eman-uele. It culminated in a triumphal entrance into the Norman cathedral, massive, austere, darkening in the wintry skies, another benediction, and then (for me, as I lived just a few steps away) the vision of the procession moving steadily back to Saint Francis amidst the occasional stirrings of flutes and violins.

In the following days I tried to find out more about the statue but the information I found was minimal. It apparently dated to the Spanish occupation (1300 to 1800 CE) and was called the Genius of Palermo. More interesting was the fact that it was not a man being attacked by a serpent. Rather, it was a duke sitting serenely on his throne as the serpent fed at his breast. And, as it turned out, the sculptural theme was a popular one: there are at least five of these stat-ues scattered about the city, one discovered the year I was there behind a decrepit wall. In at least one instance the Genius's throne rises from a scallop shell, the Conca d'Oro, symbol of the alluvial plain upon which the city sits, and in another a dog lies obediently at his feet. Giuseppe Pitrè, Palermo's renowned folklorist, collected the following account of the Genius:

> Our elders say that in ancient—but very ancient—times there was a lord both rich and powerful who sailed here and there about the world simply for pleasure. One time it hap-pened that a great tempest arose on the open sea and his ship was tossed from one side to the other; miraculously his ship wasn't overcome by the waves but after three days and three nights of terror—when he was next to death from fear and hunger—his ship was driven ashore on our land. He wandered here and there but found not one living soul—though the providence of God was everywhere. He fed on the fruits of our abundant plain until this lord—nearly half dead—was restored. And so he fell in love with this land—thinking it an earthly paradise—and because no one lived here and because he was very rich, he decided to found a city here. He gathered engineers and masons who constructed the city which was named, after the lord, Palermo. The same engineers and masons who built the city sculpted the marble statue of this rich lord, father and patron of the city, when he was already old. And this statue is the one found in the square of the Old Market.[24]

In this story, the Genius sounds suspiciously like a daemon: the tutelary spirit of a cove, a shore, a mysterious island that is so common in the folklore of sea-faring peoples in the Mediterranean.

Pitrè goes on to say that this story must surely be older than the statue and that seems likely. But this story contains no mention of the serpent at the Genius' breast—much less the dog that, in one instance, lies at his feet—and thus is only a partial explanation of the statue. I, at some point, did become aware that the motif was characteristically commissioned by the Jurists' Guild which apparently viewed it as a kind of emblem for its profession but, still, that knowledge didn't lessen my quandary as to its meaning beyond offering me a vague sense that the statue had something to do with justice in some indeci-pherable way. But how? And the fact that it was the Jurists' Guild that adopted the emblem only quickened the mystery because the Guild was likely a manifestation of the ancient Islamic *madhhab*, or legal school, which may have found its origins when a "group of Sicilian notables" were taken to Ifriqiya—North Africa—in order "to be inducted into the 'school' (*madhhab*) of the imam-caliph."[25] The suggestion that the *madhhab* was the ultimate source of the Guild is furthered by the fact that the Muslim institution shares so many characteristics to the later European legal guilds which sprang up first in Italy, later in France and Spain, and particularly tellingly in England. According to George Makdisi, the striking morphological similarities between the early Muslim *madhhabs* of Palermo and the later English Inn of Court (for instance, a school with a dormitory—i.e., an Inn—attached to a church or mosque) is better explained by the fact of "the continuous interchange in administrative personal between Norman England and Norman Sicily" then the usual explanation for the emergence of the English Inn of Court: that its origins are "exceedingly obscure."[26] Thus, there was certainly the possibility that the Genius preceded the Spanish occupation of Sicily. Perhaps it was as old as the Jurist Guild itself.

I continued to nose around for some explanation of the mysterious depiction: some people said that the statue represented the father and patron of the city; some people said that it somehow represented the classes of Palermitan society—but they could not say precisely how. I was perplexed! The Genius in the Old Market is probably the most popular inasmuch as it was used to affix notes of protest during various insurrections. It was in fact thought to so much represent Palermitan rebelliousness that it was removed from the Old Market by the repressive Bourbon government—a government rendered almost paranoiac by the execution of the queen's sister, Marie Antoinette, in Paris. Only after the unification of Italy, 1860–1870, was it restored to the Market, a symbol of the people's victory over their Bourbon oppressors. The Genius which today stands near the Quattro Canti—Palermo's Four Quarters, the spiritual heart of the city—admits a further explanation for it carries the following inscription: "Palermo, golden shell, you devour your own; you feed the foreigners." In effect, then, the serpent represents the foreigners who feed off the fruits of Palermo's abundant plain while Palermitans starve. While such sentiments certainly must have existed, they could hardly have been patronized on five separate occasions through the commissioning of these statues. This inscription is of the nature of the people's less durable protests attached to the Genius in the Old Market. Though interestingly, this inscription seems to have given rise to speculation among the Palermitan populace that the Genius is the descendant of Saturn, the ancient Greco-Roman patron of the city, who both gave birth to and devoured his own children. Perhaps, it is this last speculation (transporting a putative Spanish emblem not only back to Arabic but even to Roman Sicily) that has given rise to a little-known belief, nearly lost in the murky depths of time, that the serpent which the duke, an emblem of the aristocracy, nurtures is his child, the Palermitan people. Thus, an apparent act of nurturance—a suckling serpent—could as easily be reread as a venomous and deadly attack, as if representing the people's warning to the aristocracy that—if the foreign ruler did not become one with the indigenous populace—the child, as did Jupiter, could turn on the parent. The Genius, then, appeared to be a cryptonym: an image which rhetorically revealed its message through an apparent concealment. And as if to underscore its cryptic message, menacing fangs were a notable feature of the suckling serpent.

It was the Genius—that ancient Roman divinity, Arabic *djinn*, and Spanish daemon—which finally allowed me to understand the peculiar dichotomy presented by Roland and Renaud. In a masterful rhetorical flourish, the cycle created of the two premier Paladins a brilliant cryptonym. Through embroidering an elaborate allegory, Palermitan storytellers subjected the two knights— Roland and Renaud—to a process of condensation whereby they were cast as a single entity: a kind of double Christ. One half was based on Christ himself. The other half was based on Christ's mythic progenitor, David. And each half was as proficient as the other in felling giants (epic's ancient remembrance of Goliath) and dragons (epic's ancient remembrance of the Beast of the Apocalypse). Thereupon, through the artful employment of dialogism, these storytellers continuously displaced their audiences' acclaim from the putative hero—Roland, with his priestly diction and Christ-like obedience—to the true hero—Renaud, with his lawless diction and David-like rebelliousness. In this, the laws of obedience and rebellion were not exactly opposites but rather two sides of the same coin. And on this basis Palermitans, in the not so distant past, formed a deep sense of identification with these knights.

This sense of identification was strong, every bit as strong as that which so many other societies we have encountered maintain with their deities. This, I think, was what the café owner was intimating to me when he said that, while they had brought the Carolingian Cycle to Palermo, the Normans didn't take it back with them. And what my friend meant when she exclaimed, "These old people think those characters are real." At Palermo the Carolingian heroes were considered the ancestors of the Normans. And the Normans were considered the ancestors of the Palermitan populace. Thus, the Carolingian heroes were necessarily viewed by Palermitans as their own progenitors. This genealogical principle is precisely that which we earlier witnessed in the conception of Palermo's patron, Santa Rosalia. In this, Charlemagne and his Paladins—like Palermo's own patron saint—functioned very much like the Kachinas and Koyemcis did for the Zuni. They were, likewise, the Sicilian counterpart to

India's Pandavas and Kauravas. And, as we will momentarily see, they fulfilled the exact function that Orishas—African ancestral Spirits—do to this day in Haiti. Certainly, given such circumstances, the Carolingian Cycle now belonged to Palermo. And, further, legend at Palermo—in the form of the Carolingian Cycle and centered on ancestral genii imbued with divine attributes—effectively took on the function of myth.

Nowhere does the mythic function of legend become more apparent than in the apocalyptic imagery of the Carolingian Cycle, imagery which resonated so strongly in Sicilian society that not only did the Carolingian Cycle become the mainstay of Palermo's folkloric repertoire but *The Song of Roland* became the apex of that repertoire.[27] Such imagery displays remarkable contiguity with Christianity's *Book of Revelation*: particularly when Roland blows his Oliphant, announcing the cataclysmic battle between the forces of Christendom and Islam and dying as a result. But it also resonates with the cryptic message encapsulated in the Genius of Palermo: a message suggesting that the troubling nature of the social contract at Palermo carries within itself the roots of its own destruction. Still apocalyptic imagery is not exclusive to Palermo. We have witnessed a number of apocalypses in the course of this study: those presented in Handsome Lake's *Gaiwiio* and Wovoka's Ghost Dance, for instance. Black Elk's Great Vision likewise offered apocalyptic imagery for in his shamanic journey he witnessed the Lakota's passage along a perilous road where they, first, became separated from the animals that were their simultaneous allies and livelihood and, second, suffered terrible debilities before they found their way onto a good road and restoration. The Great War at the center of the *Mahabharata* and Nat Turner's Vision are likewise rife with apocalyptic imagery as is the Nordic Ragnarok. In fact, so widespread is the apocalypse in the world's mythologies that it might constitute its own archetype. Perhaps, as is the case with a number of the societies we have just enumerated, the harsh social conditions under which Sicilians too often labored seemed to occasion the emphasis which apocalyptic imagery received in Sicily's folkloric repertoire.

But there must have been something more. Otherwise, why construct such a complex allegory? And one so replete with apocalyptic imagery? Why imbue one's ancestral genii with so many divine attributes? And why transfer the sociological function of myth to legend in the first place? The answer, I suspect, lies once again in the stultifying nature of the priestly appropriation of mythology. If the priest employs mythology to teach obedience to a populace, mythology has lost its dynamic social function. Rather than a tool of transcendence, it becomes a tool of suppression. Little wonder, under such circumstances, that the Palermitan populace transferred the normative function of myth to legend and rescripted the mythic law of obedience into one of rebellion.

In so doing, it rescripted as well the Carolingian Cycle of medieval Europe so that a story which ostensibly pit Christians against Saracens, in actuality pit the *popolino* against the aristocracy. And while epic seemed to uphold the priestly law of obedience, so sacrosanct to the aristocracy which it protected, through holding out Roland as its preeminent hero, it in actuality extoled the bandit's law of retribution, the people's last resort against an oppressive aristocracy, and held out the Mafioso, Renaud, as its true hero. In the final analysis, the meaning of Palermo's epic is (like that of the Genius) apparent—even if cryptonymically shrouded. The people feed off the aristocracy. If the aristocracy continues to provide the people with sustenance, the symbiosis is benign. But if the aristocracy oversteps the bounds of this peculiar social contract through tyranny, or simply fails to provide for the people through ineptitude, this benign suckling becomes a venomous sting, rebellion and retribution, the apocalyptic double-edged sword of a tyrannized people.

Yet as my comprehension of the apocalyptic heft of Sicily's folkloric repertoire came slowly into focus, the holiday season, which so auspiciously opened with the Feast of the Immaculate Conception, continued to make its eternal round through the Feast of Saint Lucy, Christmas, and New Year. Soon, with the Feast of the Epiphany and the close of the holiday season, I would be taking my leave of Palermo—my wallet sadly depleted but my notebooks chock full of jottings. As the stroke of midnight on New Year's Eve, that moment of symbolic closures and openings approached, I found myself once again on a Palermitan rooftop, a pistol in my hand, and my hostess urging me to shoot. So along with hundreds of other Palermitans, and to the accompaniment of firecrackers and bottle rockets, I shot a bullet straight into the sky. A gaggle of children, two dogs, and a duck scattered, screaming, barking, and quacking gleefully about the roof and were herded back to a protective overhang by my hostess, only to press once again to the edge of the roof. As each man shot the pistol in turn, I wondered if this act were simply an augment to the noise of the firecrackers and bottle rockets, an assertion of Palermitan independence, or some admixture of both. I took the pistol again as it went the round, shot once more, and ran with the children, dogs, and duck to the edge of the roof to watch Palermo grow crimson beneath a fire-streaked sky.

8. Identity: Myth, Memory and Affirmation

Orisha and the Cryptonym

Émile Durkheim postulated that one of the premier functions of religion was that of solidifying group identity. We have already witnessed as much in the context of San medicine dances and Jewish calendrical ritual. Let us now turn our attention to Orisha religion: religion that centers on the worship of Orishas, or West African gods, both in the homeland, Africa, and abroad, in the New World to which Africans were so brutally transported. Inasmuch as the slave context which defined the period of New World Orisha development was so destabilizing to one's sense of self and self-determination, it may be the case that New World Orisha worship contains within itself a special imperative to fulfill the function of inculcating a positive group identity—and offering its adherents thereby an affirmation of self and the sense of control that such an affirmation could instill. If so, it would seem that the inculcation of social identity that is one of religion's imperative functions may not, at least in the case of Orisha, be entirely distinct from the sense of self-determination—ecological, social, and especially political—that religion offers its adherents.

New World Orisha religions are often said to be syncretic: that is, based in a merging of two or more religious traditions, in this case West African and Christian. But in fact, all religions—including Christianity, as our consideration of Sicily just suggested—are syncretic. It's just not as easy to see some of the ruptures between the various parent religions as one can sometimes see with Orisha religion. Rather than describing Orisha religion as syncretic, then, we might say that Orisha religion functions very much like the Genius of Palermo: cryptonymically. The cryptonym—as we just witnessed—offers a particularly distinctive rhetorical device because it is a symbol (a signifier) which enigmatically alludes to its referent (the signified) through an apparent act of concealment. The isolation of the cryptonym depended on two psychoanalysts: Nicolas

Abraham and Maria Torok. As such, it is a rhetorical figure fraught with Freudian significance.

There is a long history of Freudian—as well as Jungian—analysis of mythologies. Sigmund Freud, on the basis of reports that Australian Aborigines generally did not eat their totem, postulated that religion grew out of a cataclysmic act: the sons of a primal horde slaying and eating their tyrannical father who was denying them access to women—most notably their mother. But, in their remorse over their act against the tyrant, whom they simultaneously loved and hated, they restored their father through the creation of the totem—the ancestral spirit—which they could venerate through the primal taboo: the rule against slaying and eating the totem. However, the sacred nature of the totemic spirit (generally, as we have seen with the Euahlayi, an animal) was reinforced by the annual ceremony in which the horde did indeed kill and ingest the totemic animal: an act that, according to Freud, finds modern resonance in the Christian act of communion. Notably, even among the Euahlayi, who could not be reasonably expected to deny a segment of the populace a food source as important as the emu, a vestigial taboo seemed to be maintained in the symbolic act of feigning disgust when the young initiate—who was temporarily denied emu—took a bite of emu flesh in his first-kill ceremony.

Intriguingly, Freud suggested that it was the symbolic maintenance—and periodic breaking—of the primal taboo that lent religion its emotional charge. But, he somewhat ominously added that, over time, the symbolic alternative, which did not explicitly but rather unconsciously, signified its referent, would offer the celebrants less satisfaction and instinct would inevitably draw them "nearer and nearer to the activity which was originally prohibited."[1] This is precisely the movement represented by the Genius of Palermo: the venomous sting that was occluded by the gentle suckling—though deemphasized—would inevitably, under the right conditions, resurface. Then, the peaceful social contract that was tenuously maintained between "*un bel dittatore*" (a benevolent dictator) and the "*popolino*" (the commoners) could at any moment—and under the right conditions—break out into vendetta or even rebellion. The isolation of the cryptonym depends precisely on such observations. That famous patient of Freud, the Wolf Man, a Russian émigré who complained that the psychoanalyst—despite his claims to the contrary—had never managed to heal him of his malady, was victim to a recurrent dream: a pack of six wolves (though sometimes offered as seven and drawn as five) lurking outside a door behind which he was secreted or sitting upon the branches of a tree outside his bedroom window. Abraham and Torok came to the conclusion that the Wolf Man's dream was hiding the signification *siestorka* (little sister) behind the Russian term *shiestorka* ("a lot of six"). The Wolf Man's primal repression, according to the psychoanalysts, was the memory of his sister's molestation at the hands of his father. *Shiestorka* ("a lot of six") was, then, a cryptonym which hid the concept *siestorka*, little sister, even as it attempted to reveal it.[2]

The cryptonym that lurks at the center of New World slaveholding society functions similarly: Since the furthering of Christianity was regularly offered as a justification for the enslavement of people who practiced indigenous religions, and since Christian doctrine seemed to slaveholders to offer a means of making slaves tractable, Christianity over time became compulsory for African and African American slaves. Yet, at the same time, Africans and African Americans in the New World combated the hegemony of Christian slaveholders by refusing to acquiesce to demands of conversion. Over time, remembering African Nations and their gods became in Haiti, the Dominican Republic, Cuba, Puerto Rico, Jamaica, Brazil, New Orleans, even the English speaking American Southeast, a strategy for combating not only white demands of conversion but also white hegemony. Memory was the central feature of this strategy and, notably, this memory was not unidirectional. Even as Africans in the New World looked back to their homelands, those left behind remembered those who had been taken from them. In Dahomey, today Benin, the following prayer—contained within the worship of ancestral cults—could be heard:

> Oh, ancestors, do all in your power that princes and nobles who today rule never be sent away from here as slaves to Am'ica [America], to Togbome, to Gbulu, to Kankanu [Dutch colonies], to Gbuluvia, to Rarira. We pray you to do all in your power to punish the people who bought our kinsmen whom we shall never see again. Send their vessels to Whidah harbor. When they come, drown their crews, and make all the wealth of their ships come back to Dahomey.[3]

If memory in the Old World could be explicit and condemnatory, memory in the New World had to be circumscribed and disguised. Thus, African gods were cryptically secreted within the iconography of Christian saints where they could not only be remembered in the New World but also actively worshipped—each according to his or her own nation. Nowhere did this process become more explicit than Haiti where, as we will shortly see, the ancient African gods were openly referred to as *sints*, saints, but cryptically referred to as *Franginè*: Real Africans.[4]

The Yoruba

One of the many African sources for New World Orisha worship is presented by the Yoruba of Southwestern Nigeria. In fact, Orisha (*òrìṣà*) is a Yoruban term that translates as the spirits or gods. Vodun—the source of the contemporary word Vodou (Voodoo)—carries the same meaning in the Fon language of Benin (formerly Dahomey). Like a number of West African societies, the Yoruba developed a distinctive agricultural complex centering on the intensive cultivation of yams, maintaining on its basis a thriving market-based economy: this despite the fact that almost every Yoruba man was (ideally, if not actually) a farmer. And, notably, much of their culture was transported to and preserved in the New World during the forcible migration to which they were subjected. In fact, sizable Yoruba populations were still recognized in the New World into the 20th century as the Lecumi of Cuba (particularly in and around Havana) and the Nago of the Brazilian state of Bahia. And though the Yoruba suffered inordinately from the European slave trade, Yoruba Orisha religion formed a template for resistance to enslavement in the emerging African diaspora.

Yoruba farming, before mechanization, centered on the hoe rather than the plow because the presence of the tsetse fly proved a hardship to the maintenance of large draft animals. Still, Yoruba hoe farming, along with the practice of crop rotation, yielded an intensive increase in productivity which led to the development of craft specialization and mercantilism. In fact, Yoruba society developed a series of state level civilizations including the Nok (900 BCE to 200 CE) and the Classical (or Ife) Civilizations (950 to 1400 CE). As William Bascom reports, both the Nok and Ife periods of Yoruba history were characterized by intensive artistic production, especially in the adornment of the palace complex of the Oni, the king of the city of Ife: bronze, terra cotta, and wood statuary dominated the palace art complex, but finely carved stools and monoliths of both granite and quartz were also present. Moreover, at Ife, a 40-foot-high town wall, 8 miles in circumference in the 1800s and fronted by a dry moat, greeted the outsider. And in the early 1900s, eight guarded gates (manned by the Oni's tax collectors) had to be passed to enter the city. As in European towns of the same period, these eight gates were closed at night.

In the days when agriculture was nearly universal, farming—and especially farming that king of crops, the yam—was in the hands of men. "Clearing, hoeing, planting, weeding, and harvesting" a garden plot assigned to him by his clan was expected of every industrious man. His wife might "carry seed yams" to his garden, "lay them out on the yam" mounds where he would plant them, and perhaps help him in "harvesting corn, beans, or cotton." Yet, Bascom reports, if she were asked to carry the sticks used to stake the yams to the garden, her husband would be "called a tyrant." Beyond yams, which were reserved for special meals, Yoruba farmers regularly cultivated cassava, taro, maize, beans, and plantains. They distilled palm wine, an intoxicant, and gathered kola nuts, a stimulant, both used in offering hospitality to a guest and feasting the Orishas.

They likewise raised goats, sheep, pigs, chickens, and guinea fowl but they tended to eat meat only if an animal had died of natural causes or, more commonly, was sacrificed. Women did the family's domestic work but also, as was the case throughout West Africa, tended to marketing: from selling their husbands' produce, either raw to other families from market booths, or cooked to young, especially unmarried men, sometimes right from their doorways. At

Door panel protecting a granary (author's photograph).

dinner time, Yoruba towns would be bustling with women cooking and selling dishes to the local bachelors and men coming back from a day spent working their gardens. And while the money a woman earned from marketing her husband's produce was put back into his hands, she could likewise earn her own fortune through the careful marshaling of her own produce and profits.

Beyond subsistence activity, there was a significant amount of craft specialization among the Yoruba: weaving, dying, iron-working, brass-casting, calabash carving, bead-working, leather working, pottery making, hunting, fishing, drumming, divining, circumcising, importing, money lending, offering scarification services, and compounding charms and medicines. Each profession had a guild which served to protect trade secrets and punish offenders by taking them to court. Craft specialization added vibrancy to the Yoruba market economy and exchange could be carried out via barter or with general purpose money subject to a very specific counting system: cowrie shells "were counted out in strings of 40, in bunches of 200 (5 strings), in 'heads' of 2,000 (10 bunches), and in bags of 20,000 (10 heads) weighing 60 pounds." Further, a thriving market was indicative of a vigorous town. Conversely, a moribund market indicated a town in decline.[5]

With regard to religion, the Yoruba maintained a large number of deities: sometimes it was said that there were either 400 or 401; others that there were either 600 or 601. In either case, the numbers signified many. Except for the great sky god Olorun, all Yoruba gods were men who lived on earth but never died. The Yoruba Creation, as reported by Bascom, tells of a time when the gods lived in the sky with nothing but the primeval waters beneath them. Olorun, gave Orishala, the God of Whiteness, to whom the disabled are sacred, a chain, a snail containing some dirt, and a five-toed chicken, and told him to descend to the waters and create earth. But Orishala stopped at a party at the gate of heaven, drank too much palm wine generously offered to him by his younger brother Odua, and fell asleep. And Odua, taking the sacred items from his sleeping brother, went, along with Chameleon, "to the edge of heaven." He thereupon climbed down the chain, threw some dirt from the snail shell upon the water, and placed the five-toed chicken upon the newly created earth. The chicken immediately began scratching the earth, kicking "it out in all directions." Thereby, the world was formed and Odua usurped his elder brother's position as its creator. His creative act accomplished, Odua sent Chameleon to test "the firmness of the earth" and then he, Odua, stepped upon it himself at the precise spot where Idio, the sacred grove of the city of Ife, stands today. Orishala, upon awakening, tabooed palm wine (a taboo that Orishala's followers keep to this day), went "down to earth," and claimed "it as his own" because he was the elder brother. Orishala and Odua fought and—just as the Greek gods did at Troy—all the heavenly deities took sides. But Olorun ordered the fighting to cease, sending the brothers back to earth along with Shango, the thunder god, to keep the peace between them. Odua, Olorun declared, would— from that moment—have sovereignty over earth, because he created it, and become the first king of Ife. And the lineal descendants of his sixteen sons would become the other Yoruba kings who had the right to wear the beaded crown (perhaps 50 out of the 100 or so Yoruba kings in the previous century). Orishala, because he was the elder brother and was destined to create the earth, would instead be "the Creator of Mankind." He carved the Yoruba people one by one in the darkness of the womb with a knife, much as the Yoruba artisan would carve a statue from a piece of wood, forming the basic figure, separating "arms, legs, fingers, and toes," and opening "the eyes, ears, nose, and mouth." He purposely made albinos, hunchbacks, dwarfs, the deaf, mutes, and other disabled people, none of whom are mistakes but are particularly precious to Orishala whom, among all the Yoruba gods, they especially venerate.

The creation myth sanctified Yoruba politics and its loose centralization on Ife. Yorubaland was historically comprised of a number of independent kingdoms, each with its own king. Each Yoruba kingdom (represented by about 100 kings) was autonomous but the Oni (King) of the city of Ife—on the basis of his lineal descent from Odua and sanctification by Olorun—was "first among equals." The royal patrilineal clan, from which the Oni was selected, was the largest at Ife, with 20 compounds and 5000 members. Beyond the Oni, there existed the Ife Ward and Town Chiefs: Ife had five wards, each ward being divided into precincts with a number of compounds. Each ward had its Ward chief and each precinct had its Town Chiefs. Moreover, each compound was headed by the eldest clan member. He was considered the Clan Chief. Still, another level of political authority was represented by the Palace Chiefs. Though, strictly speaking, the Palace Chiefs ranked below Ife Ward and Town Chiefs, they had a certain degree of advantage over them through proximity to the Oni. Under the authority of the Palace Chiefs were the Police who acted as the Oni's bodyguard and the Pages: one hundred, in number, who occupied the palace's verandah. Their heads were shaved on alternate sides every four days to demarcate their status and their principle function was to run errands for the Oni and the Palace Chiefs. There was also, situated in the palace, a Senior Law Court which would hear disputes along with, in the most serious cases, the Oni himself. When a Palace Chief died, his eldest son joined the Police, his second son became a page, and his youngest son became a member of the law court. Interestingly, the Yoruba Creation has at times sanctified modern, as well as classical, Yoruba politics. For instance, a society founded in 1948 to unite the disparate Yoruba kingdoms into a single political entity before—

and perhaps partly in preparation for—Nigerian independence from Britain in 1960 was called the Society of the Children of Odua.

As we will soon see, a number of Yoruba Orishas are to be found in Haiti as well as in Yorubaland. Further, Haitian Orishas are said—as are their Yoruba counterparts—to "mount" their devotees when they possess them and (again in both Haiti and Yorubaland) the possessing Orisha is said to enter the devotee's head at the moment of possession and the one possessed is spoken of as the Orisha's horse. A few of the Yoruba Orishas which we will encounter in Haitian worship include Elegba, Ogun, Shango, and Oshun. Elegba, the Divine Messenger, was the portal to all other Orishas. Thus one had to go through Elegba first before propitiating other Orishas and, indeed, the other Orishas had to go through Elegba to grant the wishes of their petitioners. Elegba was, therefore, he who opens the portal or road to all blessings. For example, one would pray to Elegba to bring down other Orishas to possess, or "mount," their human worshippers. Ogun, the god of iron, supported Odua in his fight with Orishala. He was the patron of blacksmiths, woodcarvers, leatherworkers, barbers, circumcisers, and those who provide cicatrization (scarification). He became, as a result of his association with iron and other metals, the god of war. In fact, he represented so many facets of Yoruba life that he was said to have seven manifestations. Interestingly, his Haitian counterpart was likewise said to have seven manifestations. Shango, the god of thunder, whose thunderbolts are transformed into the "prehistoric stone celts which farmers sometimes find while hoeing their fields," is considered one of Ogun's manifestations in Haiti. Some of his Yoruba mounts seem to have been male to female transvestites. Oshun is a River Spirit who encompasses multiple meanings: maternity, erotic love, the household, and the hearth. It is especially Oshun who watches over the women who are, as we have seen, the preeminent Yoruba marketers and one of her Haitian counterparts, Kouzen Azaka (Cousin Azaka), performs the same role in Haiti. But her preeminent Haitian manifestation is Ezili, the sensuous goddess of love.[6]

Yoruba beliefs have found their way into a number of New World religions, offering, along with other West African religions, the basis for not only Vodou in Haiti but also Santería in Cuba, Candomblé in Brazil, Obeah, Pocomania, and Balm in Jamaica, Conjure and Roots in the United States and even a number of modern Afrocentric religious practices—which characteristically look to Yorubaland for spiritual inspiration—found in various New World locales. Each of the major Yoruba deities has his or her counterpart in the various New World Orisha religions. I am particularly conversant with the Haitian counterpart to Elegba known, in Haiti, as Papa Legba and my best friend is particularly conversant with his Cuban manifestation: Elegua. In both traditions, Haitian and Cuban, this deity must, like his Yoruban progenitor, be propitiated before any of the other Orishas can be approached. Like Elegua, his mother, Oshun is found throughout the African diaspora in the New World. In Haiti, she is reconfigured as Ezili Freda, the god of love, who—when she possesses a Vodou participant—is exotically flirtatious and, though she comes into the room laughing, she very often is unable to achieve her desires, and hastily leaves the *ounfò* (temple) in tears. In Cuba, her name is Oshun (or Ochun) and she behaves in much the same manner as Haiti's Ezili Freda but, at the same time, much of her nature has been transferred to Cuba's national patron saint: La Virgen de Caridad de Cobre (The Virgin of Charity of Cobre). In this guise, she is much like the Virgin with Child and maintains all her maternal healing propensities. I, in fact, encountered her as a burlap doll, with a single red dot for her face and the same red dot adorning her torso. But I have also encountered her—along with a number of the remnants of Orisha religion—in African American society. One such encounter unexpectedly happened not so long ago.

African American Orisha Service

"Do you remember when the whites got Charles?" The statement, offered around the kitchen table by Mrs. Jones, the mother of the family I was visiting, caused me to start. What was I going to hear? As it turned out, Charles, Mrs. Jones' eldest son, had been arrested for possession of a small amount of marijuana and was in the county jail. The family—Mrs. Jones along with her younger son, not quite yet a teenager, and her young daughter—trundled themselves into the family car and headed across the border, from Florida to Alabama, in order to consult the most famous spiritual healer in the region. Though the tradition that Mrs. Jones described to me that day has its origins in what is called Roots or Conjure, I most often heard it referred to as Spirit Work—a term which aptly illustrates its relationship to Haitian Vodou which is generally not referred to as Vodou by practitioners but rather with a verbal phrase such as "serving the Spirits." Notably, the Haitian and American Spirit Worker alike generally resist the call of the Spirits—invariably citing the story of Job when explicating both their initial reticence and their eventual capitulation to the difficult calling. And they both must be adept at remembering their dreams—by means of which the Spirits regularly speak to them. The term Conjure seems to have fallen out of use among my friends, while the term Roots seems to be reserved for actions that are a bit nefarious—or, at least, self-serving. That said, the Spirit Worker and the Root Doctor are not neatly distinct entities.

The healer that Mrs. Jones relied upon in times of need was nicknamed Pops and he practiced on a large working farm: Mrs. Jones's son telling me that as a boy he watched a cow being slaughtered and butchered while his mother awaited her consultation. The farm was equipped with cabins to lodge those who stayed overnight, a store and a diner, and—most importantly—a small chapel. The chapel consisted of the sanctuary, furnished for sermons, with pulpit and pews, as well as an office where clients consulted with Pops. In the sanctuary, where patients waited to be called into the office for consultation, Mrs. Jones found her own father and mother, simultaneously seething with resentment over the arrest and fearful of what might happen to Charles while in police custody. "Michael," Mrs. Jones turned to me and said, "You just waited until you were called, sometimes for two or three days. He called you when it was time." I have been told by a number of people that Pops had no list of who was there, that there was no signing in, but he simply knew the names of even strangers and called them out when he was ready. And I have likewise been told that no money changed hands in the chapel. The ability of Pops to know things is acknowledged in a story in which someone had stolen some newly born piglets from the farm and hidden them in the trunk of a car. Pops came out into the sanctuary and announced that there would be no more consultations until the piglets had been returned—which they were in a matter of minutes. I have also been told that the hand-to-hand exchange of money would be considered dangerous, as a jinx could be passed into the chapel in that manner. Thus, money exchanges (if there were any) would have had to have occurred elsewhere.

In this instance, Mrs. Jones was called quickly—she alone—in a matter of an hour or so. And she was told not to worry, that nothing had to be done, to just get in the car and go home, for Charles would be released unharmed. "I didn't even have the chance to tell Pops what had happened," Mrs. Jones exclaimed. "He just knew. And, moments after returning home—along with the "knot," the conjure bundle consisting of assorted herbs and roots, that Pops had prepared for her—and unloading the car, Mrs. Jones looked out the window to see her son Charles walking up the driveway. There were, of course, legal dilemmas—obtaining a lawyer, appearing in court, paying court fees, contending with a criminal record—to be attended to but the important thing was that Charles had not been hurt.

The most potent of roots used by the Spirit Worker is called by the name High John the Conqueror. High John was said to have been a slave who could never be beaten. Though he worked the fields unceasingly during the day, each night he took his flight across the sea to regenerate himself in the well of his African homeland, and in the morning he would be found, once again, back upon

American soil, toiling in the fields of a cruel master who might (for the time being) own him but who could (despite such unhappy circumstances) never raise a hand against him. His essence encapsulated in the root—said to have been brought from Africa and introduced to America—was already in use in the slaveholding era and I suspect that Frederick Douglass is speaking about that root in *Narrative of an American Slave*. He opens an episode of his *Narrative* with the words, "You have seen how a man was made a slave." But, he provocatively continues, now "you shall see how a slave was made a man." After receiving a severe beating from a slave breaker by the name of Covey, Douglass took refuge at the house of a fellow slave, Sandy, who had a free wife. Sandy advised Douglass that he had no choice but to return to Covey as the repercussions of fleeing were too perilous. But, Sandy told him, before returning, the two would go together into the woods, "where there was a certain root," which, if Douglass carried it back with him, would render him immune to any further beatings from Covey, "or any other white man." Sandy claimed that "he had carried it for years; and since he had done so, he had never received a blow, and never expected to while he carried it." While all parts of medicinal plants are potent in Orisha religion, roots are especially so. In fact, Karen McCarthy Brown reports that, in Haiti, when the roots are extracted with the leaves of a plant, a coin must be left on the spot from which the plant is uprooted.[7] Douglass admits to being skeptical as to the power of the root but he, nonetheless, carried it in his right-hand pocket as Sandy had instructed him to do. A few days later, when Covey was resolved to beat Douglass yet again, Douglass reports that "the virtue of the ROOT was fully tested." As Douglass was caring for Covey's horses, Covey "entered the stable with a long rope," and, catching hold of Douglass's legs, attempted to tie him up. "As soon as I found what he was up to, I gave a sudden spring, and as I did so, he holding to my legs, I was brought sprawling on the stable floor. Mr. Covey seemed now to think he had me, and could do what he pleased; but at this moment—from whence came the spirit I don't know—I resolved to fight; and, suiting my action to the resolution, I seized Covey hard by the throat." Douglass reports that he seized Covey so forcefully that his fingernails drew blood, whereupon Douglass and Covey embarked upon a struggle that lasted a full two hours. Douglass continues, "Covey at length let me go, puffing and blowing at a great rate, saying that if I had not resisted, he would not have whipped me half so much. The truth was that he had not whipped me at all. I considered him as getting entirely the worst end of the bargain." Perhaps, more tellingly, Douglass further maintains that the "battle with Mr. Covey was the turning-point in my career as a slave. It rekindled the few expiring embers of freedom, and revived within me a sense of my own manhood. It recalled the departed self-confidence, and inspired me again with a determination to be free."[8]

What immediately struck me about the conversation that I heard at the Jones's home was the fact that, for most white people, the incident which occasioned the conversation would have simply been described as an arrest. But, in this circumstance, there was much more at stake than an imprisonment, a conviction, and a criminal record. It wasn't simply that law enforcement had gotten hold of Charles. It was rather that law enforcement was part of a hostile camp, "the whites," that hearkened back to the days of Frederick Douglass and, after that, the Jim Crow era. It could, I suppose, be countered that perhaps there were Black officers on the police force, that the police force was not synonymous with white society. But that sort of argument, I think, entirely misses the point of Mrs. Jones' initial statement. In a very real way, Mrs. Jones was absolutely correct in her assessment of what had happened to her son. Charles was caught up in a circumstance that was fraught with racial tension and potential danger. The trust of law enforcement in the community of which I was a guest was not a given. Rather, just the opposite. Danger, for a young Black man was a real possibility. And, thus, the visit to Pops not only presented the Jones family a mechanism for combatting a significant injustice. It presented, as well, a mechanism which spoke to the ancient mysteries of remembrance: memories not only encapsulated in the figure of High John the Conqueror, but also in such mysterious entities as the *Franginè*, the Seven African Powers, and the Sankofa, all of which we will shortly encounter. But first let us turn to one particular, and probably the most famous, New World Orisha religion: Haiti's Vodou.

The Case of Vodou

"What do you want to know about Haitian politics," my interlocutor asked suspiciously, her brow knit, an eyebrow arched acutely, her eyes narrowed and fixed intently on my own. "The most important thing you need to know is that Haiti was born in 1804 from a slave revolt. It is the only nation in the world founded upon the principle that slavery is wrong. That is what you need to know about Haitian politics." Thus opened my interviews on Haitian politics, religion, and the intersection between the two—interviews which inevitably led to the topic of Vodou. Perhaps the best known, and least understood, of all Orisha religions is Haitian Vodou, popularly called Voodoo. In Vodou, a veneration of the Spirits—the *Lwa* (or *Loa*) in Creole—allowed enslaved Haitians a mechanism to empower themselves through remembering their African homelands. In fact, the first stirrings of the Haitian Revolution occurred in a Vodou ceremony undertaken in 1791 during which the Spirits possessed the rebels and allowed them to attack and temporarily overcome their oppressors. Likewise, the Spirits were, according to several of my respondents, called upon to effect the successful Haitian Revolution of 1804: that Revolution which definitively drove the French slaveholders from Haiti and repulsed Napoleon's troops when they attempted to retake the newborn nation. And the Spirits were called upon yet again to drive Americans from the island during the Marine occupation of 1914–1938 when Haiti essentially became an American colony.

Vodou, like other New World Orisha traditions, is syncretic: the product, in the case of Haiti, of the merging of a number of West African traditions with France's Roman Catholicism. That said, it is never entirely clear how African or how Catholic this syncretization is. Sometimes the Vodou Spirits are more closely associated with African gods, sometimes with Catholic saints. Perhaps the strongest statement on the subject comes from Zora Neale Hurston:

Two vodou spirits (author's photograph).

And right here, let it be said that the Haitian gods, *mysteres*, or *loa*, are not the Catholic calendar of saints done over in black as has been stated by casual observers. This has been said over and over in print because the adepts have been seen buying the lithographs of saints, but this is done because they wish some visual representation of the invisible ones, and as yet no Haitian artist has given them an interpretation or concept of the *loa*. But even the most illiterate peasant knows that the picture of the saint is only an approximation of the *loa*. In proof of this, most of the *houngans* [priests] require those who place themselves under their tutelage in order to become *hounci* [devotees] to bring a composition book for notes, and in this they must copy the *houngan*'s concept of the *loa*. I have seen several of these books with the drawing and none of them even pretend to look like the catholic saints. Neither are their attributes the same.[9]

What Hurston asserts is, in my experience as well, true. One man, for instance, declared to me unequivocally that Ogou, the Spirit of War, represented by Saint Jacques, was much older than his European namesake. Ogou was celebrated on the Feast Day of Saint Jacques—and depicted with Saint Jacques' image—in order to circumvent French prohibitions against celebrating African religions. "This is what we call camouflage in Vodou. It is a consequence of the colonial regime." He went on to say that "the same thing happened with Ezili," the Vodou Spirit of Love. "She has been represented by the Virgin Mary. But we have Ezili Freda and Ezili Dantò. Ezili Freda is the White Virgin and she is Legba's principle wife. Ezili Dantò is the Black One and Legba's second wife. But they are the same. If you go to the *ounfò*, that is the Vodou church, you are going to see a picture of the Virgin Mary." The camouflage continues, this man said, telling me that his mother had to hide her Vodou practices in order to insure that he, her son, could be confirmed in the Catholic Church, receive Communion, and continue to attend the parish's parochial school. Karen McCarthy Brown—in charting the life of Alourdes, a *mambo* (priestess) in the Haitian immigrant milieu of Brooklyn affectionately called Mama Lola—found the same bifurcated loyalty. While attending a mass with a friend in Haiti, she was taken aback by a priest's anti–Vodou diatribe. When Brown asked her friend how she felt about the priest's attack, the friend nonchalantly replied, "Oh, didn't you know, Karen? That's the way priests talk!"

Still, there is a strong aspect of Catholic imagery at play in Vodou, particularly in the Service: the ceremony in celebration of the Spirits. For instance, the opening ceremonies consist of prayers, presided over by a *prètsavann* (literally, bush priest): always a man and perhaps—like Black Elk—a catechist. This portion of the Service includes a salutation of Bondye (explicitly the Judeo-Christian God), recitations of the Our Father, the Hail Mary, and the Apostles' Creed, the singing of hymns (commonly learned at Catholic Mass) in celebration of Mary and various saints. It also includes the baptism of the altar, its offerings, and the participants with Holy Water provided by the parish.

But when turning to the Service proper, Vodou ceremonies are no longer overseen by the *prètsavann*. Rather an *oungan* (priest) or a *mambo* (priestess) take charge. And while smoking and drinking are not permitted during the opening ceremonies, they are permitted once the *oungan* or *mambo* are in control. Thereupon, the Service consists of lighting candles, rattling the *asson* (the beaded gourd rattle of the priesthood), and feasting the Spirits with animal sacrifices, festive stews of rice, beans, cassava, plantains, coconut, and generous libations of liquor—particularly rum and clairin. As the ceremony progresses, ecstatic drumming, singing, clapping, and dancing allow the Servers, in an idea reminiscent of the San medicine dance, to heat up (*echofe*).[10] Thereupon, the Servers undergo possession. As in Africa, the possessed one is described as the Spirit's *chwal* (horse) and is "ridden" by the Spirit. The metaphor expresses a very specific conceptualization. Among the practitioners of Vodou, there are three souls, all residing in their host's head. The *Gwo Bonanj* (Big Guardian Angel) is the place where divinity in the form of Bondye exists within the individual. On a person's death, the *Gwo Bonanj* will—because Bondye stands at the apex of the Spirit world—return to Africa. The *Ti Bonanj* (Little Guardian Angel) imparts to each individual his or her personality. Upon death, the *Ti Bonanj* will go to heaven. The *Mét Tét* (Master of the Head) is, a bit like the Euahlayi *yunbeai*, the essence of one of the many Vodou Spirits. With possession, it temporarily displaces the *Gwo Bonanj* and makes its presence manifest. In time, and perhaps a ritual marriage to the Spirit, the *Mét Tét* becomes—along with the *Gwo Bonanj* and *Ti Bonanj*—a major aspect of its host's spiritual essence and is particularly tasked with safeguarding its host's well-being. Upon the host's death, the *Mét Tét* will, like the *Gwo Bonanj*, return to the Spirits' homeland: Africa.

I have heard from more than one Haitian the fascination which would lead him as a boy to creep stealthily from his parents' home and follow the sound of drums and chanting voices to the temple. And in one case, the parents of one of my respondents, being evangelical Christians, feared that their son was worshipping the devil as a result of his nocturnal wanderings. In yet another, a respondent declared that—despite his Catholic parents' wariness over any interaction he might have with Vodou—he one night, while his parents were out and he was just 14 years old, took the opportunity to sneak out of the house and travel to the place from which he regularly heard drumming. He claimed that his parents never talked about Vodou and it certainly wasn't discussed in school. In fact, he claimed, "some foreigners know more about Vodou than many Haitians do." Still, having some suspicions as to what he would find at the temple, he was surprised to discover that the differences between Vodou and Catholicism were not—at least from his perspective—so great. And, interestingly, he noted that the Evangelical practice of speaking in tongues, with which he was also familiar, was indistinguishable from Vodou possession. "The Spirit comes into their head," he noted, "and they start speaking another language." Another respondent suggested as much when he said "there is no difference between a Vodou ceremony and a ceremony in a Catholic or a Protestant church. And, let me tell you, this is the reason why they use drums (*tanbou*) in the Catholic and Protestant churches, and why they sing songs in the same way as do the Vodouists: to catch more people!" But, if there are many points of correspondence between Catholicism, Protestantism, and Vodouism, the Vodou temple structure is unique. It has a covered peristyle, generally open to the air, and a closed altar room. At the center of the peristyle, where the drumming, dancing, and possession trances take place, is the *poteau-mitan*, the central pole, likely representative of sacred trees in which some Spirits are said to live and under which open-air services sometimes take place. It is the poteau-mitan round which the Servers dance and down which the Spirits descend in order to mount them. The altar room—which houses the deities—is reserved for special ceremonies such as the seclusion of an initiate to the priesthood.

A particularly renowned Service is described in the story of the Vodou priest Zandolite: As the revelers danced round the poteau-mitan of Zandolite's temple, a multitude of "chickens, goats, and bulls were sacrificed and the finest drummers in the country were drumming. Everyone danced, and the celebration went on day after day, night after night, without stopping. The noise was deafening. God heard it. It kept him from sleeping at night, and in the daytime he could not concentrate on his work." So God sent Saint John down to earth to put an end to the revelry but as Saint John entered the temple, singing, "Guard, open the gate for me to pass," Zandolite took him by the hand,

Vodou deity (detail): Papa Legba. This statue has the name San Pierre carved upon its base (author's photograph).

singing: *Wa was ile longja londja!*" This was *langay*, a kind of speaking in tongues, and it was enough to cause Saint John to forget his duty and join the revelry. He spilled some water on the temple floor, honoring the Spirit "who had entered his head," and began to dance. Within a week, God sent Saint Michael to quell the frenzy, but Saint Michael suffered the same fate as Saint John before him and Saint Peter thereafter. With Saints John, Michael, and Peter possessed by the Spirits, God deemed it prudent to set things aright himself. As he entered the temple singing, "Guard, open the gate for me to pass," Zandolite took him too by his hand and set him to dancing. "God suddenly staggered and reeled from one end of the habitation to the other. The drummers beat a special salute, and the singers sang loudly and clapped their hands, for God had a Spirit in his head."[11] Notable in this story is the fact that though the Judeo-Christian god stands at the apex of the hierarchy of Spirits, it is likely that this fact is a bit of a ruse of the sort which hides the African Spirit behind the white face depicted on saints' cards. For, in the final analysis, Zandolite causes Bondye (God) himself to be possessed by a *Franginè*, a Real African.

Still the Spirits are not deities. Godhead is retained in the personage of Bondye. Spirits are rather the intermediaries between mankind and Bondye, essential because Bondye rarely involves himself in the concerns of humanity. Therefore, the Spirits—sometimes referred to as *Mysteres* (Mysteries) and *Angs* (Angels) as well as *Sints* (Saints), *Franginè* (Real Africans), and *Lwa* (Spirits)— are the central focus of the Service.[12] These Spirits, transformations of the Orishas of the Yoruba and other West African nations, are as numerous in Haiti as they are in their African homelands. They inhabit wells and springs, trees and groves, outcroppings of rock, rivers and the sea. They dot the geography of Haiti as did the satyrs and nymphs dot the Grecian landscape or the totems dot the topography of Australia. One Spirit seems specific to a particular geographic area, another to a single shrine. One pertains to a household altar, the object of family devotions, venerated in much the way ancestors were in classical China; another belongs to the entire nation. There are Earth Spirits, Water Spirits, and Spirits of the Dead. Individuals are often dedicated to a specific Spirit as are families and villages. But any of the various Spirits may be turned to as the occasion demands. One man asked me, "You know the boat people? Before leaving on such a perilous journey over dangerous waters, they undertake a ceremony in honor of Agwe, the Chief of the Spirits of the Sea, asking him for safe passage." Still, collectively, the natural habitat of the Spirits is said to be in the earth's waters which are often referred to as *Ginen*: Africa. In fact, another man told me that when his mother wanted to get him and his siblings out of the small pond behind their home in which they used to swim, she would say it was time to let the Spirits who dwelt there get some rest.

That there is such diversity among the Spirits should come as no surprise. It is the result of a complex act of remembering the great pantheons of African deities and their nations (*nanchons*) which was so central to the creation of a New World African identity. As one man expressed it: "Let's go back. When they took people from Africa, they took them from everywhere. They put them in a boat and took them from Africa to America. The only thing they had as a remembrance (*souvenir*) of Africa was Vodou. Since they were different peoples, since they came from different places, they had different expressions, different practices. But the Spirits were the same." The most notable Nation in Haiti is the Rada (or Arada of Dahomey). It consists of the major Vodou Spirits: (1) Danbala Wèdo, a colorful boa constrictor associated with the rainbow; (2) Ayida Wèdo, his wife, also associated with the rainbow, and sometimes envisioned as a small green snake; (3) Ezili Freda, the Spirit of love and maternity; (4) Agwe, the Spirit of the sea which is called Ginen, Africa, and considered the realm of the Spirits; (5) La Sirene, a mermaid-like fertility spirit whose likeness may chillingly be inspired by the figureheads on slave ships; (6) Legba, the guardian of crossroads, to whom one must go before approaching any other Spirit; (7) Loko, master of the *ounfò* (temple) and its priesthood; (8) Aizan, his wife (these last two closely associated with Legba); (9) Azaka, an agricultural spirit depicted as a hungry peasant who always carries the *makout* (market basket) at his side and is adept in the use of the medicinal leaves and roots which he collects; (10) Ogou, the Spirit of war, politics, and metalworking, he who carries a machete and wears a red jacket with gold epaulettes and buttons, the uniform of the Haitian Revolution; and (11) Shango, the Spirit of Thunder, often seen as a manifestation of Ogou.

	Thunder	*Crossroads*	*Love*	*War*
Yoruba	Shango	Elegba	Oshun	Ogun
Dahomey	Shango	Legba	Ezili	Gu
Cuba	Chango	Elegua	Ochun	Ogun
Haiti	Shango	Legba	Ezili	Ogou

Table Four: Corresponding Orishas in Four Nations

Other nations include the Nago (Yoruba), Mande (Mandinka), Nangol (Angola), Ibo (Igbo), and Petro (Congo). Besides these nations, the Gede— Spirits associated with the Realm of the Dead—are said not to be African and, rather than considered a nation, they are spoken of as a family with Papa Gede (also called Baron Samedi) at its head. Many of the Haitian Spirits are said to have seven manifestations, some of which are, like Ogou or Ezili, split up among the various nations that form the Vodou pantheons. But in Port-au-Prince— as in Miami and New York—the nations have often been pared down to two:

the Rada and the Petro. Brown explicates the distinction between them: "The Rada spirits are sweet-tempered and dependable; their power resides in their wisdom. If a promised sacrifice cannot be offered to them now, they can easily be convinced to wait until later." Thus, they are conceived as "*lwa rasin*," root Spirits. "They are intimate, familial spirits who are given family titles such as Papa," Mama, Cousin, and their Devotees refer to themselves as the Spirits' Children. Petro Spirits are, rather, "hot-tempered and volatile. They must be handled with care and precision. Debts must be paid and promises kept, or they will badger and harass those who serve them." While the Rada Spirits are more dependable, the Petro are more powerful.[13]

That said, there is great diversity in the way various communities, families, and even individuals understand Vodou's hundreds of Spirits. For instance, the Yoruba and Ibo Nations seemed still to be propitiated when Hurston visited Haiti at the turn of the last century and in the northern city of Gonaives, one man told me, the Mande Nation was still actively propitiated—some villages maintaining festivities especially directed toward Mande Spirits while others centered their local festivals on Rada or Petro Spirits. He claimed that Vodou was more organized in Gonaives than in the southern city of Port-au-Prince because Gonaives was "more African." As evidence, he pointed out—in what seems to be a local tradition—that Toussaint L'Ouverture, the hero of Haitian independence, was from Gonaives. And, though Toussaint was born (and captured) at Gonaives, his father was a True African, born in Africa. He likewise said that the *lakout*—a compound composed of several related families' houses and not unusually anchored by a common courtyard and its own temple—was still to be found among the various neighborhoods and outlying villages of Gonaives when he was growing up. Interestingly, he drew a distinction between Ginen, or African, Spirits (which included, among others, the Rada Nation) and Congo Spirits (which included, again among others, the Petro Nation). Zora Neale Hurston found the same Ginen/Congo distinction among some (but not most) of her respondents and suggested it was an outlier to Haitian culture but I suspect it is rather a regional manifestation of the many potential organizations of Vodou Nations.

In fact, during the course of my discussions on Vodou, it often seemed to me that the Yoruba, Mande, and other West African Spirits are more often today treated as analogous to the Rada/Ginen Spirits, while the Gede are not unusually treated as analogous to the Petro Spirits—and some claim that the Petro, like the Gede, are not African. Further, some of my respondents associated the Petro Nation and the Gede Family alike with secret societies—such as Bizango and Secte Rouge—that have served to maintain justice in the face of severe abuse at the hands of first slaveholders and later foreign powers and corrupt regimes. In this, such societies do not seem dissimilar to the various secret societies that have characterized Sicilian society: the Beati Paoli and the Mafia. It seems possible, on the basis of the similarity, that the secret societies of each of these two islands—one at the crossroads of the Mediterranean, the other at the crossroads of the Caribbean—may be the inevitable result of the severest sorts of oppression.

Among the most important Petro Spirits is Ezili Dantò and her son Ti Jean Petro. Ezili Dantò is sometimes said to be the mother of the Petro Spirits and, because she is known to take female as well as male lovers, she is particularly venerated by lesbian practitioners of Vodou. Her major Spirit lover is the warrior Spirit Ogou. Mama Lola's daughter, Maggie, in speaking of Ezili Dantò, said, "That lady is from Africa." And, further, maintained that she is "pretty— and black, black, black." She fought in the Revolution and carries the scars on her cheek that she received in that conflagration. Further, she is especially associated with childbirth and, thus, images of Mary holding the infant Christ are often used to represent her, especially the Black Virgin, Our Lady of Czestochowa, who carries two scars on her cheek. And though she is characterized by a gentle maternal love, she is likewise characterized by an uncontrollable rage. One cannot sacrifice an animal in front of her for at the very sight of blood "she might," as Mama Lola put it, "turn." And, if she turns, she might become a *baka*, an evil spirit, who can readily carry death to an enemy. Worse yet, if her rage reaches an insurmountable peak, she might begin to vomit blood— and even her human mount has been known to do so. Ti Jean, who is sometimes said to be the preferred lover of his mother, Ezili Dantò, carries an attribute reminiscent of High John the Conqueror. He cannot be burned by fire—a reference to the punishment of burning slaves alive that was sometimes practiced in Haiti.

How dissimilar Petro's Ezili Dantò is from her Rada namesake Ezili Freda Dahomey! Named perhaps for the Dahomean River Spirit from Ouidah (corrupted as Whydah), Ezili Freda is, like her Yoruba counterpart, Oshun, lightskinned, if not white, meticulously dressed, and bedecked in jewelry. She is voluptuous, flirtatious and petulant. She is extremely jealous of her many lovers, among them both Spirits and mortals. And if she doesn't get what—or whom— she wants, she is liable to leave the temple in tears. She will affectedly use French instead of Creole. She is particularly venerated by gay men whom she regularly possesses. If Ezili Dantò is depicted as the scarred Black Virgin, Our Lady of Czestochowa, Ezili Freda is depicted by the Maria Dolorosa del Monte Calvario: "The Virgin Mary with a jewel-encrusted sword plunged into her heart. Her arms, crossed over her breasts, are dripping in rings. On her head is a jeweled tiara, and she wears heavy gold earrings and half a dozen weighty necklaces." Yet—despite their dissimilarities and their depiction through one of the various manifestations of the Virgin—both Ezilis make one think of Dahomean Legba's wife, Nunde, who brazenly proclaims that her husband's penis is not enough for her.[14] It is as if Ezili Dantò and Ezili Freda share a bit in the nature of Roland and Renaud: they are a singular entity with two distinct manifestations. But there is truly a difference between the two: Dantò's sensuality in in the service of having babies. Freda's is in the service of having lovers. And, intriguingly, while most Haitians agree that Dantò received her scars in the Revolution, some suggest that Ezili Freda slashed her face with her jewel-encrusted sword when she learned that "Dantò was sleeping with her man."[15]

The Gede—Spirits of the Dead—are presided over by Gede himself: perhaps in the guise of the famous Baron Samedi, always dressed in a dark suit, fedora, sunglasses, speaking in a pronouncedly deep and nasal voice, and incessantly smoking a cigar; perhaps again in the guise of Ti Malice, the preeminent Vodou trickster. Baron Samedi presides over the realm of the dead and his cross, the *Cwa Baron*, is found at the center of Haitian cemeteries. The *Cwa Baron* in Port-au-Prince's cemetery stands, ominously, in the shadow of the family tomb of the Duvaliers, Haiti's infamous dictators, one of whom (as we will shortly see) modeled his behavior on that of Baron Samedi. Ti Malice, the Little Mischief Maker, like Dahomean Legba, is extremely virile and heavily sexualized. He carries the nickname Big Penis (*Gwo Zozo*; literally, Big Bone-Bone) and his horse (again, like that of Dahomean Legba) may wield a large phallus with which he accosts various celebrants: particularly attractive women but also women who are deemed to behave with too much propriety and even an occasional man.[16] Like his Winnebago counterpart, Ti Malice is incessantly hungry

Vodou spirit (detail). Perhaps Kouzinn Zaka (author's photograph).

but loath to work for his keep. And he is often lascivious. Once, when Ti Malice had possessed Mama Lola, he reminded Brown to be sure to come to his upcoming birthday celebration. When Brown asked what she should bring, Ti Malice boisterously replied, "Bring a clean cunt!" It goes without saying that Mama Lola herself would never speak in such a brazen manner. It was, after all, Ti Malice, the Little Mischief Maker, who was speaking through her.[17] Yet, the very brashness of such speech serves to remind us that, from the start of our discussion when we considered San respect and joking relationships, through our exploration of the Native American hero and trickster traditions, to our current consideration of Rada and Gede Spirits, dialogism—in which the voices of gods, heroes, and spirits are reflections of real, indigenous voices— demands that that which is socially sanctioned must be starkly set against that which is rampantly unbecoming in order to have any meaning.

Dialogism is, in fact, a constant feature within the world of Vodou, extending well beyond the realms of social decorum and sexual license. Brown reports that the Spirits known as the Ancestors, family Spirits which are inherited through households and are collectively represented by the Rada Spirit Danbala Wèdo, speak as a group "in the thin, cracked voice" that allows us to understand that they are, indeed, the Ancients. And Danbala Wèdo himself is so aged that he has no voice. Rather, "his horse hisses" or incessantly sputters out the syllable ke-ke-ke. Likewise, the *Franginè*, they who were born in Africa and fought in the Haitian Revolution, display their own linguistic peculiarities. They effect a greater nasalization in their speech and they distort their words. For instance, "*pale* (to speak) becomes *poule* and *bagay* (thing) becomes *bougay*." Rather than *siga*, for cigar, the Spirit will say *shouga*. Loko, a particularly aged Spirit, patron of the priesthood whose badge of office is the beaded *asson*, speaks "in a breathy, cracked voice indicative of advanced age." Kouzen Azaka (Cousin Azaka, masculine), the rustic Spirit of agriculture, employs an especially nasal tone indicative of the Haitian peasantry. His companion, Kouzinn Zaka (Cousin Zaka, feminine), is a market woman (*machann*) and uses the language of her sociological counterpart—raucously calling out her wares and inviting servers to inspect and purchase them. In the distinction between Kouzen and Kouzinn Azaka, Brown sees a reflection of the ancient West African practice of leaving farming in the hands of men while marketing and the handling of money exclusively in the hands of market women. Ezili Freda will, as we have seen, affectedly speak French rather than the Creole of her fellow Spirits. Some Spirits will come speaking "langay, the sacred language of Vodou composed of partially remembered African words and disguised Creole." And "the only sound" that Ezili Dantò can utter "is a uniform '*dey-dey-dey.*'" Her malady arises from the fact that, during the Revolution, she was about to give evidence to the enemy. The *Franginè*, to safeguard their secrets, cut out Ezili Dantò's tongue. Chillingly, Zora Neale Hurston claims that this inability to talk is the fate that is suffered by the zombie and, further, that the zombie suffers it for the same crime as that which was imputed to Ezili Dantò.[18]

Vodou, History and Memory

Particularly in the past, and perhaps still in rural areas, to remember one's gods is to remember one's people and homeland. And this complex act of remembering is not only characteristic of Orisha religion in Haiti but also in Cuba, the Dominican Republic, Puerto Rico, Brazil, Louisiana, and Florida. Further, this act of remembrance is explicitly understood as empowerment. When, in 1791, the Jamaican born *oungan* Dutty Boukman gathered his rebels in the *Bwa Kayman* (Forest of the Alligators) to undertake Haiti's initial revolt against their French slaveholders, he had them call upon their respective *Spirits*. As a friend of mine described it, Boukman rallied his troops by having them taste a drop of blood supplied by Ezili Dantò who—either herself or in the guise of a woman possessed by her—sacrificed a pig in the midst of the gathering. Here, illustrating that seminal moment, my friend held out a trembling fore-finger before his eyes, slightly crossing in his concentration, and lifted the tip of the finger to his tongue. After becoming possessed by their ancestral gods, the rebels began (in an act that brings to mind Sicily's uprising against the French 500 years earlier) to slaughter their French oppressors. Plantations were burned and a number of slaveholders—perhaps as many as a thousand—were killed. And, for those killed in the battle, one man told me, it was promised, "If you die fighting for your independence, your soul is going to come back to get a new life in Africa."

Boukman's revolt ended in failure. Boukman himself was killed and beheaded. And his head was displayed on a pike to dissuade his supporters from carrying forth his project. But the revolution spearheaded by the Haitian born Toussaint L'Ouverture ten years later eventually led to Haitian independ-ence and the definitive abolition of slavery in Haiti: even if French duplicity didn't allow him to witness the ultimate success of his movement. A story told of him throughout Haiti, and even used in the lessons of Haitian school chil-dren, reports on the last days of the French colony, then called Saint-Domingue. General Charles Leclerc, brother-in-law to Napoleon and sworn enemy to the Haitian people, "was afraid of Toussaint in the colony."

> That was what made him one day decide to have Toussaint arrested. Finally, they prepared
> a trap for him. They caught him. They made him travel to Gonaives on foot, on a rope.

There they embarked him on board a boat they called La Creole. The captain who had arrested him was making fun of him. He said to him: "Yes, Brother, we succeeded in taking you today." Toussaint answered: "Fortunately it is only the head you took, but you didn't take the heart." (The heart was Dessalines, Christophe, Petion and the other generals he had left behind.) They took him to Cap Haitien. They put him on board another boat called: Le Heros (The Hero). When he was going onboard, he said: "You have taken me, very well, but know that you have only cut down the tree of Liberty in Saint-Domingue. Its root is there. It will grow again for it is very much alive."[19]

I was told nearly this same story by a respondent who added a striking detail:

Toussaint L'Ouverture came up with the strategy but he wasn't able to see it accomplished. The French lied to him; they kidnapped him. But he said to them, "You may have taken the tree but the roots are still here firmly planted in the soil." Do you understand me? Touissant L'Ouverture set everything in motion and there was no stopping the Revolution. It took the other men to finish it: Dessalines, Christophe, Petion. White people think that the slaves simply broke out in revolt. But it took years to prepare! They used tactics. They used strategy. Do you know what a biological weapon is? This is what they used. Do you know Yellow Fever? They selected a spot in every department and emptied a calabash (*kwi*) of Yellow Fever on that spot. And the French were dying of Yellow Fever!

Another respondent concurred with that story and added that the slaves, whenever possible, slipped poisons into the food of slaveholders. The distillation of these poisons is common knowledge to *oungans* and *mambos* though most choose not to use them. Mama Lola, in fact, knew how to distill a poison from soursop leaf. But she said she never worked this sort of left-hand *maji* (magic), preferring always to maintain herself within the realm of right-hand healing.[20]

Toussaint L'Ouverture died, a prisoner in France, in 1803. But true to his word, the Revolution was not crushed. In 1804, L'Ouverture's general, the Fierce Dessalines, African born and a slave until he joined L'Ouverture's movement, declared independence, and—in a quotation known to all my respondents— his aide-de-camp is reported to have said, "We will write this act of independence using a white man's skull for an inkwell, his skin for parchment, blood for ink and a bayonet for a pen." Dessalines, perhaps in a final slap to the face of European hegemony, restored to Saint-Domingue its Arawak name Ayiti: Haiti. Of him, one man told me, "They call him the Fierce Dessalines but it is unfair! He had to be fierce under the circumstances in which he found himself." Jean-Jacques Dessalines ruled Haiti firmly and his administration, like Toussaint's before him, was characterized by a policy of forced labor (assées), a policy which was meant to reinvigorate Haiti's post–Revolution export economy.[21] Thereafter, Henri Christophe and Alexandre Pétion, two more of L'Ouverature's generals, splitting Haiti in half so that both could succeed Dessalines, continued the policy. Finally, President Jean-Pierre Boyer, another hero of the Revolution who governed Haiti from 1818 to 1843, reunited the nation and gained France's recognition of Haiti's independence: but at the cost of restitution for the loss of French life, a 60 year debt that is seen by a number of my respondents as a contributing factor to Haiti's history of economic turmoil. It is likewise seen as one more example of American indifference to Haitian affairs. Indeed, the United States—frightened that Haiti's slave rebellion would wash upon American shores—did not act as an ally to the second Western Hemisphere nation to free itself in a revolution, refusing to recognize Haiti until 1864 when its own history as a slaveholding nation was coming to a violent close.

From 1844 to 1915—the start of the infamous American Marine occupation of Haiti—central government was relatively weak and African style wattle-and-daub villages as well as agricultural practices still remembered from Africa began to dominate the Haitian countryside. Government during this period was generally weak and not always functional outside the capital, Port-au-Prince. The vacuum seems to have been filled, in a circumstance reminiscent of what we witnessed in Sicily, by secret organizations: Bizango, Secte Rouge, Cochon Gris, and Champwel, among numerous others. These societies, which may have had their roots in pre–Revolution, slaveholding Haiti, maintained a function (not unlike that of the Beati Paoli) of rectifying injustices and they seemed to have been attached to Vodou temples with directions perhaps emanating from the temple's *oungan*.[22] Of the Marine occupation (curiously defended by Hurston) which attempted to stabilize the situation in which Haiti found itself, one man told me that when the Haitian people tired of their presence, they afflicted the Marines with a curse. "They couldn't put on their shoes. They couldn't button up their shirts. Their skin was falling off. It was like they had a disease. It was like the Yellow Fever." The occupation was terminated in 1934 as more pressing concerns (a looming World War) hovered upon the horizon.

With the restoration of central governmental control over the countryside and the emergence of the post–World War II Cold War ideology that too often dominated American politics, Haiti came under the rule of the infamous Duvaliers: François (Papa Doc) and Jean Claude (Baby Doc), whose vicious security forces, the Tonton Makout, terrorized the citizenry from 1957 to 1986. The Tonton Makout were named after Uncle Gunnysack, a Spirit who collected errant children in his straw shoulder bag. He is associated with Kouzinn Azaka and, like him, speaks to Haiti's agrarian countryside where Tonton, Uncle, is a common term of respect that a youngster would offer a man whose hair is greying and Makout, Gunnysack, would be used in town to refer to a peasant carrying his produce to market in a straw basket slung over his shoulder. The Tonton Makout's reign of terror ended with the flight of Baby Doc from Haiti and the election of Jean-Bertrand Aristide, a Catholic priest who adhered to the theology of liberation: a radical theology of empowering the poor. He, in turn, found himself removed from the presidency by Duvalier loyalists. His return to the presidency was compelled by a multinational coalition of military forces under the direction of the Clinton administration. The man who told me about the curse upon the occupying Marines added that, when the U.S. coalition forces entered Haiti to restore Aristide to the presidency, the non–American members of the coalition came ashore only after the Americans landed because they wanted to see if anything like what had happened to the earlier American forces would happen to the Americans in this second occupation. When no curse was forthcoming, he said, the forces realized that they would be welcomed by the Haitian people and came ashore. Yet, the hopes of a restored democracy in Haiti were short lived. Aristide seemed to take upon himself some of the corrupt actions of his predecessors—perhaps as a result of his earlier deposition from the presidency. Still, Haiti seemed, following his presidency, to gain some sense of political and economic security only to see its hopes dashed by the devastating earthquake of 2010.

As can readily be seen from this brief overview of Haitian history, every seminal moment was in one way or another in consonance with the Vodou belief that memory of Africa is the mechanism by which one achieves empowerment. In fact, Vodou, in this context, provides a kind of rhetoric of identity, a rhetoric that is expressed, at times, in the emotionally palpable form of the mnememe: a nostalgia laden memory encapsulated in a metaphor, a proverb, or a parable. The mnememe, according to William Engel, is a figure of speech that acts as a "discursive prompt" or a "mnemonic cue." It functions a bit like the orator's famed "method of loci" in which a mental image of an item is placed in a familiar landscape, perhaps one in each building that borders the forum in Pompeii. Then, the orator can simply imagine himself walking the forum and, as he sees himself passing each building, the mental image he has placed within reminds him of the next portion of his speech. The mnememe, Engel suggests, employs a suggestive metaphor, or "a historical anecdote," or perhaps "a saying deemed worthy of memory" in order "to preserve it from oblivion, to resuscitate it in a novel context, or to validate or authorize another point."[23] Expanding on Engel's formulation, we might think of the mnememe as a meme—a vital constituent of a cultural complex—committed to the evocation of memory. A mnememe then forces one to *remember* and, perhaps, even thereby to *become*.

The role that the memory of Africa played in the African diaspora cannot be overstated. Not only did it underpin the Haitian Revolution, the only revolution that created a nation out of a slave revolt, but it also is reiterated on a daily basis in the metaphors, the stories, and the songs that underpin Vodou worship. Brown records one particularly telling hymn that would be sung at Mama Lola's services in Brooklyn:

> Janmè, janmè,
> M'pa bliye Ginen ray-o.
> Janmè, janmè,
> M'pa bliye zenfan-la yo.
>
> Never, never,
> I'll not forget the ranks of Africa.
> Never, never,
> I'll not forget their children.[24]

But it is not only in Haiti's Vodou religion that such memory is venerated. In fact, the memory of Africa is the basis of much African American folklore inside Haiti and without. In my own household, we occasionally burn candles to High John the Conqueror—the American slave with miraculous powers among which was the ability to fly back to Africa in order to rejuvenate himself at the well of African ancestry and the ability to overcome any slaveholder who attempted to beat him—as well as the Seven African Powers, Orishas based upon the major deities of the Yoruban pantheon, and venerated with a special candle on the alter in African American Orisha households. So notable, in fact, is the idea that empowerment is in essence the memory of Africa, that it has spilled out of the Orisha religion—to which it is native—to find its way into African American literature: for instance, Alice Walker's *The Color Purple*. After all, Miss Celie is only able to muster her own internal strength against the abuses of Mister after she is taught of Africa—from afar—by her long-lost sister Nettie.

Perhaps one of the most potent images of empowerment through remembering Africa is offered by a simple design: one instance of which was discovered during the excavation of the African Burial Ground in lower Manhattan. Undertaken by Michael Blakey, the excavation revealed, among other things, the brutality of slavery in the Northeastern United States where, though abolished earlier than in the Southeast, it shared in the Southern legacy of excessive exploitation: The slaves "were malnourished, diseased. Infant mortality was high. Women were reproducing below population replacement." As a result of such circumstances, the "enslaved population was increasing due to importation," slaveholders replacing their slaves "by getting children ready to work." Of one of the slaves exhumed, a man with "elegantly filed teeth," likely West African by birth, somewhere in his mid-twenties to mid-thirties at death, Blakey reports that, beyond the telling signs of overwork (healed fractures in the spine), an intriguing, heart-shaped, design adorned the lid of his coffin. Blakey came to recognize it as a *sankofa*: a stylized representation, often in the abstract, of a bird, looking behind itself, a representation of the ideal of empowerment through remembering.[25] Along with a number of other mythic relics, the *sankofa*—the visual representation of the importance of remembering one's homeland, one's gods, and indeed one's sense of selfhood—suggests that remembering the homeland, Africa, was essential to combatting the dehumanizing institution that was slavery in America. Similarly, while excavating antebellum homes in Annapolis, Maryland, archaeologist Mark Leone found the remnants of what, with the help of folklorist Gladys-Marie Fry, he recognized as conjure bundles. Placed by enslaved Africans and African Americans under the thresholds of the kitchens in which they worked, the bundles contained lustrous white and blue beads; crystals and buttons; bits of glazed pottery, glass, and white clay. Some of the items were meant to represent the ocean over which one spiritually traveled to rejuvenate one's flagging strength—both physical and spiritual which, after all, are not really two different things—in the deep spiritual well of the African homeland. But, further, some of the items were meant to represent a particular African deity whose help was being sought as well as a potential recipient of the deity's potent energies: energies which could protect a petitioner or harm his tormentor.[26]

The sankofa and conjure bundles, like Haitian Spirits obfuscated within the visages of Catholic saints, are but two of the many examples of mnememes that function cryptonymically: attempting to reveal the remembrances they purportedly conceal. As such, they serve to remind us that—even in the face of severe oppression—mythology offers a primary mechanism for solidifying affiliation. In forging identification with a common group of Spirits and affirming the group's inherent dignity in the context of ritual reenactments of the Spirits' feats and attributes, Orisha religion—even if cryptonymically occluded—offered its adherents a continuous recognition of the fact that, though transported to the New World, slaves and their descendants are still—and always will be—the children of Africa. And that remembrance offers the adherent a power which no slaveholder, dictator, or segregationist can negate or even understand. And, as if to underscore this fact, there is still another, more ominous, cryptonym than the sankofa, than conjure bundles, than the Spirits themselves, which arises out of the crucible of Haitian history—one which warns against even momentarily forgetting Africa and the allegiance due her.

The Zombie

"I only believe in those things for which there is scientific proof," my friend defensively said, "like zombies." The zombie is a revenant: one who has been raised from the grave. He exists as but one of the many instances of the living dead which animates the world's folklore. But rather than a ghost, whose bodiless spirit refuses to remain at peace among the dead, the revenant is a spiritless body which continues to wander the world of the living. Still, the zombie is a very particular sort of revenant. Believed to be someone who was killed by a sorcerer, buried, and then exhumed, he thereafter becomes a slave who toils incessantly for the sorcerer's benefit. Indeed, much has been made— in the scientific and even anthropological community—about the validity of the zombie belief but as good an argument could be made that the zombie is not simply the rare survivor of a sorcerer's poison concocted from the pufferfish or sea cucumber but rather one of the most pernicious rhetorical devices to come out of the maelstrom that is Haitian history.

Of course, the zombie cannot exist without the existence of the sorcerer and my friend took pains to let me understand the nature of the sorcerer's power. Drawn out one night by the sound of the drums from a Vodou Service, he had seen a mule plodding down the street and, not hearing the clip-clop of the mule's hoofs hitting the pavement, he knew that the mule was a well-known sorcerer from his home village out to do mischief. He thus hurried back to the safety of his home and never ventured out again that night. Further, his brother had one afternoon, while walking on the side of the road with that same sorcerer, been forced to jump off the road by a speeding car. The sorcerer reportedly laughed aloud and said, "Wait and see, my friend." And, further along the road, my friend's brother saw that the car had flipped over and was just then becoming engulfed in flames. My friend was not alone in the belief that a sorcerer, or bokor, could rob a man or women of one of his or her three souls— in this case, the *Ti Bonanj* (Small Guardian Angel)—and render him or her a virtual slave.

One of my respondents claimed to know Clairvius Narcisse, the onetime zombie covered extensively by the anthropologist Wade Davis, he who perhaps isolated the zombie poisons: the first of which suspended a living individual in a temporary deathlike state; the second of which robbed the zombie of all but his motor skills. Narcisse's sister was my respondent's close neighbor and Narcisse told him that he was zombified and put, for two years, to work in the sugarcane fields. He further told my respondent that, upon eating some salted food, his memory was restored and he—along with the small group of zombies which the bokor put out to labor for pay—killed the "zombie doctor" who enslaved him. This respondent, while stating categorically that he didn't know the secret, believes that sorcerers did not give up the true secret of zombification to Davis, that neither the pufferfish nor the sea cucumber is the culprit. This belief was a common one among my respondents who invariably knew of Davis's work.[27]

The zombie as a slave is one of the most potent symbols within Haitian iconography. Still, the rhetorical significance of this symbol—growing out of a particularly vicious slaveholding society in which a recalcitrant slave could be buried alive for punishment—extends well beyond the simple metaphorical equivalence of the zombie for a slave. The more rhetorically charged aspect of the zombie belief—charged because of its use in the arena of Haitian politics— is that which suggests how a zombie is cured: through ingesting salt. I have asked about the place of salt in Vodou ritual and not been able to get much information, but I was told the following by one man. His wife, coming home from work one day, found a black cup of water, half empty, discarded in the yard. She sprinkled the cup with salt to be sure that it could present no danger. Mama Lola too employs salt, which Brown reports is "a common prophylactic in Vodou healing," in a number of her charms. "This use of salt," Brown goes on to say, "is a practice traceable to the Catholic tradition of putting salt under the tongue of a catechumen just before baptism, in order to chase away the devil."[28] As we have seen, the line of demarcation between Catholicism and Vodou has never been strongly drawn: a Catholic officiant, the *prètsavann,* was historically a constant participant in the Vodou ceremony; godparents stood up for the devotee when he or she was married to a Vodou deity and baptismal imagery was found throughout the Service. Thus, it seems incontrovertible that the salt is the *salis sapientis* of Catholic baptism by means of which an infant becomes a member of the Christian community. According to Haitian tradition, a mere taste of salt (*"goute sèl"*) will restore to a zombie his memory of what has happened to him and he will, after tearing his master limb from limb, try desperately to return to his grave.

The belief in the efficacy of salt worked its way inextricably into Haitian politics. François Duvalier, the infamous dictator of Haiti from 1957 to 1971, was a populist who, after a brief flirtation with Fidel Castro, was—perhaps with some degree of trepidation—tolerated by the United States for adopting a fierce anti-communist stance. Largely left to his own devices by the only power which could check them, Duvalier terrorized the Haitian people not only with a security force—nicknamed Tonton Makout—but also through the fear he instilled in them by means of his reputation as a powerful bokor. The Tonton Makout was, chillingly, named for a malevolent Spirit—Uncle Gunnysack— who was sometimes used to threaten disobedient children. He carried a *makout,* a roughly woven gunnysack carried at the side by means of a shoulder strap, into which he would stow an errant child whom he would later devour. The *makout,* an essential item in the Haitian peasant's toolkit, was also a major attribute of the Spirit Azaka: the Spirit—like the peasant himself, always suffering the pangs of hunger—was the spiritual representation of the Haitian farmer: whether a landowning peasant or an itinerant sharecropper. In fact, members of the Tonton Makout always wore blue denim and straw hats as did Papa Azaka to whom, apparently, they were especially devoted.

Beyond his formulation of the Tonton Makout, Duvalier wove Vodou imagery further into his administration by donning the personality of the Vodou Spirit of death and the cemetery, Baron Samedi. He dressed in a black suit, wore a black fedora, smoked a cigar, and hid his eyes behind dark sunglasses. He even affected the deep nasal tone that was attributed to Baron Samedi. Fascinatingly, among the oungans and mambos which were an integral part of Duvalier's network, "before he became president of Haiti and the ugly parts of his character revealed themselves," was Mama Lola's mother, Philomise.[29] Happily, François's son, Jean Claude Duvalier, to whom the presidency passed upon François's death, did not have the ability to hold on to the power that his father ceded him and was violently overthrown by an emboldened Haitian populace who, in some instances, employed the Tonton Makout's own mechanisms—including necklacing, hanging a tire filled with gasoline around a victim's neck and setting it on fire—against their one time oppressors. In fact, for several days after Jean Claude's flight from Haiti, Port-au-Prince's hospitals were filled with members of the Tonton Makout—sometimes beaten beyond recognition.

The new president of Haiti, Jean-Bertrand Aristide, at the time of his ascension to the presidency a Catholic priest, borrowed the image of the *salis sapientis* that cures the zombie and applied it to the political arena. His literacy program—based in Haitian Creole rather than the French language—was aptly called *goute sèl* (a taste of salt), as if to say, 'We are now combatting the zombie-like stupor that Papa Doc (François) and Baby Doc (Jean Claude) Duvalier foisted upon us. And we are doing so through education so that we, too, like the zombie, can be set free from the bokor's clutches. Not surprisingly, Aristide's detractors (generally the erstwhile followers of the Duvaliers) complained that the program was just another Catholic war on Vodou and—because the priests who promoted it were affiliated with liberation theology—communist propaganda. The program does indeed promote a kind of communalism, but it is very much a Christian ideal of communalism. In other words, it is unfair to simply label it communist. And as to the claim that the program was part of an anti–Vodou campaign, it seems unlikely. Aristide—like François Duvalier—has been accused, usually by converts to Evangelical Christianity, of using Vodou imagery in an attempt to promote a new Haitian identity.

It is true that salt is explicitly aligned with Christian theology in the literacy program which carries the subtitle: *Nou se sèl tè a*; We are the Salt of the Earth. Further, the program cites Matthew 5:13 in the prologue to its workbook: "You are the salt of the earth. But if the salt lose its savor, what use is it? It is good for nothing but to be cast out and to be trodden underfoot."[30] Yet, at the same time, salt—as we have previously seen—is used in Vodou ritual to keep the devil, or other evil spirits, at bay. Thus, it seems that the program— so aptly titled *A Taste of Salt*—is not anti–Vodou. That would be off-putting to the very people the program wished to entice. Rather, the program agitated against what in Haiti is called *maji*: magic, or working with the left hand, the very sort of practice which was attributed to Papa Doc. Mama Lola and other legitimate Vodou healers explicitly state that they work exclusively with the right hand.

There may yet be more. It is believed by a number of analysts, such as Zora Neale Hurston and Wade Davis, and has been told me by my respondents (sometimes almost conspiratorially and in a whisper), that Haiti, like Sicily, has historically harbored secret societies. These societies, my respondents almost universally claim (even if historians are divided on the issue), were initially formed by Maroons: slaves who escaped and took refuge in Haiti's mountainous interior and were among the fiercest of warriors in the Haitian Revolution. The most intriguing point of correspondence between Haitian and Sicilian secret societies is the suggestion that both served as the people's tribunals: trying and convicting anyone who has been deemed to have committed offenses against the people. Zora Neale Hurston, in discussing a zombie which she encountered, Felicia Felix-Mentor, was probably the first to suggest that zombification was caused by some poison and probably the work of secret societies. Wade Davis, following up on Hurston's observations, claims that two zombies which he encountered, Ti Femme and Clairvius Narcisse, both reviled by friends and family alike, were given over to the secret societies for zomibification. Ti Femme was a particularly venomous market woman who mercilessly overcharged her clients and would even steal from her fellow marketers. Claivius Narcisse fought over land with his own brothers, was exceedingly stingy with his family as a whole, and had fathered numerous children while never concerning himself with the welfare of them or their many mothers. Both Hurston and Davis have been roundly criticized for their analyses but, to their credit, they simply followed up on what a number of respondents reported to them—which is, after all, what anthropologists should do.[31]

One friend attempted to explain to me the nature of secret societies— and the severity of breaking the rules they were tasked with upholding. He claimed that they were under the jurisdiction of *oungans* and consisted of ceremonies which took place in the *oungan*'s temple but were celebrated for a specific Spirit and specified as secret. From his perspective, the most serious breach was to reveal the society's secrets, to talk out of turn. If it was suspected that a member of the temple had revealed the existence of such a society, or a secret ceremony, he would be thoroughly investigated and—further—the secrecy of the investigation was so absolute that the subject himself would have no idea that he was even being investigated. If the subject of the investigation were found guilty, he would suffer a fate "worse than capital punishment." As an example, this friend recounted how he had attended a ceremony at a lonely country temple—one in which the nearest farm was a ten-minute walk away— and the ceremony was specifically designated for "consecrated members" of the temple only. For some reason, perhaps because of his youth, my friend's presence was ignored. And while he participated fully in the ceremony, he was careful not to drink any of the proffered liquor, apparently in recognition that he was not consecrated to do so. At that ceremony, a woman who had been dead and buried the morning of the day before was—according to my friend— present and participating in the ceremony. At the sight of her, my friend fled the temple but, the next day, he fell ill with a condition over which—despite the fact that it lasted six weeks—he could confide in no one, least of all his parents. The woman, my friend later learned, had been zombified.

The zombie is said to be he or she who has broken the laws of social solidarity—perhaps behaving haughtily to someone of a lower socioeconomic stratum, perhaps mercilessly cheating friends and family out of their livelihood, perhaps threatening to reveal the very existence of a secret society—and thus been delivered by the verdicts of the society's tribunal to a *bokor* to do with as he will. Zombification is the most frightening result of these tribunals. Hurston suggested that it was some sort of poison, "some secret probably brought from Africa," which was used to zombify the miscreant, destroying "that part of the brain which governs speech and will power." And Davis suggested that a primary component of that poison was extracted from the pufferfish. But dwelling on the science of zombification perhaps overlooks an essential point governing the zombie belief complex. If there is indeed a poison which can create a stupor so profound that its victim might be buried, exhumed, and partially revived, there is certainly no physical antidote to such a poison. The very nature of the zombie's malady—the inability to articulate coherent thought in speech— alerts us to the fact that the zombie is yet another cryptonym, imparting to us the harsh lesson that is to be taken away from the fate of the Spirit Ezili Dantò: she who—despite the fact that she is an undeniable hero of the Revolution— is, to this day, unable to utter a single word. Inasmuch as she, in a moment of uncontrollable rage, was about to spew forth the secrets of the Revolution to its enemies, Ezili Dantò had her tongue cut out. Thus, she—like a zombie— is unable to speak, uttering a continuous, incomprehensible, Cassandra-like "*dey-dey-dey*" through those whom she possesses. It necessarily follows from such observations that salt, rather than some medical solution to zombification, some antidote to a powerful poison, should be viewed as yet another complex spiritual metaphor—and such is the case both in the context of liberating a zombie from a *bokor* or a populace from a dictator. Salt is, and always will be in this context, a baptismal symbol significant of a restored will: that is, the *salis sapientis* administered at an infant's baptism. Still, if that most severe of sentences—zombification—is indeed the result of a sentence by a tribunal of some secret society, perhaps Bizango, perhaps Secte Rouge, perhaps again Cochon Gris, the Haitian counterparts to Sicily's Beati Paoli and Mafia, the rhetorical heft of zombification becomes even more pronounced: By turning against the people, one may be made into that which the very existence of Haiti was meant to eradicate: a slave.

Conclusion:
The Legitimacy of Myth

Affiliation and Enmity

One of my Haitian friends, upon his last visit with me, left a small, crooked stick in an obscure corner of my living room. It was, of course, Papa Legba's walking stick which is not unusually to be found propped against a wall along a hall, next to a doorway, or—more often—next to Legba's altar. This is the stick with which Legba courses the world's narrow streets and alleyways looking out for, as my friend taught me, the least among us: those who have been forgotten or left behind. He exists, in this manifestation, as a kind of inverse, or benevolent, Uncle Runnysack: stowing children away in the *makout*, that he too always carries, not to devour but to protect them. The walking stick was left as a remembrance and the lesson it imparted was a good one. This stick, crooked as Papa Legba himself and topped like a crutch with a crosspiece, exists as a sign that the pathway between the material world and the spiritual world is always open and that remembering Africa is, in and of itself, a continuous affirmation of the unity and dignity of Papa Legba's scattered children—wherever in the far-flung world they might find themselves.

But such a singular remembrance raises a question: Why was it necessary? Though we have thus far explored mythology as a mechanism for establishing group identity, and thereby fostering intragroup affiliation, we have at moments noted that such identity is not unusually forged at the expense of someone else, that our sense of *Self* too often depends upon the isolation, and perhaps even abuse, of an *Other*, that intragroup affiliation is too often married to intergroup enmity. Remembering Africa became essential in the context of a dehumanizing racism that was sanctified in a particular interpretation, as misguided and pernicious as it might be, of Christian myth. The notorious trope embedded in the "Curse of Ham," that the enslavement of Africans was ordained by God himself, underwrote some of the worst abuses of slaveholding society in

Haiti, Cuba, Brazil, and—of course—the United States. It would be disingenuous to pretend, in such a study such as this, that some of the worst prejudices which have marked human history are, if not inspired, at least enabled by religion.

Anti-Semitism

Anti-Semitism, especially in a world lurching toward the Holocaust, offers a case in point. But it has sometimes proven to be a difficult prejudice to unravel. Among the more intriguing explanations for its existence is that offered by Sigmund Freud in *Moses and Monotheism*. Here Freud views Christian anti-Semitism as a kind of Oedipal response to the moral authority of the Father (Judaism). Many have dismissed that explanation out of hand but there does often seem to be a negative response on the part of a religious splinter group for its parent. One thinks of Protestant forms of anti-Catholicism, for instance. Another potential source of Christian anti-Semitism seems to result from a strange mythological debacle. For Christians, apparently sometime in the late Roman or very early medieval period, Judas Iscariot became a symbol for the Jewish people as a whole and, with that conflation, anti-Semitism took on a new virulence.

A number of theories have attempted to explicate this conflation, generally postulating a conscious attempt on the part of the authors of the gospels to conflate Judas with a rebellious Jewish state or with Judaism at a time when Christianity was becoming more independent of its parent religion. Still, a conscious manipulation of texts held to be sacred seems unlikely. The more probable source of the conflation lies in the fact that four disparate gospels came to be treated as one single story. Whereas the Gospels of Matthew, Mark, and Luke tend to situate betrayal firmly in the lap of Judas, the Gospel of John—while maintaining the figure of Judas—shifts some of the blame to some unnamed body of Jews present at the anointing of Jesus by an unnamed woman of Bethany. In Mark 14, for instance, it is reported that "Judas Iscariot, one of the twelve, went to the chief priests, to betray him to them (*et Iudas Scariotis unus de duodecim abiit ad summos sacerdotes ut proderet eum illis*) but in John 11 it is rather stated that "many of the Jews, who were come to Mary and Martha and had seen the things that Jesus did, believed in him. But some of them went to the Pharisees and told them the things that Jesus had done (*Multi ergo ex Iudaeis qui venerant ad Mariam et viderant quae fecit crediderunt in eum. Quidam autem ex ipsis abierunt ad Pharisaeos et dixerunt eis quae fecit Iesus*)." In fact, despite the analysis of numerous apologists, John's Gospel does seem to smack of anti–Semitism with its continuous reiteration of "the Jews," in one form or another, some 70 odd times—as opposed to 5 or 6 times in each of the other gospels. If all four gospels are believed to tell a single story, that story—in sermons and in the minds of its adherents—develops its own narrative logic and rhetorical heft. This story, which exists in no single gospel, follows a very specific narrative sequence as it reaches its climax. A man, Lazarus, is raised from the dead; Mary anoints Jesus with precious ointments; Judas becomes incensed and goes to the religious authorities—except in John where some amorphous group of Jews took their report to the Pharisees. With the emergence of this syncretic story, the conflation of Judas with Jews is accomplished and the anti–Semitism inherent in John infects the gospel storyline as a whole. This process seems unlikely to have occurred until the gospels were collected into a single body, perhaps as early as the 2nd century at Rome.

What one can say with assurance is that once the strange seed of anti–Semitism was emplaced in the European mind, it there festered. In the medieval period, European Jews were subjected to even more virulent abuse than they had received in late Roman times. A particularly vicious accusation leveled against medieval Jews, and one that finds voice in tales reported by both Thomas of Monmouth and Chaucer, is encapsulated in the phrase blood libel. In various forms, the blood libel charged that Jews sacrificed Christian children and used their blood—at times obtained through impromptu circumcisions— to bake their Passover matzo. An early instance of the blood libel arose in Norwich, England, when in 1144 the body of a 12-year-old boy, William, was found discarded in a forest. It began to be whispered about that the murder was accomplished by a band of Jews who had placed a crown of thorns on William's head, tortured him unmercifully, and crucified him. Some years later, Thomas of Monmouth—a monk at Norwich's Benedictine monastery—alleged that Theobald, a Jew who had converted to Christianity and become a monk, confessed that Jews believed they had been banned from their homeland because they had crucified Christ. Thus, according to Thomas's report of Theobald's confession, a council of Jews in Spain would yearly appoint a European Jewish community to crucify a Christian at Passover—and collect his blood—if they ever hoped to return to Israel. It may be that Thomas had a vested interest in relating such a diseased tale. If William were made a saint, Norwich's Benedictine monastery could be expected to reap the monetary benefits of a pilgrimage site. Still, such tales, despite their seemingly obvious lack of credibility and without any obvious benefit to those who spread them, became a constant in European culture wherein they, at times, gave rise to deadly consequences: Edward the First's expulsion of England's Jews in 1290, Ferdinand and Isabella's expulsion of Iberian Jews in 1492, the infamous pogroms of Russia, and—

of course—the Holocaust wherein the particularly European brand of anti–Semitism took on an almost unthinkably virulent form. Jews came to be described as vermin (*Ungeziefer*) subject to extermination.

Though he claims not to be speaking of anti–Semitism at all in his chilling novella, *The Metamorphosis*, it is hard to imagine that Franz Kafka was completely unaware of the rhetorical heft of the *Ungeziefer* metaphor which he uses to express his personal sense of alienation: not as a Jew in the sometimes virulently anti–Semitic Austro-Hungarian Empire but rather as a son who cannot live up to a domineering father's expectations. Yet when Kafka's alter ego, Gregor Samsa, wakes up one morning to discover that he has been transformed into a monstrous vermin (*zu einem ungeheueres Ungeziefer*), one's mind inevitably wanders to a consideration of anti–Semitism. In fact, Peter Arnds describes Kafka's use of the infamous metaphor as a cryptonym evoking a "sinister premonition of the atrocities" that would occur "in the camps more than two decades later."[1] And when considering the fact that Kafka's own early death is perhaps the only thing which precluded him from dying, like his sisters, in Germany's infamous death camps, not to mention the fury that Kafka's writings evoked in Nazi Germany, the metaphor which Kafka presciently chose to describe his alienation becomes all the more chilling. And Gregor's fate in the novella seems to confirm one's darkest suspicions about Kafka's cryptic message.

Perhaps, though, the simplest explanation for anti–Semitism is found by returning to Bassani's *The Garden of the Finzi-Contini*. Perturbed at his father's inability to see the danger that Mussolini presented the Jewish community of Ferrara, Bassani suggests that it is simply the fact of being the preeminent minority within European society that has so endangered Ferrara's Jews. When Ferrara banned Jews from playing at the city tennis club, and the Finzi-Contini family opened their private tennis court to the city's Jewish youth, Bassani attempts to make his father see the danger foreshadowed in this edict. Citing the warning offered by Trotsky in 1931, "the year in which Hitler's real rise had begun," Bassani claims that "capitalism, in the phase of industrial expansion, cannot help but be intolerant of all national minorities, and of the Jews, in particular, who are *the* minority by antonomasia," that is using a proper name as an epithet.[2] Leaving Trotsky's critique of capitalism aside, we might note that the penchant for fascist society to use the term Jew not *denotatively* (that is, not to refer to an individual of the Jewish faith or at least an individual of Jewish ethnic affiliation) but rather *connotatively* (to pejoratively signify minority and even outsider) created a circuitous communication (at once anti–Semitic and fascistic) in Europe's, and particularly Germany and Italy's, rising tide of nationalism which targeted not only Jews but also Gypsies, gay men and lesbians, Communists, and even that decidedly more amorphous category of "foreigners."

Islamophobia

Islamophobia offers yet another case in point. If we allow ourselves to become attentive to the language that is often used to express Western views of Islam, we begin to find a rhetoric that is steeped in a particularly nefarious brand of scapegoating and perhaps cannot help but spur an Islamic cultural response. For instance, during a particularly heated interval in the Church's pedophilia scandal, I encountered a most peculiar circumlocution in the *New York Times*. In an op-ed column which suggested that Pope Benedict XVI had been forced to clean up messes left unattended by John Paul II, Ross Douthat almost off-handedly suggested that "this pattern extends to other fraught issues that the last pope tended to avoid—the debasement of the Catholic liturgy, or the rise of Islam in once-Christian Europe."[3] I was startled, to say the least; it wasn't the liturgy thing, though its "debasement" didn't really seem to rise to the level of severity as, say, pedophilia. It was the suggestion that "the rise of Islam in once–Christian Europe" could be described as a "fraught" issue which Pope John Paul II, like some inattentive father, heedlessly neglected. What the statement reminded me of—making me feel, once again, as I had the evening I took Faisal to the marionette theater, as if I'd been hit with a spit wad—was the small monologue which I reported earlier. In that monologue—presented in the very first episode of the Carolingian Cycle, *The Death of King Pepin*, Pepin proclaimed: "I am content that peace reigns in our land, after the many wars that we have withstood against these vile Saracens who wanted to conquer France, who wanted to aggrandize the false faith of Muhammad. We have destroyed them, causing them to repent having ever set foot on Christian soil."

How could the *New York Times*—even in an op-ed piece—offer up an as unabashed anti–Islamic sentiment as I would occasionally encounter in Sicilian epic where, at least, history—marked as it was by 250 years of Arabic occupation being broken only when the Norman invasion ushered in Sicily's century long golden era—while not exactly *exonerating* such sentiments at least rendered them rhetorically comprehensible. Of course, one could claim that 9/11 was the historical antecedent to American Islamophobia—had not Islamophobia already been a cogent element of American rhetoric previous to 9/11. In America, however, as well as in Sicily, a peculiar mythological antecedent to Islamophobia comes into play: the Isaac/Ishmael dichotomy as the mythic precedent to Judeo-Christian/Muslim antipathy. In other words, mythologically,

Isaac is viewed as a progenitor of the Judeo-Christian tradition while Ishmael is viewed as a progenitor of Islam. This mythic archetype sets the Judeo-Christian and Islamic traditions up as two eternally feuding clans: clans that have clashed in the initial expansion of Islam into Spain, Sardinia, and Sicily, the retributive Crusades, the creation of the modern state of Israel, Islamic terrorism, Christian apocalyptic fantasies, and more recently 9/11 and the resultant wars in Afghanistan and Iraq.

Perhaps nothing throws into bold relief the rhetoric of Islamophobia in America more than the controversy which erupted over the proposed name for an Islamic community center which was to be built near Ground Zero in Manhattan: the Cordoba House. The center was to contain, among other features, conference facilities dedicated to interfaith dialogue and a mosque. A small group of politicians and activists claimed that the name evoked an Islamic conquest of a Christian land, Spain, and rechristened the center the "Mosque at Ground Zero." In fact, the violent connotation of Cordoba was solely a western Christian construct, evocative of the medieval conception of "Christian soil" or the contemporary construct of "once Christian Europe," ascribed to Islamic culture. In the Islamic context, the proposed name, Cordoba House, connoted something almost diametrically opposed to such signification. Cordoba was the ancient capital of Muslim Spain, al-Andalus (Andalucia, in modern Spanish). The concept of al-Andalus, in the folklore of a good portion of the Islamic world, is emblematic of a Golden Era when the Islamic world entered its Enlightenment (a full 700 years before Christian Europe) and during which Muslims, Christians, and Jews lived in harmony under a benevolent Islamic caliphate. Nowhere is this conception more prevalent than in the genre of folksong referred to in both the Maghrib and Mashriq as Andalusian.[4] How, then, could it be reasonably claimed that the name Cordoba cryptically suggested an Islamic desire to conquer (once again) "Christian" soil? As the controversy dragged on, and the proposed center became embroiled in financial as well as political difficulties, the Cordoba House was never built.

It seems worth noting here that the world's Islamic population is expansive and diverse. It includes ethnic Arabs in the Mashriq and the Maghreb as well as Turks, Persians, Pakistanis, and Berbers. It also includes a dramatically multiethnic Indonesia: the most populous nation where Islam is the dominant religion. With over a billion adherents and well on its way to becoming the world's dominant religion, Islam is—along with China, India, sub-Saharan Africa, and the West—providing the world with one of its most significant population blocks. And it seems unlikely that it could be defined in its entirety as uniformly concerned with a conquest of the Christian West. Certainly, my Tunisian friends, scrambling to make a difficult living in "once Christian Europe," were—even

if fundamentalist in their approach to Islam—not concerned with such ideologies. Still, we might productively ask if—given such a wide-ranging, hetero-
geneous population—there could possibly be such a thing as a global Islamic
identity with any overarching principles? Of course, just as the rich ritual life
of Judaism has helped maintain Jewish life in the diaspora, the Five Pillars of
Islam could act as a potentially unifying factor. But, perhaps more significantly,
and not unlike what we have witnessed with the diasporic Jewish community,
a sense of religious marginalization could as well foster a sense of pan-cultural
identity within a disparate populace. Thus, it seems likely that if a global Islamic
identity emerges it may do so not in the context of Pan-Islamist ideologies but
rather in response to a world which at times too easily disparages its Muslim
citizens.

Homophobia

   Homophobia, like anti–Semitism and Islamophobia, involves an attempt
to establish group identity at the expense of the Other—with the added dimension that the Other in this instance is neither an ethnic or religious minority.
Rather, LGBTQ people—as we have earlier seen—live among every society
in every epoch. And though some analysts have suggested that gay, lesbian, or
transgender identities are social constructs, same-sex attraction seems to rather
be a constant feature of humanity. Given the various *responses* to same-sex attraction that we find globally, it might not be out of place to ask why such a virulent
anti-gay animus has marked so much of the history of the West. In fact, homophobia in western societies is nothing new. The ancient story of Sodom was
always there to instill the fear of homosexuality from Western pulpits and justify
a myriad of abuses—from torture and execution to shaming and ostracization.
The story itself is a brief one:

> And there came two angels to Sodom at even. And Lot sat in the gate of Sodom: and Lot
> seeing them rose up to meet them; and he bowed himself with his face toward the ground;
> And he said, Behold now, my lords, turn in, I pray you, into your servant's house and tarry
> all night, and wash your feet, and ye shall rise up early, and go on your ways. And they said,
> Nay; but we will abide in the street all night. And he pressed upon them greatly; and they
> turned in unto him, and entered into his house; and he made them a feast, and did bake
> unleavened bread, and they did eat. But before they lay down, the men of the city, even the
> men of Sodom, compassed the house round, both old and young, all the people from every
> quarter: And they called unto Lot, and said unto him, where are the men which came into
> thee this night? Bring them out unto us, that we may know them. And Lot went out at the
> door unto them, and shut the door after him, and said, I pray you, brethren, do not so wick-
> edly. Behold now, I have two daughters which have not known man; let me, I pray you,
> bring them out unto you, and do ye to them as is good in your eyes: only unto these men

do nothing; for therefore came they under the shadow of my roof. And they said, stand back. And they said again, this one fellow came in to sojourn, and he will needs be a judge: now will we deal worse with thee than with them. And they pressed sore upon the man, even Lot, and came near to break the door. But the men put forth their hand, and pulled Lot into the house to them, and shut to the door. And they smote the men that were at the door of the house with blindness, both small and great: so that they wearied themselves to find the door.

There is something chilling and sinister in the depiction of the men of Sodom and, despite apologists who sometimes claim that we have misunderstood the story, that the crime of Sodom is inhospitality at a minimum, rape at the worst, but not homosexuality, Lot's offering of his daughters seems to confirm the worst. Rather than seek out alternate explanations for the Bible's homophobia, it seems best to just accept that homosexuality, like shellfish and foreskins, was not acceptable to those who framed Biblical narratives—either in the Torah or the New Testament—and, as do many gay and lesbian Jews and Christians today, ignore the less palatable segments of an ancient religious tradition while celebrating those tenets that speak to a benevolent spirit.

In fact, despite the rhetorical heft of the myth of Sodom and Gomorrah, homophobia no longer gains much political traction in most of the West—where the Judeo-Christian tradition maintains significant religious dominance. But something seems to magnify its intensity in American society and offer it greater political weight. In fact, while harassment of gay and lesbian Americans has a long history, the *politicization* of homophobia is relatively recent and has its birth in Southern religiosity. As segregationist messages from Southern pulpits became increasingly less tenable—particularly in the late 1970s—homophobia took on greater theological immediacy: even helping to create an Evangelical voting bloc. The pivotal moment in this metamorphosis is telling: When, in 1977, the Southern Baptist minister Jerry Falwell joined ranks with Anita Bryant's Save Our Children movement in order to overturn Miami-Dade County's gay rights ordinance, the politicization of homophobia was inevitable.[5] But a question remains: How could a metamorphosis from church-sponsored segregation to church-sponsored homophobia find any mythic rationalization? We have already witnessed the use of the myth of the "Curse of Ham" to justify slavery and segregation in the context of Southern white religiosity. What makes this mythic justification of racism significant in the context of evangelical homophobia is the reading (correctly or incorrectly, as the case may be) of a homosexual subtext into the Noah-Ham story. Following ancient precedent, beginning with Jewish commentators, continuing through Greek, Latin, and medieval traditions, and finding expression in the King James translation of the Bible where Ham was cursed for 'seeing his father's nakedness,' a phrase which is at times employed euphemistically to mean intercourse, the incident which led to Noah's horrific curse became covertly inscribed with homosexual incest. That is to say, a story that contained—perhaps misperceived, perhaps otherwise—a breach of a double taboo (homosexuality and incest) gave rise to the Southern theological justification of mistreatment of African Americans. Then, just as such mistreatment became less and less tenable in the context of modern American society, a new recipient of censure—the homosexual proper—stepped in to reformulate the emotional vortex of Southern Christianity. And a different facet of Ham came into focus: not his supposed Blackness but rather his alleged homosexuality. It was rarely so baldly stated in sermons, but—frighteningly—at times it was. Still, even when simply insinuated, the sting of the barb was inescapable. The American LGBTQ community now took on the burden that had earlier been inhabited by the African American community.[6] And, oddly, as theologically moderate Christian denominations began losing their congregants beginning in the late 1960s but accelerating in the 1980s, the Southern brand of evangelicalism began to become the dominant religious force not only in the Southeast but—largely through a kind of evangelical exportation—throughout the United States. Today, we find that this exportation is, while rapidly losing traction in the United States, continuing overseas in such locales as South America and the Caribbean, Uganda and Nigeria, and—surprisingly given the strength of the Orthodox Church—Russia. Even in a tolerant society like Samoa, we have found that converts to American brands of evangelicalism have reinterpreted Samoa's creator god, Tagaloa, as one of Satan's fallen angels and decried fa'afafines as symptomatic of a perverse intrusion of Western secular values into Samoan society.[7] But, even if such exportations exacerbate the severity of homophobia in these nations, the American LGBTQ community reaches out to its overseas constituents and overseas LGBTQ communities look to the American LGBTQ rights movement—and even to Stonewall—to brace itself against the new wave of violence.

While charting this unfortunate history might seem a bit judgmental, it is important to point out that, once prejudice works its way into religion, it only with difficulty works its way back out. Happily, however, we seem to be witnessing a diminution in doctrinal homophobia within Christianity. Even as Pope Francis I displays a remarkable acceptance of same-sex relationships, a number of Protestant denominations—the United Church of Christ, for instance, or the Episcopal Church—have discarded their old prohibitions against gay and lesbian parishioners and even ministers. And myths other than that of Sodom and Gomorrah or the Curse of Ham have been given new life and allowed to speak to issues of same-sex relationships: David's love for Jonathan, a love that is as obscured to American Christians as is David's banditry;

or Ruth's love for Naomi, which is understood as an exemplum by lesbian Christians; or Christ's love for John, which—along with David's for Jonathan—is understood as an exemplum by gay male Christians.

Pan-Indian Identity

The refutation of prejudicial interpretations of Judeo-Christian myth and the elucidation of positive mythic archetypes by the LGBTQ community allow us to think about another feature of mythic rhetoric: the rhetorical constructs—linguistically formulated and infused with mythic signification—that animate prejudices animate as well almost innumerable responses to prejudice. In other words, when a society builds its sense of community at the expense of an Other, the members of the group that have been scapegoated not unusually begin the arduous task of constructing their own sense of community as a response to their Othering. Not surprisingly, they will coalesce around the principle that their detractors are the Other. And they will inevitably, as Ward Goodenough alerted us, refuse to become invested in the peculiar social contract constructed on their back.

Similar circumstances to that which we have seen in the context of anti–Semitism, Islamophobia, and homophobia have been suffered by Native Americans and, if prejudice has helped to maintain Jewish identity in the diaspora, spurred global Islamic responses despite the great diversity within the Islamic world, and led to the adoption of positive mythic exempla on the part of LGBTQ Christians, anti–Native American sentiments have helped to forge a sense of pan–Indian cultural identity in the United States, Canada, Mexico, and beyond. Such diverse societies as the Maya, Lakota, Zuni, and Iroquois define themselves not only by their national identity but also their Native American or (as most of my Native American friends say) Indian identity. The public face of pan–Indian identity in North America is the Powwow, originally an outgrowth of the Kiowa Gourd Dance, which has grown to encompass huge gatherings of Indians from the Great Plains and beyond in dance and song competitions, vibrant displays of Indian arts and crafts, and calls for political action asserting Native American rights and contesting treaty violations.[8] But quite distinct from its public face, the ultimate source of pan–Indian identity is the commonality with which the Native American—whatever his or her national affiliation—has had to contend with a history of conquest, broken treaties, and sometimes crushing levels of prejudice.

We have already witnessed one common response to a history of abuse: the revitalization movement. The Iroquois were among the earliest Native

Americans who—having become entangled in the colonial rivalries of first Britain and France, then Britain and America—had to adjust radically to their transformation from essential and equal participants in the French and Indian Wars to a conquered and dispossessed people as a result of their alliance with the British in the American Revolution. The uneasy transformation was largely facilitated by Handsome Lake's *Gaiwiio*. A century later, the Lakota as well had to contend with a dehumanizing conquest and the piecemeal dismantling of their Great Sioux Reservation—undertaken by the American government without regard to treaty or decency. Their initial response came in the form of the Ghost Dance movement—the terrible culmination of which was the massacre at Wounded Knee. But in Black Elk's reformulation of traditional Lakota religion, the Lakota perhaps found the framework which would aid them in their adjustment to a vastly different world than that which had centered their existence as roving bison-hunters on the Great Plains.[9] Still, with warfare more than a century past, and treaties the subject of lengthy court proceedings, prejudice is the more pressing issue with which Native Americans must continuously grapple.

I once asked a Dine (Navaho) woman what it was like living in the Anglo world and she said, without missing a beat, "A fish out of water." It was pretty clear that she had had to think about her place in society more than once. Then again, a Lakota man told me that—because of his easy adjustment to life away from the reservation—he was taunted with the epithet Apple—red on the outside, white inside—on his many returns home. It can be very difficult to be Native American in America. Off reservation, one has to deal with non–Indians' expectations of what an Indian is supposed to be like. On reservation one has to deal with often limited economic opportunities—even if one is insulated from some of the worst prejudices. Sherman Alexie cogently explores the intersection of off-reservation and on-reservation life, and its profound effect on one's sense of identity, in his screenplay for *Smoke Signals*. The film—under the direction of Chris Eyre—follows the adventures of two friends from the Coeur d'Alene reservation, Victor Joseph and Thomas Builds-the-Fire, dramatically reminiscent of the Iroquois's Elder Brother and Younger Brother. Victor and Thomas are traveling from Idaho to Phoenix to retrieve the ashes of Victor's father, Arnold Joseph: himself reminiscent of the distant but loving Father of the Iroquois Creation. Waiting on the reservation for their return is Thomas's grandmother, whose calmness and wisdom speaks to the essence of Grandmother Sky Woman, and Victor's mother who, when she miraculously multiples 50 pieces of her magic frybread in order to feed 100 Indians by ripping each piece in half, is a visible remembrance of the Iroquois Mother. In exchange for a ride off the reservation, Thomas trades a story of his friend's father, Arnold, who—in Thomas's vivid and not always literal imagination—beats up a National Guardsman in an anti-war protest. When one of the women with whom he barters for the ride asks the outcome of the event, Thomas says: "Arnold got arrested, you know. But he got lucky. They charged him with attempted murder. Then they plea-bargained that down to assault with a deadly weapon. Then they plea-bargained that down to being an Indian in the Twentieth Century. Then he got two years in Walla Walla." If Victor and Thomas reenact the essence of Elder Brother and Younger Brother, Lucy and Velma, the two wise-cracking women who drive them off reservation, reenact the essence of the Lakota Heyoka or the Zuni Koyemci. They are Contraries—sacred clowns—whose car, perennially stuck in reverse, still allows them to act as the escort between two worlds—the Rez and the United States—just as Contraries are the most fitting emissaries between the worlds of the sacred and profane. Tellingly, they tease Victor and Thomas as they drop them off, saying, "Hope you got your passport," and finally, "Hope you got your vaccinations!"[10]

Examples of an anti–Native American animus—particularly just off reservation—are innumerable but let me choose just one haphazard incident that occurred during a period in which I was visiting some Iroquois friends and happened to stumble upon one of their non–Indian detractors. "Congress could solve the problem with a stroke of a pen," my American interlocutor—whose home was on a tract of land claimed by one of the Iroquois nations—declared, suggesting that the United States should recognize all treaties signed between American states and Native American nations. "It can't," I argued. "Some of those treaties were obtained dishonestly."

"No, they weren't," he argued.

"How do you know that?" I countered.

"How do you know they were?" he countered right back.

"I've read about them," I said.

"No you haven't," he blustered. "Nothing has been written about them."

"Yes something has," I assured him, "and I've read it."

"Well, it was written by Indians," he claimed as he stalked away.

His wife came over and said, "There's no use arguing with him. He's a … he's a … he's an Archie Bunker!"

"A bigot?" a woman passing by helpfully offered.

"Yes, that's it! A bigot! He won't even pull into a gas station to buy gas if he sees an Indian pumping it."

Despite a successful revitalization of Iroquois society by means of Handsome Lake's *Gaiwiio*, difficulties—truly serious difficulties—remain in adjusting to the sometimes hostile treatment received from non–Indians and the sometimes troubling limitations of reservation life. Alcoholism is, likely, one of them. Though alcohol was a common presence when I visited my friends in the Iroquois community, I never thought much about it, and in fact not unusually joined in the drinking. But, one day, a particular incident made me realize that I couldn't just look beyond the use of alcohol as if it were some gauzy film obstructing my view of the true culture that lay—obscured and impenetrable—just beyond it. Beneath a sheltering chestnut tree, in a vacant lot strewn with stones, pebbles, and occasional patches of grass, I joined some friends sitting in a circle made with a couple squat logs and some large, flat stones as they passed around a bottle of whiskey made on the reservation and chased their slugs with swigs from warm cans of Schlitz Tall Boys. As I sat down, one of my friends held up his Schlitz Tall Boy and said, with a grin, "You Anglos gave us this. Medicine to you; killing the hell out of us." He then held up the cigarette in his other hand and, laughing aloud, added, "But we gave you this. Medicine to us; killing the hell out of you."

Though it was clearly a joke, just part of the continuous teasing that animated any gathering of Iroquois that I experienced, it was a joke that echoed other statements I had heard. Alcohol, I was coming to learn, wasn't simply a distraction from Iroquois culture. Rather, it inhabited a very specific locus in Iroquois thought. It was medicine. Bad medicine, as it happened, for the Iroquois. But medicine in the same way that the sacred plant, tobacco, was medicine. Suddenly I realized that the use of alcohol was not any longer *apart* from the culture—a nefarious addition foisted upon the Iroquois by a rapacious Anglo populace—but that it was rather *a part* of the culture: nestled firmly within the web of signification that created for the Iroquois their own singular culture. Thereupon, it seemed to me, alcohol—viewed through the prism of the Iroquois concept of medicine—became an essential metaphor within Iroquois spiritual signification.

A second incident was, I believe, particularly telling: an Iroquois friend showed up at my apartment, needing a temporary refuge from the violence that often racked his own household. He was weeping disconsolately, so I went and sat beside him on the stairway landing, put my arm over his shoulder, and asked him what was wrong. "My brother's dead," he wailed. It was not one of his siblings who was dead but a fellow clan member who lived on the Reservation. As he told the story, his friends had been drinking, heavily, the usual reservation moonshine chased with Schlitz Tall Boys, and were driving fast on a dirt road on the reservation, very fast. Suddenly a witch, ensconced in a tree, reached into the car, wrapping his branches around the steering wheel, and wrenched the steering wheel violently. The car rolled over a number of times and only my friend's brother, who was thrown from the car, was killed. I was always struck by the explanation in my friend's story. It wasn't simply that he was explaining away culpability for the tragedy by claiming witchcraft, the interpretation that the Anglo inevitably offers when I relate this tale, but rather he was freely admitting culpability, alcohol (and speed), with a mitigating factor: witchcraft. In other words, rather than rationalizing a tragedy, my friend was explicating a cultural reality.

Many years after the above incidents took place, a non-drinking Iroquois woman attempted to relate to me her feelings about her past experiences with alcohol, casting the above cited incidents in a very particular light: "The thing I have to remember," she patiently explained to me, "is that my alcoholism too is a gift from the Creator. It's part of my path. It makes me who I am. If I disdain my alcoholism, I'm disdaining the Creator and the path that he has given me." To be able to think of the debilitating effects of alcohol as medicinal suggests, I think, another aspect of pan–Indian identity: In this context, traditional Native American medicinal concepts—such as those presented in Handsome Lake's *Gaiwiio*—have been caught up in the contemporary discourse of recovery in order to create something entirely unique: an *indigenous* discourse not only of alcoholism but also its refutation. Alcoholism is not simply a social problem: it is rather—as are all seeming problems—a gift from the Creator which brings us to an understanding to which we might not have otherwise had access.

What I took away from these disparate incidents (and many others not unlike them) was that Iroquois culture engendered an entire series of rhetorical associations. On the one hand, that which was disordering to society—war, witchcraft, alcohol and (by extension) the purveyors of such a debilitating medicine, Anglos—was animated by the spiritual power *otgont*, the earthly manifestation of the Iroquois god Younger Brother. On the other hand, that which was beneficial to society—peace, medicine societies, tobacco and (again, by extension) Native Americans, the purveyors of such a salutary medicine— was animated by the spiritual power *orenda*, the earthy manifestation of the Iroquois god Elder Brother. For the Iroquois, then, the world could be conceived of as a continuum with *otgont* representing one pole, *orenda*, the other. But, happily, there exists a fulcrum which keeps the two poles of this tenuous continuum in balance: Grandmother Sky Woman. The Iroquois, to this day, grapple with understanding their own particular place upon such a continuum. But, in addition, they grapple with understanding the place of the Euro-American upon such a continuum as well. And, tellingly, though the Euro-American may be Othered by such a rhetorical construct, he is not disparaged. In fact, from the Iroquois perspective, the Euro-American—whose frantic addiction to material consumption is the Anglo counterpart to Native American alcoholism—is not the opposite of, or the enemy to, the Iroquois whom he has dispossessed of his land, sovereignty, and—at times—culture. He is rather the Prodigal Son who will not be whispered about by the Native American, his orderly and stoic Elder Brother, to Grandmother—as was the Hebraic Prodigal Son whispered about by his diligent elder brother to their father. He will instead, as disorderly and troubled as he is, and even as he vociferously denies his addiction, be brought back into the fold for the sake of Mother: the Earth herself. When he finally—and hopefully not belatedly—recognizes his errant ways, he will turn to his benevolent Elder Brother in order to learn how to safeguard rather than despoil their common inheritance. Perhaps this is the reason that the Iroquois, as other Native American groups, regularly refer to Euro-Americans (notably, in treaties) as our Younger Brothers. In such terminology, Iroquois ideology may suggest a hopeful waiting for the reclamation and eventual forgiveness of the errant Younger Brother, the Euro-American, inasmuch as we all—Iroquois and Anglo alike—spring forth from the same Mother. It is a good lesson that the Iroquois have to offer, every bit as good as that offered by Papa Legba's crooked walking stick, and it too is a lesson that we would probably do well to embrace.

The Legitimacy of Myth

Dissecting such a rhetorical complex allows us the opportunity to consider the fact that just as the Iroquois had to rethink their relations with Euro-Americans in the context of a rapidly changing world so too do we have to rethink our relations with various Others in an increasingly multicultural world. But unfortunately, I suspect, we are often unwilling to hear other people or, perhaps more accurately, we often—as Deborah Tannen's work suggests—hear something different than what was intended, particularly when someone whom we define as the Other speaks: "Most white people," a friend said to me in a moment of exasperation, "don't know how to deal with Black people. They don't pay attention to us. But we have to study them. We have to learn them. It's their world and if we don't learn them, we won't make it." He wasn't trying to deny his own Black identity, or suggesting some need to accommodate to white expectations, in his heartfelt lament. He was rather expressing his reason for learning about white identity and protesting the fact that white folks didn't often enough see a reason to reciprocate. Perhaps it is past time that we give up the intellectual unidirectionality of which my friend lamented. Too often this unidirectionality is all that is demanded of us. Too often we take too little time to listen to one another. But such a strategy may no longer serve us well—precisely because we now live in a globalizing, multicultural world. Thus, we are living at a pivotal juncture, existing as a liminal society poised between two disparate realities—the one insular; the other interconnected—and we will have to adjust to much in order to heal ourselves of the maladies which inevitably afflict liminal societies.

The medicinal nature of stories may be just the antidote to the cultural tone-deafness that so often afflicts us. One thing we might note—if indeed we learn to listen with acuity, with intent, with engaging earnestness—is that we really aren't all that different from the various societies which we have thus far explored. Earlier in this study, for instance, we encountered a number of religious behaviors which we might term as human rights abuses: female genital mutilation among Egyptians, boys forced to fellate teenagers among the Sambia, and the mutilation of girls' fingers among the Dani. We could mention many more: the arrest and imprisonment of gay men in Egypt and Iran, the execution of suspected witches in New Guinea, the immolation of widows in India. Yet is it not a human rights abuse, as well, to marginalize a group of humanity? And, worse, to use religious ideology to do so? Our mythologies, perhaps, too often circumscribe our lives in some of the worst prejudices: prejudices which preclude good, solid, human empathy; prejudices which not only harm their victimized objects but also eat away at the souls of their unhappy hosts. Anti-Semitism, Islamophobia, homophobia and an anti–Native American animus are but four of myriad examples. Yet, happily, there is another possible spiritual pathway. What we today call spirituality might offer us a productive lead in this regard.

Particularly in the West, spirituality is conceived of as being the opposite of religion, but it needn't be. Both spirituality and religion are the inevitable consequence of the myth-ritual complex that is at the center of religious signification. Still, spirituality—to its adherents—displays a marked difference from religion: the absence of a controlling priesthood with its demands for exclusivity in religious practice. Rather, spirituality liberally avails itself of non–Western traditions: Native American, African, Asian, and Oceanic. It sometimes looks to past traditions as well, particularly Celtic—or Druidic—religious practices, for inspiration. Rejecting the sometimes draconian judgments of the world's priesthoods, spirituality seeks out and borrows alternate, affirming, models of identity. Among the most fascinating of such borrowings are those of the Native American Two-Spirit, Polynesian Fa'afafine, and Indian Hijra transgender sensibilities by gay men: particularly those who participate in the Radical Faerie movement. But, likewise, second generation Haitians in both New York and Miami are returning to their parents—or grandparents—Vodou roots. African Americans, particularly those who maintained a tradition of Spirit Work, look to Yorubaland for further spiritual guidance. Sabina Magliocco discusses the fluidity that characterizes such borrowings. When a group of Neo-Pagans found the Wiccan Great Rite to be too heterosexist for its needs, it reorganized the ritual to express LGBTQ sensibilities. Rather than "plunging the atheme, or ritual dagger, into the ritual chalice" in celebration of "the union of the male and female principles in nature," two daggers and two chalices, "filled with the spirit of the deities," both the God and the Goddess, were brought into the circle of celebrants. And while two women offered each celebrant a sip from one of the chalices, two men touched the forehead of each celebrant with the tip of one of the daggers.[11]

The easy manner in which contemporary spirituality integrates so many mythic traditions into its patterns of worship cannot help but alert us to the fact that our common mythic heritage is shot through with numerous points of contiguity, that our global mythologies are characterized by more that unite than divide us: Within the arena of myth itself, we encounter the Birth of Life from a watery world in the San tale of Beautiful Python Girl, the Mesopotamian and Hebraic tales of Postdiluvian Birds, and the Siberian, Iroquois, and Ojibwa Earth-Diver tales. Various Falls from Grace—including the Hebraic Expulsion from the Garden of Eden, the San Branding of Animals, and the dissolution of both Arthur's court and Christian England—are likewise a common feature of myths globally. Further, such falls often take on Apocalyptic overtones such as those expressed in medieval Europe's *Song of Roland*, Black Elk's Great Vision, or Christianity's *Book of Revelation*. Magical Flights such as that undertaken by the San's Beautiful Python Girl are reiterated in those undertaken by African America's Beatrice, Sicily's Epomata, and Appalachia's Merrywise. And Spiritual Journeys are as much the prerogative of the Iroquois's Handsome Lake, the Paiute's Wovoka, and the Lakota's Black Elk as they are of Mesopotamia's Gilgamesh, Greece's Odysseus, and India's Yudhishthira. Our world is lodged narrowly between a Sky World and an Underworld not only for Christians but also for the Iroquois. Both the Euahlayi and the Iroquois believe the soul, upon departing the body, traverses the well-worn path of the Milky Way to an Afterworld. And, of course, the fact that our own world—whether situated on the back of Turtle, on Atlas' shoulders, or on the expanse of the Pacific—is teeming with Gods, Demigods, Ghosts, Ancestors, and Spirits of all sorts is as valid to Africans, Asians, and Native Americans as it is to the inhabitants of Oceania and Europe. Even the fact that there exists among these multitudinous spirits a Hero, or an Elder Brother, and a Trickster, or a Younger Brother, is as imperative to the San and the Iroquois as it was to the ancient Hebrews and Greeks. And if the Hero oversees the orderly progression of rites of passage and calendrical ritual, the Trickster oversees all aspects of ritual reversal. Further, among this teeming spiritual world inevitably lurk dangerous and forbidding monsters—more than a few of them voracious cannibals.

But likewise, within the arena of ritual, there is much that is found globally. The spiritual efficacy of the Dance, perhaps the Round Dance which invites the spirits into our midst, is as obvious to the San as it is to the Paiute and the Lakota. The fact that there are essential rites of passage (marking birth, puberty, marriage, and death) which universally unfold in the pattern that Victor Turner has explicated (separation, limen, and incorporation) is as valid an observation for the San and the Euahlayi as it is for Sicilians, Haitians, and Jews. There are processions and pilgrimages to the places where gods reside: the sacred peyote field of Wirakuta, the great shrine of Ise (seat of the Shinto Sun Goddess Amaterasu), and the Kaaba (where Adam first worshipped god and Ibrahim and Ishmael built a shrine to commemorate that event), or the Church of Saint Francis (Home of Palermo's Immaculate Virgin). And there are calendrical rites of intensification which depend upon that other essential concept that Turner isolated—liminality and its constant corollary, communitas—which likewise occur globally and inevitably refer in one way or another to the ecological round that the spinning globe bestows upon us. There are altars and sacrifices, ingestion of sacred foods—whether in the form of the Totem, Prasad, or the Host—and there are various punishments exacted upon the scapegoat: whether that scapegoat is the Hebraic goat, the Christian Christ, or the Iroquois witch. There are extravagant sacred items: crystals (in which both the past and the future can be seen), sacred wells and springs (entrances to and outlets from the Underworld), shells (which are exchanged at birth, marriage, and death), turtle carapaces (which may be used as rattles or censors) and aspergillums (with which to disperse holy waters). There are dietary prescriptions as well as sacred foods and there is the demand that encumbered respect language be used, particularly when addressing the Creator and his emissaries, even if the rawest sexual language may be employed when addressing the Trickster and his spirit allies. And all of this ritual activity is overseen by those personages—shamans and priests—who exist "betwixt and between" our world and the world above or below to which they might travel or simply aspire: the Inuit shaman may plumb the depths of the sea through invisible tubes to commune with Takánakapsâluk if she is holding back the sea animals on whom the people depend or the San shaman may climb the invisible threads which descend from the sky to commune with Gangwanana sitting among the teeming spirit-animals over which he has sovereignty.

Even the fact that myth inevitably inscribes itself in ritual speaks to the global nature of human spirituality. The universality of the myth-ritual complex—whether actualized in the San reenactment of the tales of Beautiful Python Girl and the Branding of Animals in the Medicine Dance, the Jewish reenactment of the night before the Flight from Egypt with a Passover Seder,

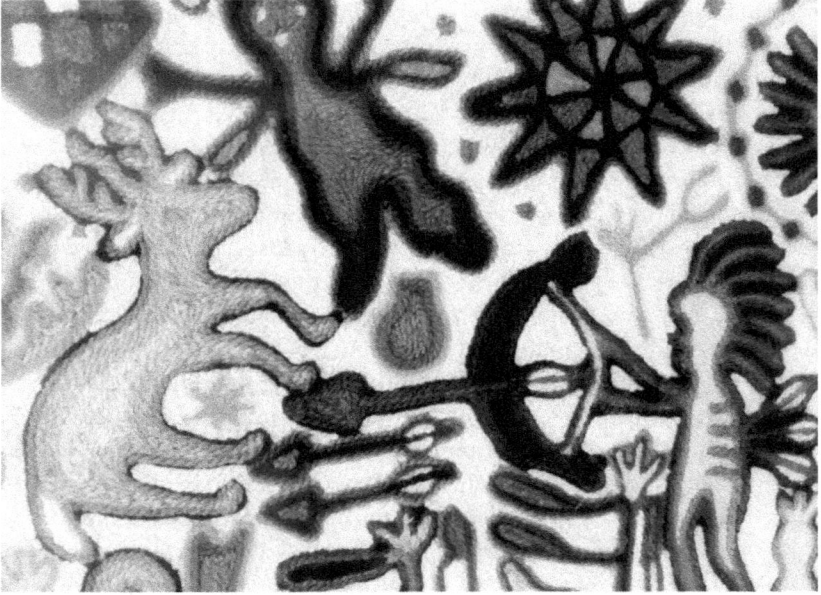

A Huichol shaman, travelling to Wirakuta, shoots an arrow into a peyote button, releasing the trifold spirit of Peyote, Deer and Corn (author's photograph).

or the Christian reenactment of the Last Supper in Holy Communion—may be the most significant point of contiguity in the world's mythologies. For, when exploring the myth-ritual complex globally, we cannot help but note that, though the world's spiritual inheritance may be differentiated according to the ecological, sociological, and anthropomorphic metaphors with which its various people's trick out their spiritual conceptions, so much that is our common spiritual inheritance lurks behind those indigenous metaphors: concerns for life and death; health and sickness; fear and ecstasy; affiliation and enmity; the Self and Other; ethnicity and gender; obedience and rebellion; order and disorder; poverty and happiness; affluence and malaise; conformance and orthodoxy; artistry and transcendence.

Taken as a whole, the numerous points of contiguity that define our spiritual life might make us wonder if there is not something beyond the cold, empirical facts to which we generally resort in order to explain our rich spiritual life. In fact, it seems worth pondering—as so many others have done—if there is not something more at play in our mythologies than mere science. The constant features which define our global mythologies may, in fact, suggest that there is perhaps a divine spark, a kind of celestial energy, setting everything in motion: a force (not unlike that which the Iroquois maintain informs our dreams) that we can tap into and, thereby, create our various communities. And, perhaps again this force is (as the Lakota seem to suggest and as Pope Francis has cogently argued) not some magician waving his wand and, thereby, conjuring all creation into being. Perhaps this force is rather (as the Greeks seemed to imagine when Zeus, rather than proclaiming Hector's fate, took the measure of it) the sum total of all consciousnesses—not only that of deities and humans but even plants and animals, rocks and stars—coming together and communicating to one another. Perhaps just as the roots of plants communicate to one another through chemical markers, one human consciousness communicates to another: the one having a thought, the other comprehending it; the one dreaming, the other interpreting that dream. Then, the striking similarity of both San and Inuit shamanic journeys—the first to Gangwanana in his home in the sky along miraculous threads, the second to Takánakapsâluk in her home at the bottom of the sea through magical tubes, both to the accompaniment of percussive singing and dancing—would be less a coincidence and more a comprehension of some mythic reality. And, perhaps further, this force—this infinite set of multiple consciousnesses—might be animated by a mandate that we consider the various communities with which we have affiliated ourselves (and perhaps even those with which we have only wearily treatied) and seek out some sort of accommodation (uneasy at times, at others nearly effortless to maintain) among them.

After all, as Zora Neale Hurston posited so long ago when considering her place in a racially charged America, "in the main, I feel like a brown bag of miscellany propped against a wall. Against a wall in company with other bags, white, red and yellow."

> Pour out the contents, and there is discovered a jumble of small things priceless and worthless. A first-water diamond, an empty spool, bits of broken glass, lengths of string, a key to a door long since crumbled away, a rusty knife-blade, old shoes saved for a road that never was and never will be, a nail bent under the weight of things too heavy for any nail, a dried flower or two still a little fragrant. In your hand is the brown bag. On the ground before you is the jumble it held—so much like the jumble in the other bags, could they be emptied, that all might be dumped in a single heap and the bags refilled without altering the content of any greatly. A bit of colored glass more or less would not matter. Perhaps that is how the "Great Stuffer of Bags" filled them in the first place—who knows?[12]

Or, then again, as one San shaman, a woman whom Richard Lee described as "the most charismatic" among the San healers, explained: God created us all—the San, the Bantu (Blacks in San parlance), and the Europeans—with our own particular medicine. "The Blacks have their medicine in divination and sorcery, the Europeans have their medicine in pills and steel needles, and the San have their medicine in the kowhedile," the mysterious shrieks that well up in a shaman as he or she enters into a healing trance state. "Different medicine, very different ways of living," the shaman continues. "But when you cut any one of them their blood flows the same color."[13] Certainly, Swamiji concurs when he claims that the force which he variously calls Bhagavan (masculine) and Bhagavati (feminine) consists of all the codes which people everywhere rely on in order to treat one another with sympathy and kindness. The soul, *ātman*, which exists within each of us, Swamiji maintains, comprehends "what is good to do." And it is thus that people know that they should "live in justice, in right-eousness," that they should "not do ill to others." And it is the rules of peaceable comportment, whether those rules pertain to "the Hindus, the Muslims," or "the Buddhists," that are the true form of Bhagavan. Thus, all religions every-where, Swamiji concludes, are the same.[14] And Black Elk maintains as much when he says, "And I saw that the sacred hoop of my people was one of many hoops that made one circle, wide as daylight and as starlight, and in the center grew one mighty flowering tree to shelter all the children of one mother and one father. And I saw that it was holy."

Chapter Notes

Preface

1. I use the term respondent to describe individuals with whom I have conversed on the subject of spirituality. But, because life happened to place me in a number of singular cultural milieus, I will often be citing friends or relatives and when such is the case, I will note as much. The conversations have almost always been informal. Though I audiotape at times, I most often listen and take notes. Thus, quotations from respondents, while extremely close to the original, are not always verbatim. Further, since I sometimes deal with sensitive subjects, I use pseudonyms and avoid geographic specifiers for almost all respondents. Finally, when quoting respondents, as well as analysts and mythic texts, I make slight emendations for the sake of legibility. I omit ellipses, normalize spellings, and regularize terminology while maintaining strict fidelity to the originals. My special thanks to Leah Nusman, Hitendra Chowdury, and Gregory Hill for generously contributing their expertise on Jewish American, Indian, and African American spirituality to this project.

Introduction

1. I use the term medicine man here because that's the term my interlocutor used to describe himself. Also, I am reconstructing this conversation, as accurately as possible, from memory.

2. Joseph Campbell and Bill Moyers, *The Power of Myth* (New York: Anchor Books, 1991), pp. 77–78; Kirin Narayan, *Storytellers, Saints, and Scoundrels* (Philadelphia: University of Pennsylvania Press, 1989), pp. 160–188.

3. Joseph Campbell, *Myths of Light* (Novato: New World Library, 2003), p. xxii.

4. On my use of the names Blowgun Hunter and Little Jaguar see *Popol Vuh*, trans. Delia Goetz and Sylvanus Griswold Morley (Los Angeles: Plantin Press, 1954), pp. 94–95, and *Popol Vuh*, trans. Dennis Tedlock (New York: Simon and Schuster, 1996), pp. 211 and 234.

5. Takeshi Inomata, "Maya Collapse and Modern Society," *New York Times* (April 14, 2011): Online.

6. Quotations from Samuel Butler's translations of *The Iliad* and *The Odyssey*.

7. Dennis Tedlock, *Finding the Center* (Lincoln: University of Nebraska Press, 1999), pp. 75–124.

8. C. Scott Littleton, "Japanese Religions," *Religion and Culture, 2nd Edition*, ed. Raymond Scupin (Upper Saddle River: Pearson/Prentice Hall, 2008), pp. 331–337.

9. Madeline Slovenz, "Lion Dancing in Chinatown," *Drama Review* 31/3 (1987), pp. 74–102.

10. Justin McDaniel, *The Lovelorn Ghost and the Magical Monk* (New York: Columbia University Press, 2011), p. 17.

11. Parichat Jungwiwattanaporn, "In Contact with the Dead," *Asian Theatre Journal* 23/2 (2006), pp. 374–395.

12. McDaniel, pp. 1–71.

Chapter 1

1. Dorothy Lee, "Religious Perspectives in Anthropology," *Magic, Witchcraft, and Religion, 6th Edition*, eds. Arthur Lehmann, et al. (Boston: McGraw Hill, 2000), p. 20.

2. Jane Goodall, *The Chimpanzees of Gombe* (Cambridge: Harvard University Press, 1986), *passim*.

3. John Skoyles, "Human Balance, the Evolution of Bipedalism and Dysequalibrium Syndrome," *Medical Hypothesis* 66/6 (2006), pp. 1060–1068; C. Owen Lovejoy, "Evolution of Human Walking," *Scientific American* 259/5 (1988), p. 118.

4. C. Owen Lovejoy, "The Origin of Man," *Science* 211/4480 (1981), pp. 341–350.

5. Michael Winkelman and John Baker, *Supernatural as Natural* (Upper Saddle River: Pearson/Prentice Hall, 2010), p. 106.

6. National Geographic Society, *Among the Wild Chimpanzees*, dir. Barbara Jampel (1984): Film.

7. Winkelman and Baker, pp. 101, 105

8. *Among the Wild Chimpanzees.*

9. Edward Wilson, "The Riddle of the Human Species," *New York Times* (February 24, 2013): Online; David Sloan Wilson, et al., "Multilevel Selection Theory and Major Evolutionary Transitions," *Current Directions in Psychological Science* 17/1 (2008), pp. 6–9.

10. Winkelman and Baker, p 110.

11. T.M. Luhrmann, "To Dream in Different Cultures," *New York Times* (May 13, 2014): Online.

12. Arthur Parker, *Seneca Myths and Folktales* (Lincoln: University of Nebraska Press, 1989), p. 5.

13. Richard Lee, *The Dobe Ju/'hoansi, 4th Edition* (Belmont: Wadsworth, 2013), pp. 137–148; Karl Heider, *Grand Valley Dani, 3rd Edition* (Boston: Cengage, 1996), pp. 124–129; 173–174.

14. J.K. Rowling, *Harry Potter and the Deathly Hallows* (New York: Arthur A. Levine, 2007), p. 723.

15. T.D. Stewart, "The Neanderthal Skeletal Remains from Shanidar Cave, Iraq," *Proceedings of the American Philosophical Society* 121/2 (1977), pp. 154–161.

16. Arlette Leroi-Gourhan, "The Flowers Found with Shanidar IV," *Science* 190/4214 (1975), pp. 562–564; Ralph S. Solecki, "Shanidar IV," *Science* 190/4217 (1975), pp. 880–881; Anna Belfer-Cohen and Erella Hovers, "In the Eye of the Beholder," *Current Anthropology* 33/4 (1992), p. 468; Arlette Leroi-Gourhan, "Comment," *Current Anthropology* 30/2 (1989), p. 182.

17. William Haviland, et al., *Evolution and Prehistory, 8th Edition* (Belmont: Wadsworth, 2008), p. 209; M. Aubert, et al., "Pleistocene Cave Art from Sulawesi," *Nature* 514 (2014), pp. 223–227.

18. Winkelman and Baker, p. 121.

19. Megan Biesele, *Women Like Meat* (Bloomington: Indiana University Press, 1993), pp. 70–71.

20. John Neihardt, *Black Elk Speaks* (Albany: SUNY Press, 2008), pp. 17–36.

21. Knud Rasmussen, "A Shaman's Journey to the Sea Spirit," *Reader in Comparative Religion, 4th Edition*, ed. William Lessa and Evon Vogt (New York: Harper Collins, 1979), pp. 308–311.

22. Dale Peterson and Jane Goodall, *Visions of Caliban: On Chimpanzees and People* (Athens: University of Georgia Press, 1993), p. 207; Jane Hill, "Apes and Language," *Annual Review of Anthropology* 7 (1978), p. 11; most analysts delicately translate "Dirty-Dirty" as excrement.

23. Ursula Goodenough, "Did We Start Out As Self-Domesticated Apes?" *National Public Radio* (February 5, 2010): Online; Terrence Deacon and Ursula Goodenough, "The Evolution of Symbolic Language," *National Public Radio* (March 18, 2010): Online.

24. Deborah Tannen, "I Can't Even Open my Mouth," *Annual Editions: Anthropology* 4/5, ed. Elvio Angeloni (Guilford: McGraw Hill/Dushkin, 2003), pp. 38–46.

25. Ursula Goodenough (2010).

26. Marcel Danesi, *A Basic Course in Anthropological Linguistics* (Toronto: Canadian Scholars' Press, 2004), pp. 18–20.

27. More accurately, Upper Paleolithic.

28. Simon Armitage, et al., "The Southern Route Out of Africa," *Science* 331/6068 (2011), pp. 453–456; Irina Pugach, et al., "Genome-Wide Data Substantiate Holocene Gene Flow From India to Australia," *Proceedings of the National Academy of Sciences* 10/5 (2013): Online.

29. Ewen Callaway, "First Aboriginal Genome Sequenced," *Nature News* (September 22, 2011), Online; Morten Rasmussen, et al., "An Aboriginal Australian Genome Reveals Separate Human Dispersals into Asia," *Science* 352/6288 (September 22, 2011): Online.

30. Andrew Curry, "Ancient Migration: Coming to America," *Nature* 485 (May 2, 2012): Online; Manfred Kayser, et al., "Melanesian and Asian Origins of Polynesians," *Molecular Biology and Evolution* 23/11 (2006), pp. 2234–2244; Pedro Soares, et al., "Ancient Voyaging and Polynesian Origins," *The American Journal of Human Genetics* 88 (2011), pp. 239–247.

31. Barbara Tedlock, *The Woman in the Shaman's Body* (New York: Random House, 2005), pp. 30–33.

32. Vincenzo Formicola, "From the Sunghir Children to the Romito Dwarf," *Current Anthropology* 48/3 (2007), pp. 446–453.

33. Catherine Yonsa and Kristin Adams, "Mastodons and Mammoths in the Great Lakes Region," *Geography Compass* (2012), pp. 1–14; Reuven Yeshurun and Alla Yaroshevich, "Bone Projectile Injuries and Epipaleolithic Hunting," *Journal of Archaeological Science* 44 (2014), pp. 61–68.

34. Jean-Pierre Bocquet-Appel, "The Agricultural Demographic Transition During and After the Agriculture Inventions," *Current Anthropology* 52/4 (2011), pp. 497–510.

35. Matthew Bandy, "Fissioning, Scalar Stress, and Social Evolution in Early Village Societies," *American Anthropologist* 106/2 (2004), pp. 322–333.

36. Kent Flannery, "The Origins of Agriculture," *Annual Review of Anthropology* 2 (1973), pp. 271–310; B. Bramanti, et al., "Genetic Discontinuity between Local Hunter-Gatherers and Central Europe's First Farmers," *Science* 326/5949 (2009), pp. 137–140.

37. Dani Nadel, et al., "Earliest Floral Grave Lining From 13,700–11,700 Year Old Natufian Burials at Raqefet Cave," *Proceedings of the National Academy of Sciences* 110/29 (2013), pp. 11774–11778.

38. Leore Grosman, et al., "A 12,000-Year-Old Shaman Burial from the Southern Levant (Israel)," *Proceedings of the National Academy of Sciences* 105/46 (2008): Online.

39. Carlos Driscoll, et al., "From Wild Animals to Domestic Pets," *Proceedings of the National Academy of Sciences* 106/1 (2009), pp. 9971–9978; Melinda Zeder, "The Domestication of Animals," *Journal of Anthropological Research* 68/2 (2012), pp. 161–190.

40. Brian Hare, et al., "The Domestication of Social Cognition in Dogs," *American Association for the Advancement of Science* 298/5598 (2002), pp. 1634–1636.

41. Anna Belfer-Cohen, "The Natufian in the Levant," *Annual Review of Anthropology* 20 (1991), p. 172.

42. Carlos Driscoll, et al., "The Taming of the Cat," *Scientific American* (2009), p. 71.

43. James Mellaart, "A Neolithic City in Turkey," *Avenues to Antiquity*, ed. Brian Fagan (San Francisco: W.H. Freeman, 1967), p. 141–150.

44. "The Epic of Gilgamesh," trans. E.A. Speiser, *The Ancient Near East, Vol. 1*, ed. James Pritchard (Princeton: Princeton University Press, 1958), p 41.

45. *The Epic of Gilgamesh*, trans. N.K. Sanders (London: Penguin, 1972), pp. 111.

46. *Ibid.*, pp. 108–113.

47. Typology draws on Elman Service, Morton Fried, and Marshall Sahlins.

48. E.A. Wallace Budge, *The Gods of the Egyptians, Volume Two* (New York: Dover Publications, 2013), pp. 123–126.

Chapter 2

1. Mark Niesse, "Scientists, Hawaiians Debate Taro Plan," *Associated Press* (April 3, 2007): Online.

2. Madhur Singh, "Cow's with Gas: India's Global Warming Problem," *Time* (April 11, 2009): Online; Jackie Northam, "Indian State Bans the Slaughter, Sale and Consumption of Beef," *National Public Radio* (March 3, 2015): Online.

3. S.A. Tishkoff, et al., "Convergent Adaptation of Human Lactase Persistence in Africa and Europe," *Nature Genetics* 39/1 (2007), pp. 31–40.

4. George Perry, et al. "Diet and the Evolution of Human Amalyse Gene Copy Number Variation," *Nature Genetics* 39/10 (2007), pp. 1256–1260.

5. Kevin Laland, et al., "How Culture Shaped the Human Genome," *Nature Reviews Genetics* 11 (2010), p. 142.

6. Genesis 4: 1–12 (NJPS).

7. Mary Douglas, *Purity and Danger* (London: Routledge and Keegan Paul, 1966), pp. 41–57.

8. Matthew 25: 31–46 (KJV).

9. Marvin Harris. *Culture, People, Nature, 7th Edition* (*Upper Saddle River: Pearson,* 1997), pp. 98–99.

10. Quotations from Kisari Mohan Ganguli's translation of *The Mahabharata* (Volume I).

11. More properly Ju/'hoansi; I have opted for the name San (used by journalists and ethnographers though not the Ju/'hoansi) in order to avoid diacritic marks.

12. Sarah Tishkoff, et al., "The Genetic Structure and History of Africans and African Americans," *Science* 324/5930 (2009), pp. 1035–1044.

13. Bernd Heine, "Khoisan," *Encyclopedia of Linguistics,* ed. Philipp Strazny (New York: Routledge, 2005), pp. 574–575.

14. Quentin Atkinson, "Phonemic Diversity Supports a Founder Effect Model of Language Expansion from Africa," *Science* 332/6027 (2011), pp. 346–349 and "Response to Comments on Phonemic Diversity," *Science* 335/6069 (2012), p. 657.

15. Tishkoff (2009), pp. 1035–1044; Hie Lim Kim, et al., Khoisan Hunter-Gatherers Have Been the Largest Population throughout Most of Modern Human Demographic History," *Nature Communications* 5 (2014): Online.

16. Richard Lee, *The Dobe Ju/'hoansi, 4th Edition* (Belmont: Wadsworth, 2013), pp. 25–33; 56–58; 73.

17. Lorna Marshall, "Marriage Among !Kung Bushmen," *Africa* 29/4 (1959), p. 339; Johannes Fabian, "!Kung Bushman Kinship," *Anthropos* 1/6 (1965), pp. 692–693.

18. Lorna Marshall, "The Kin Terminology System of the !Kung Bushmen," *Africa* 27/1 (1957), pp. 21–22.

19. Megan Biesele, *Women Like Meat* (Bloomington: Indiana University Press, 1993), p. 17.

20. Richard Katz, *Boiling Energy* (Cambridge: Harvard University Press, 1986), p. 29; I use Richard Lee's names (minus diacritic marks) for the gods to draw attention to the interrelationship of Gangwanana, Gangwa Matse, and the Gangwasi that seems to be implied by the common root in their names (2013), p. 141.

21. Lorna Marshall, "!Kung Bushman Religious Beliefs," *Africa* 32/3 (1962), p. 225; Katz (1986), p. 29.

22. Marshall (1962), p. 238; Lee, p. 141.

23. Biesele, pp. 17–20; Biesele suggests that the heroine's name may translate as "beautiful antbear maiden" and that she sometimes appears as a python. In either case, her animal "characteristics do not outweigh her human ones. (22)." For clarity, I have called her Beautiful Python Girl, building off Biesele's phrase, "a lovely python girl (p. 134)." Also, so I could integrate Biesele's terminology into my summaries, I have slightly edited most of the quotations from Biesele's collection of San folklore.

24. *Ibid.,* pp. 19–28; 61; 124–134.

25. Marshall (1962), p. 228; Katz (1986), pp. 112–113; Biesele, p. 34.

26. Biesele, pp. 25; 227; Katz (1986), p. 30.

27. Andrey Korotayev, et al., "The Return of the White Raven," *Journal of American Folklore* 119/472 (2006), pp. 203–235; Frank Speck, *Myths and Folklore of the Timiskaming Algonquin and Timagami Ojibwa* (Ottawa: Government Printing Bureau, 1915), pp. 34–38.

28. Biesele, pp. 23; 116–138; 153; 165; 197.

29. Carl Lindahl, "Two Tellings of Merrywise," *Journal of Folklore Research* 38/1–2 (2001), pp. 39–54.

30. Laura Gozenbach, *Beautiful Angiola*, trans. Jack Zipes (New York: Routledge, 2004), pp. 68–73.

31. Zora Neale Hurston, *Mules and Men* (New York: Harper and Row, 1935), pp. 47–53.

32. Biesele, pp. 161–170.

33. Lee, pp. 137–148.

34. Katz (1986), p. 62.

35. Richard Katz, "Boiling Energy," *Ethos* 10/4 (1982), pp. 353, 365.

36. Katz (1986), *passim*.

37. Biesele, pp. 67–69; 81–94; 106–107.

38. Katz (1986), p. 44, 140.

39. Beisele, pp. 81, 24.

40. Katz (1982), p. 365; Biesele, p. 24; Lorna Marshall, "N!ow," *Africa* 27/3 (1957), pp. 232–240.

Chapter 3

1. Melville Herskovitz, "A Note on 'Woman Marriage' in Dahomey," *Africa* 10/3 (1937), p. 338; Nancy Oestreich Lurie, "Winnebago Berdache," *American Anthropologist* 55/5 (1953), p. 708.

2. Lee, pp. 65–83.

3. Matthew 1: 1–17 (KJV).

4. Julian Rice, *Ella Deloria's The Buffalo People* (Albuquerque: University of New Mexico Press, 1994), pp. 61–63.

5. Ward Goodenough, *Culture, Language, and Society* (Menlo Park: Benjamin/Cummings, 1981), p.79.

6. A general typology; exceptions abound!

7. *Mahabharata* (Volume VI).

8. Genesis 9: 18–27 (KJV).

9. Andrey Korotayev, et al., "The Return of the White Raven," *Journal of American Folklore* 119/472 (2006), pp. 206–207.

10. Katie Langloh Parker. *The Euahlayi Tribe* (London: Archibald Constable, 1905), p. 88.

11. Marvin Harris. *Culture, People, Nature, 7th Edition (Upper Saddle River: Pearson, 1997)*, pp. 208–209; Nancy Scheper-Hughes, *Death Without Weeping* (Berkeley: University of California Press, 1992), *passim*.

12. E. Kathleen Gough, "The Nayars and the Definition of Marriage," *Journal of the Royal Anthropological Institute of Great Britain and Ireland* 89/1 (1959), pp. 24–25.

13. Gilbert Herdt, "Fetish and Fantasy in Sambia Initiation," *Rituals of Manhood*, ed. Gilbert Herdt (Berkeley: University of California Press, 1982), pp. 44–98.

14. Johanna Schmidt, *Migrating Genders* (New York: Routledge, 2010), pp. 60–82.

15. Lowell Holmes and Ellen Rhodes Holmes, *Samoan Village Then and Now, 2nd Edition* (Fort Worth: Harcourt, 1992), pp. 13–16.

16. Dan Taulapapa McMullin, "Fa'afafine Notes," *Queer Indigenous Studies*, ed. Qwo-Li Driskill, et al. (Tucson: University of Arizona Press, 2011), pp. 81–94; I use the pronoun he because McMullin, though fa'afafine, speaks of himself as a man.

17. George Turner, *Samoa* (London: London Missionary Society, 1884), p. 73.

18. Matilda Coxe Stevenson, "The Zuni Indians," *23rd Annual Report of the U.S. Bureau of American Ethnology* (Washington: Smithsonian Institute, 1904), pp. 310–313.

19. Serena Nanda, "Hijra and Sadhin," *Gender Diversity*, ed. Serena Nanda (Prospect Heights: Waveland Press, 2000), pp. 27–41.

20. Evelyn Blackwood, "Tombois in Western Sumatra," *Cultural Anthropology* 13/4 (1998), pp. 491–521.

21. Nanda (2000), pp. 27–41; Dan Bilefsky, "Albanian Custom Fades," *New York Times* (June 25, 2008): Online.

32. Parker (1905), *passim*; Katie Langloh Parker. *Australian Legendary Tales* (London: David Nutt, 1896), *passim*.

23. Victor Turner, *The Ritual Process* (Chicago: Aldine, 1969): *passim*; Douglas, p. 100.

Chapter 4

1. Claude Lévi-Strauss, *Tristes Tropiques*, trans. John and Doreen Weightman (New York: Harper and Row, 1974), pp. 48–49.

2. Metaphor borrowed from Emerson's *Self-Reliance*.

3. Grandmother becomes the Moon in the version told me. In others, the mother's face becomes the Moon, her breasts the Sun.

4. Literally: These Sustain Us.

5. Arthur Parker, "The Code of Handsome Lake," ed. William Fenton, *Parker on the Iroquois* (Syracuse: Syracuse University Press, 1968), p. 47.

6. Arthur Parker, *Seneca Myths and Folktales* (Lincoln: University of Nebraska Press, 1989), pp. 59, 73; *otgont* sometimes conceived as a single power with orderly and disorderly manifestations.

7. *Ibid.*, pp. 64, 71.

8. Sally Roesch Wagner, "Feminism, Native American Influences," *Encyclopedia of American Indian History, Vol. 1,* ed. Bruce Johansen and Barry Pritzker (Santa Barbara: ABC-CLIO, 2008), pp. 383–388.

9. *Gaiwiio* quotations from Parker (1968), pp. 20–24; 64–67.

10. Anthony F.C. Wallace, "Revitalization Movements," *American Anthropologist* 58/2 (1956), pp. 264–281.

11. Kecia Ali, "Many Views of Muhammad, as a Man and as a Prophet, *National Public Radio* (October 19, 2014): Interview.

12. Elizabeth Grobsmith, *Lakota of the Rosebud* (Long Grove: Waveland Press, 1981), pp. 5–21, 69; š (sh)," č (ch).

13. Neihardt, pp. 155–156.

14. Grobsmith, p. 3.

15. Julian Rice, *Ella Deloria's The Buffalo People* (Albuquerque: University of New Mexico Press, 1994), pp. 67–126.

16. Neihardt, pp. 2–5.

17. Grobsmith, p. 69.

18. Jeannette Mirsky, "The Dakota," *Cooperation and Competition Among Primitive Peoples,* ed. Margaret Mead (New Brunswick: Transaction Publishers, 2003), pp. 412–413.

19. Alice Beck Kehoe, *The Ghost Dance* (Long Grove: Waveland Press, 2006), pp. 3–17.

20. James Mooney, "The Ghost Dance Religion and the Sioux Outbreak of 1890," *Annual Report of the Bureau of Ethnology* 14/2 (Washington: Smithsonian Institution, 1892), p. 784.

21. *Ibid.*, pp. 18–20.

22. Neihardt, pp. 210–211.

23. Kehoe, pp. 53–72; 81–82.

24. Jessica McBride, "Peltier Backers see FBI's Lobbying as Example of Repression. *Milwaukee Journal Sentinel* (April 21, 2000): Online.

Chapter 5

1. Kenneth Burke, *The Rhetoric of Religion* (Berkeley: University of California Press, 1970), *passim.*

2. Zora Neale Hurston, *Tell My Horse* (New York: Harper and Row, 1938), p. 219.

3. Gary Gutting. "What Would Krishna Do? Or Shiva? Or Vishnu?" *New York Times* (August 3, 2014): Online.

4. Kirin Narayan (1989), p. 52.

5. *Mahabharata* (Volume I).

6. Alan Beals, *Gopalpur* (Belmont: Wadsworth/Thompson, 1962), pp. 47–48.

7. *Mahabharata* (Volume I).

8. Nanda (2000), pp. 27–41.

9. Serena Nanda, *Neither Man Nor Woman: The Hijras of India, 2nd Edition* (Belmont: Wadsworth, 1999), pp. 20–21.

10. Michael Edison Hayden. "Tears and Broken Glass as India's Largest Transgender Festival Closes." *New York Times* (May 7, 2012): Online.

11. Narayan (1989), p. 210.

12. Kirin Narayan, "The Ascetic Practice of Eating Sweets," *Interval(le)s* 4/5 (2008), pp. 597–606.

13. Narayan (1989), pp. 22–25; 219.

14. Narayan (2008), pp. 600–604.

15. Narrayan (1989), p. 183.

16. Arthur Parker harbored the same reservations.

17. Paul Radin, *The Trickster* (New York: Philosophical Library, 1956), *passim.*

18. Ella Deloria, *Dakota Texts* (Lincoln: University of Nebraska Press, 2006), pp. 43–46.

19. I. Eph'al, "'Ishmael' and 'Arab(s),'" *Journal of Near Eastern Studies* 35/4 (1976), pp. 228–229, 235; Yvonne Sherwood, "Binding-Unbinding: Divided Responses of Judaism, Christianity, and Islam to the 'Sacrifice' of Abraham's Beloved Son," *Journal of the American Academy of Religion* 72/4 (2004), p. 830.

20. Thomas Malory's and (Morganic incest) stanzaic *Death of Arthur.*

21. *Odyssey* (Book XI).

22. Karl Heider, *Grand Valley Dani*, 3rd *Edition* (Boston: Cengage, 1996), *passim*; Robert Gardner, *Dead Birds* (Cambridge: Peabody Museum, 1963): Film.

23. Conrad Arensberg, *The Irish Countryman* (Long Grove: Waveland Press, 1988), pp. 166–167.

24. Jeremiah Curtin, *Tales of the Fairies and of the Ghost World* (Boston: Little, Brown, and Company, 1895), pp. 19–22.

25. Arensberg, pp. 38–41.

26. Curtin, pp. 6–18.

27. Sebastian Evans' translation of Chretien de Troyes' *High History of the Holy Graal.*

28. R.B. Anderson's translation of Snorri Sturluson's *Prose Edda.*

29. Sarah Semple, "A Fear of the Past," *World Archaeology* 30/1 (1998), p. 109–113.

30. Katz (1986), pp. 226–227.

31. David Hufford, *The Terror that Comes in the Night* (Philadelphia: University of Pennsylvania Press, 1982), *passim.*

32. Agnes Murgoci, "The Vampire in Roumania," *Folklore* 37/4 (1926), pp. 320–349.

33. Ward Goodenough, *Culture, Language, and Society* (Menlo Park: Benjamin/Cummings, 1981), *passim.*

34. Roland Barthes, *Mythologies*, trans. Annette Lavers (New York: Noonday Press, 1972), pp. 107–111.

Chapter 6

1. C. Scott Littleton, "Japanese Religions," *Religion and Culture*, 2nd *Edition*, ed. Raymond Scupin (Upper Saddle River: Pearson/Prentice Hall: 2008), p. 344.

2. Rebecca Stein and Phillip Stein, *The Anthropology of Religion, Magic, and Witchcraft* (Boston: Pearson, 2008), p. 100; Raymond Scupin, "Islam," in *Religion and Culture*, 2nd *Edition* (Upper Saddle River: Pearson/Prentice Hall: 2008), pp. 432–433.

3. Stein and Stein, p.100.

4. Gil Atzmon, et al., "Abraham's Children in the Genome Era," *American Journal of Human Genetics* 86/6 (2010), pp. 850–859; Nicholas Wade, "Studies Show Jews' Genetic Similarity," *New York Times* (June 9, 2010): Online.

5. Giorgio Bassani, *The Garden of the Finzi-Contini*, trans. William Weaver (San Diego: Harcourt, 1977), pp. 14; 22–23.

6. Henrietta Szold, *The Legends of the Jews* (Vol. I), trans. Louis Ginzberg (Baltimore: Johns Hopkins University Press, 1909), pp. 65–66.

7. Ruth Bunzel, "Introduction to Zuni Ceremonialism," *47th Annual Report of the Bureau of American Ethnology* (Washington: Smithsonian Institute, 1932), p. 515.

8. Dennis Tedlock, *Finding the Center* (Lincoln: University of Nebraska Press, 1999), pp. 243–318.

9. Ruth Bunzel, "Zuni Origin Myths," 47th *Annual Report of the Bureau of American Ethnology* (Washington: Smithsonian Institute, 1932), p. 584–585; the blocked portion of this story is not a quotation but a retelling that depends heavily on quotations from Bunzel's translation of the Emergence—augmented by Dennis Tedlock's (i.e., "entered upon my road")—in order to give the reader a sense of how a Zuni story unfolds.

10. Bunzel, "Zuni Ceremonialism," p. 512.

11. Tedlock, pp. 125–164.

12. Bunzel, "Zuni Ceremonialism," pp. 473–544.

13. Winkelman and Baker, p. 148.

14. I use the Sicilian, rather than the Neapolitan or Italian, term here as it was most commonly used among my interlocutors. It is often translated as co-mother rather than godmother in anthropological literature but it is explicitly translated as godmother among my interlocutors who speak both Italian and English.

Chapter 7

1. Earlier versions of portions of this chapter appeared in Michael Buonanno, *Sicilian Epic and the Marionette Theater* (Jefferson, North Carolina: McFarland Press, 2014) and *The World Observed*, eds. Bruce Jackson and Edward Ives (Champagne/Urbana: University of Illinois Press, 1996), pp. 84–99.

2. Leonardo Sciascia and Rosario La Duca, *Palermo Felicissima* (Palermo: Edizioni il Punto, 1974), pp. 24–30.

3. Absolute figures are difficult to obtain given the presence of an underground economy and significant levels of underemployment.

4. Booker T. Washington, *The Man Furthest Down* (New York: Doubleday, 1912), pp. 193–196, 232.

5. Mary Taylor Simeti, *On Persephone's Island* (San Francisco: North Point Press, 1986), pp. 37–38.

6. Giuseppe Pitrè, "Le Tradizioni Cavalleresche Popolari in Sicilia," *Romania* 13 (1884), p. 359.

7. Denis Mack Smith, *A History of Sicily* (London: Chatto and Windus, 1968), p. 13.

8. The elements of Giuliano's story presented here are those that are commonly included in any recitation with narrative detail added from two sources: the first is Giuseppe Sciortino Giuliano's, *La Vera Storia di Salvatore Giuliano*, a website version of the narrative offered by Salvatore Giuliano's family which is no longer available online; the second is a 1986 marionette theater playbill printed by the *Cooperativa Teatrale Nuove Proposte* (Enna, Sicily) entitled *Salvatore Giuliano*.

9. Giuseppe Pitrè, *Il Vespro Siciliano* (Palermo: Edizioni "Il Vespro," 1979), pp. 11–12.

10. Steven Runciman, *The Sicilian Vespers* (Baltimore: Penguin, 1960), pp. 237–238; 313–318.

11. Vincenzo Linares, *I racconti popolari* (Palermo: Luigi Pedone Lauriel, 1886), pp. 2–33.

12. There is no Monte Olivieri today but rather a Castello di Oliveri which sits upon a promontory hard by the village of Oliveri in Messina. The topographic feature was called Mons Olivierius by Godfrey of Viterbo in the 12th century and probably did not (as Godfrey suggests) relate to the Paladin but rather to the olive groves which were a mainstay of the local economy.

13. Norman Cohn, *The Pursuit of the Millennium* (New York, Oxford: Oxford University Press, 1961), pp. 71–72.

14. Giuseppe Argento, et al., *Morte dei Paladini* (Palermo: Antonio Pasqualino Museo Internazionale delle Marionette, 1980): Audiotape.

15. The number for Renaud's band is variously given as 600 or 700.

16. M.I. Finley, et al., *A History of Sicily* (New York, Viking 1986), p. 50.

17. *Ibid.*, pp. 3–5; 56; Steven Runciman, *The Sicilian Vespers* (Baltimore: Penguin, 1960), p. 18.

18. Giuseppe Quatriglio, *A Thousand Years in Sicily*, 2nd *Edition*, trans. Justin Vitiello (Brooklyn, New York: Legas, 1997), p. 10.

19. Finley et al., p. 53.

20. Nicolas Abraham and Maria Torok, *The Wolfman's Magic Word*, trans. Nicolas Rand (Minneapolis: University of Minnesota Press. 1986), p. 132.

21. Ronald Loewe, "Euphemism, Parody, Insult, and Innuendo," *Journal of American Folklore* 120/477 (2007), p. 287.

22. Deborah Tannen, "My Mother Speaks Through Me," *New York Times* (September 19, 2017): Online.

23. 1 Samuel 17: 44 (KJV).

24. Giuseppe Pitrè, "Le tradizioni cavalleresche popolari," Romania 13 (1884): 345–398.

25. Alex Metcalfe, *Muslims of Medieval Italy* (Edinburgh: Edinburgh University Press, 2009), pp. 44–45.

26. George Makdisi, "The Guilds of Law in Medieval Legal History," *Cleveland State Law Review* 3 (1985), pp. 4, 14; George Makdisi, "Scholasticism and Humanism in Classical Islam and the Christian West," *Journal of the American Oriental Society* 109/2 (1989), pp. 175–182.

27. The *Song of Roland* is known in Palermo as *The Death of the Paladins*.

Chapter 8

1. Sigmund Freud, *Totem and Taboo*, trans. James Strachey (London: Routledge, 1950), p. 36.

2. Abraham and Torok, *passim*; little sister is figurative since the Wolfman's trauma involves his older sister.

3. Melville Herskovitz and Frances Herskovitz, "A Footnote to the History of Negro Slaving," *Opportunity* 11/6 (1933), p. 180.

4. Karen McCarthy Brown, "Voodoo," *Magic, Witchcraft, and Religion*, 2nd *Edition*, ed. Arthur Lehmann and James Myers (Mountain View: Mayfield, 1989), pp. 322–323.

5. William Bascom, *The Yoruba of Southwestern Nigeria* (New York: Holt, Rinehart, Winston, 1969), pp. 7–28; 37; see also Andrew Apter, "The Blood of Mothers," *Journal of African American History* 98/1 (2013), p. 78.

6. Bascom, pp. 9–12; 70–97; I have used the Yoruba names for the deities that are more similar to the names of their Haitian counterparts (i.e., Elegba for Eshu); see also Marilyn Houlberg, "Social Hair," *The Fabrics of Culture*, ed. Justine Cordwell and Ronald Schwarz (Hague: Moulton Publishers, 1979), p. 383.

7. Brown (1991), p. 188.

8. Frederick Douglass, *Narrative of the Life of Frederick Douglass, an American Slave* (Boston: Anti-Slavery Office, 1849), pp. 58–77.

9. Hurston (1938), p. 114.

10. Karen McCarthy Brown, *Mama Lola* (Berkeley: University of California Press, 1991), pp. 43–59; 276–285.

11. Harold Courlander, *The Drum and the Hoe* (Berkeley: University of California Press, 1960), pp. 24–25.

12. Brown (1989), pp. 321–326.

13. Brown (1991), pp. 100–101.

14. *Ibid.*, pp. 222–232; 246; 321–331; see also Ina Fandrich, "Yoruba Influences on Haitian Vodou and New Orleans Voodoo," *Journal of Black Studies* 37/5 (2007), p. 783; Robin Law, *Ouidah: The Social History of a West African Slaving Port* (Athens: Ohio State University Press, 2004), p. 2; Bascom, p. 90; Melville Herskovitz and Frances Herskovitz, *Dahomean Narrative* (Evanston: Northwestern University Press, 1958), p. 148.

15. Brown (1991), p. 256.

16. *Ibid.*, pp. 198, 357–358; see also Herskovitz (1958).

17. Brown (1991), pp. 356–361.

18. *Ibid.*, p. 229; Hurston p. 196.

19. Robert Hall, *Haitian Creole* (Philadelphia: American Folklore Society, 1953), pp. 215–216.

20. Brown (1991), p. 188.

21. Wade Davis, *The Serpent and the Rainbow* (New York: Warner Books, 1985), pp. 68–71.

22. *Ibid.*, pp. 257–261.

23. William Engel, *Mapping Mortality* (Amherst: University of Massachusetts Press, 1995), p. 110.

24. Brown (1991), p. 282.

25. Michael Blakey, "Return to the African Burial Ground," *Archaeology* (2003): Online.

26. Mark Leone and Gladys-Marie Fry, "Conjuring in the Big House Kitchen," *Journal of American Folklore* 112/445 (1999), pp. 372–403.

27. Davis, *passim*; my respondent's account of the death of the *bokor* differs slightly from Davis's.

28. Karen McCarthy Brown, "Healing Relationships in the African Caribbean," *Medicine Across Cultures*, ed. Helaine Selin (New York: Kluwer, 2003), pp. 291–292.

29. Brown (1991), p. 75.

30. Two translations elided for clarity.

31. Hurston, pp. 179–198; Davis, pp. 62–64; 84–92; 260–263; 312–313.

Conclusion

1. Peter Arnds, *Lycanthropy in German Literature* (London: Palgrave Macmillan, 2014), pp. 97–121.

2. Bassani, p. 44.

3. Ross Douthat, "The Better Pope," *New York Times* (April 12, 2010), p. A25.

4. Jonathan Shannon, "Performing al-Andalus, Remembering al-Andalus," *Journal of American Folklore* 120/477 (2007), pp. 308–334.

5. Then Dade County.

6. See William Eskridge, "Noah's Curse," *Georgia Law Review* 45/3 (2011), pp. 657–720.

7. McMullin, p. 84.

8. Luke Lassiter, *The Power of Kiowa Song* (Tucson: University of Arizona Press, 1998), *passim*.

9. Kehoe, pp. 81–82.

10. Sherman Alexie, *Smoke Signals*, dir. Chris Eyre (Santa Monica: Miramax, 1998): Screenplay.

11. Sabina Magliocco, "Ritual is my Chosen Art Form," *Magical Religion and Modern Witchcraft*, ed. James Lewis (Albany: SUNY Press, 1993), pp. 93–119.

12. Zora Neale Hurston, "How It Feels To Be Colored Me," *World Tomorrow* 11 (1928), pp. 215–216.

13. Richard Lee, *The Dobe Ju/'hoansi* (Belmont: Wadsworth, 2013), pp. 150–151.

14. Narayan, pp. 227–228.

References

Abraham, Nicolas, and Maria Torok. *The Wolfman's Magic Word*. Translator: Nicolas Rand. Minneapolis: University of Minnesota Press, 1986.

Alexie, Sherman. *Smoke Signals*. Director: Chris Eyre. Santa Monica: Miramax (1998): Screenplay.

Ali, Kecia. "Many Views of Muhammad, as a Man and as a Prophet. *National Public Radio* (October 19, 2014): Interview.

Apter, Andrew. "The Blood of Mothers." *Journal of African American History* 98/1 (2013), pp. 72–98.

Arensberg, Conrad. *The Irish Countryman*. Long Grove: Waveland Press, 1988.

Argento, Filippo, et al. *Morte dei Paladini*. Palermo: Antonio Pasqualino Museo Internazionale delle Marionette (1980): Audiotape.

Armitage, Simon, et al. "The Southern Route Out of Africa." *Science* 331/6068 (2011), pp. 453–456.

Arnds, Peter. *Lycanthropy in German Literature*. London: Palgrave Macmillan, 2014.

Atkinson, Quentin. "Phonemic Diversity Supports a Founder Effect Model of Language Expansion from Africa." *Science* 332/6027 (2011), pp. 346–349.

_____. "Response to Comments on Phonemic Diversity." *Science* 335/6069 (2012), p. 657.

Atzmon, Gil, *et al.* "Abraham's Children in the Genome Era." *American Journal of Human Genetics* 86/6 (2010), pp. 850–859.

Aubert, M., et al. "Pleistocene Cave Art from Sulawesi, Indonesia." *Nature* 514 (2014), pp. 223–227.

Bandy, Matthew. "Fissioning, Scalar Stress, and Social Evolution in Early Village Societies." *American Anthropologist* 106/2 (2004), pp. 322–333.

Bar-Yosef, Ofer. "The Natufian Culture in the Levant." *Evolutionary Anthropology* 6/5 (1998), pp. 159–177.

Barthes, Roland. *Mythologies*. Translator: Annette Lavers. New York: Noonday Press, 1972.

Bascom, William. *The Yoruba of Southwestern Nigeria*. New York: Holt, Rinehart, Winston, 1969.

Bassani, Giorgio. *The Garden of the Finzi-Contini*. Translator: William Weaver. San Diego: Harcourt, 1977.

Beals, Alan. *Gopalpur*. Belmont: Wadsworth/Thompson, 1962.

Belfer-Cohen, Anna. "The Natufian in the Levant." *Annual Review of Anthropology* 20 (1991), pp. 167–186.

Belfer-Cohen, Anna, and Erella Hovers. "In the Eye of the Beholder." *Current Anthropology* 33/4 (1992), pp. 463–471.

Biesele, Megan. *Women Like Meat*. Bloomington: Indiana University Press, 1993.

Bilefsky, Dan. "Albanian Custom Fades." *New York Times* (June 25, 2008): Online.

Blackwood, Evelyn. "Tombois in Western Sumatra." *Cultural Anthropology* 13/4 (1998), pp. 491–521.

Blakey, Michael. "Return to the African Burial Ground." *Archaeology* (November 20, 2003): Online.

Bocquet-Appel, Jean-Pierre. "The Agricultural Demographic Transition During and After the Agriculture Inventions." *Current Anthropology* 52/4 (2011), pp. 497–510.

Bramanti, B., et al. "Genetic Discontinuity between Local Hunter-Gatherers and Central Europe's First Farmers." *Science* 326/5949 (2009), pp. 137–140.

Brown, Karen McCarthy. "Healing Relationships in the African Caribbean." *Medicine Across Cultures*. Editor: Helaine Selin. New York: Kluwer, 2003, pp. 285–304.

_____. *Mama Lola*. Berkeley: University of California Press, 1991.

_____. "Voodoo," *Magic, Witchcraft, and Religion, 2nd Edition*. Editors: Arthur Lehmann and James Myers. Mountain View: Mayfield Publishing, 1989, pp. 321–326.

Budge, E.A. Wallace. *The Gods of the Egyptians, Volume Two*. New York: Dover Publications, 2013.

Bunzel, Ruth. "Introduction to Zuñi Ceremonialism." *47th Annual Report of the Bureau of American Ethnology*. Washington: Smithsonian Institution, 1932, pp. 467–544.

_____. "Zuni Origin Myths." *47th Annual Report of the Bureau of American Ethnology*. Washington: Smithsonian Institute, 1932, pp. 545–609.

Buonanno, Michael. "The Genius of Palermo." *The World Observed*. Editors: Bruce Jackson and Edward Ives. Champagne/Urbana: University of Illinois Press, 1996, pp. 84–99.

_____. *Sicilian Epic and the Marionette Theater*. Jefferson: McFarland Press, 2014.

Burke, Kenneth. *The Rhetoric of Religion*. Berkeley: University of California Press, 1970.

Callaway, Ewen. "First Aboriginal Genome Sequenced." *Nature News* (September 22, 2011): Online.

Campbell, Joseph. *Myths of Light*. Novato, California: New World Library, 2003.

Campbell, Joseph, and Bill Moyers. *The Power of Myth*. New York: Anchor Books, 1991.

Cohn, Norman. *The Pursuit of the Millennium*. New York, Oxford: Oxford University Press, 1961.

Copeland, Sandi, et al. "Strontium Isotope Evidence of Landscape Use by Early Hominins." *Nature* 474/7349 (2011), pp. 76–79.

Courlander, Harold. *The Drum and the Hoe*. Berkeley: University of California Press, 1960.

Curry, Andrew. "Ancient Migration." *Nature* 485 (May 2, 2012): Online.

Curtin, Jeremiah. *Tales of the Fairies and of the Ghost World*. Boston: Little, Brown, and Company, 1895.

Danesi, Marcel. *A Basic Course in Anthropological Linguistics*. Toronto: Canadian Scholars' Press, 2004.

Davis, Wade. *The Serpent and the Rainbow*. New York: Warner Books, 1985.

Deacon, Terrence, and Ursula Goodenough. "The Evolution of Symbolic Language." *National Public Radio* (March 18, 2010): Online.

Deloria, Ella. *Dakota Texts*. Lincoln: University of Nebraska Press, 2006.

Douglas, Mary. *Purity and Danger*. London: Routledge and Keegan Paul, 1966.

Douglass, Frederick. *Narrative of the Life of Frederick Douglass, an American Slave*. Boston: Anti-Slavery Office, 1849.

Douthat, Ross. "The Better Pope." *The New York Times* (April 12, 2010): Online.

Driscoll, Carlos, et al. "From Wild Animals to Domestic Pets." *Proceedings of the National Academy of Sciences* 106/1 (2009), pp. 9971–9978.

_____. "The Taming of the Cat." *Scientific American* (June 2009), pp. 68–75.

Engel, William. *Mapping Mortality*. Amherst: University of Massachusetts Press, 1995.

Eph'al, I. "Ishmael and Arab(s)." *Journal of Near Eastern Studies* 35/4 (1976), pp. 225–35.

Epic of Gilgamesh. Translator: E.A. Speiser. *The Ancient Near East, Volume 1*. Editor: James Pritchard. Princeton: Princeton University Press, 1958, pp. 40–75.

Epic of Gilgamesh. Translator: N.K. Sanders. London: Penguin, 1972.

Eskridge, William. "Noah's Curse." *Georgia Law Review* 45/3 (2011), pp. 657–720.

Fabian, Johannes. "!Kung Bushman Kinship." *Anthropos* 1/6 (1965), pp. 663–718.

Fandrich, Ina. "Yoruba Influences on Haitian Vodou and New Orleans Voodoo." *Journal of Black Studies* 37/5 (2007), pp. 775–791.

Finley, M.I., et al. *A History of Sicily*. New York: Viking, 1986.

Flannery, Kent. "The Origins of Agriculture." *Annual Review of Anthropology, 2nd Edition* (1973), pp. 271–310.

Formicola, Vincenzo. "From the Sunghir Children to the Romito Dwarf." *Current Anthropology* 48/3 (2007), pp. 446–453.

Freud, Sigmund. *Totem and Taboo*. Translator: James Strachey. London: Routledge, 1950.

Gardner, Robert. *Dead Birds*. Cambridge: Peabody Museum (1963): Film.

Geertz, Clifford. *The Interpretation of Culture*. New York: Basic Books, 1973.

Goodall, Jane. *The Chimpanzees of Gombe*. Cambridge: Harvard University Press, 1986.

Goodenough, Ursula. "Did We Start Out as Self-Domesticated Apes?" *National Public Radio* (February 5, 2010): Online.

Goodenough, Ward. *Culture, Language, and Society*. Menlo Park: Benjamin/Cummings, 1981.

Gough, Kathleen. "The Nayars and the Definition of Marriage." *The Journal of the Royal Anthropological Institute of Great Britain and Ireland* 89/1 (1959), pp. 23–34.

Gozenbach, Laura. *Beautiful Angiola*. Translator: Jack Zipes. New York: Routledge, 2004.

Grobsmith, Elizabeth. *Lakota of the Rosebud*. New York: Holt, Rhinehart, Winston, 1981.

Grosman, Leore, et al. "A 12,000-year-old Shaman Burial from the Southern Levant, Israel." *Proceedings of the National Academy of Sciences* 105/46 (2008): Online.

Gutting, Gary. "What Would Krishna Do? Or Shiva? Or Vishnu?" *New York Times* (August 3, 2014): Online.

Hall, Robert. *Haitian Creole*. Philadelphia, American Folklore Society, 1953.

Hare, Brian, et al. "The Domestication of Social Cognition in Dogs." *American Association for the Advancement of Science* 298/5598 (2002), pp. 1634–1636.

Harris, Marvin. *Culture, People, Nature, 7th Edition*. Upper Saddle River: Pearson, 1997.

Haviland, William, et al. *Cultural Anthropology, 13th Edition*. Belmont: Cengage, 2010.

_____. *Evolution and Prehistory, 8th Edition*. Belmont: Wadsworth, 2008.

Hayden, Michael Edison. "Tears and Broken Glass as India's Largest Transgender Festival Closes." *New York Times* (May 7, 2012): Online.

Heider, Karl. *Grand Valley Dani, 3rd Edition*. Boston: Cengage, 1996.

Heine, Bernd. "Khoisan." *Encyclopedia of Linguistics*. Editor: Philipp Strazny. New York: Routledge, 2005, pp. 574–575.

Herdt, Gilbert. "Fetish and Fantasy in Sambia Initiation." *Rituals of Manhood*. Editor: Gilbert Herdt. Berkeley: University of California Press, 1982.

Herskovitz, Melville. "A Note on Woman Marriage in Dahomey." *Africa* 10/3 (1937), pp. 335–341.

Herskovitz, Melville, and Frances Herskovitz. *Dahomean Narrative*. Evanston, Illinois: Northwestern University Press, 1958.

_____. "A Footnote to the History of Negro Slaving." *Opportunity* 11/6 (1933), pp. 178–181.

Hill, Jane. "Apes and Language." *Annual Review of Anthropology, 7th Edition* (1978), pp. 89–112.

Holmes, Lowell, and Ellen Rhodes Holmes. *Samoan Village Then and Now, 2nd Edition*. Fort Worth: Harcourt, 1992.

Houlberg, Marilyn. "Social Hair." *The Fabrics of Culture*. Editors: Justine Cordwell and Ronald Schwarz. Hague: Moulton Publishers, 1979, pp. 349–397.

Hufford, David. *The Terror that Comes in the Night*. Philadelphia: University of Pennsylvania Press, 1982.

Hurston, Zora Neale. "How It Feels to Be Colored Me." *World Tomorrow* 11 (1928), pp. 215–216.

_____. *Mules and Men*. New York: Harper and Row, 1935.

_____. *Tell My Horse*. New York: Harper and Row, 1938.

Inomata, Takeshi. "Maya Collapse and Modern Society." *New York Times* (April 14, 2011): Online.

Jungwiwattanaporn, Parichat. "In Contact with the Dead." *Asian Theatre Journal* 23/2 (2006), pp. 374–395.

Katz, Richard. *Boiling Energy*. Cambridge: Harvard University Press, 1986.

_____. "Boiling Energy." *Ethos* 10/4 (1982), pp. 344–368.

Kayser, Manfred, et al. "Melanesian and Asian Origins of Polynesians: mtDNA and Y Chromosome Gradients Across the Pacific." *Molecular Biology and Evolution* 23/11 (2006), pp. 2234–2244.

Kehoe, Alice Beck. *The Ghost Dance*. Long Grove, Illinois: Waveland Press, 2006.

Kim, Hie Lim, et al. "Khoisan Hunter-Gatherers Have Been the Largest Population throughout Most of Modern Human Demographic History." *Nature Communications* 5 (December 4, 2014): Online.

Korotayev, Andrey, et al. "The Return of the White Raven." *Journal of American Folklore* 119/472 (2006), pp. 203–235.

Laland, Kevin, et al. "How Culture Shaped the Human Genome." *Nature Reviews Genetics* 11 (February 2010), pp. 137–148.

Lassiter, Luke. *The Power of Kiowa Song*. Tucson: University of Arizona Press, 1998.

Law, Robin. *Ouidah*. Athens: Ohio State University Press, 2004.

Lee, Dorothy. "Religious Perspectives in Anthropology." *Magic, Witchcraft, and Religion, 6th Edition*. Editors: Arthur Lehmann, *et al.* Boston: McGraw-Hill, 2000, pp.19–25.

Lee, Richard. *The Dobe Ju/'hoansi, 4th Edition.* Belmont: Wadsworth, 2013.
Leone, Mark, and Gladys-Marie Fry. "Conjuring in the Big House Kitchen." *Journal of American Folklore* 112/445 (1999), pp. 372–403.
Leroi-Gourhan, Arlette. "Comment." *Current Anthropology* 30/2 (Apr 1989), p. 182.
_____. "The Flowers Found with Shanidar IV." *Science* 190/4214 (1975), pp. 562–564.
Lévi-Strauss, Claude. *Tristes Tropiques.* Translators: John and Doreen Weightman. New York: Harper and Row, 1974.
Linares, Vincenzo. *I racconti popolari.* Palermo: Luigi Pedone Lauriel, 1886.
Lindahl, Carl. "Two Tellings of Merrywise." *Journal of Folklore Research* 38/1–2 (2001), pp. 39–54.
Littleton, C. Scott. "Japanese Religions." *Religion and Culture, 2nd Edition.* Editor: Raymond Scupin. Upper Saddle River: Pearson/Prentice Hall (2008), pp. 322–349.
Loewe, Ronald. "Euphemism, Parody, Insult, and Innuendo." *Journal of American Folklore* 120/477 (2007), pp. 284–307.
Lovejoy, Owen. "The Origin of Man." *Science* 211/4480 (1981), pp. 341–350.
_____. "Evolution of Human Walking." *Scientific American* 259/5 (November 1988), pp. 118–125.
Luhrmann, T.M. "To Dream in Different Cultures." *New York Times* (May 13, 2014): Online.
Lurie, Nancy Oestreich. "Winnebago Berdache." *American Anthropologist* 55/5 (1953), pp. 708–712.
Magliocco, Sabina. "Ritual is my Chosen Art Form." *Magical Religion and Modern Witchcraft.* Editor: James Lewis. Albany: SUNY Press, 1993, pp. 93–119.
Makdisi, George. "The Guilds of Law in Medieval Legal History." *Cleveland State Law Review* 3 (1985), pp. 3–18.
_____. "Scholasticism and Humanism in Classical Islam and the Christian West." *Journal of the American Oriental Society* 109/2 (1989), pp. 175–182.
Marshall, Lorna. "The Kin Terminology System of the !Kung Bushmen." *Africa* 27/1 (1957), pp. 1–25.
_____. "!Kung Bushman Religious Beliefs." *Africa* 32/3 (1962), pp. 221–252.
_____. "Marriage Among !Kung Bushmen." *Africa* 29/4 (1959), pp. 335–365.
_____. "N!ow." *Africa* 27/3 (1957), pp. 232–240.
McBride, Jessica. "Peltier Backers see FBI's Lobbying as Example of Repression. *Milwaukee Journal Sentinel* (April 21, 2000): Online.
McDaniel, Justin. *The Lovelorn Ghost and the Magical Monk.* New York: Columbia University Press, 2011.
McMullin, Dan Taulapapa. "Fa'afafine Notes." *Queer Indigenous Studies.* Editors: Qwo-Li Driskill, et al. Tucson: University of Arizona Press (2011), pp. 81–94.
Mellaart, James. "A Neolithic City in Turkey." *Avenues to Antiquity.* Editor: Brian Fagan. San Francisco: W.H. Freeman, 1967, pp. 141–150.
Metcalfe, Alex. *Muslims of Medieval Italy.* Edinburgh: University Press, 2009.
Mirsky, Jeannette. "The Dakota." *Cooperation and Competition among Primitive Peoples.* Editor: Margaret Mead. New Brunswick: Transaction Publishers, 2003.
Mooney, James. "The Ghost Dance Religion and the Sioux Outbreak of 1890." *Annual Report of the Bureau of Ethnology* 14/2 (1892), pp. 641–1136.
Murgoci, Agnes. "The Vampire in Roumania." *Folklore* 37/4 (1926), pp. 320–349.
Nadel, et al. "Earliest Floral Grave Lining from 13,700–11,700 Year Old Natufian Burials at Raqefet Cave. *Proceedings of the National Academy of Sciences* 110/29 (2013), pp. 11774–11778.
Nanda, Serena. "Hijra and Sadhin." *Gender Diversity.* Editor: Serena Nanda. Prospect Heights: Waveland Press, 2000, pp. 27–41.
_____. *Neither Man Nor Woman, 2nd Edition.* Belmont: Wadsworth Publishing, 1999.
Narayan, Kirin. "The Ascetic Practice of Eating Sweets." *Interval(le)s* 4/5 (2008), pp. 597–606.
_____. *Storytellers, Saints, and Scoundrels.* Philadelphia: University of Pennsylvania Press, 1989.
National Geographic Society. *Among the Wild Chimpanzees.* Director: Barbara Jampel (1984): Film.
Neihardt, John. *Black Elk Speaks.* Albany: SUNY Press, 2008.
Niesse, Mark. "Scientists, Hawaiians Debate Taro Plan." *Associated Press* (April 3, 2007): Online.
Northam, Jackie. "Indian State Bans the Slaughter, Sale and Consumption of Beef." *National Public Radio* (March 3, 2015): Online.
Parker, Arthur. "The Code of Handsome Lake." *Parker on the Iroquois.* Editor: William Fenton. Syracuse: Syracuse University Press, 1968, pp. 5–159.

_____. *Seneca Myths and Folktales*. Lincoln: University of Nebraska Press, 1989.
Parker, Katie Langloh. *Australian Legendary Tales*. London: David Nutt, 1896.
_____.*The Euahlayi Tribe*. London: Archibald Constable, 1905.
Perry, George, et al. "Diet and the Evolution of Human Amalyse Gene Copy Number Variation." *Nature Genetics* 39/10 (2007), pp. 1256–1260.
Peterson, Dale, and Jane Goodall. *Visions of Caliban*. Athens: University of Georgia Press, 1993.
Pitrè, Giuseppe. *Il Vespro Siciliano*. Palermo: Edizioni "Il Vespro," 1979.
_____. "Le tradizioni cavalleresche popolari." *Romania* 13 (1884), pp. 345–398.
Popol Vuh. Translators: Delia Goetz and Sylvanus Griswold Morley. Los Angeles: Plantin Press, 1954.
Popol Vuh. Translator: Dennis Tedlock. New York: Simon & Schuster, 1996.
Pugach, Irina, et al. "Genome-Wide Data Substantiate Holocene Gene Flow from India to Australia." *Proceedings of the National Academy of Sciences* 10/5 (2013): Online.
Quatriglio, Giuseppe. *A Thousand Years in Sicily*, 2nd Edition. Translator: Justin Vitiello. Brooklyn: Legas, 1997.
Radin, Paul. *The Trickster*. New York: Philosophical Library, 1956.
Rasmussen, Knud. "A Shaman's Journey to the Sea Spirit." *Reader in Comparative Religion, 4th Edition*. Editors: William Lessa and Evon Vogt. New York: HarperCollins, 1979, pp. 308–311.
Rasmussen, Morten, et al. "An Aboriginal Australian Genome Reveals Separate Human Dispersals into Asia." *Science* 352/6288 (2011): Online.
Rice, Julian. *Ella Deloria's The Buffalo People*. Albuquerque: University of New Mexico Press, 1994.
Rowling, J.K. *Harry Potter and the Deathly Hallows*. New York: Arthur A. Levine, 2007.
Runciman, Steven. *The Sicilian Vespers*. Baltimore: Penguin, 1960.
Scheper-Hughes, Nancy. *Death Without Weeping*. Berkeley: University of California Press, 1992.
Schmidt, Johanna. *Migrating Genders*. New York: Routledge, 2010.
Sciascia, Leonardo, and Rosario La Duca. *Palermo Felicissima*. Palermo: *Edizioni il Punto*, 1974.
Scupin, Raymond. "Islam." *Religion and Culture, 2nd Edition*. Upper Saddle River: Pearson/Prentice Hall: 2008, pp. 430–454.
Semple, Sarah. "A Fear of the Past." *World Archaeology* 30/1 (1998), pp. 109–126.
Shannon, Jonathan. "Performing al-Andalus, Remembering al-Andalus." *Journal of American Folklore* 120/477 (2007), pp. 308–334.
Sherwood, Yvonne. "Binding-Unbinding: Divided Responses of Judaism, Christianity, and Islam to the Sacrifice of Abraham's Beloved Son." *Journal of the American Academy of Religion* 72/4 (2004), pp. 821–861.
Simeti, Mary Taylor. *On Persephone's Island*. San Francisco: North Point Press, 1986.
Singh, Madhur. "Cow's with Gas: India's Global Warming Problem." *Time* (April 11, 2009): Online.
Skoyles, John. "Human Balance, the Evolution of Bipedalism and Dysequalibrium Syndrome." *Medical Hypothesis* 66/6 (2006), pp. 1060–1068.
Slovenz, Madeline. "Lion Dancing in Chinatown." *The Drama Review* 31/3 (1987), pp. 74–102.
Smith, Denis Mack. *A History of Sicily*. London: Chatto and Windus, 1968.
Soares, Pedro, et al. "Ancient Voyaging and Polynesian Origins." *The American Journal of Human Genetics* 88 (2011), pp. 239–247.
Solecki, Ralph. "Shanidar IV." *Science* 190/4217 (1975), pp. 880–881.
Speck, Frank. *Myths and Folklore of the Timiskaming Algonquin and Timagami Ojibwa*. Ottawa: Government Printing Bureau, 1915.
Stein, Rebecca, and Phillip Stein. *The Anthropology of Religion, Magic, and Witchcraft*. Boston: Pearson, 2008, p. 100.
Stevenson, Matilda Coxe. "The Zuni Indians." *23rd Annual Report of the U.S. Bureau of American Ethnology*. Washington: Smithsonian Institute, 1904.
Stewart, T.D. "The Neanderthal Skeletal Remains from Shanidar Cave." *Proceedings of the American Philosophical Society* 121/2 (1977), pp. 121–165.
Sturluson, Snorri. *The Prose Edda*. Translator: R.B. Anderson. Chicago: S.C. Griggs, 1879.
Szold, Henrietta. *The Legends of the Jews, Volume I*. Translator: Louis Ginzberg. Baltimore: Johns Hopkins University Press, 1909.

Tannen, Deborah. "I Can't Even Open my Mouth." *Annual Editions: Anthropology* 4/5. Editor: Elvio Angeloni. Guilford: McGraw-Hill/Dushkin, 2003, pp. 38–46.
_____. "My Mother Speaks Through Me." *New York Times* (September 19, 2017): Online.
Tedlock, Barbara. *The Woman in the Shaman's Body*. New York: Random House, 2005.
Tedlock, Dennis. *Finding the Center*. Lincoln: University of Nebraska Press, 1999.
Tishkoff, Sarah, et al. "Convergent Adaptation of Human Lactase Persistence in Africa and Europe." *Nature Genetics* 39/1 (2007), pp. 31–40.
_____. "The Genetic Structure and History of Africans and African Americans." *Science* 324/5930 (2009), pp. 1035–1044.
Turner, George. *Samoa*. London: London Missionary Society, 1884.
Turner, Victor. *The Ritual Process*. Chicago: Aldine Publishing, 1969.
Tylor, E.B. *Primitive Culture, Volume 1*. London: John Murray, 1871.
Wade, Nicholas. "Studies Show Jews' Genetic Similarity." *New York Times* (June 9, 2010): Online.
Wagner, Sally Roesch. "Feminism, Native American Influences." *Encyclopedia of American Indian History, Volume 1*. Editors: Bruce Johansen and Barry Pritzker. Santa Barbara: ABC-CLIO (2008), pp. 383–388.
Wallace, Anthony. "Revitalization Movements." *American Anthropologist* 58/2 (1956), pp. 264–281.
Wilson, David Sloan, et al. "Multilevel Selection Theory and Major Evolutionary Transitions." *Current Directions in Psychological Science* 17/1 (February 2008), pp. 6–9.
Wilson, Edward. "The Riddle of the Human Species." *New York Times* (February 24, 2013): Online.
Winkelman, Michael. *Shamanism*. Santa Barbara: Praeger, 2010.
Winkelman, Michael, and John Baker. *Supernatural as Natural*. Upper Saddle River: Pearson/Prentice Hall, 2010.
Yeshurun, Reuven, and Alla Yaroshevich. "Bone Projectile Injuries and Epipaleolithic Hunting." *Journal of Archaeological Science* 44 (2014), pp. 61–68.
Yonsa, Catherine, and Kristin Adams. "Mastodons and Mammoths in the Great Lakes Region." *Geography Compass* (2012), pp. 1–14.
Zeder, Melinda. "The Domestication of Animals." *Journal of Anthropological Research* 68/2 (2012), pp. 161–190.

Index

www.ingramcontent.com/pod-product-compliance
Lightning Source LLC
Chambersburg PA
CBHW021220270326
41929CB00010B/1204